# HARDENING
## Linux

# HARDENING
## Linux

John Terpstra, Paul Love,
Ronald P. Reck, Timothy Scanlon

**MCGRAW-HILL**/OSBORNE

New York   Chicago   San Francisco
Lisbon   London   Madrid   Mexico City   Milan
New Delhi   San Juan   Seoul   Singapore   Sydney   Toronto

The **McGraw·Hill** Companies

**McGraw-Hill**/Osborne
2100 Powell Street, 10th Floor
Emeryville, California 94608
U.S.A.

To arrange bulk purchase discounts for sales promotions, premiums, or fund-raisers, please
contact **McGraw-Hill/**Osborne at the above address. For information on translations or book
distributors outside the U.S.A., please see the International Contact Information page
immediately following the index of this book.

## Hardening Linux

1234567890 CUS CUS 01987654

ISBN 0-07-225497-1


**Publisher**
   Brandon A. Nordin
**Vice President & Associate Publisher**
   Scott Rogers
**Editorial Director**
   Tracy Dunkelberger
**Project Editor**
   Julie M. Smith
**Acquisitions Coordinator**
   Athena Honore
**Technical Editor**
   Makan Pourzandi
**Copy Editor**
   Lunaea Weatherstone

**Proofreader**
   Linda Medoff
**Indexer**
   Claire Splan
**Composition**
   Apollo Publishing Services
**Illustrators**
   Melinda Lytle, Kathleen Edwards
**Series Design**
   Kelly Stanton-Scott, Peter F. Hancik
**Cover Series Design**
   Theresa Havener

This book was composed with Corel VENTURA™ Publisher.

This book is dedicated to the army of skilled people
who have a vision for a world in which ideas may be freely
communicated and where the application of those ideas can benefit
all of society. The Linux operating system platform is one of the
fruits of the exchange of such ideas, their implementation
and ultimately their use the world over.
This book can not cover everything that is to be known
about securing Linux, but without input from many generous
folks who gave their time and who continue to take great care and
have pride in their efforts this book could not be a powerful
tool in helping you to secure your Linux servers.

John Terpstra

For my wife, my children, and John and Bill.
Your presence in my life has been my inspiration.

Paul Love

I would like to dedicate my work to my wife and best friend
Olga M. Lorincz-Reck, and to my mother Dr. Ruth A Reck.

Ronald P. Reck

I would like to dedicate my work to my parents
and siblings. You guys are the best.

Timothy Scanlon

# About the Authors

**John Terpstra** is the CTO/President of PrimaStasys, Inc., a company that mentors information technology companies and facilitates profitable change in business practices. He is a member of the formation committee of the Desktop Linux Consortium, a long term member of the Samba Team (a major Open Source project), and a well known contributor and visionary in the open source community with a very active commercial focus. He is a member of the Open Source Software Institute Advisory Board. He has worked with the Linux Standard Base, Li18nux (now OpenI18N.Org), the Linux Professional Institute, and is a best selling author of *The Official Samba-3 HOWTO and Reference Guide, and Samba-3 by Example: Practical Exercises to Successful Deployment by Prentice Hall.*

John has worked with The SCO Group (previously Caldera Inc.) and Turbolinux® Inc. in VP level positions. Prior to moving to the USA in 1999, John founded Aquasoft Pty Ltd (Aust.) and managed the group for 10 years. He has a Graduate Diploma in Marketing (with Credit), UTS Aust. and an Applied Science Certificate in Chemistry, QUT (Aust.).

**Paul Love**, CISSP, CISA, CISM, Security+, has been in the IT field for 15 years. Paul holds a Master of Science degree in Network Security and a Bachelor's degree in Information Systems. He has been the technical editor for over 10 best selling Linux and Unix books, and ran a successful Linux portal site during the dot com era. Paul is currently a Security Manager at a large utilities service provider.

**Ronald P. Reck** was raised and educated in the Detroit Metropolitan area and on occasion has enough time to miss the friends and culture of the place he still calls home. He is formally trained in theoretical syntax and remains fascinated by language and what it reveals about being human. A passion for linguistics and intensity with computers afford him gainful employment using Perl, XML, and Semantic Web technologies running, of course, under *nix. He prides himself on developing scalable, open source architectural strategies for difficult problems. He resides near our nation's capital with his lovely wife Olga and two cats.

**Timothy Scanlon** is an IT industry veteran who has worked in the US and internationally on a variety of IT and security projects. He has done work in the public and private sectors for a number of Fortune 500 firms, as well as startups like UUNet. In the public sector he has worked as a civilian contractor at various R&D facilities, departments, and branches. His professional interests include cryptography, application & infrastructure design, security, games theory, and simulation and modeling. He thinks that Linux has come a long way from the days when it would all fit on a few floppies.

# About the Contributors

**Mike Shema** is Director of Research and Development at NT Objectives, where he focuses on assessment and mitigation strategies for web application security. During Mike's previous work as a consultant he performed network penetration tests, Web Application security assessments, and wireless network security audits. His experience with Web application security led to co-authoring *Hacking Exposed: Web Applications* and authoring *Hack Notes: Web Application Security.* He also co-authored *The Anti-Hacker Toolkit,* now in its second edition. He also finds enough time to squeeze in a role-playing game or board game every now and then.

**Paul Robertson** has been in information technology and security over 20 years; highlights include being stationed at the White House while in the United States Army and putting *USA Today*'s website on the Internet. Paul currently helps manage risk for hundreds of corporate clients at TruSecure®, and he participates in computer forensics, advocating www.personalfirewallday.org and moderating the Firewall-Wizards Mailing List.

# About the Technical Editor

**Makan Pourzandi** received his Ph. D. degree on parallel and distributed computing in 1995 from the University of Lyon, France. He works for Ericsson Research Canada in the Open Systems Lab Department. He has more than 25 publications in technical reviews and scientific conferences. He first began working with Linux 9 years ago and is involved in several Open Source projects. He was the editor for security requirements for Carrier-Grade Linux Server (CGL) 2.0 and is member of the working group for security requirements for CGL 3.0 from Open Source Development Lab (OSDL).

# About the Series Editor

**Roberta Bragg** (Grain Valley, MO), CISSP, MCSE:Security, MVP, Security+, ETI -Client Server, Certified Technical Trainer, IBM Certified Trainer, DB2-UDB, Citrix Certified Administrator, has been a "Security Advisor" columnist for *MCP* magazine for six years, is a "Security Expert" for searchWin2000.com, and writes for the "Security Watch" newsletter, which has over 55,000 subscribers. Roberta designed, planned, produced, and participated in the first Windows Security Summit, held in Seattle, WA in 2002. Roberta is the author and presenter of the "Windows Security Academy," a three-day hands-on secure network-building workshop. She has taught for SANS and MIS. She was selected by Microsoft to present the IT Professional advanced track for their 2004 Security Summits. Roberta is a Security Evangelist, traveling all over the world consulting, assessing, and training in network and Windows security issues. She is featured in the *Cool Careers for Girls* book series by Ceel Pasternak and Linda Thornburg. Roberta has served as adjunct faculty member at Seattle Pacific University and the Johnson County Community College, teaching courses on Windows 2000 Security Design and Network Security Design. Roberta is the author of the *MCSE Self-Paced Training Kit (Exam 70-298): Designing Security for a Microsoft Windows Server 2003 Network*. Roberta is the lead author of McGraw-Hill/Osborne's *Network Security: The Complete Reference*. She has written on SQL Server 2000, CISSP, and Windows Security for QUE and New Riders.

# At a Glance

# Contents

**PART III**    Once Is Never Enough!

# Foreword

## From Dave Wreski

Security is all about trade-offs. Make the right decision, and users will be satisfied with their level of access to information and resources. Make the wrong decision, and users discover the hard way that maintaining security of of information and resources, is more than than just choosing the right password or defining a policy (which is seldom ever followed(.

Instant access to information is expected these days. With the prevalence of Linux systems and off-the-shelf distributions designed to accomplish any number of tasks, administrators are often caught between unachievable deadlines for getting online systems up and running and the constant barrage of Internet threats posed by malicious individuals (both inside and outside) looking to gain access for their own benefit.

Adding to the difficulty of finding the right balance between controlling access and protecting information, the administrators of today's Linux servers have to juggle access control (security) in addition to other numerous day-to-day tasks. Linux vendors also struggle with the task of providing compelling tools for the administrator while not compromising system security and performance.

Hardening Linux takes a proactive approach to securing the general Linux systems used today, and does an excellent job of managing the tradeoffs and pitfalls many administrators face.

Its comprehensive coverage of technical and corporate policy issues deliver a step-by-step approach for those who need to get security done without understand all that runs under the hood.

This highly regarded group of authors does a tremendous job of ensuring that the average reader achieves a solid understanding of how to harden their Linux systems and how to develop and deploy a sustainable security strategy Although general Linux distribution vendors are making great progress in improving the security of their products, *Hardening Linux* is an invaluable resource for those seeking the perfect balance to improve security while meeting their core business needs.

While on the pursuit towards the "secured" server, a copy of this book, along with other valuable resources including LinuxSecurity.com, are sure to provide the guidance necessary to be vigilant, and learning how to act instead of react, when addressing real-world security issues.

Dave Wreski
Chief Executive Officer, Guardian Digital Corporation
Co-author Linux Security HOWTO
EnGarde Secure Linux Project Lead

*Dave Wreski has been in information technology and security for more than ten years. Founding Guardian Digital in early 1999, Wreski has grown the company to serve hundreds of corporate clients interested in using open source to solve critical business security issues. Prior to launching Guardian Digital, Wreski served as senior architect for UPS Worldwide where he managed the security architecture of the company's data centers. He enjoys advocating open source security and improving acceptance of Linux to the enterprise.*

# Foreword

## From Corey D. Schou

Your system just halted when your customers need it most. You just realized that someone just downloaded your bank information. Your computer just became a zombie and is now attacking other systems on the Internet. The life-support system in the hospital just administered the wrong medicine to a critically ill patient. You awaken in a cold sweat!

These nightmare scenarios—and worse—happen every day because users and managers do not understand how to make a computer system secure enough to provide assurable information systems. They make simple mistakes such as attaching a new computer system to the Internet without tightening it the operating system down. This makes as much sense as parking a new Porsche on a downtown street with the doors unlocked, keys in the ignition, and registration on the passenger seat.

In our day-to-day lives, we take basic precautions without even thinking. When you leave your house, you lock the doors. When you have unneeded copies of documents containing your bank account numbers, you shred them. When you park your car, you take your keys away with you. You should do the same for your computer.

Once you are aware of the potential problems, you learn how to protect your system. This book is an excellent resource for both the novice who wants to learn how to improve security and the expert who wants to make sure he has covered all the bases.

A secure operating system is the first line of defense for computer systems. This book provides a unique perspective on securing Linux systems. The authors lead you through the critical steps to ensure your Linux based systems are secure.

Their concise style makes it clear that as you tighten down your system you must be able to enforce five primary security services: confidentiality, availability, integrity, nonrepudiation, and authentication.

These security services protect valuable information assets while they are transmitted, stored, and processed. For example, Chapter Two jumps right into the protection of transmitted data by hardening network access while Chapter Ten deals with communications security. Throughout the book, the protection of stored data is addressed in a straightforward discussion that includes cryptology tools. The integrity of the processing is dealt with a discussion of hardening the kernel and patch management.

The book is made more interesting with a clear discussion of security policies. Security policies provide a formal structure for secure operations. If the policies fail, you have to learn what to do to when your system has been compromised. The authors demonstrate how to employ monitoring techniques, how to determine system damage by keeping logs, and how to read these logs.

They even discuss the often-overlooked subject of building and justifying the budget. For most technologists, this is usually the last thing they think of. If management does not know how much security services cost, they will not pay the bill. The authors help the reader recognize that technological countermeasures must be complimented by getting management buy-in to the security process. Even if management knows what security services cost, they will not pay for something they do not understand. If they will not pay the bill, the technology will not be implemented and security program will fail.

As you read the book, keep looking for the three nformation states (transmission, storage, and process), five srvices, and three countermeasure (technology, policy, and training).[1]

When you complete the book and use your knowledge well, you can be assured that your system is secure. Don't forget the authors' admonition from Section III: Once is not enough. You must keep working with your system to make sure the security is current. You should monitor your system and read the logs. You must personally apply the training countermeasure every day to keep policy current and technology protected. This book can be summed up by the motto of my research center:

*Awareness – Training – Education*
*There is no patch for ignorance.*

Corey D. Schou, PhD
University Professor of Informatics
Professor of Computer Information Systems
Director of the National Information Assurance Training and Education Center
Idaho State University

---

1    V. Maconachy, C. Schou, D. Welch, and D. J. Ragsdale, "A Model for Information Assurance: An Integrated Approach ," Proceedings of the *2nd Annual IEEE Systems, Man, and Cybernetics Information Assurance Workshop*, West Point, NY, June 5–6, 2001, pp. 306–310

# Note on Security-Enhanced Linux (SeLinux)

Chapter Five discusses hardening the kernel. This is important given operating system security mechanisms are the foundation for ensuring the confidentiality, availability, and integrity of the data on a system. Mainstream operating systems lack the critical security feature required for enforcing separation: mandatory access control. Application security mechanisms are vulnerable to tampering and bypass, and malicious or flawed applications may cause system security failures.

The National Security Agency has had an ongoing open source research project, called SeLinux, (see URL at end of document) to create a security-enhanced Linux system for several years. It has a strong, flexible mandatory access control architecture incorporated into the major subsystems of the kernel. The system provides a mechanism to enforce the separation of information based on confidentiality and integrity requirements.

SeLinux enforces mandatory access control (MAC) policies to confine user programs and system servers to the minimum amount of privilege required. This reduces or eliminates the capability of programs and system daemons to cause harm via buffer overflows or mis-configurations. It further confines damage caused through exploitation of flaws during processing that requires a system-process or privilege-enhancing (`setgid` or `setuid`) program.

SeLinux can be installed on a standard Red Hat installation provided with the book. It is compatible with existing Linux applications and provides source compatibility with existing Linux kernel modules. It addition, it is compatible with existing Linux applications. Existing applications run unchanged if the security policy authorizes their operation.

SeLinux is not a complete security solution for Linux; it demonstrates how mandatory access controls can confine the actions of any process. Some of the important security issues it addresses are:

- Caching of Access Decisions for Efficiency
- Clean Separation of Policy from Enforcement
- Controls over File Systems, Directories, Files, and Open File Descriptions
- Controls over Process Initialization and Inheritance and Program Execution
- Controls over Sockets, Messages, and Network Interfaces
- Controls over Use of "Capabilities"
- Independent of Specific Policies and Policy Languages
- Independent of Specific Security Label Formats and Contents
- Individual Labels and Controls for Kernel Objects and Services
- Support for Policy Changes
- Well-Defined Policy Interfaces

If you want to experiment with SeLinux, you can download a complete package including documentation from http://www.nsa.gov/SeLinux/.

# Introduction

We live in a consumer-oriented society. Symptomatic of the consumer attitude is the notion that everything can be bought and disposed of with great convenience.

Computers have become almost a commodity, so it is not surprising to hear business managers make statements like, "We need to buy a new network," or "Where can we buy a firewall?" One office manager recently stated with absolute indignation that the server he had "bought recently was not secure because someone had been able to hack into it and mess up our files."

This book is designed to help you, the administrator or the the "IT person" cut through the noise on the bookshelves and on the Web and secure your Linux environment. Hardening your system is more like a way of traveling than a destination. A hardened server is the result of a process that begins with a number of definitive proactive steps. Security, reliability, and integrity are states that, once achieved, must be maintained . Hardening Linux provides the principles of system hardening that are applicable regardless of the Linux distribution being used. The concepts and techniques presented in this book go beyond the technical and cover critical political and budgetary considerations that must be achieved or recognized in order to deploy an effective and holistic security strategy.

The information systems cracker is the modern equivalent of the person who breaks into a safe or a bank vault. Some network crackers practice their craft just for thrills, while others may have sinister motives. One thing we can be sure of is that the best defense available is only effective until someone learns to break through and compromise it.

Perpetual vigilance is the price of peace of mind. The cost of vigilance is determined by the measures taken in anticipation of malicious attack against your organization. Vigilance and the associated actions can be borne in an economically sustainable manner. This book is your friend in the quest against an enemy who remains invisible until it is too late. It is our challenge to make his or her efforts uneconomic and unrewarding.

Linux servers are increasingly subject to scurrilous activity, as are all other server and desktop platforms. The majority of attacks and intrusions that occur are the result of inadequate measures taken to harden the network and its resources. So let's start with the right steps to close the door on the potential for a security breach, and then work toward putting an iron safety net around your information systems.

It has been often pointed out that the only totally secure server is one that is turned off and sealed inside concrete. Unfortunately, that is not a practical solution to business and organizational needs. A server can also be secured by isolating it from all users, but that too is seldom feasible. In the real world, computer systems must be secured and hardened while they exist in a production environment. Securing a running production system is somewhat like refurbishing a firing range while ducking to avoid flying bullets. The safest advice is to secure a server offline, then introduce it into active service when it has been fully hardened.

Hardening involves more than security. It includes all action that must be taken to make the total Linux server suitable for the task for which it is being used. A holistic approach is necessary if the results of hardening are to be acceptable in the long run. New computer security legislation is being enacted almost daily and increases the burden and responsibilities of system administration. An organization may be held responsible for spam that appears to have originated from one of its network systems. Executive management is being held to greater account to assure data integrity and security. A leak of confidential information, such as credit card information, may send a victimized business to its doom.

Our journey begins with seven initiatives that will help you take control of your servers. The remaining chapters should be followed with a resolute determination to gain and hold effective control over all network resources, never giving a criminal opportunity to do more harm.

# Overview

This book approaches the system hardening challenge from a position that is rather uncommon in the Linux world. It assumes that you have purchased a commercially supported Linux server product from a reputable company that does all the right things to help secure your server. Bear in mind that you are responsible for applying the security updates your vendor provides, but we assume that they are the experts in providing a secure system, particularly when the patches and updates they provide have been applied.

## Chapter 1

The first chapter will help you to verify that the Linux server is in a condition that is suitable for hardening. If these steps provide cause for concern you should ask yourself, "Is this system worthy of hardening?" If the system has been compromised before the hardening process has even begun you should consider reinstallation from installation media that is known to be safe.

Assuming that your server shows no evidence of intrusion or of having been compromised your server is in good shape to commence the hardening process.

# Chapter 2

Following the principle that a safe computer is one that has been shut down, you will ensure that only essential processes are running. This closes the door to potential intrusion through exploitation of services that are not needed and possibly not monitored.

# Chapter 3

Now that the system is providing only essential services the next step is to make the server almost invisible to prying eyes from the public Internet. Your new firewall configuration will make it difficult for an intruder or an assailant to gain system access. Internal network interfaces are assumed to be trusted, but external interfaces can not be trusted and must reflect this as a fact.

# Chapter 4

A proactive security policy will do everything possible to ensure that an intruder will find as few tools to make easy any intended alien activities. True to this sentiment, you will remove all software that is not needed for the services that the Linux system must provide.

# Chapter 5

In light of the increasing presence of people who have nasty intent and who make an art out of exploiting newly discovered security holes or weaknesses, one must assume that sooner or later the server may need to be reinstalled. This chapter will help you to prepare for the inevitable encroachment that we all hope will never happen.

# Chapter 6

Intruders want root level access because they know that is the only way they can get around all system restrictions, but we must fully anticipate system misuse by the normal user also. In this chapter you will learn how to use techniques to help protect files from the prying eyes and wanton access attempts by the ordinary user. You will learn how to protect even directories that are world writable so that only the owner of a file will be able to write to it.

## Chapter 7

Learn how to protect the most sensitive information through the use of cryptography. You will take positive steps to deprive an intruder as well as the curious user of access to sensitive data. Learn how to secure identity information and sensitive financial records. Make use of the crypto-filesystem that can add a great deal of peace of mind to your business.

## Chapter 8

Understanding of how authentication and system access controls function will help you to provide better locks and improved safeguards against unauthorized system access. This chapter covers the pluggable authentication modules (PAM) and the name service switcher (NSS) that handle the core identity validation and access control for the Linux system.

## Chapter 9

The UNIX system permits processes to be run from a branch in the file system that looks like it is the whole machine. In reality, the process is running in a tightly sealed off part of the real file system, but a user who happens to intrude into the protected process will be able to damage only the sealed-off area, not the whole machine. This means that it is possible to contain intrusion damages to only the affected service thereby helping to keep unaffected service operative. This chapter is very detail oriented, as it must be, so you can gain a sure foothold on system integrity.

## Chapter 10

Communication over local as well as public networks can not be avoided. Learn how to secure all private traffic that must traverse a public network infrastructure. You will learn how to use secure data tunneling techniques as well as use of secure communication tools.

## Chapter 11

In this chapter you will experience the use of system monitoring as well as the use of sophisticated tools to probe and prove your Linux system against security weaknesses.

## Chapter 12

Scattered throughout this book you will find reference to logging or critical information. Here you will learn how to configure a centralized log server that can be equipped with automated log file scanning and reporting tools. Never give a criminal an even break; instead you will most likely be alerted to an intruder before he even knows you are watching him.

## Chapter 13

Just when you think that the application of patches and security updates is so easy, you stumble upon this chapter to help you to take hold of a most intensely important responsibility. Seasoned security veterans are well aware that change management is part of the patching and update process. This chapter may seem so obvious, but do not let the benefits of proper controls pass you by. There is something for even the most experienced security plumber in this chapter.

## Chapter 14

What more can be done to find the cancer within? This chapter provides a cogent answer to nagging doubts regarding system security – system self monitoring is an indispensable technique in integrity management. This chapter puts it in perspective.

## Chapter 15

Find out how to get management buy-in for Linux system hardening. The tips and tools presented here are worth more their weight in gold – they will help you to get total commitment to the return on investment opportunity that management expects.

## Chapter 16

Finally, your server has been secured and management has "bought into" your security goals and objectives. Now to maintain that support you'll learn how to set goals and implement sustainable security policies and practices that work.

# Linux Naming Conventions Used in This Book

In this book we use several abbreviations for SUSE and Red Hat products, as well as for the Security-enhanced Linux kernel from NSA.

- Security-enhanced Linux is abbreviated SELinux.
- SUSE LINUX Enterprise Server is abbreviated SLES, and you will see frequent mention of SLES8, SLES9 and SLES8/9. SUSE products include:
  - SUSE LINUX 9.1 Personal
  - SUSE LINUX 9.1 Professional
  - SUSE LINUX Desktop
  - SUSE LINUX Enterprise Server 8

- SUSE LINUX Enterprise Server 9
- SUSE LINUX Openexchange Server 4.1

- Red Hat products are also referred to by their abbreviated forms. Red Hat Enterprise Linux Server 3.0 is referred to as RHEL, and Red Hat Enterprise Linux Advanced Server 3.0 is called RHAS. Red Hat Linux products include:

  - Red Hat Linux 9
  - Red Hat Fedora Core 1
  - Red Hat Fedora Core 2
  - Red Hat Enterprise Linux Server 3.0
  - Red Hat Enterprise Linux Advanced Server 3.0

The authors would especially like to thank Red Hat Linux and Novell (the new owners of SUSE) for their support, most valued assistance, and generous access to products that made possible the preparation of this book.

# Part I

# Do These Seven Things First

# Chapter 1

## Critical First Steps

- Examine Systems for Evidence of Compromise
- Check System Stability and Availability

It takes time to develop and deploy a comprehensive hardening plan. Meanwhile systems may already be compromised or may not be operating properly. They may be leaking information, be busy infecting other systems on your network, or even be part of coordinated attacks on other machines. Regardless of their security status, systems that are unstable due to hardware or power issues may be further weakened by your hardening efforts. Adding security controls to systems you no longer control, or toppling already subperforming servers, serves no purpose. Before you harden a current production system, you must determine if it's still your system to harden. You must make sure it is operating correctly. After you harden systems, you must have a way to determine if the steps you've taken are keeping the system secure.

Stop and do this now. Test the system to determine its status. If you find evidence of an unauthorized intrusion, presence of malware of the presence of a root kit, or of evidence of attack, use approved methods to reclaim the system. Cleaning and reclaiming may entail obtaining and running special software, following instructions for removing files and reconfiguring settings, or wiping the hard drive and reinstalling. Next, ensure that the system is operating properly. This chapter provides the steps that will teach you how.

## HEADS UP!

Before you attempt to recover a system that has been compromised, sit down and count the costs and the final results. You should consider which is more cost effective, to reinstall or to recover. Past experience suggests that the real cost of recovery is often more than double the initial estimate. The cost of reinstallation is often premised on a worst-case scenario. In other words, there is a tendency to underestimate the costs of system recovery and to overestimate the costs of reinstallation. In addition, it is wise to consider the possibility that a compromised machine may have hidden backdoors installed. When evidence of one successful attack is discovered, you must consider if it's possible that cleaning the system of some recognizable Trojan horse or other results may still leave hidden modifications or software that will allow an attacker to manage the system. There are no hard and fast rules that can be used to make the decision of recovery versus reinstall. You will have to weigh the cost and the risk.

# Examine Systems for Evidence of Compromise

Perform the following steps to determine if the system is clean and not under attack.

1. Terminate unauthorized users.

2. Identify and shut down unauthorized processes.

3.  Check log files for evidence of intrusion attempts.

4.  Check for potential file system damage.

# Terminate Unauthorized Users

Unauthorized users can originate from inside or outside the organization. Unauthorized external system access must be terminated with extreme urgency, particularly if the user appears to be hiding his or her identity. Unauthorized internal users may necessitate disciplinary action depending on the nature of the access.

Our hypothetical server is at IP address 10.0.0.95. Follow these steps now:

1.  Log in at the console to the server as the user root.

2.  Execute the following command:

```
linux:~ # w
```

The listing in Figure 1-1 is obtained. The **w** command produces a listing of all users currently logged in. It lists the source of the login and shows the process currently being run. In this case we see a user called l33t (most likely meant to be pronounced as "elite"), who could be a cracker.

The fact that this user has logged in from three different systems on our internal network, one of which is the external gateway machine, demands investigation. The login from the system at IP address 10.0.0.98 has subsequently logged onto our gateway to the Internet. This is potentially alarming.

The login from the system at IP address 10.0.0.12 has an outgoing FTP connection to ftp.gateway.com. We do not know what this user may be doing. The connection may be being used to download or upload software we do not want to have anything to do with.

It is apparent that the user is also using the utility called **top** to monitor who is on the system. Immediate action should be taken to cut the user off, but it would appear that this potential intruder may already have compromised our gateway machine and at least two internal systems. The safest solution is to log into the gateway system to

```
linux:~ # w
  1:48am   up   8:31,   9 users,   load average: 0.07, 0.03, 0.00
USER     TTY      FROM           LOGIN@   IDLE    JCPU    PCPU  WHAT
root     :0       console        8:52pm   ?       0.00s   ?     -
root     pts/0    -              8:52pm   4:55m   0.00s   ?     -
root     pts/1    -              9:10pm   0.00s   0.11s   0.01s w
root     pts/3    -              9:56pm   12:55   0.07s   0.07s /bin/bash
133t     pts/2    10.0.0.98      1:23am   12:48   0.18s   0.13s ssh root@10.0.0.1
133t     pts/4    10.0.0.1       1:24am   17.00s  0.24s   0.22s top
133t     pts/5    10.0.0.1       1:25am   12:48   0.03s   0.03s -bash
133t     pts/6    10.0.0.12      1:29am   17:08   0.06s   0.01s ncftp ftp.gateway.com
root     pts/7    10.0.0.1       1:33am   13:47   0.03s   0.00s ncftp ftp.dwdg.de
linux:~ # []
```

**Figure 1-1.**   Output of **w** command

see if this user has originated from an external Internet location. This is the action we follow and it reveals the following line in the output from running the **w** command:

```
l33t    pts/93   dang.xployt.us  1:34am 0.00s  1.12s  ssh 10.0.0.95
```

This means that our gateway machine, which should have no user accounts at all, has been compromised by an intruder who has created an account called l33t and who is using it to intrude further on internal systems. It is now clear that we must take immediate drastic action. The intruder may have replaced system executable files so that he has control of the machine at all times. We know that he has logged in as the user root from our gateway machine and is using it to access an FTP server at ftp.dwdg.de, so this means that he has root level access on the gateway server.

This situation demands that the gateway connection to the outside world must be shut down until it has been again secured. Additionally, we must now investigate all servers and clients on our internal network to identify what damage may have been done.

The action warranted by anyone who is paranoid about security would be to immediately reinstall the gateway system and secure it before reopening our connection to the Internet. By shutting off the connection to the Internet, we have immediately frozen the intruder's activities. If possible the gateway machine should be replaced so that the compromised system can be examined to identify what the intruder may have been doing. Intrusion evidence that demonstrates unauthorized system access should be reported to the police in case criminal activity may have taken place.

To avoid all risk, it is likely that we will reinstall all critical internal servers, but that decision should wait until the issue has been more fully investigated.

Had no unusual activities been noted on the machine, the next step would be to check for abnormal accounts.

As a precautionary move, all suspect accounts should be locked by executing

```
linux:~ # passwd -l username
```

Duplicate accounts in /etc/passwd that have the same UID should also be disabled this way. It is not uncommon for an intruder to set up an account that has UID=0 (a duplicate of the root account) so that he or she can access the system with root level privilege and yet minimize the risk of early detection. In many cases this would warrant suspicion of serious system compromise. This would again be treated in a manner consistent with the gravity it deserves.

When a system intrusion has occurred, it is important that essential evidence is recorded before deleting unauthorized accounts. Be careful not to destroy evidence you may later need in order to be able to prosecute an intruder.

Another useful tool for identifying unauthorized user logins is the tool called **last**. A sample of its use is shown in Figure 1-2. This shows the logins by the users l33t and drule. A check of the user account for drule reveals suspicious facts. The user's UID is 0, and the home directory is /var/adm/drule. This could well be a backdoor account and must be blocked until its ownership and purpose can be determined.

```
linux:~ # last
root      pts/2                       Thu May 20 13:30    still logged in
root      pts/1                       Thu May 20 12:58    still logged in
root      pts/0                       Thu May 20 12:55    still logged in
root      :0           console        Thu May 20 12:55    still logged in
reboot    system boot  2.4.19-4GB     Thu May 20 12:54          (00:36)
root      pts/7        10.0.0.1       Thu May 20 01:33 - 02:50  (01:17)
133t      pts/6        10.0.0.12      Thu May 20 01:29 - 02:01  (00:32)
133t      pts/5        10.0.0.1       Thu May 20 01:25 - 02:01  (00:36)
133t      pts/4        10.0.0.1       Thu May 20 01:24 - 02:01  (00:37)
133t      pts/2        10.0.0.98      Thu May 20 01:23 - 02:01  (00:37)
root      pts/2        10.0.0.98      Thu May 20 01:11 - 01:11  (00:00)
drule     pts/4        localhost      Wed May 19 22:05 - 22:58  (00:53)
root      pts/4        localhost      Wed May 19 22:04 - 22:05  (00:00)
root      pts/4        localhost      Wed May 19 22:02 - 22:04  (00:02)
133t      pts/2        10.0.0.98      Wed May 19 22:00 - 22:58  (00:58)
root      pts/3                       Wed May 19 21:56 - down   (05:20)
root      pts/2        10.0.0.98      Wed May 19 21:50 - 21:59  (00:08)
root      pts/2        10.0.0.98      Wed May 19 21:11 - 21:33  (00:21)
root      pts/1                       Wed May 19 21:10 - down   (06:06)
root      pts/0                       Wed May 19 20:52 - 03:15  (06:23)
root      :0           console        Wed May 19 20:52 - 03:15  (06:23)
root      pts/3                       Wed May 19 18:22 - 21:56  (03:33)
root      pts/3                       Wed May 19 17:44 - 18:22  (00:37)
root      pts/2                       Wed May 19 17:27 - 21:11  (03:44)
root      pts/1                       Wed May 19 17:21 - 21:10  (03:48)
root      pts/0                       Wed May 19 17:18 - 20:52  (03:34)
root      :0           console        Wed May 19 17:18 - 20:52  (03:34)
```

**Figure 1-2.**   Example output from the last log file

The **last** utility reports activity from the /var/log/wtmp file. Every system user access is recorded in this file. Smart crackers will often delete the /var/log/wtmp file to remove evidence of their activities. They will frequently also delete any history file they may have created. In both cases, evidence that this may have happened is present when logs show a logout without a matching login record. If this is found, you must immediately raise suspicion and alarm until investigation clears the air.

In the event that no unusual activity is noted and no unusual accounts are found, simply move on to the next steps. You can be thankful that the Linux system does not currently appear to be under threat, but do not breathe easy just yet. Lurking beneath harmless-looking parts of the system software could be something more sinister than a currently logged-in user, so get ready for the next steps.

## Identify and Shut Down Unauthorized Processes

Once a Unix or Linux system has been compromised, any application can be made to appear as a standard system utility. Applications can be downloaded to the system either in ready-to-execute form or in cleverly disguised source code form later to be compiled and run on the system.

On a system that had been compromised, someone found a harmless-looking file in the /usr/lib directory. This started a process of investigation that ultimately found a backdoor to the system as well as how it was being initiated.

For some days, the administrator was perplexed that shortly following a system reboot a process called **sndme** was running. A system scan found no file by that name on the system. When the command **netstat -ap** was run, the following line was present in output:

```
udp      0    0  *:32145       *:*         LISTEN   1118/sndme
```

This means that the process called **sndme** was waiting for something to happen on UDP port 32145. It had been easy to identify the fact that this unusual process was running, but it took a little genius to find how this exploit was able to hide from view.

The key to unlocking the mystery was the finding of a file called sendmail.txt. A careful search of startup files isolated a shell script being called during startup that did the following:

1. Created a directory called /var/sndtmp.
2. Copied the sendmail.txt file to that directory and renamed it to snd.Z.
3. Executed **uncompress snd.Z**.
4. Executed the file as a shell script by running **sh snd**. This extracted a file called snd.c.
5. Compiled the file with the command **gcc -o sndme snd.c**.
6. Linked the file sndme to /bin/sndme.
7. Deleted the /var/sndtmp directory.
8. Executed /bin/sndme.
9. Delete /bin/sndme.

The **sndme** process was waiting for a specific UDP message that would open a root exploit to the system. The frightening part of this exploit is that, according to system logs, it went undetected for over six months. Someone had obviously penetrated the Unix system and had opened the door for a future revisit. What the intruder had done remains a mystery to this day. The server ran an application that held very sensitive data. No damages could be found to the database, as a printout of the data matched printed records. Management of that company do not know whether their sensitive customer information has fallen into enemy hands or not.

The moral: Unauthorized processes may originate from any source. They may be Trojan horses that have been planted by an intruder, or they can be legitimate processes that should not be running or that should not have been executed by a particular person.

As an administrator you should run the **ps** utility and validate that every process found running is legitimate. You should execute the **netstat -ap** utility to find which processes are active on particular TCP/IP ports. Each such process should be validated. If a process is not known, raise the alarm at once. If an unknown process involves network activity, disconnect the Linux system from all external sources of system access until it has either been killed off or validated as a legitimate service.

## Check Log Files for Possible Evidence of Intrusion Attempts

The main system log file can be a gold mine of information. It is an essential first port of call in the search for evidence that might demand an answer. One such source is the file /var/log/messages. An example log file fragment is shown in Figure 1-3.

This file should be scanned for two keywords: **fail** and **repeat**. The following commands can be used to do this:

```
[root@linux /] # grep fail /var/log/messages
[root@linux /] # grep repeat /var/log/messages
```

A positive response for either keyword must be investigated. The example shows repeated failed login attempts. It also shows a successful login shortly following a failed one. The successful root login at the start of the log file fragment could have been done by a legitimate user who logged out to leave the terminal. But the sequence of failed logins compels investigation due to the fact that the Linux system may have been compromised.

Any Linux system found in this condition should immediately be presumed to be in need of recovery or reinstallation. Do your homework before jumping to unwarranted conclusions. Contact the users who experienced an apparent login problem if they can recall the incident. If not, you may need to dig deeper to find the right answer. When it appears that the cost of elucidating what really happened seems to get out of control, consider each option and its cost. It may be more cost effective to reinstall the system, or to replace it, than to find a totally conclusive answer to why or how the log entries may have occurred.

```
May 21 02:40:26 linux sshd[1654]: Could not reverse map address 10.0.0.98.
May 21 02:40:26 linux sshd[1654]: Accepted password for root from ::ffff:10.0.0.98 port 4174
May 21 02:40:44 linux sshd[1673]: Could not reverse map address 10.0.0.98.
May 21 02:40:44 linux sshd[1673]: Failed password for jht from ::ffff:10.0.0.98 port 4175
May 21 02:41:05 linux last message repeated 7 times
May 21 02:41:24 linux sshd[1676]: Could not reverse map address 10.0.0.98.
May 21 02:41:24 linux sshd[1676]: Failed password for drule from ::ffff:10.0.0.98 port 4177
May 21 02:41:40 linux last message repeated 5 times
May 21 02:41:57 linux sshd[1678]: Could not reverse map address 10.0.0.98.
May 21 02:41:57 linux sshd[1678]: Failed password for l33t from ::ffff:10.0.0.98 port 4178
May 21 02:42:22 linux last message repeated 7 times
May 21 02:42:40 linux sshd[1680]: Could not reverse map address 10.0.0.98.
May 21 02:42:40 linux sshd[1680]: Failed password for jht from ::ffff:10.0.0.98 port 4179
May 21 02:42:44 linux sshd[1680]: Accepted password for jht from ::ffff:10.0.0.98 port 4179
May 21 02:44:26 linux sshd[1675]: Did not receive identification string from ::ffff:10.0.0.9
linux:~ # []
```

**Figure 1-3.**    Example var/log/ messages file entries showing attempted failed intrusions

# Check for Potential System File Damage

You can breathe a little easier now that you have found no early immediate evidence of system intrusion or compromise. Both Red Hat Linux and SUSE Linux use a system software management system known as the Red Hat Package Manager (RPM).

There were several precursors to RPM that permit software to be packaged in a manner that facilitates system maintenance. The RPM packaging method creates and maintains a database of all files that it installs. This database contains vital information from which RPM can determine which files have been changed since installation. It is therefore also possible to compare the list of files that are on the system with the list of known files. From this, a listing of non-system files can be obtained. This is in part what is done by the SUSE YaST2 backup tool to create a system backup.

Find out now which files and file system settings are no longer as they were when the system was installed. This method works the same on Red Hat Linux as it does on SUSE Linux. Log in as the root user, then execute the following command:

```
[root@linux /] # rpm -Va > /tmp/rpmVa.log
```

The output from running this command consists of a line for each file RPM has installed on the system. The format of each line consists of an eight-character status field followed by a space, a letter *c* denoting a file, another space, then the file or directory name. The eight-character field contains the following characters only if a change has been noted:

- **S**   File size has changed.
- **M**   Mode (permissions and file type) has changed.
- **5**   The MD5 checksum has changed.
- **D**   The characteristics of a device node have changed.
- **L**   A symbolic link has been changed.
- **U**   The owner of the file/directory/device node has changed.
- **G**   The group owner of the file/directory/device node has changed.
- **T**   The modification timestamp has changed. If a file is found to be missing, the word "missing" is printed in place of the status field.

Examine each line of the report that RPM generated to identify what types of changes may have been made. Configuration files will have changed during system configuration. Binary files must never change. Binary files are placed in well-known locations such as /bin, /sbin, /usr/bin, /usr/sbin, /usr/X11R6/bin, and so on. Changes in binary files must be treated with great alarm. If the change cannot be clearly identified as one implemented by deliberate action taken during installation or as part of system administration, the file should be replaced from its original binary source RPM package.

An example of immediately actionable output would be an entry that says

```
.M......    /usr/bin/write
```

which means that the executable file called write has been modified. This is unlikely to have occurred if the system has been properly maintained by installation only of RPM updates.

Where a binary file must be updated or changed, the safe and normal method of change involves installation of an update via RPM. This keeps the RPM database up to date. You could reinstall the RPM package that provides the modified binary file.

---

## HEADS UP!

Seasoned Linux administrators often generate a snapshot report using this tool as soon as system configuration is complete. This reference snapshot is then stored in a safe location, typically on a floppy disk or on another network file system. At a future time the original reference copy can be compared with a freshly generated report to isolate files that may have changed. It is easier to deal with reports of incremental change to save having to wade through long listings. Fortunately, a typical report from a freshly installed system will seldom be more than 400 lines long.

---

If a binary file is found to differ from the RPM database record, immediately reinstall the package it came from. The originating RPM package name can be found by executing

```
[root@linux /] # rpm -qf fully_qualified_path_and_file_name
```

Assuming that the report generated by **rpm -Va** indicates that /bin/splash has changed, its source binary package can be found by executing

```
[root@linux] # rpm -qf /bin/splash
bootsplash-1.0-71
```

This means that reinstallation of the package bootsplash-1.0-71-i586.rpm will restore this file to its original contents. Always take a backup copy of the modified file for later analysis and so it can be produced as evidence in court in case the ability presents itself later to prosecute an intruder or a perpetrator of an unauthorized change.

The file RPM package can be reinstalled by executing the following from a directory containing the source binary RPM:

```
[root@linux /] # rpm -Uvh --nodeps --force bootsplash-1.0-71-i586.rpm
```

Hopefully the report will have generated no alarm. There are two final steps to complete before commencing the process of hardening the entire system.

# Check System Stability and Availability

A stable system is able to do the job it is asked to do. An unstable system uses resources unnecessarily and may cause problems for other systems. It may also unexpectedly go offline, crash, and/or become unrecoverable. You should look for any evidence of instability and correct it. Availability is part of the securities domain, and external denial-of-service attacks are not the only threat to continued operation. Two tasks are necessary:

- Validate hardware operation.
- Ensure that power is stable.

## Validate Hardware Operation

A transport company spent four days and over $35,000 installing a new firewall. Staff had been complaining about poor server performance. The administrator noticed that base system load had gone up dramatically following a major virus problem that affected all MS Windows desktop systems. During times of poor Linux server performance there was no notable network traffic. The assumption was made that the Linux system might have been affected by a virus or may have been intruded upon by someone from the Internet connection. The administrator was instructed to put in a new firewall and then sort out the server. The real problem was not a virus or compromise, it was hardware malfunction. If the administrator had initially looked for hardware failure, a great deal of frustration, expense, and loss of productivity could have been avoided.

Hardware failures are mostly easy to detect. Monitor, keyboard, mice, and serial port failures are generally very obvious. Failures in storage media will almost certainly generate error logs in the system log file. To see if there may be a storage media problem, execute the following:

```
[root@linux /] # grep error /var/log/messages
```

A telltale hardware fault will produce an error message such as

```
Ide: sector buffer error
ide: I/O error, dev XX:xx (had), ...
```

It is not uncommon to find error messages pertaining to CD-ROM and DVD drive use. These can be treated symptomatically.

Hard disk storage–related errors must never be ignored. If a hard disk is defective, replace it. It never pays to gamble with file storage hardware integrity.

## Make Sure Power Is Stable

Unstable power sources pose great risk to data integrity. File system data can be damaged by power fluctuations, spikes, and surges. Brownouts and blackouts can do damage to hardware also. One fact is often overlooked: most damage to hardware is incurred as power is restored following a brownout or a blackout.

When power supply is interrupted briefly, the computer may show no immediate symptoms. Switch mode power supplies store power that is in flux while the power unit is in normal use. Depending on the design of the power unit, the power that is in flux may take a few milliseconds to be fully dissipated in the event of an unplanned interruption to power supply. When power flow is interrupted and restored before the power unit loses all power, the condition known as a brownout has occurred. The computer generally does not need to be rebooted following a brownout.

A complete power loss means that the system will have to be rebooted. This condition is caused by a blackout. Following a brownout or a blackout in the electrical supply grid, as power supply is restored there may be a sag and/or a surge in voltage as equipment comes back into service or recovers from the loss. The use of power conditioning equipment, an uninterruptible power system (UPS), is essential to protect computer equipment from exposure to such events.

Table 1-1 lists the most common hardware failures.

UPSs are manufactured in many different types. The basic types of UPSs sold today include

- Power conditioning (filters)
- Failover battery backup
- Always-on UPS

Failover battery backup UPSs generally provide a filtered mains supply. When the mains supply fails, a battery operated inverter will cut in to provide power continuity. On the whole, failover UPSs must experience an interruption in supply before cutting over. This causes symptoms equivalent to a brownout to pass through to the computer system.

Always-on UPSs supply the computer equipment with power that is generated by an inverter. This generally results in the best quality of power that can be obtained. The inverter will run off rectified mains power with an active online battery that operates in parallel. When the grid power supply fails, the battery continues to provide power to the inverter. When power is restored, the battery is simply recharged while online.

Uninterruptible power supply technology is a specialist art. Make sure you obtain sound advice in selecting the right type of UPS for your installation. Also, be certain to follow the manufacturer's advice regarding planned maintenance for the UPS.

| Failure Type | Cause |
|---|---|
| Hard drives, monitors | Power sags and surges |
| Motherboards and peripherals | Power spikes |
| Serial ports and network interfaces | Power spikes and lightning strikes |

**Table 1-1.**    The Most Common Hardware Failures

# Part II

# Take It From The Top: The Systematic Hardening Process

# Chapter 2

# Hardening Network Access: Disable Unnecessary Services

- Step 1: Take the Machine Off the Network
- Step 2: Determine Required Services
- Step 3: Determine Services' Dependencies
- Step 4: Prevent Services from Running
- Step 5: Reboot
- Step 6: Check Configuration for Unnecessary Services
- Step 7: Check Configuration for Necessary Services
- Step 8: Return the Machine to the Network

The main reason to put a computer on a network is so that it can communicate with other computers. Computer security is often an afterthought when deploying a new server. Unfortunately, correctly configuring system security requires delicately balancing system access. You must provide just enough access, but not too much.

The best strategy to adopt when hardening any system is to limit machine-to-machine communication to just the necessary communications. The first step in limiting communication is to only allow a service to be enabled or running if it is fulfilling a requirement.

The best time to configure services is right after installation. However, when creating a server it may be difficult to determine exactly what is needed. If this is the case, the following nine steps present a quick recipe for turning off all unnecessary network services and ensuring they remain off. You can return to this fundamental process over and over again as your system requirements change. You can also use the steps right after an installation, before placing the system on the network. Each individual step in the following list is explained in its own section.

1. Remove the machine from the network.

2. Identify the services you intend to support.

3. Determine the dependencies of the supported services.

4. Alter the system configuration so only necessary services are enabled.

5. Reboot the system.

6. Check to see that unnecessary services are not running.

7. Check to see if the services you require are running.

8. Return the machine to the network and verify network connectivity.

---

**NOTE**   For the work in this chapter, you are going to need to be root to make changes and to check or test configurations.

---

# Step 1: Take the Machine Off the Network

If you have just installed the server's operating system it is likely that the current condition poses an unnecessary security risk. To minimize your exposure it is safest to take the server off the network until the services are tightened down. Merely unplug the Ethernet cable for now. It will get plugged in during step 8. If you cannot unplug the Ethernet cable, it is possible to temporarily disable the server's network interface by typing the following from a command prompt (as root):

```
ifconfig interface down
```

For example:

```
ifconfig eth0 down
```

Repeat this step for as many network interfaces as the server has.

## Runlevels

Linux systems, like Unix systems, are designed for doing multiple tasks. A runlevel, or run state, as it is sometimes called, is a number between 1 and 6 that describes the role the system is playing. All the applications that are running at a runlevel are intended to work together. Easy transition between different configurations is considered one of the strengths that Linux systems have. Changing the machine runlevel is easy; it requires just one command, **init**. You can change the runlevel by typing **init** *newrunlevel* at the command line (as root). For example, **init 6** would reboot the system since runlevel 6 is for reboot. The default runlevel your computer has is set in /etc/inittab on the line that looks like **id:3:initdefault:.** Servers with a text login have a default runlevel of 3, and servers with a graphic login have the default runlevel of 5. The difference between a text and graphical login is whether the X server is running. To maximize your server's available power, it makes good sense to have a default runlevel of 3 and to not be logged into the window manager for no reason for days at a time. Table 2-1 lists possible runlevels and what they mean.

| Runlevel | State |
|----------|-------|
| 0 | Shutdown |
| 1 | Single user mode |
| 2 | Multiuser without network |
| 3 | Multiuser text based |
| 4 | Multiuser with X server Slackware/BSD) |
| 5 | Multiuser with X server (Red Hat, SUSE, Debian) |
| 6 | Reboot |
| S | Single user (Slackware) |
| M | Multiuser (Slackware) |

**Table 2-1.**    Runlevels

# Step 2: Determine Required Services

The second step in hardening network services is to determine which services need to be supported. Does the server need to act as a shared drive for Windows? Is the machine a corporate web server? Do you need an e-mail server? It is likely that the server will fulfill a combination of different purposes. Requirements may change over time as new tasks are delegated to an existing server, but you should not turn on unnecessary services now. When they become necessary, you can enable them. Unless you know what you are trying to achieve, it is impossible to determine the correct balance between too much and too little access. If you are eager to get started, but are not absolutely sure which services you will need, look at the service configuration suggestions for SLES8 and Red Hat Enterprise Linux AS 3.0 in Tables 2-2 and 2-3. They will give you an idea of what

| Service | On by Default? | Turn Off? | Leave On When Using... | Purpose |
|---|---|---|---|---|
| freeWnn | Yes | Yes | Japanese | Japanese conversion engine |
| apmd | Yes | Yes | A laptop | Monitors battery status for laptops |
| arptables_jf | Yes | Yes | | Automates a packet filtering firewall with **arptables** |
| atd | Yes | | | AT batch job daemon |
| autofs | Yes | | | **autofs** daemon |
| canna | Yes | Yes | Japanese | Canna Japanese conversion engine |
| crond | Yes | | | Cron job service |
| cups | Yes | Yes | Printing | CUPS printer daemon |
| gpm | Yes | Yes | Cut and paste on the console | Allows mouse on console |
| hpoj | Yes | Yes | An HP OfficeJet | HP OfficeJet support |
| ip6tables | Yes | | | **ip6tables** firewall |
| iptables | Yes | | | **iptables** firewall |
| irqbalance | Yes | | | Distributed interrupts across CPU on multiprocessor systems |
| isdn | Yes | Yes | ISDN | ISDN drivers |
| kkeytable | Yes | | | Keyboard settings |
| kudzu | Yes | Yes | Run this by hand if hardware changes | Hardware probe for configuring new hardware |
| mdmonitor | Yes | Yes | RAID | Software RAID monitoring |
| microcode_ctl | Yes | | | Applies CPU microcode |

**Table 2-2.**    Red Hat Enterprise Linux AS 3.0 Services Baseline

| Service | On by Default? | Turn Off? | Leave On When Using... | Purpose |
|---|---|---|---|---|
| netfs | Yes | Yes | NFS | Mounts and unmounts NFS, SMB, and NCP file systems |
| network | Yes | | | Configures network interfaces and routing |
| nfslock | Yes | Yes | NFS | NFS locking daemon |
| pcmcia | Yes | Yes | A laptop | PCMCIA card configuration database |
| portmap | Yes | Yes | NFS | DARPA port to RPC program number mapper |
| random | Yes | | | Random number generator |
| rawdevices | Yes | | | Enables raw I/O |
| rrhnsd | Yes | Yes | A service contract | Program for querying Red Hat network for updates |
| sendmail | Yes | Yes | E-mail server | SMTP server |
| sgi_fam | Yes | | | File monitoring daemon |
| sshd | Yes | | | OpenSSH SSH daemon |
| syslog | Yes | | | System logging daemon |
| xinetd | Yes | | | Internet daemon |

**Table 2-2.**    Red Hat Enterprise Linux AS 3.0 Services Baseline *(continued)*

services are on by default in runlevel 3 after the initial operating system install. The tables also make suggestions about some services you can turn off unless you are sure you need them.

## Red Hat Enterprise Linux AS 3.0 Services Baseline

Table 2-2 lists the services that are running by default in Red Hat Enterprise Linux AS 3.0 at runlevel 3. As you scan the table, look for services that are not necessary on the server. For example, if your server is not a mail server, you should be sure to turn off Sendmail. Mail is one of the most likely network services to be targeted by hackers. This is partly because it is widely deployed and partly because it is a critical infrastructure component that administrators are reluctant to upgrade or patch, even though many vulnerabilities have been discovered and are widely recognized.

## SLES8 Services Baseline

Table 2-3 shows the services baseline for SLES8.

| Services | On by Default? | Turn Off? | Leave On When Using | Purpose |
|----------|----------------|-----------|---------------------|---------|
| alsasound | Yes | Yes | Sound | Loads ALSA driver |
| atd | Yes | | | AT batch job daemon |
| cron | Yes | | | Cron job service |
| evlog | Yes | | | Event logging daemon |
| hotplug | Yes | | | Linux hotplugging support |
| hwscan | Yes | | | Hardware scan and reconfiguration |
| ippl | Yes | | | IPPL protocols logger |
| iscsi | Yes | Yes | Remote SCSI devices | Access to remote SCSI devices |
| joystick | Yes | Yes | A joystick | Joystick drivers |
| kbd | Yes | No | | Keyboard settings |
| ldirectord | Yes | Yes | A cluster | Linux Director daemon for clustering |
| microcode | Yes | | | Updates Intel CPU microcode |
| network | Yes | | | Configures network interfaces and routing |
| nscd | Yes | | | Name service caching daemon |
| portmap | Yes | | | DARPA port to RPC program number mapper |
| postfix | Yes | | | Postfix mail transfer agent |
| random | Yes | | | Random number generator |
| rawdevices | Yes | | | Enables raw I/O |
| rpmconfigcheck | Yes | | | rpm config file scan |
| smbfs | Yes | | | Imports remote SMB/CIFS file systems |
| splash_early | Yes | | | Kills animation after network start |
| splash_late | Yes | | | Starts animation before shutdown |
| sshd | Yes | | | OpenSSH SSH daemon |
| SuSEfirewall2_final | Yes | | | |
| SuSEfirewall2_init | Yes | | | |
| syslog | Yes | | | System logging daemon |

**Table 2-3.**    SLES8 Services Baseline

# Consider Additional Services

In addition to the services installed and turned on by default, many other services are available for enabling. Do not configure these services unless you know that they are needed. However, if these services are already installed and enabled, you should investigate each service to see if it is required for that specific server. The first bit of information you will need to know is what each service is used for. Table 2-4 lists many Linux services and their purposes. Use this information, additional information provided by the man pages on these services, and your knowledge of what role a specific server plays to determine if a specific service is necessary. Use caution; it may not be immediately obvious if a service is needed. Its role on the server may be to support some other necessary service or component. The section "Step 3: Determine Services' Dependencies" can help you determine if this is the case. Before you disable or remove any service, thoroughly investigate it.

| Service | Purpose |
| --- | --- |
| freeWnn | Japanese conversion engine |
| acct | Process accounting |
| adsl | Starts Roaring Penguin ADSL |
| aep1000 | AEP coprocessor driver |
| alsasound | Loads ALSA driver |
| amd | Automount daemon for NFS |
| apache | Loads Apache HTTP daemon |
| apmd | Monitors battery status for laptops |
| argus | Starts Argus |
| arpwatch | Starts **arpwatch** daemon |
| arptables_jf | Automates a packet filtering firewall with **arptables** |
| atalk | AppleTalk TCP/IP daemons |
| atd | AT batch job daemon |
| autofs | autofs daemon |
| avgate | Anti-Virus Mail Gateway Service |
| bcm5820 | Hardware cryptographic accelerator support |
| bgpd | BGP routing daemon |
| Canna | Canna Japanese conversion engine |
| cipe | CIPE tunnel |
| cron | Cron job service |
| crond | Cron job service |
| cups | CUPS printer daemon |
| dc_client | Distcache, a distributed SSL session cache client proxy |
| dc_server | Distcache, a distributed SSL session cache server |
| dhcpd | DHCP server |
| dhcrelay | DHCP relaying across network segments |
| evlog | Event logging daemon |

**Table 2-4.**    Services and Their Purposes

| Service | Purpose |
|---------|---------|
| fam | File access monitoring |
| fbset | Frame buffer setup |
| gpm | Allows mouse on console |
| heartbeat | Starts heartbeat HA services |
| hotplug | Linux hotplugging support |
| hpoj | HP OfficeJet support |
| httpd | Apache HTTP server |
| hwscan | Hardware scan and Reconfiguration |
| inetd | Internet daemon |
| inn | InterNetNews server |
| innd | InterNetNews server |
| ippl | IPPL protocols logger |
| ip6tables | ip6tables firewall |
| iptables | iptables firewall |
| ipsec | Encrypted and authenticated communication |
| ipvsadm | Virtual server administration |
| ipxmount | Access to Novell network via IPX |
| ipxrip | IPX routing daemon |
| ircd | Internet Relay Chat daemon |
| irda | Infrared Data Association support for infrared communication |
| irqbalance | Distributed interrupts across CPU on multiprocessor systems |
| iscsi | Access to remote SCSI devices |
| isdn | ISDN drivers |
| joystick | Joystick drivers |
| kadmin | Kerberos 5 server |
| kdc | Kerberos 5 server |
| kbd | Keyboard settings |
| keytable | Keyboard settings |
| kprop | Kerberos 5 service |
| krb524 | Kerberos 5 credential converter |
| krb5kdc | Kerberos 5 service |
| ksysguardd | Remote monitor daemon for **ksysguard** |
| kudzu | Hardware probe for configuring new hardware |
| ldap | Open LDAP2 server |
| ldirectord | Linux Director daemon for clustering |

**Table 2-4.**   Services and Their Purposes *(continued)*

| Service | Purpose |
|---|---|
| lisa | LAN browser daemon |
| mailman | The **mailman** mailing list program |
| mdmonitor | Software RAID monitoring |
| microcode | Update Intel CPU microcode |
| microcode_ctl | Applies CPU microcode |
| mon | Heartbeat HA services |
| mrtd | Multithreaded routing toolkit daemon |
| mysql | MySQL database server |
| nagios | Network monitor |
| named | Domain Name Server |
| nessusd | Allow security scans from this host |
| netdump | Initialize netconsole and netcrashdump facility |
| netdump-server | Server to send oops data and memory dumps over the network |
| netfs | Mount and unmount NFS, SMB, and NCP file systems |
| network | Configure network interfaces and routing |
| nfs | Imports remote network file systems |
| nfslock | NFS locking daemon |
| nfsserver | Kernel-based NFS daemon |
| nmd | Samba NetBIOS naming service over IP |
| nscd | Name service caching daemon |
| ntop | Monitor network usage |
| ntpd | Network time protocol daemon |
| nwe | Starts the nwe-server (marsnwe) |
| ospf6d | OSPF IPv6 routing daemon |
| ospfd | OSPF routing daemon |
| pcmcia | PCMCIA card configuration database |
| pcscd | pcscd daemon |
| pkcipe | CIPE public key server |
| pkcsslotd | pkcsslotd daemon |
| portmap | DARPA port to RPC program number mapper |
| postfix | Postfix mail transfer agent |
| postgresl | PostgreSQL daemon |
| powertweakd | Performance tuning utility |
| pptpd | PoPToP PPTP daemon |
| psacct | Process accounting |

**Table 2-4.**    Services and Their Purposes  *(continued)*

| Service | Purpose |
|---|---|
| pxe | Preboot execution environment for network booting other machines |
| quota | Turns **quota** on |
| quotad | Starts **quota** daemon |
| radiusd | Authentication, authorization, and accounting server |
| radvd | Router advertisement daemon |
| random | Random number generator |
| rarpd | Server for reverse address resolution request |
| raw | Raw devices for raw I/O |
| rawdevices | Enables raw I/O |
| rhnsd | Queries Red Hat network for updates |
| rinetd | Internet redirection server |
| ripd | RIP routing daemon |
| ripngd | RIPNG routing daemon |
| rpmconfigcheck | rpm config file scan |
| rpasswdd | Secure remote password updates |
| rstatd | Network status monitor RPC protocol server |
| rsyncd | rsync daemon |
| rusersd | Checks who is logged on other machines |
| rwhod | Gets a list of users logged on a remote machine |
| saslauthd | SASL authentication server |
| scanlogd | scanlogd portscanner daemon |
| sendmail | Sendmail mail transfer agent |
| setserial | Initializes serial ports |
| sgi_fam | File monitoring daemon |
| slurpd | OpenLDAP2 server |
| smartd | Self-monitoring and reporting technology daemon |
| smb | Samba SMB/CIFS file and print server |
| smbfs | Imports remote SMB/CIFS file systems |
| smpppd | Internet dial-up connections daemon |
| snmpd | University of California at Davis Simple Network Management Protocol |
| snmptrapd | Receives and logs SNMP trap messages |
| snort | Packet sniffer/logger |
| spamassassin | Mail filter to identify spam |
| splash | Splash screen setup |
| splash_early | Kills animation after network start |

**Table 2-4.**   Services and Their Purposes   *(continued)*

| Service | Purpose |
|---|---|
| **splash_late** | Starts animation before shutdown |
| **squid** | SQUID web cache daemon |
| **sshd** | OpenSSH SSH daemon |
| **SuSEfirewall2_final** | Sets all the firewalling rules. Phase 3 of 3 of SuSEfirewall setup. |
| **SuSEfirewall2_init** | Does some basic setup and is Phase 1 of 3 of the SuSEfirewall initialization. |
| **SuSEfirewall2_setup** | Does some basic setup and is Phase 2 of 3 of the SuSEfirewall initialization. |
| **syslog/syslogd** | System logging daemon |
| **tux** | Threaded kernel-based HTTP server |
| **vncserver** | Virtual network computing server |
| **vtun** | VPN daemon |
| **vsftpd** | Very Safe FTP daemon |
| **winbindd** | NSS daemon for name resolution from NT servers |
| **wwwoffle** | Proxy server |
| **xdm** | X display manager |
| **xfs** | X font server |
| **xinetd** | Internet daemon |
| **xntpd** | Time protocol daemon |
| **ypbind** | Finds server for NIS domains |
| **yppasswdd** | Allows NIS users to change passwords |
| **ypserv** | Distributes NIS maps |
| **ypxfrd** | Faster NIS maps transfers |
| **zebra** | Routing manager daemon |

**Table 2-4.**    Services and Their Purposes *(continued)*

# Step 3: Determine Services' Dependencies

Sometimes a particular service requires one or more other daemons to be running (a daemon is a process that runs without an associated console). For instance, the **samba** service needs these three daemons to be running: **smbd**, **nmbd**, and **winbindd**. This can pose a problem when some daemons are not running or not configured. In their effort to make a server as functional as possible, most distributions are likely to have all possible services running and operational out of the box. After the initial operating system installation, you need to shut down some of the unnecessary services. A properly hardened server runs only the necessary services. The rationale is that any bit of code may have vulnerabilities; if the service is not running, no one can take advantage of it. The question is, how do you know which services are necessary? A difficult way to determine this might be to turn off each service one at a time, and then check to see if everything you need is still working. This approach is both tedious and impractical. Tables 2-2 and 2-3 list the default services that are running and guidelines for determining which ones you might not need.

However, many other services exist, and there are many interdependencies between services, and between services and other components. Simple trial and error will not be the most productive approach. The best way to configure services is to learn which services are necessary and turn off the rest. The definition of what services are necessary, as you have seen, may vary from server to server.

Once you have determined that a specific service is necessary, you may be able to determine if another service is also required by seeing if it is required by the ones that you know are necessary. This is the process of checking to see if a service has prerequisites or dependencies. To find the dependencies, check the man page with the man command. Type **man** *servicename,* such as **man sendmail**. The man page will list any requirements a service has. If you are not sure what man page to look at, try using **man**'s keyword capability, as follows:

```
man -k keyword
```

For example, the command

```
man -k sendmail
```

would show you all the man pages that contain information pertaining to sendmail.

You should also refer to the "See Also" section at the end of the man page and investigate these other sources of service information.

---

**TIP**  Under SLES8, the Runlevel Editor program that is described in the next section will warn you if you attempt to turn on a service but neglect to start services it depends on.

---

Tables 2-5 and 2-6 list common Linux services and their dependencies. The services are listed down the first column, and the services they require are listed across the top.

Finding service dependencies is not difficult in Linux distributions that are compliant with the Linux Standard Base (LSB) version 1.3. Both Red Hat Enterprise Linux AS 3.0 and SLES8 are LSB 1.3 compliant. LSB requires that the headers in the scripts that start and stop services contain a field showing exactly what each service is dependant upon. For instance, the script that starts the ypserver /etc/rc.d/ypserv contains a line like **Required-Start: portmap**. This means that the ypserver requires the **portmap** service in order to run correctly. When **portmap** is started by the init script and the **start** argument, the information specified in the **portmap** script's "Provides" header is considered present. This fulfills the ypserver's requirement, and ypserver is then eligible to run. The converse is also true, if the init script is run with the **stop** argument, the facilities described in the "Provides" header are considered no longer present. For these reasons it is important that startup scripts contain all the correct header information. Do not delete or alter header information from the scripts without a good reason, especially in the section that is delimited by the following lines:

```
### BEGIN INIT INFO
### END INIT INFO
```

If you are interested in the rest of the fields in the script header, you are encouraged to check out the LSB specification at http://www.linuxbase.org. This is also a way to get exposed to the other useful information contained in the headers of the init scripts.

| Service | Required Services | | | | | | | |
|---|---|---|---|---|---|---|---|---|
| | network | syslog | route | quota | zebra | nmb | ypserv | inetd |
| acct | Yes | Yes | | | | | | |
| adsl | Yes | Yes | | | | | | |
| apache | Yes | | | | | | | |
| arpwatch | Yes | Yes | | | | | | |
| atalk | Yes | | | | | | | |
| autofs | Yes | Yes | | | | | | |
| bgpd | Yes | | | | Yes | | | |
| cipe | Yes | | | | | | | |
| cron | Yes | Yes | | | | | | |
| cups | Yes | Yes | | | | | | |
| dhcpd | Yes | | | | | | | |
| dhcrelay | Yes | | | | | | | |
| evlog | Yes | | | | | | | |
| fam | Yes | Yes | | | | | | |
| gpm | Yes | Yes | | | | | | |
| heartbeat | Yes | Yes | | | | | | |
| hotplug | Yes | Yes | | | | | | |
| httpd | Yes | | | | | | | |
| inetd | Yes | Yes | | | | | | |
| innd | Yes | | | | | | | |
| ippl | Yes | | | | | | | |
| ipsec | Yes | Yes | | | | | | Yes |

**Table 2-5.**    Services and Dependencies Part 1

| Service | Required Services | | | | | | | |
|---|---|---|---|---|---|---|---|---|
| | network | syslog | route | quota | zebra | nmb | ypserv | inetd |
| ipvsadm | Yes | | | | | | | |
| ipxmount | Yes | Yes | | | | | | |
| ipxrip | Yes | Yes | | | | | | |
| ircd | Yes | Yes | | | | | | Yes |
| irqbalance | | | | | | | | |
| iscsi | Yes | Yes | | | | | | |
| kdc | Yes | | | | | | | |
| ksysguardd | Yes | | | | | | | |
| lisa | Yes | Yes | | | | | | |
| mailman | Yes | Yes | | | | | | |
| mon | Yes | Yes | | | | | | |
| mrtd | Yes | | | | | | | |
| mysql | Yes | | | | | | | |
| nagios | Yes | Yes | | | | | | |
| named | Yes | Yes | | | | | | |
| nessusd | Yes | | | | | | | |
| nfs | Yes | Yes | | | | | | |
| nfslock | Yes | Yes | | | | | | |
| nfsserver | Yes | Yes | | | | | | |
| nmd | Yes | Yes | | | | | | |
| ntop | Yes | | | | | | | |
| new | Yes | Yes | | | | | | |
| ospf6d | Yes | | | | Yes | | | |
| ospfd | Yes | | | | Yes | | | |
| pcscd | Yes | Yes | | | | | | |
| pkcipe | Yes | | | | | | | |
| portmap | Yes | Yes | | | | | | |
| postfix | Yes | Yes | | | | | | |
| postgres | Yes | | | | | | | |
| powertweakd | Yess | Yes | | | | | | |
| pptd | Yes | | Yes | | | | | |
| quota | Yes | Yes | | | | | | |

**Table 2-5.** Services and Dependencies Part 1 *(continued)*

| Service | Required Services | | | | | | | |
|---|---|---|---|---|---|---|---|---|
| | network | syslog | route | quota | zebra | nmb | ypserv | inetd |
| quotad | Yes | Yes | | Yes | | | | |
| radiusd | Yes | Yes | | | | | | |
| radvd | Yes | Yes | | | | | | |
| ripd | Yes | | | | Yes | | | |
| ripngd | Yes | | | | Yes | | | |
| rpasswdd | Yes | Yes | | | | | | |
| rstatd | Yes | | | | | | | |
| rsyncd | Yes | Yes | | | | | | |
| rusersd | Yes | | | | | | | |
| rwhod | Yes | | | | | | | |
| scanlogd | Yes | Yes | | | | | | |
| sendmail | Yes | | | | | | | |
| smb | Yes | Yes | | | | Yes | | |
| smbfs | Yes | Yes | | | | Yes | | |
| smpppd | Yes | Yes | | | | | | |
| snmpd | Yes | | | | | | | |
| snmptrapd | Yes | | | | | | | |
| snort | Yes | | | | | | | |
| squid | Yes | | | | | | | |
| syslog | Yes | | | | | | | |
| vtun | Yes | Yes | | | | | | |
| winbindd | Yes | Yes | | | | Yes | | |
| wwwoffle | Yes | Yes | | | | | | |
| xfs | Yes | | | | | | | |
| xinetd | Yes | | | | | | | |
| xnlpd | Yes | Yes | | | | | | |
| ypbind | Yes | Yes | | | | | | |
| yppasswdd | Yes | Yes | | | | | Yes | |
| ypserv | Yes | Yes | | | | | | |
| ypxfrd | Yes | Yes | | | | | Yes | |
| zebra | Yes | | | | | | | |

**Table 2-5.**   Services and Dependencies Part 1  *(continued)*

| Service | Required Services | | | | | | | | |
|---|---|---|---|---|---|---|---|---|---|
| | ldap | portmap | sshd | hotplug | alsasound | cron | nfslock | cipe | z90crypt |
| slurpd | Yes | | Yes | | | | | | |
| ipsec | | Yes | | | | | | | |
| nsf | | Yes | | | | | | | |
| nsflock | | Yes | | | | | | | |
| nfsserver | | Yes | | | | | Yes | | |
| quota | | Yes | | | | | | | |
| quotad | | Yes | | | | | | | |
| ypbind | | Yes | | | | | | | |
| yppasswdd | | Yes | | | | | | | |
| ypserv | | Yes | | | | | | | |
| ypxfrd | | Yes | | | | | | | |
| ircd | | | Yes | | | | | | |
| Cups | | | | Yes | | | | | |
| Joystick | | | | | Yes | | | | |
| mailman | | | | | | | | | |
| Pkcipe | | | | | | | | Yes | |
| Pkcsslotd | | | | | | | | | Yes |

**Table 2-6.** Services and Dependencies Part 2

# Step 4: Prevent Services from Running

Once you have determined the services that should be and should not be running, the first thing you should do to control services is to alter configuration so that unnecessary services do not get turned on at startup. Your goal is not just to shut down unnecessary services, but to make sure they don't accidentally get started again. Instead of turning the service off, you can configure it to not start and then reboot. For instance, if the **sendmail** service is running right now and you do not need the SMTP service it provides, change its configuration to prevent startup and reboot. The service will not be running anymore. The next thing to do to control services is to change the startup scripts and configurations so that services you do require start only when you intend. Finally when all service configurations are changed, the next step (step 5) is simple: reboot.

One aspect of the Linux services model can be confusing if you are new to it. Some services run as their own daemon and some are started from a special daemon called the Internet daemon.

The services that run as their own program are called daemons. One group of daemons, called network daemons, are services that are listening on the network interface for connections from clients. Once the client connects to a daemon, the daemon usually performs some action. On Linux systems, daemons have their startup scripts under either the /etc/init.d directory or /etc/rc.d directory depending on which distribution is being used.

The second group of services are started by the Internet daemon. The Internet daemon is **inetd** in the SUSE and Debian distributions and **xinetd** in the Red Hat distribution. These daemons' configurations are in /etc/inetd.conf and /etc/xinetd.d, respectively. Service configuration changes of this type involve changing only this single daemon. Fortunately, some configuration tools, such as the text-based **chkconfig**, do not require knowledge about where the configuration occurs because the knowledge of the service differences is built into the tool. It will not require you to know which it is changing, but it will change the correct one. The **chkconfig** command is detailed later in the section "Use chkconfig."

# Use Tools to Alter Startup Scripts

There are several different tools that can help alter the startup scripts of a Linux system. Table 2-7 lists the tools available on a few distributions.

The correct tool to use depends on which distribution you are using and what you are trying to accomplish. The GUI tools described here are YaST2 for SLES8 and serviceconf for Red Hat Enterprise Linux AS 3.0. A third type of tool, called System V Init tools, is also briefly described.

In all cases, you will need root authority in order to make changes. Start by logging in as root or type **su - root** in a terminal window if you are invoking the tool from the command line. When you are invoking a GUI from the command line, but are not logged into the window manager as root, you may need to type **xhost +localhost** to authenticate your session to the window manager. If you get an error saying something like "could not open display," this is the problem. This depends entirely upon the flavor of Linux you are using, because different versions of Linux use different models.

There is no additional risk if you type the **xhost** command with **+localhost**, however, if you do not include **localhost** you are making a serious security error.

| Distribution | Service Configuration Tools |
|---|---|
| Debian | rcconf<br>chkconfig |
| Red Hat | ntsysv<br>serviceconf<br>chkconfig |
| SUSE | YaST2<br>chkconfig |

**Table 2-7.** Tools for Altering init Scripts and the Distributions in Which They Occur

# HEADS UP!

Sometimes people solve window manager authentication problems with **xhost +**.
This is not the right way to use the **xhost** command because it allows *anyone* to
authenticate to the display on your window manager.

## Use YaST2 with SUSE

If you are running SUSE, use the GUI service configuration tool YaST2. You can invoke
YaST2 by clicking the hammer and wrench icon, then YaST2 Modules | System | Runlevel
Editor. You can see an example of traversing the menu hierarchy in Figure 2-1.

Once the YaST2 Runlevel Editor comes up, the next step is to select the default
runlevel for your system. If the system is a dedicated server, the correct runlevel is 3.
Next, click Runlevel Properties. This will bring up a list of services that looks like
Figure 2-2.

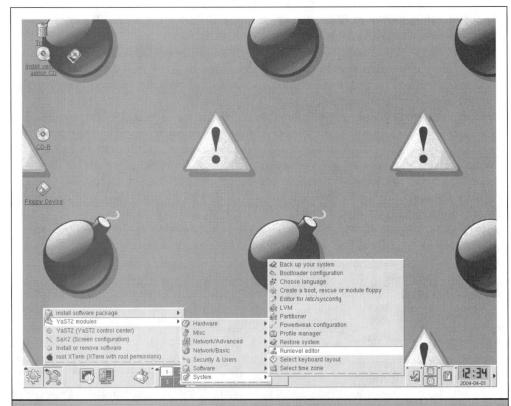

**Figure 2-1.** SLES8 YaST2 menu hierarchy for the Runlevel Editor

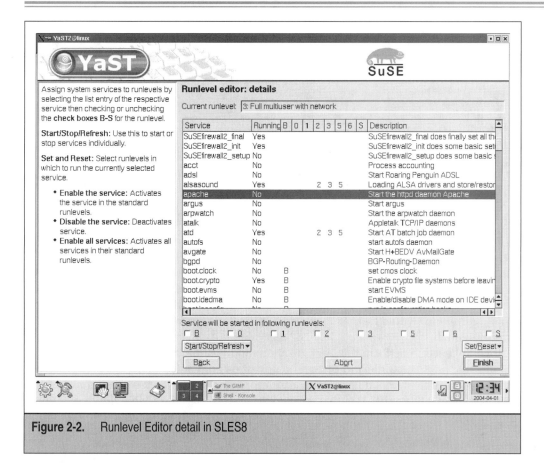

**Figure 2-2.** Runlevel Editor detail in SLES8

Scroll through the list of services and make sure the only services with a "Yes" in the second column of Table 2-2 are the services you chose when determining your requirements in step 2. It is better to err on the side of caution, since you can always come back here and enable something else later. If you are unsure what something does, look the service up in Table 2-4. At the bottom of the Runlevel Editor window is a group of checkboxes that indicate for each runlevel whether that service will be running. Concentrate first on your default runlevel 3 since that is the most important. When you are done with your changes, click Finish.

To finish your services configuration in SUSE, check which services are started by **inetd**. Again, click the hammer and wrench icon, then YaST2 Module | Network/Basic | Start/Stop Services (inetd), as shown in Figure 2-3.

The first step in working with the **inetd** configuration GUI is to select the radio button for "on with custom configuration" and the click Next (the Finish button changes to Next after you choose to do the custom configuration). The next screen has instructions on the left. All the services are off by default as evidenced by the number symbol (#) on the left of each line. This # is carried over from the configuration file itself. To have any

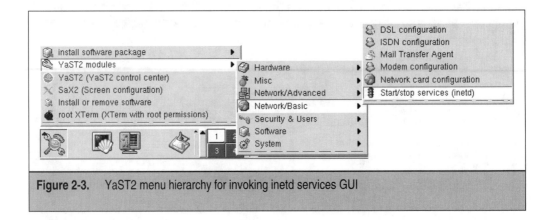

**Figure 2-3.** YaST2 menu hierarchy for invoking inetd services GUI

of the configurations turned on, merely click on the line and then click the Activate or Deactivate button. Repeat this step as many times as there are changes to make. When you are done, click Finish. Notice the word "Active" appears in the list next to the service name. Conversely, if you were turning off services, you should do this exact procedure and the difference would be that the word "Active" disappears and is replaced by the number symbol.

If you wanted to perform this configuration modification by hand, you would merely edit the /etc/inetd.conf file and put a # on any line you wanted to make inactive. After saving the file, the Internet daemon needs to reread its configuration by restarting or by being sent a SIGHUP (**kill -1**) signal. You could do this by typing the following at the command line:

```
kill -1 process-id
```

## Use serviceconfig with Red Hat

Service configuration is easier in Red Hat since both daemons and **xinetd** services can be turned on and off from the same GUI tool.

Invoke serviceconf by clicking the Red Hat icon, then System Settings | Server Settings | Services, as shown in Figure 2-4. The window that comes up has a single list, as shown in Figure 2-5.

The serviceconf tool is simple to use:

■ At the top of the window is the Edit Runlevel pull-down menu that indicates which runlevel's configuration you are currently configuring. The first thing to do is make sure the runlevel you are configuring is the runlevel that your server will be at when it is deployed. Click Edit Runlevel | Runlevel 3. Shown in Figure 2-5, Runlevel 3 allows your server to be working on tasks instead of running a Window Manager and is therefore the desirable runlevel for your deployed server.

■ Each of the possible services is presented in a list. Next to each item is a checkbox for turning on and off the service. If the checkbox has a check in it, the service is

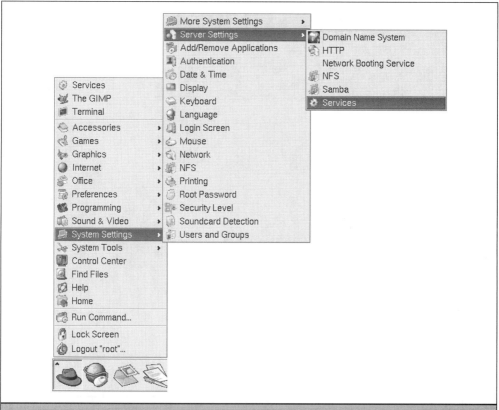

**Figure 2-4.**   Menu hierarchy for serviceconf in Red Hat Enterprise Linux AS 3.0

"on." Go through the list and make sure there is a reason for each service that has a check next to it. At the same time, make sure there are no checks next to services you do not need. After you make a change, you can click the Start button at the top of the window if you want to turn the service on immediately, or click the Stop button if you want to stop the service immediately.

■ Save your changes by clicking File | Save Changes before closing the window, as shown in Figure 2-6.

## HEADS UP!

After you are done, be sure to save your changes. If you just exit the program, your changes will not be saved and services that you do not want to run will still be able to do so. The Start and Stop buttons only affect the current state of the server.

**Figure 2-5.**   serviceconf window with default services enabled

## Use System V Init Type Programs

Another group of GUI tools are available in some Linux distributions or can be installed separately. They are common, have been around a long time, and are standard in distributions other than Red Hat and SUSE. They are very similar to each other and are referred to as System V Init type programs. They include **tksysv**, **ntsysv** (Red Hat), and **ksysv**. These tools operate almost identically—in fact according to its "About" message, **ntsysv** was inspired by **tksysv**. There are minor differences between these tools, for instance, **ksysv** has drag and drop support. If any of these tools are installed, they can be invoked from the command line by typing the name, such as **tksysv**. Figure 2-7 shows what the **tksysv** GUI looks like.

To add a service:

1.   Determine the name of the service.

**Figure 2-6.**    Save changes in serviceconf

2. Locate the service in the left column.

3. Select the service, then click Add.

4. At the prompt requesting the runlevel for the service, select a runlevel checkbox, then click Done.

5. At the prompt for the order to initiate the service, "The number for [service] is," a proposed possible order for service startup is displayed. This is only important if the service is *required* to start before another service at that runlevel.

To remove a service at a runlevel is even easier:

1. Locate the service listed at the runlevel you would like to remove and select it.

2. Click Remove and the service will not be invoked at that runlevel at the next bootup.

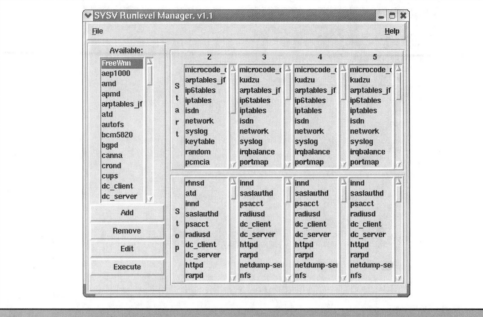

**Figure 2-7.**   The TKSYSV GUI

# Turn Off Unnecessary Services: Command Line Tool

There are at least two different ways you can turn off system services from the command line. One method uses a command like **chkconfig**. The command **chkconfig** is available in both SUSE and Red Hat. It operates a little differently in the two environments. In SLES8, typing the command returns a list of each service and whether it is running or not. For Red Hat you need to use the flag **-list**, as in **/sbin/chkconfig -list**.

## Use chkconfig

If you find that the display is too long, you can pipe the output to the **more** filter to make it readable, like this:

```
/sbin/chkconfig --list | more
```

Figure 2-8 shows what the **chkconfig** information looks like.

If you are not the root user you can still run the command if you supply the complete path /sbin/chkconfig, but you will not be able to make any changes to the configurations. If you were using Red Hat and trying to turn off sendmail, you could run the following:

```
chkconfig --list sendmail
```

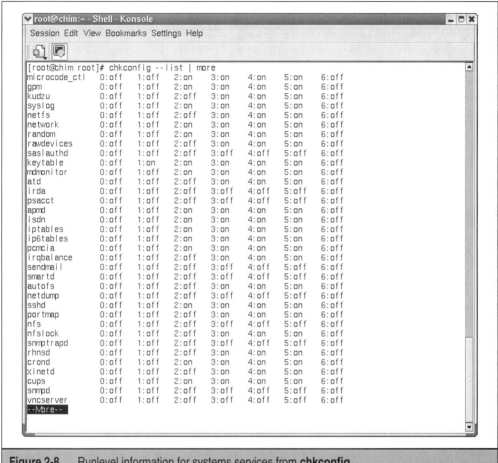

```
root@chim:~ - Shell - Konsole                                    _ □ ✕
Session  Edit  View  Bookmarks  Settings  Help

[root@chim root]# chkconfig --list | more
microcode_ctl  0:off  1:off  2:on   3:on   4:on   5:on   6:off
gpm            0:off  1:off  2:on   3:on   4:on   5:on   6:off
kudzu          0:off  1:off  2:off  3:on   4:on   5:on   6:off
syslog         0:off  1:off  2:on   3:on   4:on   5:on   6:off
netfs          0:off  1:off  2:off  3:on   4:on   5:on   6:off
network        0:off  1:off  2:on   3:on   4:on   5:on   6:off
random         0:off  1:off  2:on   3:on   4:on   5:on   6:off
rawdevices     0:off  1:off  2:off  3:on   4:on   5:on   6:off
saslauthd      0:off  1:off  2:off  3:off  4:off  5:off  6:off
keytable       0:off  1:on   2:on   3:on   4:on   5:on   6:off
mdmonitor      0:off  1:off  2:on   3:on   4:on   5:on   6:off
atd            0:off  1:off  2:off  3:on   4:on   5:on   6:off
irda           0:off  1:off  2:off  3:off  4:off  5:off  6:off
psacct         0:off  1:off  2:off  3:off  4:off  5:off  6:off
apmd           0:off  1:off  2:on   3:on   4:on   5:on   6:off
isdn           0:off  1:off  2:on   3:on   4:on   5:on   6:off
iptables       0:off  1:off  2:on   3:on   4:on   5:on   6:off
ip6tables      0:off  1:off  2:on   3:on   4:on   5:on   6:off
pcmcia         0:off  1:off  2:on   3:on   4:on   5:on   6:off
irqbalance     0:off  1:off  2:off  3:on   4:on   5:on   6:off
sendmail       0:off  1:off  2:off  3:off  4:off  5:off  6:off
smartd         0:off  1:off  2:off  3:off  4:off  5:off  6:off
autofs         0:off  1:off  2:off  3:on   4:on   5:on   6:off
netdump        0:off  1:off  2:off  3:off  4:off  5:off  6:off
sshd           0:off  1:off  2:on   3:on   4:on   5:on   6:off
portmap        0:off  1:off  2:off  3:on   4:on   5:on   6:off
nfs            0:off  1:off  2:off  3:off  4:off  5:off  6:off
nfslock        0:off  1:off  2:off  3:on   4:on   5:on   6:off
snmptrapd      0:off  1:off  2:off  3:off  4:off  5:off  6:off
rhnsd          0:off  1:off  2:off  3:on   4:on   5:on   6:off
crond          0:off  1:off  2:on   3:on   4:on   5:on   6:off
xinetd         0:off  1:off  2:off  3:on   4:on   5:on   6:off
cups           0:off  1:off  2:on   3:on   4:on   5:on   6:off
snmpd          0:off  1:off  2:off  3:off  4:off  5:off  6:off
vncserver      0:off  1:off  2:off  3:off  4:off  5:off  6:off
--More--
```

**Figure 2-8.**    Runlevel information for systems services from **chkconfig**

You would see that sendmail is running under runlevels 2, 3, 4, and 5. The command to turn sendmail off during these runlevels would look like this:

```
chkconfig --level 2345 sendmail off'
```

You need to put the runlevels you are changing right next to each other without spaces or commas. To make sure the change happens the way you intend, you can run the following command again and notice that Off is next to runlevels 2, 3, 4, and 5 instead of On:

```
chkconfig --list sendmail
```

The SUSE distribution uses the SMTP server postfix instead of sendmail. To check if mail is on in SLES8, type **chkconfig postfix**.

## Use Startup Scripts

The second command line method for turning off and on a system service requires you to know what runlevel the service starts at, and whether the service is invoked as a daemon or from the Internet daemon. When your server starts up, the scripts for each runlevel are run. The same type of thing happens at shutdown time too. The startup scripts can be found in a directory named after each of the runlevels under the /etc/ directory. For instance, the scripts for runlevel 5 are under /etc/rc.d/rc5.d/. When a system starts, it runs all the scripts in that directory that start with the letter "S." When a system is shutting down or rebooting, all the scripts in the directory that start with a "K" will be executed. The nice thing about these scripts is that they run in numerical order. For example, **S09sshd** will be executed before **S17cron**. Since the order of execution is based on the numerical order, this allows precise control over which program runs before which other program.

In SLES8, the startup scripts for each runlevel are in /etc/rc.d/rc*.d. For example, in runlevel 3 the startup scripts are in /etc/rc.d/rc3.d. Technically, the scripts themselves reside in the /etc/rc.d directory, and special files called soft links are made in each directory to point back at the /etc/rc.d directory. This is useful for a few reasons. One reason is that if changes need to occur in the startup scripts, the changes can be made in one place, but they affect each instance where a script is used. Another reason to use soft links instead of files is that if you would like to disable a service at a certain runlevel, you can merely remove the soft link and the startup script itself is unchanged. To remove a soft link, treat it like a file and type

```
rm filename
```

For example:

```
rm /etc/rc.d/S01isdn
```

The easiest way to create a soft link is to **cd** into the directory where you want the link to be and type

```
ln -s script-to-link-to soft-link-to-make
```

For example, the following creates the soft link deleted in the previous listing:

```
ln -s /etc/rc.d./isdn S01isdn
```

Type **ls -l** and notice that all the files in the directory are actually soft links pointing at the actual files that are up one directory.

The directory layout for startup scripts in Red Hat Enterprise Linux AS 3.0 is slightly different than in SLES8. In Red Hat, the startup scripts are in the directory /etc/rc.d/ init.d instead of /etc/rc.d/. The soft linking process is the same except the soft link points at a different directory structure. To create the soft link to start the **isdn** service, first **cd** into the desired runlevel, such as **cd /etc/rc.d/rc3.d**. Then type the following:

```
ln -s /etc/rc.d/init.d/isdn S09isdn
```

Linux distributions that are Linux Standard Base compliant have an elegant mechanism for dealing with the soft linking process. The packager installer program (**rpm**) runs a postinstall script, which in turn uses the program /usr/lib/lsb/install_initd to configure the distribution's boot script system to call the package's init.d file at the appropriate time. The **install_initd** program takes a single argument, the pathname to the /etc/init.d file. When removing a package the converse is also true. When a software package is removed, the package's preuninstall script should call /usr/lib/lsb/remove_initd and pass the path name to the /etc/init.d file. The package manager is still required to remove the /etc/init.d file. The **remove_initd** program is provided in case the distribution needs to clean up any other modifications in the distribution's boot script system that might have been made by the **install_initd** program.

Another benefit provided by LSB-compliant startup scripts is that each script can take the arguments **start**, **stop**, **restart**, **force-reload**, and **status**. Also, LSB compliance dictates that startup scripts need to "behave sensibly if invoked with **start** when the service is already running, or with **stop** when it isn't, and that they don't kill unfortunately named user processes."

This is added to the fact that "the **init** script must return an exit status of zero if the action described by the argument has been successful." This ensures that a consistent approach toward working with startup scripts yields predictable behavior no matter which distribution you are working with. It is unlikely that you will need to be able to recite these details from memory because tools like YaST2 perform all these behaviors behind the scenes. You can read more about this at http://www.linuxbase.org/spec/refspecs/LSB_1.3.0/gLSB/gLSB.html#INITSRCINSTRM.

One last approach to consider allows you to leave the scripts intact but not have them execute. All that is needed is to change the case of the **init** script from a capital letter to a lowercase letter. If the script doesn't begin with a capital, it will not be executed. If you decide you want the script to execute, change the case of the first letter back to a capital.

# Step 5: Reboot

Now that the changes to the startup configuration are complete, you should restart your system to see if the committed changes are correct. The step is simple yet important. The point of this step is to verify that the changes you made will be persistent. Before your server returns to the network, it is good to verify that a power cycle will not put your server in a state you did not anticipate. As was shown in Table 2-1, runlevel 6 reboots the computer. As the root user, type the following at the command line to restart your computer:

```
sync;sync; init 6
```

The **sync** command here tells your hard drive to flush its buffers to disk. The reason that you do it twice is a longstanding tradition. Once your computer comes back up, log in to the machine as root again and proceed to the next step to verify what you did in step 4.

Another method for restarting your computer is the **reboot** command. All you need to do is type **reboot** at a command prompt. As stated in the **reboot** man page, this is not recommended in older **sysvinit** releases.

# Step 6: Check Configuration for Unnecessary Services

Before returning the system to the network, double-check that there are no unnecessary services running. Until you get familiar with the process, the GUI can help you through the steps. Once you are more comfortable, the command line tool, **chkconfig**, is a more direct method for checking what is configured to start up at boot time. If you find that some service you have identified as unnecessary is running, return to step 4 and shut it down, then continue following the procedure.

## Check Configuration: GUI

This step should be simple: if you are using Red Hat, restart the serviceconf GUI. If you are only viewing the service configurations under Red Hat, you will need root privileges, but not under SUSE. Check to make sure that there are no checks next to any of the services you intended to turn off. If there is a check next to a service that should not be running, repeat the procedure in step 4 to turn it off. If you have tried this a couple of times but it doesn't seem to keep the changes, make sure you are selecting File | Save Changes as shown previously in Figure 2-6.

## Check Configuration: Manual

In Red Hat Enterprise Linux AS 3.0, there is the command **service** which can be very helpful in determining whether a service is on or not. If you type **service --status-all** it returns a list of the state of all services it knows about. The easiest way to look for unwanted services is to type the following:

```
service --status-all |grep -v "stopped"
```

You will get a list of the services that are on. If you see something running that should be off, return to step 4. This is a quick way to get through the service list without missing anything.

In SLES8, there is a similar method for checking to see which services are running. At the command line, type

```
chkconfig |grep -v "off"
```

What is returned to you is a list of all the services that are running at the current runlevel.

# Step 7: Check Configuration for Necessary Services

Technically speaking, it is possible to have a service running but not be able to access it because of the security configuration of the network interface. Network interface security controls like iptables can be configured so that access is denied even though the service is configured and operating correctly on the server. In the next chapter, you will learn more about iptables and how you can use it to protect your system. The best system configuration is one where there is continuity between the services and security restrictions of the network interfaces.

There are three different approaches you can use to determine if a service is running:

- Check the configuration
- Probe the service
- Look for the service in memory

## Check the Configuration

Go back and start the GUI you used to turn off the services. Check and make sure things are configured the way you meant them to be. Make sure you did not leave anything still running that isn't necessary. Alternatively, you can take a more direct method and try the **chkconfig** command as shown in step 4.

## Probe the Service

In Chapter 14, you are shown how to scan the ports of your server for services. After reading Chapter 14, try a port scan and compare your findings to verify that only the services you expect are answering on a port. If a service is responding that shouldn't be, go back to step 4 and alter the services configuration. Complete the rest of the cycle by rebooting and checking again. If **nmap** is used, it generally gives you enough info about the services. Otherwise, it's a good idea to use the /etc/services file to define what ports correspond to what services.

## Look for the Service in Memory

This technique can be used to determine if any kind of program is currently running. This will not determine whether the Internet daemon would start something up, since those services will only be in memory when a client program's activity initiates it.

To do so, you can use commands like **ps**, **netstat**, or **lsof** to make sure that service daemons are not running. The following examples show how each command could be used to look for the mailer daemon. In Red Hat, type

```
ps aux |grep -v grep | grep sendmail
```

In SUSE, type

```
ps aux |grep -v grep | grep postfix
```

If you intend to turn off the mailer daemon but these commands return any information, you have made a mistake and the mailer daemon is indeed in memory. If the command does return information, return to step 4 and try again.

The **netstat** command can supply a lot of useful information, but we can't review it all here. Use **netstat** to see your network connections. Type the command

```
netstat -ap | grep -i listen | more
```

and it will list the network services that are listening for connections. This works the same in both Red Hat and SUSE. If you see a line with SMTP and you have intended to turn the mail daemon off, return to step 4.

Another powerful tool, **lsof**, can show what files are open on your computer. This is another approach for looking for which services are running. In either Red Hat or SUSE, type

```
lsof |grep smtp
```

If you are trying to turn off the mail daemon but this command returns content, return to step 4.

# Step 8: Return the Machine to the Network

Now that your checking is complete, it's time to put the machine back on the network. Plug the Ethernet cable(s) back into your network card(s). If you used the method of shutting down the interface manually with the **ifconfig** command, your machine should have come back on the network after rebooting in step 5. If the interface is not back up, use a tool like **netconfig** to correctly configure your network interface(s). The network device could be brought up manually, but the configuration would not be persistent through a reboot.

## Test Network Connectivity

The quickest way to test whether you are back on the network is to ping the gateway. If you are not sure what your gateway IP is, type **ip route** and take the IP address that is on the default line. You may need to add a **-b** to the ping line; the command will tell you if it is necessary. Type **ping** *gatewayIP*, as in **ping 192.168.1.1**. If you are back on the network, you should get messages showing the time it takes the packets to reach your gateway.

Congratulations, you are done hardening your network services. Go on to Chapter 3 and harden the security of your network interface.

# Chapter 3

## Installing Firewalls and Filters

- Take Stock
- Identify Protective Firewall Needs

**M**any network managers have an intense dislike for firewall and network filtering technologies. This is not surprising given the complexities and the prevalence of conflicting beliefs regarding firewall design and implementation.

This chapter steps you through the following tasks:

1. Identify firewall rules that may be present before you make changes

2. Understand the difference between firewall rules and network filters

3. Identify the level and type of protection necessary for your system

4. Install minimum protective measures to ensure the system's safety

Before moving on, take stock:

- The Linux operating system has been installed and is operational.

- Nonessential services have been turned off or disabled. A service that has been turned off will restart the next time the system is restarted (or when the runlevel changes). A service that has been disabled will not restart when the system is restarted or when the runlevel is changed.

- There are many areas of vulnerability to be addressed immediately—you must get ready to take the steps that are outlined in the chapters that follow this one.

# Take Stock

During installation of the Linux operating system, firewall rules may already have been created. Those new to Linux may simply accept defaults that are offered during installation. Beware of options that appear to sidestep the configuration of firewall settings but actually cause it to be implemented. This can be a trap for new players. Before moving on, you should prove beyond doubt whether or not firewall rules already exist.

## Check for Existing Firewall Rules

The Linux operating system kernel supports the loading of application modules that allow you to add kernel-level processes as they are required. This design helps to minimize the size (memory requirements) of the kernel while still permitting the addition of device drivers as well as kernel-level (privileged) processes as needed. The Linux kernel design makes it possible to maintain and use older drivers even where newer technologies may have replaced the earlier one. One example of this is firewall support. In version 2.4.$x$ of the Linux kernel, it is possible to use the older style **ipchains**-based firewall facilities, or to use the newer **iptables**-based filters simply by loading the respective kernel modules.

Immediately after the firewall filtering module has been loaded into kernel memory, it is autoconfigured to accept all network traffic as the default setting. Each module includes a user-level utility that can be used to set firewall rules in place. It can also be used to report what rules are currently in effect.

Firewall rules are normally set as early as possible to minimize the opportunity for potential system intrusion during system startup.

The firewall rules may be examined using the following command:

```
iptables -L -v
```

The command for **ipchains**-based facilities is

```
ipchains -L -v
```

To discover what rules are in effect on your system, follow these steps:

1. Start your Linux server.

2. Log in as root.

3. Open a terminal session:

   - For Red Hat Enterprise Linux AS 3.0, select Red Hat | System Tools | Terminal.

   - For SLES8/9, click the Terminal button on the toolbar.

4. When the terminal shell has opened up, execute **iptables -L -v**.

The output you obtain will show whether firewall settings have been implemented. Figure 3-1 shows output from a system that is in its default state where rules have not been applied.

The firewall rules have a policy to accept all network traffic as the setting. In other words, there are no protective rules.

When firewall rules have been applied during system startup, the output of this command will be similar to that shown in Figure 3-2.

```
[root@sandpiper root]# iptables -L
Chain INPUT (policy ACCEPT)
target      prot opt source             destination

Chain FORWARD (policy ACCEPT)
target      prot opt source             destination

Chain OUTPUT (policy ACCEPT)
target      prot opt source             destination
[root@sandpiper root]# []
```

**Figure 3-1.**    Red Hat Linux, no firewall rules present

```
[root@sandpiper root]# iptables -L
Chain INPUT (policy ACCEPT)
target     prot opt source              destination
RH-Firewall-1-INPUT  all  --  anywhere            anywhere

Chain FORWARD (policy ACCEPT)
target     prot opt source              destination
RH-Firewall-1-INPUT  all  --  anywhere            anywhere

Chain OUTPUT (policy ACCEPT)
target     prot opt source              destination

Chain RH-Firewall-1-INPUT (2 references)
target     prot opt source              destination
ACCEPT     all  --  anywhere            anywhere
ACCEPT     icmp --  anywhere            anywhere            icmp any
ACCEPT     ipv6-crypt--  anywhere           anywhere
ACCEPT     ipv6-auth--  anywhere            anywhere
ACCEPT     all  --  anywhere            anywhere            state RELATED,ESTABLISHED
ACCEPT     tcp  --  anywhere            anywhere            state NEW tcp dpt:http
ACCEPT     tcp  --  anywhere            anywhere            state NEW tcp dpt:ftp
ACCEPT     tcp  --  anywhere            anywhere            state NEW tcp dpt:ssh
ACCEPT     tcp  --  anywhere            anywhere            state NEW tcp dpt:smtp
REJECT     all  --  anywhere            anywhere            reject-with icmp-host-prohibited
[root@sandpiper root]# []
```

**Figure 3-2.**    Red Hat Linux, firewall rules enabled

In this example, the settings the user implemented offer little protection as the policy settings on the input rules permit traffic to be accepted.

The steps you have just completed have positively determined whether firewall rules are present. The point of this chapter is that you need appropriate rules to ensure that the Linux system is hardened against unwanted activities or assault. Firewall rules and filters are only part of the answer, but they are most important and should not be glossed over.

The firewall rules can be easily enabled on a SLES 8 system using the YaST tool that will be described later in this chapter. The resulting firewall rules are complex and lengthy. You can gain valuable insight in how complex firewalls function by examining the script that is produced on SLES8/9 systems. A brief review is provided at the end of this chapter. If you delight in simpler solutions, the alternative script provided may also prove useful.

## HEADS UP!

A simple firewall rule set may not offer the level of protection necessary, while undue complexity is a maintenance liability. Every firewall configuration must be rigorously validated to prove its adequacy. It must log intrusion attempts, port scans, and any connection attempts to ports and services from blocked source addresses.

## Dealing with Existing Firewall Rules

If you find that a firewall configuration has already been implemented, it is necessary to determine its suitability. Obviously, if the rules presently in effect are sufficient they should not be tampered with. On the other hand, if inadequate or inappropriate the rules must be replaced with the correct solution.

If a firewall is found on a freshly installed Linux system, it can be removed or reconfigured using standard operating system tools. If a firewall script is found on a Linux system that has been installed for some time, your best recourse is to find the person who performed the installation to identify how the firewall rules were implemented.

It is important to realize that a Linux system that has been within network reach, and has been inadequately protected, may already have been compromised. In many situations like this the most time-effective way to deal with the problem is to reinstall the system from an installation source that is of known integrity. Correction of damage done to a compromised system will almost certainly be more costly (at least in time) than reinstallation.

## Check Packet Filter Configuration

Commercial Linux servers like Red Hat Enterprise Linux AS 3.0 and SLES8 implement a facility known as **tcp_wrappers**, a technique that was designed to protect services that are implemented using the internetworking superdaemon (**inetd** or **xinetd**).

The tcp_wrappers are implemented using two files, one controlling what is specifically accepted and the other that specifies denials. The files are respectively called /etc/hosts.allow and /etc/hosts.deny. These files provide the ability to define access to network services based on IP addresses or hostnames.

Many programs have the capability to support tcp_wrappers, including FTP and telnet, as well as other popular protocols except for HTTP and the X Windows System, among the most notable exceptions that use their own logging and access control systems.

Some open source applications have built-in support for tcp_wrappers. The best known example of this is Samba, where control of tcp_wrappers is effected using control statements inside Samba's smb.conf file. The two parameters that effect **tcp_wrappers** are **hosts allow** and **hosts deny**. You should refer to the online manual page for Samba's smb.conf file for specific guidance regarding these parameters.

For example, to find the manual entry for **hosts allow** in the smb.conf file, execute:

```
[root@sandpiper root]# man smb.conf
```

The **tcp_wrappers** facility can log connections as they come in, so your service sessions that weren't necessarily logged can be logged with detailed information on the nature of the connection. The syntax for entries in both files is

```
daemon_list: client_list [: options]
```

The *daemon_list* and *client_list* entries are mandatory. The options shown in brackets are optional. The most common option is to specify a shell script that can be executed when a rule is invoked as a result of the matching of an allow or deny rule with an incoming connection packet.

The default setting does not include rules and therefore allows all communications to take place. The default behavior of tcp_wrappers is to deny access to services defined in hosts.deny unless there is a specific rule in hosts.allow to allow it (/etc/hosts.allow takes precedence over /etc/hosts.deny). Each rule is evaluated from the top down. Rules are evaluated starting at the top of the hosts.deny and the hosts.allow files so that a later rule can override an earlier rule. The ordering of rules within each file is significant.

## HEADS UP!

Careless and incorrect ordering of rules within the hosts.allow and hosts.deny files may result in incorrect tcp_wrappers operation and may result in many hours lost trying to debug a tcp_wrappers rules file. Always build the rules file one step at a time and test each entry as soon as it is added.

SLES8/9 are provided with Web (HTML) formatted man pages. Many sites object to providing external access to man pages. The default SUSE **tcp_wrappers** configuration disables external access to the remote man pages. This is effected using an entry in the /etc/hosts.deny file as follows:

```
http-rman: ALL EXCEPT LOCAL
```

## HEADS UP!

Most documentation available on the Internet will tell you to put **ALL : ALL** in /etc/hosts.deny and then define services allowed in /etc/hosts.allowed. This is fine in most cases, but doesn't achieve what the user thinks it does, as someone with proper privileges can add a service to /etc/hosts.allow or accidentally remove /etc/hosts.deny, removing all restrictions that **ALL: ALL** had in the /etc/hosts.deny file. A better way to block all services not explicitly defined is to make the last entry in /etc/hosts.allow **ALL: ALL: DENY** removing the need for a /etc/hosts.deny file (for better security it should be present with the **ALL: DENY** statement as well).

The client list in both hosts.allow and hosts.deny can be set up to show the types of entries shown in Table 3-1.

| Client List Entry Types | Example |
|---|---|
| IP address | 192.168.1.100 matches single IP<br>192.168.1. matches entire class C network of 192.168.1.0 (if a portion of the entry is left out, everything to the right of the entry are treated as zero) |
| Hostname | fake.domain would match any requests from the fake.domain<br>.fake.domain would match any requests from anything within the fake.domain |
| Network/Netmask | 192.168.0.0/255.255.255.0 would match everything in the class C 192.168.0 network |
| NIS (YP) netgroup | Anything with @ as the leading character is treated as an NIS netgroup |

**Table 3-1.**   hosts.allow and hosts.deny Entry Types

Note that when using domain names or hostnames, DNS failures can cause problems accessing the machines, especially when used with the wildcards described in Table 3-2. When possible, use IP addresses for maximum safety.

**tcp_wrappers** also can use the **EXCEPT** operator to allow you to exclude certain clients from a match.

So if your server, which is linux1 (192.168.1.1), needed to allow SSH connections from linux2 (192.168.1.100) and deny connections from other machines, you could set up your /etc/hosts.allow to show:

```
[root@sandpiper root]# cat /etc/hosts.allow
#
# hosts.allow   This file describes the names of the hosts which are
#               allowed to use the local INET services, as decided
#               by the '/usr/sbin/tcpd' server.
#
sshd: 192.168.1.100
ALL: ALL: DENY
```

| Wildcard | Description |
|---|---|
| ALL | Always matches |
| KNOWN | Matches a host whose name and address are known (via name services) |
| LOCAL | Any name that does not contain a dot (linux2 would match, linux2.domain would not) |
| PARANOID | Matches a host whose name does not match the address (putting **ALL: PARANOID** in /etc/hosts.allow would deny access to all machines whose IP didn't match its host address) |
| UNKNOWN | When a hostname or address is unknown because it cannot be resolved using the gethostbyXXXX() system calls that implement name resolution services |

**Table 3-2.**   TCP Wrappers Wildcards

In the following hosts.allow file you can see additional entries that demonstrate the principals of operation recommended in this book:

**Listing 3-1: A typical hosts.allow configuration file**

```
#
# hosts.allow    This file describes the names of the hosts which are
#                allowed to use the local INET services, as described
#                by the '/usr/sbin/tcpd' server.
#
sshd: .domain EXCEPT bad.domain
in.telnetd: 192.168.1.6, 10.0.0.0/255.0.0.0 EXCEPT 10.0.0.5
portmap: 192.168.1.100
ALL: ALL : DENY
```

In this example, you are allowing all machines on the .domain network to connect to your server using SSH except for bad.domain, which is denied. On line 2, you allow 192.168.1.6 and the whole class A range of 10.0.0.0 except for 10.0.0.5 access this machine via telnet. On the next line, you allow **portmap** from 192.168.1.100 since this is the NFS server, and for NFS to work properly you need to allow portmapper access for machines using NFS. On the last line, you deny all connections not specifically noted.

Another interesting capability of tcp_wrappers is that it can run commands when a condition is matched. This should be used sparingly, but for advanced customization it can provide some important functionality. For instance, you can place the following line in your /etc/hosts.deny file to have an e-mail be sent to jdoe@my.domain whenever a connection fails:

```
ALL:ALL : spawn (/bin/echo Security Alert from %a on %d on 'date' | \
tee -a /var/log/security_Alert | mail jdoe@linux1.domain)
```

You are having anything that doesn't match any of the rules in /etc/hosts.allow and that matches the **ALL:ALL** condition in /etc/hosts.deny write

```
Security Alert from hostname on daemon_process on date
```

and sending that to /var/log/security_alert as well as e-mailing the information to jdoe@linux1.domain. The **%a** and **%d** within the spawned command are expansions available from tcp_wrappers. The listing of available expansions are shown in Table 3-3.

**tcp_wrappers** can provide an extra layer of security even when using **iptables** or other firewalling software, and can provide some interesting alerting mechanisms with the **spawn** option.

**tcp_wrappers** support is supplied in an unconfigured state by default on commercial Linux systems. It is left to the discretion of the administrator to configure this facility.

| Expansion | Description |
|-----------|-------------|
| %a | Client's host address |
| %A | Server's host address |
| %c | As much client information as available |
| %d | Daemon process information |
| %h | Client hostname or address if no hostname is available |
| %H | Server hostname or address if no hostname is available |
| %n | Client hostname (or unknown or paranoid) |
| %N | Server hostname (or unknown or paranoid) |
| %p | Daemon process ID |
| %s | As much server information as available |
| %u | Client username (or unknown) |
| %% | Expands to a single % |

**Table 3-3.**    TCP Wrapper Expansions

# Understand Network Basics

Network managers are constantly bombarded by companies that sell Internet security devices. Many pretend to offer a simple-to-use device that solves all network security problems. Nothing can be farther from the truth. Network security is not a simple issue at all, nor is a device the only viable solution to effect network security. But that does not mean network security is so complex that mortals can't understand the issues. Network security issues can be addressed in easily digestible steps.

The information provided in this section is designed to help you, the administrator, understand the basics of firewalls and network filters.

The core issue we are addressing in this chapter is that of the security of network connectivity. All network connectivity involves the use of a network interface controller (NIC). A NIC provides physical media access capability (an Ethernet connection—usually an RJ-45 connector that supports 10Base-T, 100Base-T, Gigabit Ethernet, or similar protocols).

Every NIC has a unique 48-bit address that is by convention reported as 6 octets (hexadecimal numbers), each separated by a colon. For example, 1b:23:5e:1d:7f:01. Companies that manufacture NICs can obtain from IANA a unique identifier that involves the first three octets (from left to right) of the address of the devices they produce. This address is called the media access controller address, or MAC address.

All physical network communications involve the use of MAC addresses. The MAC address contains two parts: a vendor identifier and a serial number (see Figure 3-3).

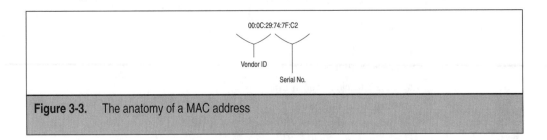

**Figure 3-3.** The anatomy of a MAC address

A NIC may be assigned a primary IP address, plus additional addresses (known as IP aliases). The relationship between the elements of the TCP/IP protocols is shown in Figure 3-4.

Network cards respond to two MAC addresses: their own unique address and the *all ones* address (ff:ff:ff:ff:ff:ff).

The Address Resolution Protocol (ARP), as well as the Reverse Address Resolution Protocol (RARP), makes use of the fact that the NIC will respond to the *all ones* MAC address. The protocols that make use of this behavior include ARP, RARP, ICMP, and UDP (broadcast). Excessive use of such protocols will interrupt the smooth operation of network devices and under extreme load may deny legitimate network operation.

TCP and UDP make use of port addresses. For example, the Hypertext Transport Protocol (HTTP) used for web services uses TCP port 80. Network traffic follows standards that document the structure of network messages or packets. It is from the contents of the network packet (the sequence of information that passes over the physical transport medium) that the TCP/IP protocol implementation can decode what type of information is being transmitted as well as how it should be handled within the computer.

A network packet may contain data that continues a current communication session. It may contain information that will attempt to start up a new session or close a session. Normal network traffic also includes packets from each end of a TCP session which inform the other end that the session is progressing correctly.

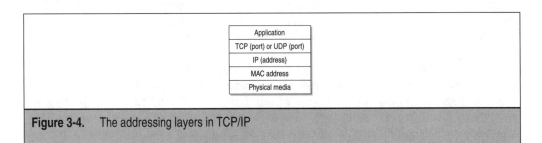

**Figure 3-4.** The addressing layers in TCP/IP

Any element of network communications can potentially be involved in firewall rules that will affect packet handling.

A network client or server may have one network interface (called a single-homed host) that is attached to an internal (private) network, or may be attached to a public network (called an external host). A network client or server that has more than one NIC is said to be multi-homed. Multi-homed machines may act as routers between each of the networks they are connected to.

The default configuration of the Linux kernel has ip_forwarding between interfaces disabled. Most Linux vendors implement a system to enable ip_forwarding (routing) when more than one NIC is enabled on the system. The TCP/IP protocol stack forwards an incoming packet that is destined for the interface that received it to the loopback adapter so that the machine can process its content. The kernel based ip_forwarding only deals with the routing of IP packets between interfaces other than the loopback adapter.

# Understand Firewall Rules

Firewall configuration involves creation and application of policies that specify default handling of incoming packets and outbound packets, as well as forwarding of packets from the receiving interface to the destination address.

Packets that are destined for the machine itself must be routed to the loopback interface (IP address 127.0.0.1). All packets that are received from a network interface that are not destined for the machine itself must be routed to the destination or dropped. A dropped packet is effectively one that is ignored and disposed of.

Rules may be applied either to accept a packet, reject (deny) the packet, or drop it. A packet that is rejected will result in a message sent to the source address advising the reason for the rejection. The advisory packet may provide information that an attacker can use to implement an attack on the system. The dropping of packets results in no information being returned to the originator, with the effect that it will appear to the originator that the destination machine does not exist.

Rules specified may cause the firewall to examine any part of the incoming packet header information and determine how the packet will be processed if particular conditions are met.

Figure 3-5 illustrates the points of control in a dual-homed host. Firewall rules may be based on conditions at each point. The implementation of the rules is based on inbound, outbound, or forwarding requirements. As a result, rules that affect points A and E are collated under the rules table for outgoing packets, for B and D as part of the rules table for incoming packets, and forwarding between the NICs and the host itself is specified in the rules table for forwarding of packets.

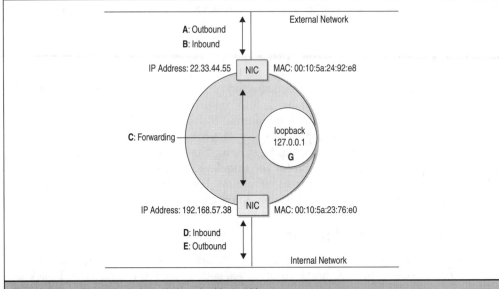

**Figure 3-5.** Firewall rule bounds in a dual-homed host

## IP Masquerading

A firewall may additionally be configured to hide the identity of hosts (IP addresses) that are present on a private (internal) network from the world at large. The most common modes of protection make use of IP masquerading or of network address translation (NAT).

IP Masquerade, also called IPMASQ or MASQ, allows one or more computers in a network without assigned IP addresses to communicate with the Internet using the Linux server's assigned IP address. The IPMASQ server acts as a gateway, and the other devices are invisible behind it, so to other machines on the Internet the outgoing traffic appears to be coming from the IPMASQ server and not the internal PCs.

It is much easier to guard a single point of entry than it is to guard many potential points of entry. The principle behind the Internet firewall is a machine that divides the network into the *inside* and the *outside*, with all traffic passing through the firewall. By protecting the single network firewall, the entire internal network can be protected. Masquerading allows machines on the inside to get out, without allowing foreign machine access to systems inside the private network. Masquerading rewrites the IP headers of outbound internal packets, making it appear that they all came from the firewall. Reply packets are treated by the reverse of the outgoing IP header translation, and are then forwarded to the appropriate internal machine. Thus, internal machines are allowed to connect to the outside world. However, external machines cannot find internal machines, since they are aware of only the IP address of the firewall external interface. The result is that they cannot attack the internal machines directly.

## Network Address Translation

Network address translation is a more general process whereby IP addresses in one address space (perhaps a private network) will be translated into another address space (say, a public address range) by a router or equivalent device. Unlike IP masquerading, NAT may map each address that originates from an internal network to its own external address. Additionally, an internal IP address that has been translated to an external address may well be capable of being reached by a foreign system simply by connecting to the unique external address that the internal address has been mapped to. This makes possible the use of NAT for a very wide range of applications, including:

- Load distribution routing
- Clustering of network servers and services
- Virtual server implementations

NAT was invented in the early 1990s. It is specified by RFC 1631 and was mainly meant to save IP address space on the Internet. Modern use of NAT extends the concept well beyond the original design intent. All modes of use, other than simple static NAT, require the maintenance of state information for each translated IP address. This adds significant overhead compared with the simplicity of IP masquerading.

The Linux kernel version 2.4 and more recent supports a wide array of IP masquerading and NAT techniques. Additionally, Red Hat Enterprise Linux AS 3.0 and SLES8 both provide the Linux Virtual Server (LVS) application, which makes it possible to implement load distribution routing as well as load distribution NAT.

NAT may be used to implement IP masquerading in the Linux operating system kernel, therefore it is important to be aware what NAT entails. It is beyond the scope of this book to address the details of IP masquerading and NAT technologies, other than to briefly mention the role each may have in the process of hardening a Linux server against external or internal assault.

## Stateless and Stateful Firewalls

Now that you know what a firewall is, there is one important factor that radically differentiates one type of firewall from another. Many old-style firewalls are *stateless*, meaning they lack capacity to remember connection states. Each connection that passes through it is a new connection. A *stateful* firewall maintains a history of connection contexts and dynamically updates the connection history.

A stateful firewall knows the context of each connection between its interfaces. This context information mitigates against the likelihood of third-party intrusion into the communication session. Connection context maintenance works in favor of the legitimate connection user and helps to prevent the hijacking of connection traffic.

The Linux kernel **iptables** facility can track connection state and permits its use to set up conditions for which an incoming packet may be accepted or rejected. The most common use of this capability is to accept only incoming connections for established outgoing connections. Incoming packets that attempt to set up a new TCP/IP connection will be rejected. **iptables** is a stateful instrument.

# Identify Protective Firewall Needs

There is sufficient weight of evidence from media reports and from professional security sources to justify the claim that all publicly exposed network interfaces must be protected. Crackers find an unprotected Unix/Linux system hard to resist.

Many network administrators argue that internal network traffic can be trusted and that internal computer systems do not require stringent protective barriers from people inside the organization. On the other hand, the conclusion of at least one researcher is that *insider jobs are the single largest financial threat* to information technology users (as found at http://research.rutgers.edu/~ungurean/610/Security.ppt).

In 2000, Global Health Trax Inc. reported that its old web site was opened to unauthorized access in January, possibly because of sabotage by disgruntled employees (see http://www2.norwich.edu/mkabay/iyir/2000.PDF). Although there was no evidence of penetration, detailed account information about hundreds of distributors was unprotected for several hours, including bank account and credit card numbers.

There is therefore a good argument that even internal network interfaces should be treated with the same suspicion that the external interface attracts. You should consider the risk and structure your firewall to provide a measure of protection that matches the level of risk you are comfortable with. If you are as paranoid as we are, you may choose to be totally paranoid.

When security is at risk, it is better to be prepared than to be sorry later. You may conclude otherwise, but the weight of evidence strongly demonstrates that computer systems and the resources they hold must be protected from insiders as much as from outsiders.

## Protective Strategy

Forward thinking is essential in firewall design. Consider what will happen in the event that specific firewall rules fail. Even though the risk may be minimal, still consider the effect of a system intrusion and exposure of critical data. The best policy is to never give a criminal a fair break. The default policy on all network interfaces should be to specifically drop (or deny) network traffic and thus prevent network interface access.

Firewall rules can be created that will specifically permit certain network traffic to pass to the Linux system. Table 3-4 provides guidelines of what may be permitted through the firewall.

Every server on your network should be assessed from a risk and exposure perspective. If a machine stores only inconsequential data, it may not warrant the effort and overhead of affording it a high level of protection. On the other hand, every

| Protocol | Inside Interfaces | External Interfaces |
|---|---|---|
| HTTP | Yes | Yes |
| HTTPS | Yes | Yes |
| SMTP | Yes | Yes |
| POP/IMAP | Yes | No |
| DNS | Yes | Yes (lookup only) |
| DHCP | Yes | No |
| NBNS | Yes | No |
| NBSS | Yes | No |
| FTP | Yes | Yes (read only) |
| Proxy | Yes | No |
| Print (515, 631) | Yes | No |
| High order ports (ports >1024) | Yes | Yes (only for existing connections) |

**Table 3-4.**    Firewall Interface Access Policy Guidelines

server that stores and/or processes sensitive data really ought to be well protected—and monitored. Simply protecting a system once is not a sufficient measure, unless it is monitored, action is taken when necessary, and regular updates are made to keep pace with new potentially aggressive methods by which the system may be compromised.

This is a good place to reiterate that all services that are running on a computer system may be attacked. In fact, the only secure computer system is one that is turned off and embedded in a steel reinforced block of concrete.

An attacker may attempt to flood your system with seemingly legitimate network service requests, effectively denying legitimate users from being serviced. This is known as a denial-of-service (DoS) attack. An attacker may attempt to exploit a known weakness or security hole in a service, or they may misuse legitimate credentials for unauthorized purposes. Your duty as a networking professional is to make unauthorized network service use as difficult as possible.

One last matter should be noted also. The firewall rules should permit network requests only to services that are actually being provided on the system. Never permit system access for services that are not operational and that are being routinely monitored.

## Configure the Firewall

Now that you have carefully considered the default policy regime as well as specific security rules that can be applied, the next challenge is to implement them.

This book encourages you to make use of standard facilities provided by Red Hat and SUSE for use with their enterprise Linux products. The building of specific, hand-crafted firewall rules requires experience and a detailed understanding of the principles of network operation. A clear, in-depth understanding of the techniques used by crackers and potential assailants is also essential to the design and implementation of a purpose-built secure firewall.

## SUSE Linux Firewall Configuration

The configuration of the standard SLES8 Linux firewall facility may be performed using the YaST2 toolset. The following procedure will take you through the necessary steps for a system that has two network interfaces, one external Internet connection and the other connected to a private network.

1. Log into the system as the user root.
2. Click the toolbar icon with the SUSE gecko logo with a hammer and a spanner through it.
3. Select YaST2 Modules | Security & Users | Firewall.
4. The panel shown in Figure 3-6 will be displayed.
5. Select the External and Internal Interfaces in the boxes shown in Figure 3-6.
6. Click Next.

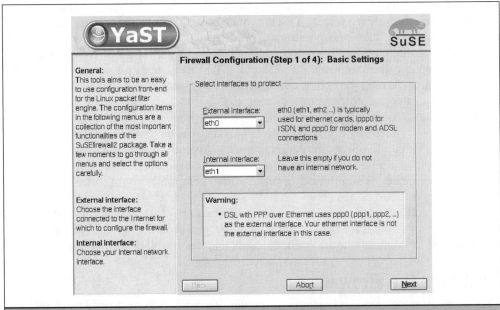

**Figure 3-6.** SUSE Linux Firewall Configuration (Step 1 of 4): Basic Settings

7. Click on the services you want to enable, as shown in Figure 3-7. If you enable protection of the internal network interface, it is necessary to select the protocols that internal users need to access via the internal interface. If you choose to not protect the internal interface, select only protocols that foreign users (outside your internal network) need to access.

8. Click Next.

9. As shown in Figure 3-8, select the features you want to enable, paying careful attention to the guidelines in the left panel regarding each option. It is essential to enable traffic forwarding and masquerading if the internal network interface uses an RFC1918 (private) class network address (in the range of 192.168.*.*, 172.16.*.*, or 10.*.*.*).

10. Click Next.

11. Select at least the top two logging options (as shown in Figure 3-9). This will permit you to identify from the system log files (/var/log/messages, /var/log /warn) the source IP address of alien requests that promoted the rules table to log this information. This is an essential part of a defense process.

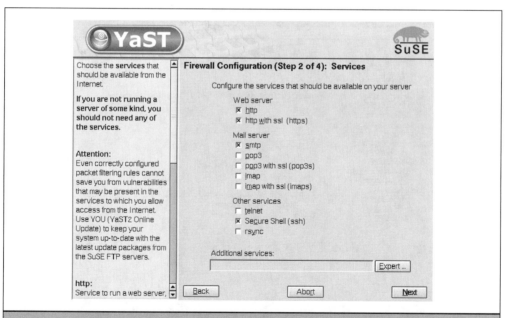

**Figure 3-7.** SUSE Linux Firewall Configuration (Step 2 of 4): Services

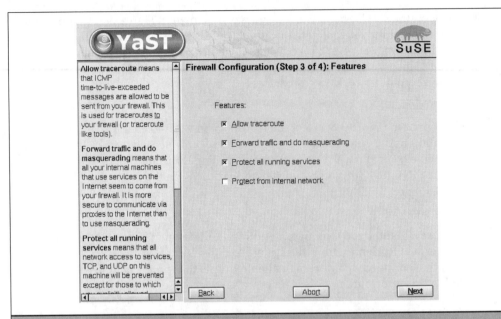

**Figure 3-8.** SUSE Linux Firewall Configuration (Step 3 of 4): Features

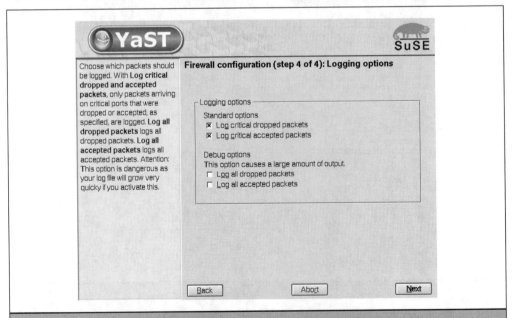

**Figure 3-9.** SUSE Linux Firewall Configuration (Step 4 of 4): Logging Options

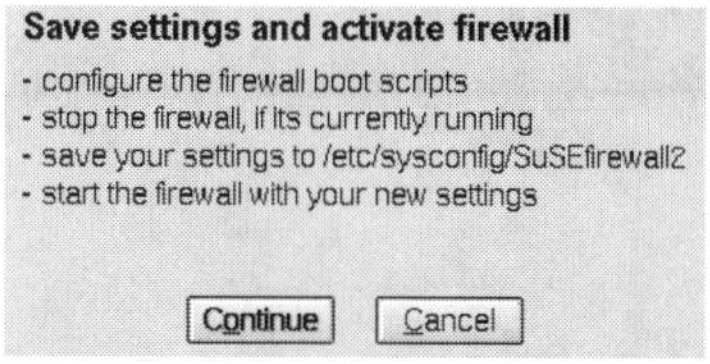

**Save settings and activate firewall**

- configure the firewall boot scripts
- stop the firewall, if its currently running
- save your settings to /etc/sysconfig/SuSEfirewall2
- start the firewall with your new settings

[ Continue ]   [ Cancel ]

**Figure 3-10.**   SUSE Linux Save settings and activate firewall

12. Click Next.

13. Figure 3-10 shows the control panel that appears. Click Continue to apply the firewall rule changes. The dialog panel shown in Figure 3-11 will report progress as the new rules are applied.

14. When the progress meter shows 100%, click Quit to exit the firewall configuration tool.

Your SUSE system firewall has now been configured.

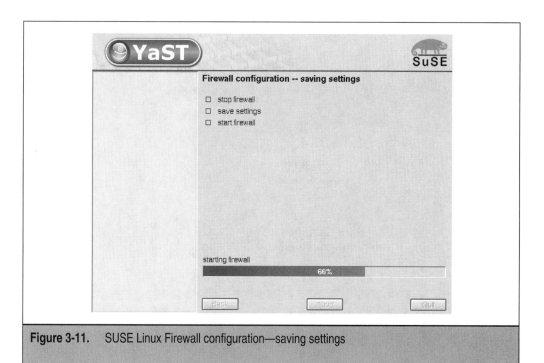

**Figure 3-11.**   SUSE Linux Firewall configuration—saving settings

## Red Hat Linux Firewall Configuration

Configuration of a basic firewall for Red Hat Enterprise Linux AS 3.0 can be achieved by following these steps:

1. Log onto the system as the root user.

2. On the desktop, click the Start Here icon.

3. Select System Settings | Security Level.

4. The panel shown in Figure 3-12 will appear. Select the Security Level and the protocols you want to permit to access this machine. Also check the network interfaces that you want to trust. Take care with your selection—any interface you enable will be configured as a trusted device.

5. Click OK.

6. The dialog box shown in Figure 3-13 provides an opportunity to void the change or to commit it. Click Yes to proceed.

The Red Hat Linux firewall is now configured and applied. Unlike the default SUSE firewall, the Red Hat default sets a default policy to accept all incoming traffic on a network interface. The correct operation of the rules is imperative.

**Figure 3-12.**    The Red Hat firewall configuration tool

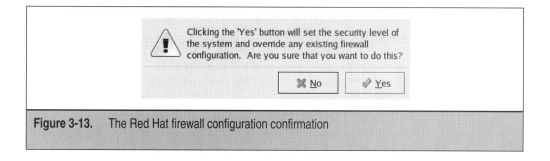

**Figure 3-13.** The Red Hat firewall configuration confirmation

## HEADS UP!

Red Hat sets a default policy to accept all incoming traffic on a network interface. This makes it critical that you configure rules to counter this.

### An Alternative Simple Linux Firewall Configuration

Listing 3-3 shown at the end of this chapter was obtained by executing the **iptables –L** command on a SLES8 system that has had a firewall enabled through use of the YaST2 facility.

The complexity of these rules is readily apparent. Both input and forwarding rules have a default policy to DROP incoming traffic. Exceptions are then made to permit desired traffic only. The substantial use of logging details of unwanted traffic is essential to permit the potential identification of sources of hostile traffic.

If you want to understand how the firewall rules operate, take some time to familiarize yourself with the structure, design, and method of implementation of firewall rules and exception handling. The exception reporting methods used in the script that has been generated on this system is extensive and provides a large volume of logged data.

## HEADS UP!

It makes sense to monitor and act on all logged data. If you do not intend to monitor *and* act on the exception reports, it does not make sense to create voluminous detailed information.

If you want to install an alternative firewall strategy, the following script must be modified to meet local needs. It can be configured to run as part of the startup process from the script /etc/rc.d/rc.local or from any alternative startup script. If you decide to use an alternative startup method, be sure to implement the firewall as early as possible, preferably before network services are started.

The nice thing about this script is the ease with which you can add or remove protocols as well as the fact that it uses a default policy to drop all incoming network requests unless a rule explicitly specifies otherwise. This leaves less room for risk of failure.

**Listing 3-2: An alternative masquerading firewall script**

```
#!/bin/sh
echo -e "\n\nLoading NAT firewall.\n"

IPTABLES=/usr/sbin/iptables
EXTIF="eth0"
INTIFA="eth1"

echo "   External Interface:  $EXTIF"
echo "   Internal Interfaces: $INTIFA"
echo -en "   loading modules: "
echo "  - Verifying that all kernel modules are ok"
/sbin/depmod -a
echo -en "ip_tables, "
/sbin/insmod ip_tables
echo -en "ip_conntrack, "
/sbin/insmod ip_conntrack
echo -en "ip_conntrack_ftp, "
/sbin/insmod ip_conntrack_ftp
echo -en "iptable_nat, "
/sbin/insmod iptable_nat
echo -en "ip_nat_ftp, "
/sbin/insmod ip_nat_ftp
echo ".  Done loading modules."
echo "   Clear existing rules, then setting default policy.."

$IPTABLES -P INPUT DROP
$IPTABLES -F INPUT
$IPTABLES -P OUTPUT ACCEPT
$IPTABLES -F OUTPUT
$IPTABLES -P FORWARD DROP
$IPTABLES -F FORWARD
$IPTABLES -t nat -F

$IPTABLES -A INPUT -i lo -j ACCEPT
$IPTABLES -A INPUT -i $INTIFA -j ACCEPT
$IPTABLES -A INPUT -i $EXTIF -m state --state ESTABLISHED,RELATED -j ACCEPT

# Enable incoming traffic for: SSH, SMTP, DNS(tcp), HTTP, HTTPS
for i in 22 25 53 80 443
do
        $IPTABLES -A INPUT -i $EXTIF -p tcp --dport $i  -j ACCEPT
done
```

```
# Allow DNS(udp)
$IPTABLES -A INPUT -i $EXTIF -p udp --dport 53  -j ACCEPT

echo "Allow all connections OUT and only existing and specified ones IN"
$IPTABLES -A FORWARD -i $EXTIF -o $INTIFA -m state --state ESTABLISHED,RELATED -j ACCEPT

$IPTABLES -A FORWARD -i $INTIFA -o $EXTIF -j ACCEPT
$IPTABLES -A FORWARD -j LOG

echo "  Enabling SNAT (MASQUERADE) functionality on $EXTIF"
$IPTABLES -t nat -A POSTROUTING -o $EXTIF -j MASQUERADE

echo "  Enabling IP_forwarding.. "
echo "1" > /proc/sys/net/ipv4/ip_forward

echo -e "\nNAT firewall done.\n"
```

The primary defense mechanism in use today is the firewall, with secondary protection afforded by **tcp_wrappers**. Your firewall rules table includes provision for logging of network access attempts that are either unexpected, originate from unacceptable sources, or exhibit potentially detrimental characteristics.

Hopefully, you will have deduced that there can be no such thing as a perfectly secure firewall. It is strongly recommended that you work with an attitude that every reported exception should be treated with suspicion and that you will identify the source of the exception and take appropriate action to protect the integrity of the system as well as that of the network resources it is designed to protect.

In a later chapter, you will configure facilities that will automate the process of monitoring firewall logs with an emphasis on inducing you to take appropriate corrective action. We hope you are ready to move on—there is more work to be done.

**Listing 3-3: SUSE SLES 8.0 firewall rules for dual interface configuration**

```
Chain INPUT (policy DROP)
target     prot opt source              destination
ACCEPT     all  --  anywhere            anywhere
LOG        all  --  loopback/8          anywhere            LOG level warning \
tcp-options ip-options prefix 'SuSE-FW-DROP-ANTI-SPOOFING '
LOG        all  --  anywhere            loopback/8          LOG level warning \
tcp-options ip-options prefix 'SuSE-FW-DROP-ANTI-SPOOFING '
DROP       all  --  loopback/8          anywhere
DROP       all  --  anywhere            loopback/8
LOG        all  --  192.168.57.128      anywhere            LOG level warning \
tcp-options ip-options prefix 'SuSE-FW-DROP-ANTI-SPOOFING '
DROP       all  --  192.168.57.128      anywhere
LOG        all  --  linux.demoworld.org anywhere            LOG level warning \
tcp-options ip-options prefix 'SuSE-FW-DROP-ANTI-SPOOFING '
DROP       all  --  linux.demoworld.org anywhere
input_ext  all  --  anywhere            linux.demoworld.org
input_int  all  --  anywhere            192.168.57.128
DROP       all  --  anywhere            192.168.1.255
```

```
DROP       all  --  anywhere              255.255.255.255
DROP       all  --  anywhere              192.168.57.255
DROP       all  --  anywhere              255.255.255.255
LOG        all  --  anywhere              linux.demoworld.orgLOG level warning \
tcp-options ip-options prefix 'SuSE-FW-ACCESS_DENIED_INT '
DROP       all  --  anywhere              linux.demoworld.org
LOG        all  --  anywhere              anywhere              LOG level warning \
tcp-options ip-options prefix 'SuSE-FW-ILLEGAL-TARGET '
DROP       all  --  anywhere              anywhere
Chain FORWARD (policy DROP)
target     prot opt source                destination
TCPMSS     tcp  --  anywhere              anywhere \
tcp flags:SYN,RST/SYN TCPMSS clamp to PMTU
ACCEPT     all  --  anywhere              anywhere
ACCEPT     all  --  anywhere              anywhere
forward_ext  all  --  anywhere             anywhere
forward_int  all  --  anywhere             anywhere
LOG        all  --  anywhere              anywhere              LOG level warning \
tcp-options ip-options prefix 'SuSE-FW-ILLEGAL-ROUTING '
DROP       all  --  anywhere              anywhere
ACCEPT     all  --  anywhere              anywhere \
state NEW,RELATED,ESTABLISHED
LOG        all  --  anywhere              anywhere              LOG level warning \
tcp-options ip-options prefix 'SuSE-FW-FORWARD-ERROR '
Chain OUTPUT (policy ACCEPT)
target     prot opt source                destination
ACCEPT     all  --  anywhere              anywhere
LOG        icmp --  anywhere              anywhere              icmp time-exceeded \
LOG level warning tcp-options ip-options prefix 'SuSE-FW-TRACEROUTE-ATTEMPT '
ACCEPT     icmp --  anywhere              anywhere              icmp time-exceeded
ACCEPT     icmp --  anywhere              anywhere              icmp port-unreachable
ACCEPT     icmp --  anywhere              anywhere \
icmp fragmentation-needed
ACCEPT     icmp --  anywhere              anywhere \
icmp network-prohibited
ACCEPT     icmp --  anywhere              anywhere              icmp host-prohibited
ACCEPT     icmp --  anywhere              anywhere \
icmp communication-prohibited
DROP       icmp --  anywhere              anywhere \
icmp destination-unreachable
ACCEPT     all  --  anywhere              anywhere \
state NEW,RELATED,ESTABLISHED
LOG        all  --  anywhere              anywhere              LOG level warning \
tcp-options ip-options prefix 'SuSE-FW-OUTPUT-ERROR '
Chain forward_dmz (0 references)
target     prot opt source                destination
LOG        all  --  192.168.1.0/24        anywhere              LOG level warning \
tcp-options ip-options prefix 'SuSE-FW-DROP-ANTI-SPOOF '
DROP       all  --  192.168.1.0/24        anywhere
```

```
LOG        all  --  192.168.57.0/24      anywhere           LOG level warning \
tcp-options ip-options prefix 'SuSE-FW-DROP-ANTI-SPOOF '
DROP       all  --  192.168.57.0/24      anywhere
LOG        all  --  anywhere             192.168.57.128     LOG level warning \
tcp-options ip-options prefix 'SuSE-FW-DROP-CIRCUMVENTION '
DROP       all  --  anywhere             192.168.57.128
LOG        all  --  anywhere             linux.demoworld.orgLOG level warning \
tcp-options ip-options prefix 'SuSE-FW-DROP-CIRCUMVENTION '
DROP       all  --  anywhere             linux.demoworld.org
ACCEPT     icmp --  anywhere             anywhere           state RELATED icmp \
destination-unreachable
ACCEPT     icmp --  anywhere             anywhere state \
RELATED,ESTABLISHED icmp echo-reply
ACCEPT     all  --  anywhere             anywhere           state \
NEW,RELATED,ESTABLISHED
ACCEPT     all  --  anywhere             anywhere           state \
RELATED,ESTABLISHED
LOG        tcp  --  anywhere             anywhere           tcp \
flags:SYN,RST,ACK/SYN LOG level warning tcp-options ip-options prefix \
'SuSE-FW-DROP-DEFAULT '
LOG        icmp --  anywhere             anywhere           icmp \
source-quench LOG level warning tcp-options ip-options prefix \
'SuSE-FW-DROP-DEFAULT '
LOG        icmp --  anywhere             anywhere           icmp redirect \
LOG level warning tcp-options ip-options prefix 'SuSE-FW-DROP-DEFAULT '
LOG        icmp --  anywhere             anywhere           icmp echo-request \
LOG level warning tcp-options ip-options prefix 'SuSE-FW-DROP-DEFAULT '
LOG        icmp --  anywhere             anywhere           icmp \
timestamp-request LOG level warning tcp-options ip-options prefix 'SuSE-FW-DROP-DEFAULT '
LOG        icmp --  anywhere             anywhere           icmp \
address-mask-request LOG level warning tcp-options ip-options prefix \
'SuSE-FW-DROP-DEFAULT '
LOG        udp  --  anywhere             anywhere           LOG level warning \
tcp-options ip-options prefix 'SuSE-FW-DROP-DEFAULT '
LOG        all  --  anywhere             anywhere           state INVALID LOG \
level warning tcp-options ip-options prefix 'SuSE-FW-DROP-DEFAULT-INVALID '
DROP       all  --  anywhere             anywhere
Chain forward_ext (1 references)
target     prot opt source               destination
LOG        all  --  192.168.57.0/24      anywhere           LOG level warning \
tcp-options ip-options prefix 'SuSE-FW-DROP-ANTI-SPOOF '
DROP       all  --  192.168.57.0/24      anywhere
LOG        all  --  anywhere             192.168.57.128     LOG level warning \
tcp-options ip-options prefix 'SuSE-FW-DROP-CIRCUMVENTION '
DROP       all  --  anywhere             192.168.57.128
ACCEPT     icmp --  anywhere             anywhere           state RELATED \
icmp destination-unreachable
ACCEPT     icmp --  anywhere             anywhere           state \
```

```
RELATED,ESTABLISHED icmp echo-reply
ACCEPT     all  --  anywhere              anywhere           state \
NEW,RELATED,ESTABLISHED
ACCEPT     all  --  anywhere              anywhere           state RELATED,ESTABLISHED
LOG        tcp  --  anywhere              anywhere           tcp \
flags:SYN,RST,ACK/SYN LOG level warning tcp-options ip-options prefix \
'SuSE-FW-DROP-DEFAULT '
LOG        icmp --  anywhere              anywhere           icmp source-quench \
LOG level warning tcp-options ip-options prefix 'SuSE-FW-DROP-DEFAULT '
LOG        icmp --  anywhere              anywhere           icmp redirect \
LOG level warning tcp-options ip-options prefix 'SuSE-FW-DROP-DEFAULT '
LOG        icmp --  anywhere              anywhere           icmp echo-request \
LOG level warning tcp-options ip-options prefix 'SuSE-FW-DROP-DEFAULT '
LOG        icmp --  anywhere              anywhere           icmp \
timestamp-request LOG level warning tcp-options ip-options prefix \
'SuSE-FW-DROP-DEFAULT '
LOG        icmp --  anywhere              anywhere           icmp \
address-mask-request LOG level warning tcp-options ip-options prefix \
'SuSE-FW-DROP-DEFAULT '
LOG        udp  --  anywhere              anywhere           LOG level warning \
tcp-options ip-options prefix 'SuSE-FW-DROP-DEFAULT '
LOG        all  --  anywhere              anywhere           state INVALID LOG \
level warning tcp-options ip-options prefix 'SuSE-FW-DROP-DEFAULT-INVALID '
DROP       all  --  anywhere              anywhere
Chain forward_int (1 references)
target     prot opt source               destination
LOG        all  --  192.168.1.0/24       anywhere           LOG level warning \
tcp-options ip-options prefix 'SuSE-FW-DROP-ANTI-SPOOF '
DROP       all  --  192.168.1.0/24       anywhere
LOG        all  --  anywhere             linux.demoworld.orgLOG level warning \
tcp-options ip-options prefix 'SuSE-FW-DROP-CIRCUMVENTION '
DROP       all  --  anywhere             linux.demoworld.org
ACCEPT     icmp --  anywhere              anywhere           state RELATED icmp \
destination-unreachable
ACCEPT     icmp --  anywhere              anywhere           state \
RELATED,ESTABLISHED icmp echo-reply
ACCEPT     all  --  anywhere              anywhere           state \
NEW,RELATED,ESTABLISHED
ACCEPT     all  --  anywhere              anywhere           state \
RELATED,ESTABLISHED
LOG        tcp  --  anywhere              anywhere           tcp \
flags:SYN,RST,ACK/SYN LOG level warning tcp-options ip-options prefix \
'SuSE-FW-DROP-DEFAULT '
LOG        icmp --  anywhere              anywhere           icmp \
source-quench LOG level warning tcp-options ip-options prefix \
'SuSE-FW-DROP-DEFAULT '
LOG        icmp --  anywhere              anywhere           icmp redirect \
LOG level warning tcp-options ip-options prefix 'SuSE-FW-DROP-DEFAULT '
```

```
LOG        icmp -- anywhere              anywhere            icmp echo-request \
LOG level warning tcp-options ip-options prefix 'SuSE-FW-DROP-DEFAULT '
LOG        icmp -- anywhere              anywhere            icmp \
timestamp-request LOG level warning tcp-options ip-options prefix \
'SuSE-FW-DROP-DEFAULT '
LOG        icmp -- anywhere              anywhere            icmp \
address-mask-request LOG level warning tcp-options ip-options prefix \
'SuSE-FW-DROP-DEFAULT '
LOG        udp  -- anywhere              anywhere            LOG level warning \
tcp-options ip-options prefix 'SuSE-FW-DROP-DEFAULT '
LOG        all  -- anywhere              anywhere            state INVALID LOG \
level warning tcp-options ip-options prefix 'SuSE-FW-DROP-DEFAULT-INVALID '
DROP       all  -- anywhere              anywhere
Chain input_dmz (0 references)
target     prot opt source               destination
LOG        all  -- 192.168.1.0/24        anywhere            LOG level warning \
tcp-options ip-options prefix 'SuSE-FW-DROP-ANTI-SPOOF '
DROP       all  -- 192.168.1.0/24        anywhere
LOG        all  -- 192.168.57.0/24       anywhere            LOG level warning \
tcp-options ip-options prefix 'SuSE-FW-DROP-ANTI-SPOOF '
DROP       all  -- 192.168.57.0/24       anywhere
ACCEPT     icmp -- anywhere              anywhere            icmp echo-request
ACCEPT     icmp -- anywhere              anywhere            state \
RELATED,ESTABLISHED icmp echo-reply
ACCEPT     icmp -- anywhere              anywhere            state \
RELATED,ESTABLISHED icmp destination-unreachable
ACCEPT     icmp -- anywhere              anywhere            state \
RELATED,ESTABLISHED icmp time-exceeded
ACCEPT     icmp -- anywhere              anywhere            state \
RELATED,ESTABLISHED icmp parameter-problem
ACCEPT     icmp -- anywhere              anywhere            state \
RELATED,ESTABLISHED icmp timestamp-reply
ACCEPT     icmp -- anywhere              anywhere            state \
RELATED,ESTABLISHED icmp address-mask-reply
LOG        icmp -- anywhere              anywhere            icmp redirect \
LOG level warning tcp-options ip-options prefix 'SuSE-FW-DROP-ICMP-CRIT '
LOG        icmp -- anywhere              anywhere            icmp source-quench \
LOG level warning tcp-options ip-options prefix 'SuSE-FW-DROP-ICMP-CRIT '
LOG        icmp -- anywhere              anywhere            icmp \
timestamp-request LOG level warning tcp-options ip-options prefix \
'SuSE-FW-DROP-ICMP-CRIT '
LOG        icmp -- anywhere              anywhere            icmp \
address-mask-request LOG level warning tcp-options ip-options prefix \
'SuSE-FW-DROP-ICMP-CRIT '
LOG        icmp -- anywhere              anywhere            icmp type 2 LOG \
level warning tcp-options ip-options prefix 'SuSE-FW-DROP-ICMP-CRIT '
DROP       icmp -- anywhere              anywhere
reject_func tcp -- anywhere              anywhere            tcp dpt:ident \
flags:SYN,RST,ACK/SYN
```

```
LOG        tcp  -- anywhere          anywhere          tcp dpt:ssh \
flags:SYN,RST,ACK/SYN LOG level warning tcp-options ip-options prefix \
'SuSE-FW-DROP '
DROP       tcp  -- anywhere          anywhere          tcp dpt:ssh \
flags:SYN,RST,ACK/SYN
LOG        tcp  -- anywhere          anywhere          tcp dpt:sunrpc \
flags:SYN,RST,ACK/SYN LOG level warning tcp-options ip-options prefix \
'SuSE-FW-DROP '
DROP       tcp  -- anywhere          anywhere          tcp dpt:sunrpc \
flags:SYN,RST,ACK/SYN
LOG        tcp  -- anywhere          anywhere          tcp dpt:x11 \
flags:SYN,RST,ACK/SYN LOG level warning tcp-options ip-options prefix \
'SuSE-FW-DROP '
DROP       tcp  -- anywhere          anywhere          tcp dpt:x11 \
flags:SYN,RST,ACK/SYN
LOG        tcp  -- anywhere          anywhere          tcp dpts:1024:65535 \
flags:SYN,RST,ACK/SYN LOG level warning tcp-options ip-options prefix \
'SuSE-FW-ACCEPT '
ACCEPT     tcp  -- anywhere          anywhere          state \
RELATED,ESTABLISHED tcp dpts:1024:65535
ACCEPT     tcp  -- anywhere          anywhere          state \
ESTABLISHED tcp dpts:ipcserver:65535 flags:!SYN,RST,ACK/SYN
ACCEPT     tcp  -- anywhere          anywhere          state \
ESTABLISHED tcp dpt:ftp-data flags:!SYN,RST,ACK/SYN
ACCEPT     udp  -- frodo.demoworld.org anywhere        state \
NEW,RELATED,ESTABLISHED udp spt:domain dpts:1024:65535
DROP       udp  -- anywhere          anywhere          udp dpt:ssh
DROP       udp  -- anywhere          anywhere          udp dpt:bootpc
DROP       udp  -- anywhere          anywhere          udp dpt:sunrpc
DROP       udp  -- anywhere          anywhere          udp dpt:sunrpc
DROP       udp  -- anywhere          anywhere          udp dpt:x11
ACCEPT     udp  -- anywhere          anywhere          state \
RELATED,ESTABLISHED udp dpts:1024:65535
LOG        tcp  -- anywhere          anywhere          tcp \
flags:SYN,RST,ACK/SYN LOG level warning tcp-options ip-options prefix \
'SuSE-FW-DROP-DEFAULT '
LOG        icmp -- anywhere          anywhere          icmp \
source-quench LOG level warning tcp-options ip-options prefix \
'SuSE-FW-DROP-DEFAULT '
LOG        icmp -- anywhere          anywhere          icmp redirect LOG \
level warning tcp-options ip-options prefix 'SuSE-FW-DROP-DEFAULT '
LOG        icmp -- anywhere          anywhere          icmp echo-request \
LOG level warning tcp-options ip-options prefix 'SuSE-FW-DROP-DEFAULT '
LOG        icmp -- anywhere          anywhere          icmp \
timestamp-request LOG level warning tcp-options ip-options prefix \
'SuSE-FW-DROP-DEFAULT '
LOG        icmp -- anywhere          anywhere          icmp \
address-mask-request LOG level warning tcp-options ip-options prefix \
'SuSE-FW-DROP-DEFAULT '
```

```
LOG         udp  --  anywhere              anywhere              LOG level warning \
tcp-options ip-options prefix 'SuSE-FW-DROP-DEFAULT '
LOG         all  --  anywhere              anywhere              state INVALID LOG \
level warning tcp-options ip-options prefix 'SuSE-FW-DROP-DEFAULT-INVALID '
DROP        all  --  anywhere              anywhere
Chain input_ext (1 references)
target      prot opt source                destination
LOG         all  --  192.168.57.0/24       anywhere              LOG level warning \
tcp-options ip-options prefix 'SuSE-FW-DROP-ANTI-SPOOF '
DROP        all  --  192.168.57.0/24       anywhere
LOG         icmp --  192.168.1.0/24        anywhere              icmp source-quench \
LOG level warning tcp-options ip-options prefix 'SuSE-FW-ACCEPT-SOURCEQUENCH '
ACCEPT      icmp --  192.168.1.0/24        anywhere              icmp source-quench
ACCEPT      icmp --  anywhere              anywhere              icmp echo-request
ACCEPT      icmp --  anywhere              anywhere              state \
RELATED,ESTABLISHED icmp echo-reply
ACCEPT      icmp --  anywhere              anywhere              state \
RELATED,ESTABLISHED icmp destination-unreachable
ACCEPT      icmp --  anywhere              anywhere              state \
RELATED,ESTABLISHED icmp time-exceeded
ACCEPT      icmp --  anywhere              anywhere              state \
RELATED,ESTABLISHED icmp parameter-problem
ACCEPT      icmp --  anywhere              anywhere              state \
RELATED,ESTABLISHED icmp timestamp-reply
ACCEPT      icmp --  anywhere              anywhere              state \
RELATED,ESTABLISHED icmp address-mask-reply
LOG         icmp --  anywhere              anywhere              icmp redirect LOG \
level warning tcp-options ip-options prefix 'SuSE-FW-DROP-ICMP-CRIT '
LOG         icmp --  anywhere              anywhere              icmp source-quench \
LOG level warning tcp-options ip-options prefix 'SuSE-FW-DROP-ICMP-CRIT '
LOG         icmp --  anywhere              anywhere              icmp \
timestamp-request LOG level warning tcp-options ip-options prefix \
'SuSE-FW-DROP-ICMP-CRIT '
LOG         icmp --  anywhere              anywhere              icmp \
address-mask-request LOG level warning tcp-options ip-options prefix \
'SuSE-FW-DROP-ICMP-CRIT '
LOG         icmp --  anywhere              anywhere              icmp type \
2 LOG level warning tcp-options ip-options prefix 'SuSE-FW-DROP-ICMP-CRIT '
DROP        icmp --  anywhere              anywhere
LOG         tcp  --  anywhere              anywhere              tcp \
dpt:http flags:SYN,RST,ACK/SYN LOG level warning tcp-options ip-options prefix \
'SuSE-FW-ACCEPT '
ACCEPT      tcp  --  anywhere              anywhere              state \
NEW,RELATED,ESTABLISHED tcp dpt:http
LOG         tcp  --  anywhere              anywhere              tcp \
dpt:https flags:SYN,RST,ACK/SYN LOG level warning tcp-options ip-options prefix \
'SuSE-FW-ACCEPT '
ACCEPT      tcp  --  anywhere              anywhere              state \
NEW,RELATED,ESTABLISHED tcp dpt:https
```

```
LOG        tcp  --  anywhere           anywhere          tcp dpt:smtp \
flags:SYN,RST,ACK/SYN LOG level warning tcp-options ip-options prefix \
'SuSE-FW-ACCEPT '
ACCEPT     tcp  --  anywhere           anywhere          state \
NEW,RELATED,ESTABLISHED tcp dpt:smtp
LOG        tcp  --  anywhere           anywhere          tcp dpt:ssh \
flags:SYN,RST,ACK/SYN LOG level warning tcp-options ip-options prefix \
'SuSE-FW-ACCEPT '
ACCEPT     tcp  --  anywhere           anywhere          state \
NEW,RELATED,ESTABLISHED tcp dpt:ssh
reject_func tcp  --  anywhere           anywhere          tcp dpt:ident \
flags:SYN,RST,ACK/SYN
LOG        tcp  --  anywhere           anywhere          tcp dpt:ssh \
flags:SYN,RST,ACK/SYN LOG level warning tcp-options ip-options prefix \
'SuSE-FW-DROP '
DROP       tcp  --  anywhere           anywhere          tcp dpt:ssh \
flags:SYN,RST,ACK/SYN
LOG        tcp  --  anywhere           anywhere          tcp dpt:sunrpc \
flags:SYN,RST,ACK/SYN LOG level warning tcp-options ip-options prefix \
'SuSE-FW-DROP '
DROP       tcp  --  anywhere           anywhere          tcp dpt:sunrpc \
flags:SYN,RST,ACK/SYN
LOG        tcp  --  anywhere           anywhere          tcp dpt:x11 \
flags:SYN,RST,ACK/SYN LOG level warning tcp-options ip-options prefix \
'SuSE-FW-DROP '
DROP       tcp  --  anywhere           anywhere          tcp dpt:x11 flags:SYN,RST,ACK/
SYN
LOG        tcp  --  anywhere           anywhere          tcp dpts:1024:65535 \
flags:SYN,RST,ACK/SYN LOG level warning tcp-options ip-options prefix \
'SuSE-FW-ACCEPT '
ACCEPT     tcp  --  anywhere           anywhere          state \
RELATED,ESTABLISHED tcp dpts:1024:65535
ACCEPT     tcp  --  anywhere           anywhere          state \
ESTABLISHED tcp dpts:ipcserver:65535 flags:!SYN,RST,ACK/SYN
ACCEPT     tcp  --  anywhere           anywhere          state \
ESTABLISHED tcp dpt:ftp-data flags:!SYN,RST,ACK/SYN
ACCEPT     udp  --  frodo.demoworld.org anywhere          state \
NEW,RELATED,ESTABLISHED udp spt:domain dpts:1024:65535
DROP       udp  --  anywhere           anywhere          udp dpt:ssh
DROP       udp  --  anywhere           anywhere          udp dpt:bootpc
DROP       udp  --  anywhere           anywhere          udp dpt:sunrpc
DROP       udp  --  anywhere           anywhere          udp dpt:sunrpc
DROP       udp  --  anywhere           anywhere          udp dpt:x11
ACCEPT     udp  --  anywhere           anywhere          state \
RELATED,ESTABLISHED udp dpts:1024:65535
ACCEPT     udp  --  anywhere           anywhere          state ESTABLISHED \
udp dpts:61000:65095
LOG        tcp  --  anywhere           anywhere          tcp \
flags:SYN,RST,ACK/SYN LOG level warning tcp-options ip-options prefix \
```

```
'SuSE-FW-DROP-DEFAULT '
LOG         icmp -- anywhere           anywhere          icmp source-quench \
LOG level warning tcp-options ip-options prefix 'SuSE-FW-DROP-DEFAULT '
LOG         icmp -- anywhere           anywhere          icmp redirect LOG \
level warning tcp-options ip-options prefix 'SuSE-FW-DROP-DEFAULT '
LOG         icmp -- anywhere           anywhere          icmp echo-request \
LOG level warning tcp-options ip-options prefix 'SuSE-FW-DROP-DEFAULT '
LOG         icmp -- anywhere           anywhere          icmp \
timestamp-request LOG level warning tcp-options ip-options prefix \
'SuSE-FW-DROP-DEFAULT '
LOG         icmp -- anywhere           anywhere          icmp \
address-mask-request LOG level warning tcp-options ip-options prefix \
'SuSE-FW-DROP-DEFAULT '
LOG         udp  -- anywhere           anywhere          LOG level warning \
tcp-options ip-options prefix 'SuSE-FW-DROP-DEFAULT '
LOG         all  -- anywhere           anywhere          state INVALID LOG \
level warning tcp-options ip-options prefix 'SuSE-FW-DROP-DEFAULT-INVALID '
DROP        all  -- anywhere           anywhere
Chain input_int (1 references)
target      prot opt source            destination
LOG         all  -- 192.168.1.0/24     anywhere          LOG level warning \
tcp-options ip-options prefix 'SuSE-FW-DROP-ANTI-SPOOF '
DROP        all  -- 192.168.1.0/24     anywhere
ACCEPT      all  -- anywhere           anywhere
ACCEPT      icmp -- anywhere           anywhere          icmp echo-request
ACCEPT      icmp -- anywhere           anywhere          state \
RELATED,ESTABLISHED icmp echo-reply
ACCEPT      icmp -- anywhere           anywhere          state \
RELATED,ESTABLISHED icmp destination-unreachable
ACCEPT      icmp -- anywhere           anywhere          state \
RELATED,ESTABLISHED icmp time-exceeded
ACCEPT      icmp -- anywhere           anywhere          state \
RELATED,ESTABLISHED icmp parameter-problem
ACCEPT      icmp -- anywhere           anywhere          state \
RELATED,ESTABLISHED icmp timestamp-reply
ACCEPT      icmp -- anywhere           anywhere          state \
RELATED,ESTABLISHED icmp address-mask-reply
LOG         icmp -- anywhere           anywhere          icmp redirect LOG \
level warning tcp-options ip-options prefix 'SuSE-FW-DROP-ICMP-CRIT '
LOG         icmp -- anywhere           anywhere          icmp source-quench \
LOG level warning tcp-options ip-options prefix 'SuSE-FW-DROP-ICMP-CRIT '
LOG         icmp -- anywhere           anywhere          icmp \
timestamp-request LOG level warning tcp-options ip-options prefix \
'SuSE-FW-DROP-ICMP-CRIT '
LOG         icmp -- anywhere           anywhere          icmp \
address-mask-request LOG level warning tcp-options ip-options prefix \
'SuSE-FW-DROP-ICMP-CRIT '
LOG         icmp -- anywhere           anywhere          icmp type 2 LOG \
level warning tcp-options ip-options prefix 'SuSE-FW-DROP-ICMP-CRIT '
```

```
DROP       icmp -- anywhere            anywhere
reject_func tcp  --  anywhere          anywhere          tcp dpt:ident \
flags:SYN,RST,ACK/SYN
LOG        tcp  --  anywhere           anywhere          tcp dpts:1024:65535 \
flags:SYN,RST,ACK/SYN LOG level warning tcp-options ip-options prefix \
'SuSE-FW-ACCEPT '
ACCEPT     tcp  --  anywhere           anywhere          state \
RELATED,ESTABLISHED tcp dpts:1024:65535
ACCEPT     tcp  --  anywhere           anywhere          state ESTABLISHED \
tcp dpts:ipcserver:65535 flags:!SYN,RST,ACK/SYN
ACCEPT     tcp  --  anywhere           anywhere          state ESTABLISHED \
tcp dpt:ftp-data flags:!SYN,RST,ACK/SYN
ACCEPT     udp  --  frodo.demoworld.org anywhere         state \
NEW,RELATED,ESTABLISHED udp spt:domain dpts:1024:65535
ACCEPT     udp  --  anywhere           anywhere          state \
RELATED,ESTABLISHED udp dpts:1024:65535
LOG        tcp  --  anywhere           anywhere          tcp \
flags:SYN,RST,ACK/SYN LOG level warning tcp-options ip-options prefix \
'SuSE-FW-DROP-DEFAULT '
LOG        icmp -- anywhere            anywhere          icmp source-quench \
LOG level warning tcp-options ip-options prefix 'SuSE-FW-DROP-DEFAULT '
LOG        icmp -- anywhere            anywhere          icmp redirect LOG \
evel warning tcp-options ip-options prefix 'SuSE-FW-DROP-DEFAULT '
LOG        icmp -- anywhere            anywhere          icmp echo-request \
LOG level warning tcp-options ip-options prefix 'SuSE-FW-DROP-DEFAULT '
LOG        icmp -- anywhere            anywhere          icmp \
timestamp-request LOG level warning tcp-options ip-options prefix 'SuSE-FW-DROP-DEFAULT '
LOG        icmp -- anywhere            anywhere          icmp \
address-mask-request LOG level warning tcp-options ip-options prefix \
'SuSE-FW-DROP-DEFAULT '
LOG        udp  -- anywhere            anywhere          LOG level warning \
tcp-options ip-options prefix 'SuSE-FW-DROP-DEFAULT '
LOG        all  -- anywhere            anywhere          state INVALID LOG \
level warning tcp-options ip-options prefix 'SuSE-FW-DROP-DEFAULT-INVALID '
DROP       all  -- anywhere            anywhere
Chain reject_func (3 references)
target     prot opt source             destination
REJECT     tcp  --  anywhere           anywhere          reject-with \
tcp-reset
REJECT     udp  --  anywhere           anywhere          reject-with \
icmp-port-unreachable
REJECT     all  --  anywhere           anywhere          reject-with \
icmp-proto-unreachable
```

# Chapter 4

## Hardening Software Accessibility

- Identify Required Software
- Determine Software Dependencies
- Remove or Restrict Unneeded Software
- Install Software Securely
- Monitor Your Systems

**S**oftware provides functionality and the ability to get things done, but it can also be used to destroy and attack a machine through vulnerabilities or misconfiguration. With the vast array of software available for Linux, it is easy to fall into the trap of installing a lot of interesting software that you may not necessarily need. The less software you have running on your Linux machine, the fewer potential vulnerabilities there are to exploit on your system. This basic truth is the basis for this chapter, and we will go over the steps you will be taking to harden your system. The first half of the chapter will discuss removing software that you may have installed or was previously installed that isn't needed for your server. The second portion of the chapter will discuss how to securely install new software that is required for your organization's objectives.

The steps you need to take to resolve this vulnerability are the following:

- Identify required software
- Determine software dependencies
- Remove or restrict unneeded software
- Install software securely
- Test and monitor your system

# Identify Required Software

The first step is to determine what your system is being used for and then determine what is required to achieve your business goals. For instance, you may have a web server running Apache that is also a file server with NFS for the sales group. This is not an optimal situation, as you should restrict functions as much as possible for critical services, so if one server is compromised, you don't lose more information than if the server was a single use machine. After some investigation, you determine that the sales group is using a completely different machine for most file sharing functions. With this discovery, you could remove NFS capabilities from the server, eliminating a whole class of NFS vulnerabilities as well as patching and administration requirements associated with NFS. This also would have the effect of mitigating a high value target, because the machine would only house web services as opposed to a web server with potentially sensitive files.

Don't be fooled by how simple this sounds—it is often the most difficult portion of the whole evolution of removing unneeded software. If you are lucky enough to be able to install Linux on the machine yourself, you should start by doing a custom install when it comes to packages and selecting the packages you need individually. If you are inheriting a system, the first step toward determining what is needed is to do a software inventory of your current system. You can do this with the **rpm** command or through the graphical package management tools included in most distributions. To get a listing of all packages on your system, from the command line use the **rpm -qa** command, which shows output similar to that in Figure 4-1.

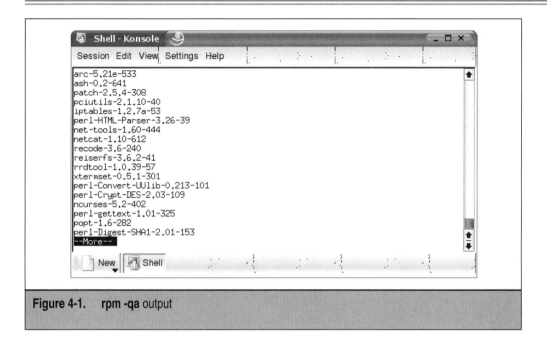

**Figure 4-1.    rpm -qa** output

---

**NOTE**   One option for testing multiple configurations with minimal cost is to set up an old machine with Linux and then run multiple virtual machines on that machine. A virtual machine provides software emulation for a hardware environment (typically x86 architecture). This saves on hardware costs and allows you to test in a safe, controlled manner. VMWare (http://www.vmware.com/) is the most widely known product available for virtual machines and is a commercially supported product.

---

To get a verbose listing of package information, you could run

```
rpm -qai
```

There is a lot of output associated with these methods, so you will want to redirect the output to a file with a command similar to rpm -qai > filename_to_send_ouptut_to.

If you want to view this type of output in a graphical format, type **yast2 sw_single** in SUSE or type **redhat-config-packages** in Red Hat at the command line and you will see screens similar to Figure 4-2 (for SUSE) or Figure 4-3 (for Red Hat).

Anything that shows up in the output of the **rpm -qa** command is installed on your system. If you are using the graphical tools, anything that has a check next to its package name is installed.

Having a list of the installed software is nice, but you really need to know what the software does. As with determining what software you have, there are multiple ways

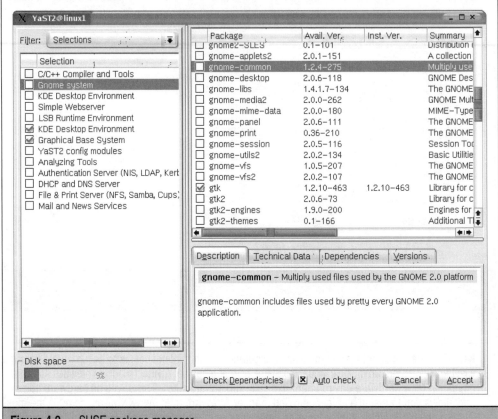

**Figure 4-2.**   SUSE package manager

to determine what the software that you have installed is supposed to do. From the command line you can type

```
rpm -qi <package name>
```

with *<package name>* replaced by the package you want information about (in this case telnet). Figure 4-4 shows the output.

To get information about a package in the graphical package managers, you only need to highlight the package you are interested in finding out about. Figure 4-5 shows how to obtain information on the telnet package in SUSE (note that the top right hand side of the screen shows where to filter the information by package groups, general search, and selections).

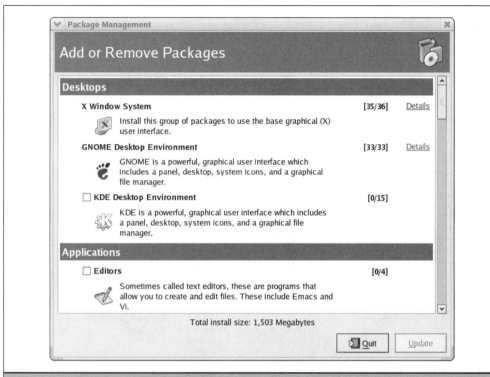

**Figure 4-3.**    Red Hat package manager

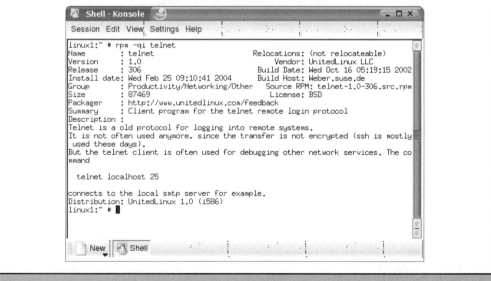

**Figure 4-4.**    **rpm -qi** telnet output

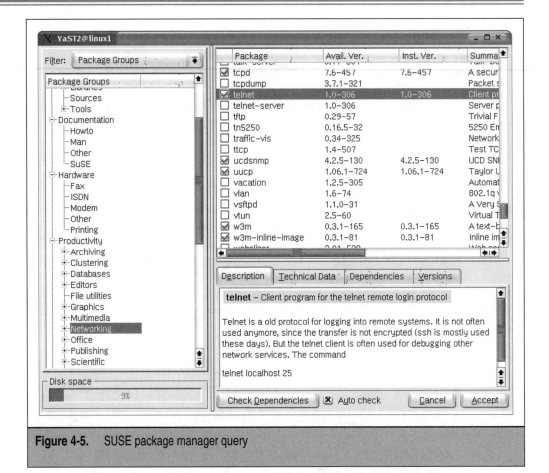

**Figure 4-5.** SUSE package manager query

Red Hat's package manager shows a brief overview of what the package does as shown in Figure 4-6 (in this case selecting Gnome packages).

Now that you know how the tools work, the next part is the time-consuming one. You need to decide if a package is needed. Create a simple spreadsheet and populate it with packages that are on the system and then determine whether the packages are needed. Figure 4-7 is an example report tracking the software installed on a server called linux1.

You can also use the **ps** command (**ps -ef** or **ps -auxww**) to see what processes are running and reference those processes to packages to determine what you need. If you are not too familiar with the machine you are hardening, you will want to contact those who are familiar with the machine for guidance. If this is not an option, watch the system logs to see what types of actions are taking place and the output of the **ps** command.

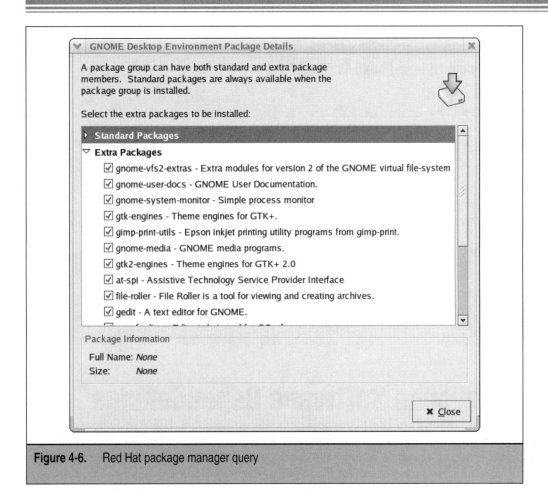

**Figure 4-6.**    Red Hat package manager query

Let's take a dedicated web server as an example of what types of software you would want and what types of software you wouldn't want. For a dedicated web server you probably don't need any type of X Window System software (X11, Gnome, KDE, and so on), audio software, web browsers, games, and other software that is generally used by workstations. You would want to install Apache and possibly Perl and PHP as well as other web-related software.

There is no default formula in determining what software you require for your business as each situation is different, so you will have to go through the process and determine if you are using the functionality described in the package. A good knowledge of your system requirements and what the machine is used for goes a long way in making the process of investigating your software requirements much easier.

**Software List for linux1 (192.168.1.1)**

Date Updated: <u>August 24, 2004</u>

| Package Name | Required | Reason |
| --- | --- | --- |
| bash-2.05b-29 | Yes | Standard shell for logins and interactive sessions |
| tcp_wrappers-7.6-34 | Yes | Allows restriction of connections for certain services |
| vim-common-6.2.98-1 | Yes | Useful text editor |
| sudo-1.6.7p5-1 | Yes | Allows users to execute commands as other users in a controlled manner |
| telnet-0.17-26 | No | SSH is being used exclusively |

**Figure 4-7.** Sample software list table

# Determine Software Dependencies

After determining your software requirements, you can now begin investigating if the software that you deemed you no longer need is required by software that you do need. Linux has interdependencies among its different programs as Linux developers will often piggyback or reuse other software packages. These interdependencies can be confusing but are manageable if documented during your investigation. An example of the types of problems that can arise with software dependencies are with SLES8 and Samba-3. Samba-3 requires heimdal-0.6 to function properly. Updating SUSE's included version of heimdal-0.4e would require updating 30 or more system packages, and the total set of packages that must be updated to meet nested dependencies is 130 or more. This means it may be necessary to update to a later version of the OS to gain access to a particular software release or version. In the case of Samba-3, an outside entity provided Samba-3 packages that were statically linked with the newer version of heimdal allowing for the installation of Samba-3.

There are a few ways to determine what the dependencies are. The first is with the **--whatrequires** option. For example, to determine what packages require openssl capability, you can run the command as shown in Figure 4-8.

It turns out there is a chain of dependencies for the openssl capability, so before removing that package, you must determine if you need the other packages shown as requiring openssl capabilities. In our example from SLES8, you know that kdebase3

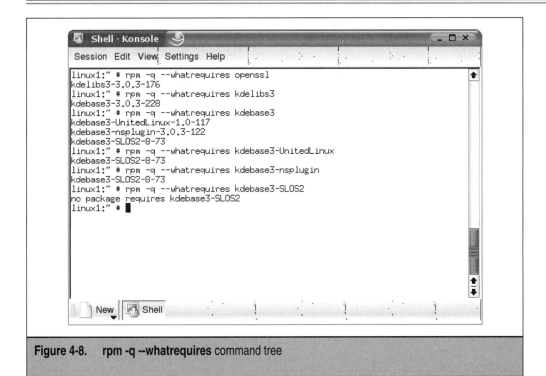

**Figure 4-8.    rpm -q --whatrequires** command tree

requires openssl, so if you determine you don't need kdelibs (after running **rpm -qi** to get more information), you can see if anything requires kdelibs—in this case, kdebase3. You would then decide if you need kdebase3 and if not, continue through the chain until you come to the end, which is shown by the "no package requires kdebase3-SLOS2" statement.

This can be misleading, though, because these wouldn't be the only things that would need to be removed if you wanted to remove a package. It only shows what other packages depend on the named capability (in this case, the capability is openssl). A better way to get the most information is to use the following command, which gives more verbose information:

```
rpm -e --test
```

The **-e** option is to erase or remove the package, while **--test** will go through the process of removing the package showing any dependency errors, without actually trying to erase the package. Figure 4-9 shows the output from **rpm -e --test openssl**.

After determining the dependencies, you will need to go through and determine which programs you will need before removing the main package. You might be tempted to use the **--force** option when removing packages, but this is not recommended because you could affect your software in unexpected ways. The time spent properly researching

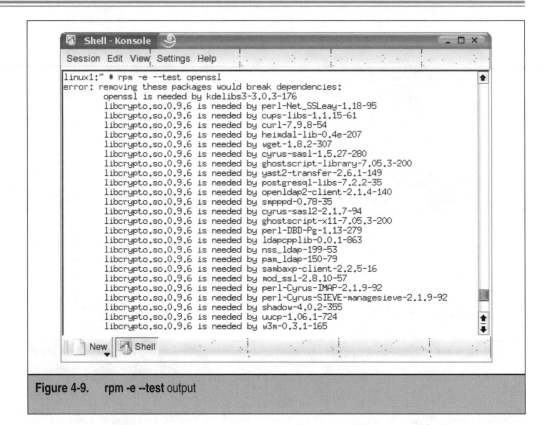

**Figure 4-9.** **rpm -e --test** output

your system will save you significant time in troubleshooting and downtime in the future. If you are installing the system, always install the least amount of software required to provide the functionality needed for your organization's mission.

You should be aware that installing software on your system, even to satisfy dependencies for approved software distributed by the vendors (Red Hat and SUSE), can create support problems. By installing certain software you can void your support contract with the distributor. With the vast array of software available to users of Linux, the majority of which is free, there can be interdependency problems or conflict with other supported software. SUSE and Red Hat have to have a baseline of software to support, as it is not feasible or reasonable to expect them to support every software configuration available. SUSE and Red Hat have a specific set of software groups they support and because of this, you should read and understand your support contract to ensure that the software you are removing or installing does not void the contract or you could find yourself in an unsupported configuration, creating problems when there is a need for support.

An example of this is with the Samba packages provided by a major distribution. The packages wouldn't support a specific configuration required by a user, and a fix was readily available from the Samba team (it was a minor update, not a full upgrade of the software). The user contacted the distribution vendor to ensure that their software would be supported as this was a critical production server. The vendor stated that applying this minor upgrade would void the support contract and that if the update were installed, they could no longer support the customer if problems arose due to the software. This presented a problem for the user as they needed the functionality provided by the latest release of Samba or the previous version. The customer was forced to upgrade to the latest version and hope for the best until the newest version was supported. The moral of this story is to be careful when upgrading or installing software and always install in a test environment where production processes will not be affected.

# Remove or Restrict Unneeded Software

You've done your research and think you know that you can safely remove those extra software packages. If some of the packages are related to services, you can use the techniques described in Chapter 2 to disable the services prior to removing the software to determine the impact on the system. If you don't have that ability or the package is not a service, try to follow a method for removing packages. Don't arbitrarily remove a large group of packages (ten or more) unless you are absolutely positive of the impact on the system. Even if you are sure, try removing packages in small groups and try to remove packages of a group (such as the ones that are related to each other in some way). By removing packages in small groups, you can let your system run a few days to determine the impact on the system. If there are no adverse effects, you can continue to the next set of packages for removal until you have removed all software deemed unnecessary. If there is a problem, you only have to roll back a small amount of packages to determine if that is the root cause. If you were to do all the packages, and problems occurred that were suspected to be related to the package removal, you would have to roll back a large group of packages. The incremental path is the best course of action in this case.

---

**NOTE** One way to track your actions during a session is to use the **script** command. This command will allow you to save everything from a terminal window to a file. You can then track all the software modified or removed by reviewing the file at a later date. One problem is that you can accidentally forget to stop the **script** command, which can create a large file if run too long. To start scripting, run **script** *<filename>*. After you have completed your logged session, you can use CTRL-D or CTRL-d (dependent on the shell you are using).

---

Before removing any packages, you absolutely must have a recent, known good backup of your system and you should always document what you are removing. If you did your homework, you will know what the dependencies are and you can start removing packages with the **rpm -e** command such as this:

```
rpm -e openssl
```

Note that you wouldn't succeed if you hadn't removed the package dependencies shown by using **rpm -e --test**. By default the packages wouldn't be removed with just **rpm -e** unless you removed the dependent packages, so it is still safe, but it is not in the best form to use **-e** as a querying tool.

If you installed software with another method than **rpm**, you will need to view the original makefile that came with your program. Or if you don't have the installation or readme files, you can try to determine where the program and its configuration files resides via the Internet or the source of your software. **rpm** is the preferred method of installing software due to the ease of removal, update capabilities, and management of the software.

# Install Software Securely

For the majority of servers you administer, you will find that you may need additional software that is not provided on the installation disks. Finding software that you can trust is always a problem, especially when dealing with noncommercial software. With commercial software, there is the perception that you have some assurance that the software is "safe" and free from malicious code. This perception is somewhat based on corporate accountability that you get from having a company behind the software that can be held responsible for problems. The open source and free software community is often seen as a rogue element, but this is not entirely appropriate.

Open source software offers some advantages over its closed source counterparts primarily because of the availability of the core components of the software. Software is comprised of hundreds, thousands, or even millions of lines of instructions for the computer. When all of these lines are put together and run on the computer, they do something, change something, or produce output on the computer. Open source software distributes the complete internals of the software with the associated binaries. This means that the lines of instructions that form the program are widely available for peer review.

The ability to review the software allows you to make configuration changes to suit your needs, but more importantly it allows anyone to review the code for malicious or undesirable activities. Having the source code available doesn't guarantee that the software will be free from Trojan horses or other malware, but it does add one more safety net, especially on large, popular programs such as Apache or Snort where there is constant peer review. You shouldn't take the availability of the source code as a guarantee that the software is free from malware, though, as the source code and the compiled version may differ. For the best security, a competent programmer should review the code for any anomalies and then you should compile the software yourself on a trusted machine. This is not always feasible, so we will discuss other options throughout this section.

Closed source software does not provide the internal code or instructions that comprise the program itself. Closed source software is usually associated with commercial applications although not all commercial applications are closed source nor is all open source software noncommercial. Software with a company behind it does provide some accountability for the software, but you have to trust the integrity and coding practices of the company that created the software.

Commercial/closed source software is often distributed by the company that created the software, so we will only discuss open source software throughout this chapter.

# Install Trusted Software from Vendors

When looking for software, one option is to obtain the software from the vendor. SUSE provides a large amount of software with the CDs provided in the installation disks allowing you to pull almost any type of software you want directly from the CD, while Red Hat provides a more convenient online installation option. Using the vendor-specific tools, with vendor-approved sources, you ensure that your system configuration remains in a supported state. This is an important consideration when determining what software to install and cannot be emphasized enough. If you have a production server that is crucial to your organization's objectives, and you have a support contract, you must weigh the advantages of voiding your support contract and the need for the new software.

## Install Software with SUSE-Specific Tools

SUSE provides a software installation module with the YaST program that allows you to install software from the thousands of programs available on the distribution CD at any time while checking for dependencies. To start a graphical interface for installing software, type the following:

```
/sbin/yast2 --install
```

At this point the install and remove software screen will appear as shown in Figure 4-10.

You have the option of selecting software provided with the distribution at this point with automatic dependency checking. The problem with this approach is that you will need to update your software immediately as discussed in Chapter 13, as your software may have patches available.

The next step in installing the software you need is to find the software. In Figure 4-10, you will see a Filter drop-down box. You can filter by

- **Selections (the default)**   Groups of software separated by preconfigured groups
- **Package groups**   Groups of software separated by type of software
- **Search**   Look for software by name or other advanced functions

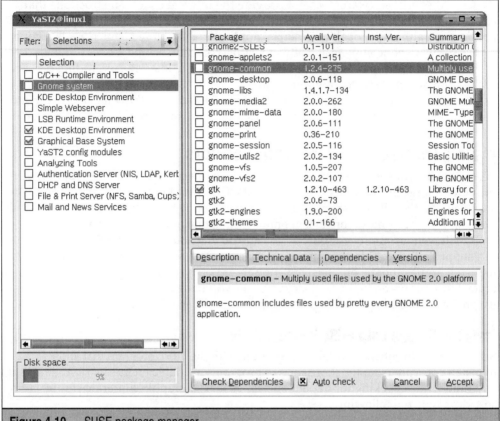

**Figure 4-10.** SUSE package manager

These tools have very robust dependency checking and conflict resolution tools built into them, providing a much needed respite to the dependency nightmares that Linux administrators had to face in the past. Let's take a package grouping to show how to install a package using YaST2. A user needs to install Nmap onto the security server that is running SLES8. Use the search filter and type **nmap** and you will see the screen shown in Figure 4-11.

Select the checkbox next to the package name listing and click Accept in the bottom right corner. At this point you will be prompted for the first (and possibly only) CD to insert for the installation to continue, as shown in Figure 4-12.

After the CD prompt, post-installation configuration scripts are run and the software install is complete. After you have installed the software, you will need to run YaST Online Update as discussed in Chapter 13 to use the latest, patched versions of the software.

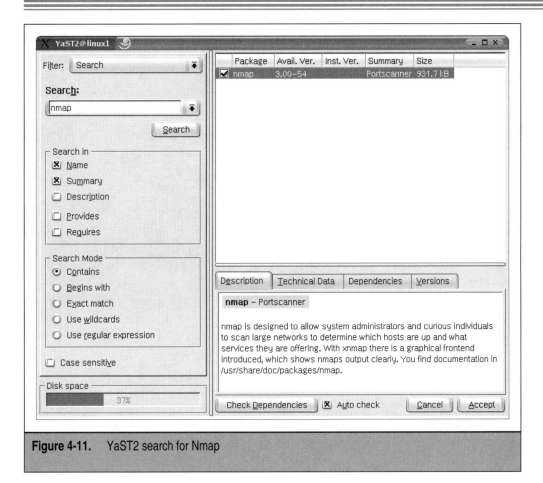

**Figure 4-11.** YaST2 search for Nmap

## Install Software with Red Hat–Specific Tools

Red Hat's **up2date** tool is an excellent example of a multipurpose installation and patching tool all in one. As with SUSE's tools, all dependencies will be resolved and the software will install seamlessly. The **up2date** tools does have one advantage over SUSE's installation program in that you do not have to initially patch your software after install to get the latest revision of the software. You are downloading directly from Red Hat's server and the package you download is the latest version available from Red Hat. To use Red Hat's installation tools, you will first need to determine the package name of the software. You can do this using the **--show-all** option, which shows all packages available for installation from the machine's Red Hat Network Channels. Use the command like this:

```
up2date --show-all
```

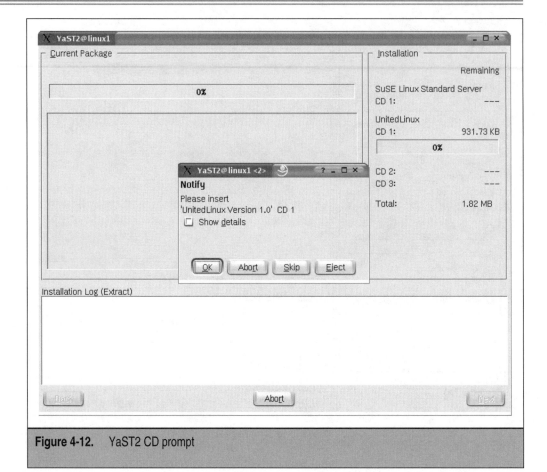

**Figure 4-12.**   YaST2 CD prompt

After determining the name of the package you want to install, you only need to type the **up2date** command with the package name following. For Nmap, you would type

```
up2date nmap
```

This gives you the latest, patched version of the software available directly from Red Hat.

## Install Software from Trusted Sources

You may find one day that the distributions do not provide some functionality that you require. This can be a predicament in regard to future support as discussed earlier, but sometimes you have to install the software for business reasons. If you do take this path, always test your software on a nonproduction machine that is an exact duplicate of the server that the software is installed on. Run the new package in the test environment for as long as possible and try to emulate the load and processes on the server to determine if there will be any conflicts with other processes or programs. This is an important phase because you are treading on dangerous ground as your support contract may not be available after the software install. The fewer surprises that you encounter, the better. Any problems that arise during the test will not affect production services if careful planning is conducted before implementation.

## Find Reputable Sources of Packages

There are many places on the Internet that provide software for use on your systems, but as with everything on the Internet, caveat emptor. There are a few well-established sites that provide RPMs or source packages for installation that are trustworthy. One thing to remember when downloading this software is that the software is made available on a public web site that may be trustworthy, but these sites only offer what the programmers make available. If the programmer of the project inserts malicious code into the software, the site that offers the download may not know about it until someone in the Linux community has reviewed the code. Also note that just because a project is well established and very popular, do not take for granted that the software is trustworthy, unless you receive it from your distribution vendor (who does a code review on software it releases). Here are some of the more popular sites for downloading new software (in **rpm** and source code format).

- http://www.sourceforge.net/
- http://www.freshmeat.net/
- http://www.rpmfind.net/
- http://www.rpmseek.com/
- http://rpm.pbone.net/
- Project's homepage (use your favorite search engine and search for the project name and the "homepage" keyword)

These sites usually offer great search capabilities as well as extended information on the **rpm** and packages you are looking for, allowing you to find alternatives to the packages you searched for. If you decide to use non-vendor released software on your system, you must consider the fact that the rigorous quality control processes that are conducted on the packages by the vendor might be absent from the package you are downloading. Developers not associated with a distribution often do not have the resources to test the quality and stability of the software they create. When downloading new software, always test it on a nonproduction machine to determine its stability on your platform, especially if it is non-vendor released.

## Use MD5 to Determine Package Integrity

After you have located the files you want to download, you will want some assurance that the file you download is the same one that the project maintainer published. A common way to do this is for the software publisher to create an MD5 checksum to create a "signature" of sorts for the file. The MD5 algorithm is described in RFC 1321, which is available at http://www.ietf.org/rfc/rfc1321.txt. It takes the input provided and creates a 128-bit fingerprint of the input that is mathematically unlikely to match another input. Even if only one portion of the input is changed, the MD5 signature will be altered, making it very obvious that the file has changed. More and more security conscious software developers in the Linux community are providing MD5 signatures of their software, so try to locate the MD5 on the web site or FTP server. Some sites will post it on the same page as the download links, such as Tripwire.org's open source version. At http://www.tripwire.org/downloads/ you will notice signatures for the differing files, with the MD5 signature for tripwire-2.3-47.bin.tar.gz being d3d1d35ee10b59a0176ca6f754825ca1. Some sites will have an md5 extension on a file in the FTP or download directory, such as Snort has at http://www.snort.org/dl/. In this instance, you would view the MD5 file (for snort-2.1.2.tar.gz the MD5 file is snort-2.1.2.tar.gz.md5) and see that the MD5 for that file is f01ae080f1571fd3e8d282dcae51f528. There is no standard location for the md5sums, but most software developers will put it on the download page in some format.

Now that you know what the MD5 is, you can test it to make sure the files you downloaded are the same ones that the author made available. To do this you run a command called **md5sum**, which is available on most major distributions.

To determine if the file is the same as what is listed on the web site, download the file and then run the **md5sum** command with the filename as an argument. Let's take a hypothetical program called exampleprogram (filename exampleprogram.0.0.1.tar.gz). We find the MD5 signature on the exampleprogram project homepage in a file called exampleprogram.0.0.1.md5 to determine the "signature" of the file.

```
md5sum exampleprogram.0.0.1.tar.gz
```

Figure 4-13 shows the contents of the exampleprogram.0.0.1.tar.gz.md5 file and then the results of the **md5sum** command against the file, showing the files match.

To show the dependability of MD5 signatures, we will take the exampleprogram.0.0.1.tar.gz file and untar and ungzip it. We will then add a very small file called badfile that contains one line of text to represent a Trojan horse program. Then the file will be tarred up and gzipped with the same filename. We can then run **md5sum** to see if the file's MD5 signature will change. Figure 4-14 shows the results of this exercise.

You will notice that we double-check the output of the original file, which has an MD5 signature of df7b941c970b3a526332ba97b39f8c24, but after our small modification, we have a completely different md5sum of ce6a8633ac74a90d7ebc5fbbcd776eb5. Remember that this only verifies the md5sum against a listed md5sum (on a web page or in the file). If the web site had been compromised and an attacker changed the file and the MD5 shown, you would only be verifying a bad file. This is unlikely, but you must consider the source of the file.

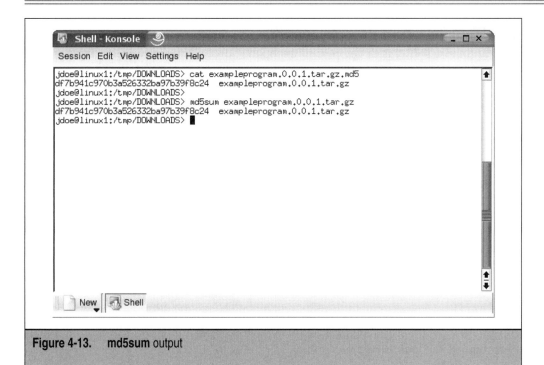

**Figure 4-13.**   **md5sum** output

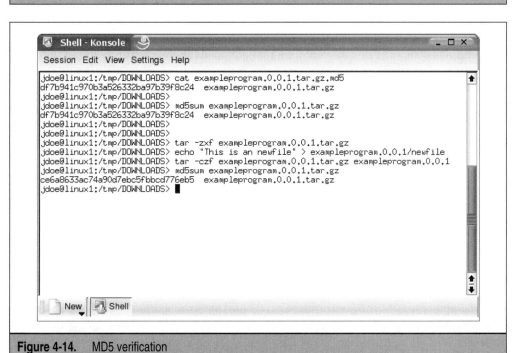

**Figure 4-14.**   MD5 verification

## Use GPG to Determine Package Integrity

More and more software developers in the open source community are utilizing gpg
keys to digitally sign their keys.

---

**NOTE** GPG (or Gnu Privacy Guard) is a free, GPL version of PGP. More information is available
in Chapter 7 and at http://www.gnupg.org/.

---

To use the developer's keys to determine file validity, you will need to find the
developer's public key, which is usually available on the download web site. For instance,
Snort provides a public key link from their download site at http://www.snort.org/dl/.
You will see a link in the text "All official snort releases are signed with this pgp key."
When you go to http://www.snort.org/public-key.html you will see the public key.
Public keys will be enclosed in

```
-----BEGIN PGP PUBLIC KEY BLOCK-----
```

and

```
-----END PGP PUBLIC KEY BLOCK-----
```

A typical key looks like the following:

```
-----BEGIN PGP PUBLIC KEY BLOCK-----
Version: GnuPG v1.0.7 (GNU/Linux)

mQGiBECCsukRBAC7pgIt5oDsSCTcDwxNI7/ZF/gN1bja5wbBQoqybCvi2mbCFzWK
yZNjTGPT2BCac6UO1Rf1c3b87hA1l11u4mvX62iglt/4EUu7slpYHJNOhnQqvBlD
CMfM9epx+mQNjtoWS2IqO1Llj9gXsxdiW/c5CHc4A1sO3UOfsd8KMKARowCg0j2h
bx4pezgOxswKEtZleNAM4bED/iZ+druCQa3KwjId+QgM9d2WYBbpfhiThcxtFl7p
Ary09eZh5Cf92Az0vgom6QUfcEQ8Rl+c0rx3S0mADqbvJlJwsNs4sBx/P2m609NU
yt5eRO2t5JGK5C8jQ5X6XLp4ImNQf6N7+J16l73m/5OC1r40ZG2Sn+Ap9ocmNRRR
H+GUBACDG6BgY1Ojxu2OYYNaAnviNG+mE4PCGkZKn2bkf4xc8CZPNrjuhAEDLbK5
70w1o8sJOnI2bq4jOBWXxHuEVjMKW1xIn7y+aYO+Wj6wq7JmbXuopEehewNTdRxa
MpfaceqVlhTcKdXYqm5FfvbwZUCscehI+6dN//fz8ro1wKM7c7QMRXhhbXBsZSBV
c2VyiFkEExECABkFAkCCsukECwcDAgMVAgMDFgIBAh4BAheAAAoJEHAkFaQblXYi
FE0An1y/BjkHktIvUitpWQi+eyUzUUixAKCa+DS0JIL29EUhSqHlnCTEdtSpL7kB
DQRAgrLtEAQAr3/oUE2KpZEvTQ23Z0M1N06NAYJk7XCiutlK08+Xn//EzsOyCKJu
tHj5gS+6tuVJ6BDOhOR7NxFOAgVCH53SFI0kwNXNoLLaFoF+UFmCocV/KhaaZCpg
CwIKUnSd7F8hrTQsEsvxnb/UZNssjq4xhEVCnkFOZMH7E62S4ePFPX8AAwcEAI47
5SvRYL/jUOuDK9vpvChwMgOPI4cAZ0YteVRHaeErgLQjDOMgy6Lx/JgCb6KNmF5A
Z9ZQ6g/7dPMKAa9+zUhX/xznn7F2HUYb3eguz20rM7g/APZbKQwdTsPwRGNKS/wm
SasoVore2haVU6RJ/hkIaWAZZi0DgMF4RerpaZWfiEYEGBECAAYFAkCCsu0ACgkQ
cCQVpBuVdiJONwCgr+NkvZub+/fpSnkxCeFXrgfTt6sAmgJHoJkIwAVY0VdJZaTS
aH5mu6MB
=WK8J
-----END PGP PUBLIC KEY BLOCK-----
```

You will need to copy everything (including the two lines stating BEGIN and END) and put them into a file, which in our case is named exampleprogram.key. After you have done this, you can import the key using

```
gpg --import keyfile name
```

We pasted everything between and including

```
-----BEGIN PGP PUBLIC KEY BLOCK-----
```

and

```
-----END PGP PUBLIC KEY BLOCK-----
```

into a file called exampleprogram.key, so you would run the command like this:

```
gpg --import exampleprogram.key
```

The results of this command are shown in Figure 4-15.

After you have imported the key, you need to locate the pgp signature file (usually with an .asc extension) and download that file in addition to the package files. You will need to download the signature file with the same versioning numbers as the file you are checking against. To verify the validity of the file you will run the following command:

```
gpg --verify signature_file.asc
```

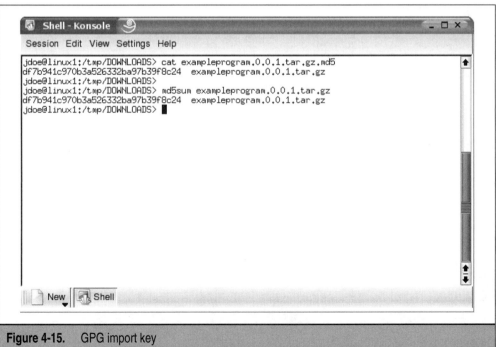

**Figure 4-15.**    GPG import key

For our exampleprogram.0.0.1 download, you would run the command

```
gpg --verify exampleprogram.0.0.1.tar.gz.asc
```

This command returns the output shown in Figure 4-16 if the file is valid.

The output of a bad signature would show "Bad signature" on the second line, in which case the file should not be installed. A bad signature means that the validity of the package cannot be verified and should not be trusted.

---

**NOTE** Another way to check the validity of your file is to use **rpm --checksig**, although this is not the preferred method due to the added complexity of using the command.

---

## Install Software with RPM

After you have verified the integrity of the software you downloaded, you need to install it. Most Linux software will have an available RPM package available. When using precompiled RPMs you are trusting the source of the RPM to not insert any malicious

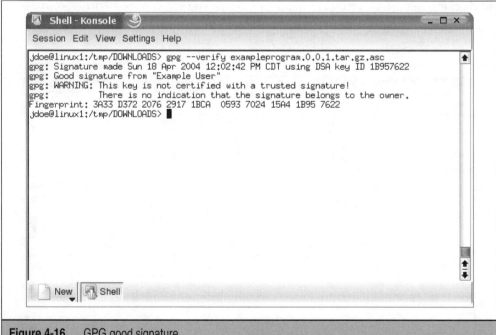

**Figure 4-16.** GPG good signature

code into the package. There are a few ways to install RPM packages depending upon your needs. The available options for installation are shown in Table 4-1.

A common method for installing RPM packages is to use the **-Uvh** option, which shows the following:

```
[root@linux2 root]# rpm -Uvh example-0.0.1.i386.rpm
Preparing...                 ########################################### [100%]
1:example                    ########################################### [100%]
```

## Install Software from Source

Possibly the safest way to acquire software, but the most difficult to manage, would be to compile the source code yourself. This is if you have a competent programmer review the software for malicious entries or poor coding. Don't assume that just because the source is available, it has been reviewed by outside programmers. Many think that just because the source code to software is available, the software is automatically safe to use. Generally this is true, especially with more popular projects, but apathy is the enemy of security. In the majority of instances where you need to compile software, you need to have a compiler (such as **gcc**) installed, which is generally not included in a default install. This is because a compiler can create a major security risk on a system. By installing a compiler on a production system, you have given an attacker a tool that will allow them to create custom-built programs for attacking systems as well as making it easier to get other malicious programs compiled and installed. Never install a compiler on a production system if it can be avoided. This is why you should have a test server and ideally a nonproduction machine for compiling programs.

With that said, you may find yourself needing to compile programs that you download for installation. There are many different ways to do this, but the majority of programs you download will be in in tar.gz format. To untar and ungzip those files, type

```
tar -xzvf package_name
```

| Option | Description |
|--------|-------------|
| **-i** (or **--install**) | Install an RPM |
| **-U** (or **--upgrade**) | Upgrade an RPM (will install the RPM whether or not there is a previous version on the machine) |
| **-F** (or **--freshen**) | Freshens an RPM (will only install if the package already existed on the machine) |
| **-v** | Provides easier to read output |
| **-h** | Shows hash marks indicating the progress of the installation |
| **Table 4-1.**   RPM Options | |

You now need to descend into the directory that the file created; you will generally find a file called README or INSTALL. Any special instructions pertaining to the program as well as any special installation instructions will be documented there. The next step generally pertains to all packages requiring compilation. These are the steps you must take (commands are run in the directory created by the **tar** command):

```
./configure
make
make install
```

At this point your program should be installed and ready to use.

One more note on installing software securely. Try to install the software as the user who requires the program or a non-root user. Some software requires that you install it as the root user. Using a non-root user to install prevents any malicious software installation scripts from installing with root permissions, possibly creating major vulnerabilities. If you install software scripts as a non-root user, the script could only damage the system with the permissions of the user installing, which will prevent major damage as non-root users don't have full access rights to the system.

# Monitor Your Systems

The most overlooked phase of software installation and removal is the monitoring phase. You should frequently monitor your system via the logs, system behavior, or failures in processes to determine if your changes are causing problems. There is no set time frame to check, but you should have a sufficient amount of time to run all major processes through their normal evolution or at a minimum of one full day and night to get a full picture of whether the system needs to be rolled back to its previous state.

Some of the commands you can use to determine your system's state and check for unusual activity are:

- **netstat -ap**   Shows any unusual ports that may be open and what programs are using those ports
- **ps -ef**   Shows any unusual processes that may be running
- **last**   Shows the last users logged into the system

These commands allow you to check for any unusual activity, although there are others as discussed throughout this book. Make sure that you monitor your systems to ensure that you do not have any unusual activity that could signal malicious software. To determine what normal conditions are, you should take a few snapshots of your system throughout the day before installing or removing software. This allows you to get a baseline condition of your system. Your software should document or note if there are any unusual processes or ports associated with the installation or removal of the program. If you see some new ports open, for instance, you can refer to your /etc/services for a listing of common services and their respective ports. You can also visit

http://www.iana.org/assignments/port-numbers/

for a listing of official/legitimate ports, or

http://www.pestpatrol.com/Support/About/About_Ports_And_Trojans.asp#portlist

for a listing of Trojan ports. You can also refer to the Internet for information on services running or ports open that you are concerned about. For example, let's say you have to install an old version of sendmail, because you were directed to. You protest installing an outdated version of sendmail, but in the end, you are overridden. One of the senior system administrators has you install version 8.12.6. You were a diligent security administrator and took a baseline of your system before installation. After installation, you continue your monitoring of the system, when you discover that port 6667 is open on your server and connected to a server you have never seen before. You look at your /etc/services file and notice that the port is assigned to ircd, which is the Internet Relay Chat daemon (IRC). You know that you aren't running IRC, and after further investigation it turns out you received a malicious version of sendmail. While this specific exploit is unlikely today, it does illustrate how monitoring can help you find problem software.

By removing unneeded software and installing software in a safe manner, you reduce the overall vulnerabilities to your system and you have the residual effects of reducing the amount of time it takes to update your software and saving disk space. Remember, less is more when it comes to software on your Linux system.

# Chapter 5

## Preparing for Disaster

- Understand Disaster Recovery
- Don't Build a Custom Kernel
- Document Server Setup and Record Changes
- Prepare Automated Reinstallation

ooner or later, systems fail. They are compromised and cannot be cleaned, hardware gives up the ghost, and forces beyond our control destroy machines and datacenters. When this happens, you may need to restore from a backup, bring up new systems quickly to replace the old, or move operations to remote sites. Speed may be of critical importance here, right alongside the need to provide platforms and systems that operate just like the ones that were doing the work before.

# Understanding Disaster Recovery

Disaster recovery is the process by which this is accomplished. However, it cannot occur unless you have made sound preparations. There should be three parts to your plan.

First, determine which systems are so critical that the business cannot remain solvent without them. While you should develop a restoration plan for all systems, these critical systems are the place to start. You may find yourself prioritizing your systems into more than just "critical" and "the rest." That's fine. In case of a major disaster, you'll want to know which systems to bring up first, which should follow, and those that can wait till later.

Next, for each group of systems, prepare the procedures that will bring them back online and train IT in how to use them. Creating the list of steps and attempting to practice them will bring to light new requirements and make the actual recovery run smoothly. Determine what type of offsite facilities might be necessary, and where backup machines are required. If your research uncovers a lack of proper backup methods and storage, add that to your list of processes to improve.

Finally, determine if current administration, installation, and maintenance processes can be improved to support rapid recovery efforts. If you find weaknesses, take the time now to correct them. Several common procedures can and should be changed.

# Do Not Build a Custom Kernel

Many Linux devotees hold the opinion that the building of a custom kernel is necessary to gain tight control over system security. They may tell you to build software from source as needed. While that may be what is best for a highly technical engineer, it is undesirable for the network administrator who expects the vendor to provide an optimal business solution platform. It is not sustainable in an enterprise environment.

A key reason for using Red Hat Enterprise Linux AS 3.0 or SUSE Linux Enterprise Server is specifically to avoid the necessity of rebuilding the kernel or operating system software. By purchasing a fully supported, packaged commercial operating system platform, you are trusting the vendor to take responsibility for kernel security updates. You are assuming that the operating system as supplied by the vendor is fully suitable for the task for which it is being deployed. Thus it is assumed that all necessary device drivers are supplied in the commercial software bundle. It is expected that a vendor provides security patches as part of the support services, and all essential system updates will be provided in a timely manner. While you should apply appropriate hardening methods to secure the system, you should not customize the kernel. If you customize the kernel, you may void your support contract with the distributor and make it harder to provide rapid recovery. In a large organization, hundreds, if not thousands, of Linux servers may be present. It is not feasible to maintain enough documentation and expertise to custom-build each of them should disaster strike.

# Document Server Setup and Record Changes

Chapter 4 provides essential information regarding software hardening as well as instructions on the elimination of unnecessary software. Maintaining a record of what software is installed on each server is a critical step in preparing for recovery. Documenting configuration is also important. Finally, make sure to record changes that are made, including configuration, software installation and removal, and patching and updating.

## HEADS UP!

It is a sound practice to document in a journal all changes made after installation, recording details of every change made. At some future time someone may need to reinstall the system without the benefit of your knowledge and common sense. Second-guessing a previous administrator's installation decisions is not pleasant and leaves risk of some important matter being overlooked.

# Prepare Automated Reinstallation

When it is necessary to rapidly install multiple systems and prepare them for production use, an automated reinstallation facility will make it easier to do so. More important, it will significantly improve the chances of commissioning a replacement server without mistakes being made. A breakdown that requires installation of a new server usually creates much stress and anxiety, thus creating a situation during which logic and a systematic approach to recovery of business operations may fail.

A secondary benefit that may be obtained from the process of creating an automated recovery facility is that it can also be used to roll out multiple identical servers. This is of considerable value in a large organization. In other words, sound administration practices can result in processes that support rapid recovery. Likewise, spending the time to prepare for recovery can improve normal operations.

It is easy to install Linux by inserting a DVD install disk and responding to a few installation process prompts. However, this type of installation is human resource intensive and requires product expertise, and the results of installation can be highly varied when performed by more than one person.

The purpose of automated installation is to reduce human resource overhead, to improve efficiencies, and to deliver a totally predictable and consistent installation result. The process begins by installing a server manually, then preparing automated installation processes.

Some sites prefer to install a temporary installation server that will be used to generate automated installation tools, after which this server is overwritten with an automatic installation. Most sites find it more practical to have a dedicated installation server. A dedicated installation server can be used to perform local network updates as well as to assist in the deployment of new systems.

Automated installations can be performed from

- CD-ROM or DVD-ROM
- A local disk partition that contains the installation and recovery files
- A network resource (via either NFS or SMB)

It is possible to generate custom installation CDs or DVDs from which a completely customized and fully configured server can be created. Considerable effort may be required to complete this, but the results are most often justified entirely by the speed of recovery in the event of a massive hardware failure.

Sites that have a large number of servers can appreciate the value of a permanently available network installation server. The same server can be used to install MS Windows servers as well as Linux servers. A low-cost dedicated installation server can be built for less than $1,000 using a relatively low-powered desktop PC with a 200GB IDE hard drive. As a precaution, do not install the installation server on the production network,

A large medical company in Sydney, Australia, had a practice of holding two spare machines in case of a hardware failure. They had a server farm of purpose-built systems, each of which was installed from a customized Red Hat Kickstart CD-ROM. Many within the company thought the Kickstart recovery CDs would never be needed. However, they were tested during emergency recovery test drills.

In 1999, the site was hit by lightning, which destroyed a number of critical servers. Using their Kickstart recovery CDs, the site was able to recover from a serious incident within two hours of loss of services.

and install server systems offline from the production network. This will help protect the installation software from any infection or malware circulating on the production network, and prevent a new server from being compromised during installation.

## Prepare Red Hat Kickstart Install Facility

Use of Red Hat Kickstart is simple, but proficiency in the flexibility of its use will take some practice. The use of Kickstart ceases to be a simple process if the ultimate solution of a single custom installation CD is the only acceptable objective.

The Red Hat installation CD-ROM uses a floppy disk that has been specially encoded to use the El Torito boot process. The disk image that has been embedded into the CD-ROM boot catalog has a standard MS-DOS FAT file system. The boot disk is specific to each particular Red Hat Linux release and must be prepared from the boot disk that is provided on the installation CD-ROM.

### Create the Kickstart CD-ROM

The following steps will permit modification of the first installation CD-ROM to include a Kickstart facility. In this instance, the multiple installation CD-ROM process will be preserved. This will permit the implementation of Kickstart with minimum change to the original CD-ROM.

1. First install Red Hat Enterprise Linux AS 3.0 on a PC. Be sure to install the packages called cdrecord and mkisofs.

2. Create a directory into which can be copied the first boot CD-ROM for your distribution. Insert the first installation CD-ROM into the drive. Follow these steps:

```
[root@localhost /]# mkdir -p /export/RHEL3
[root@localhost /]# cd /export/RHEL3
[root@localhost RHEL3]# mount /dev/cdrom /mnt
[root@localhost RHEL3]# cp -a /mnt/. .
[root@localhost RHEL3]# cd isolinux
[root@localhost isolinux]# vi isolinux.cfg
```

3. Now edit the contents of the file isolinux.cfg so it has the following information:

```
default ks
prompt 1
timeout 120
display kickstart.msg
F1 boot.msg
F2 options.msg
F3 general.msg
F4 param.msg
F5 rescue.msg
```

```
F7 kickstart.msg
label linux
  kernel vmlinuz
  append initrd=initrd.img ramdisk_size=8192
label text
  kernel vmlinuz
  append initrd=initrd.img test ramdisk_size=8192
label expert
  kernel vmlinuz
  append expert initrd=initrd.img ramdisk_size=8192
label ks
  kernel vmlinuz
  append ks=cdrom:/ks.cfg initrd=initrd.img ramdisk_size=8192
label lowres
  kernel vmlinuz
  append initrd=initrd.img lowres ramdisk_size=8192
label memtest86
  kernel memtest
  append -
```

In this example file, the following modifications have been made:

- The default installation type has been changed from an interactive installation to one controlled by the Kickstart control file.

- The timeout has been reduced from ten minutes to two minutes.

- The default boot message has been changed to our own message.

- The entry under function key F7 has been changed from snake.msg to kickstart.msg.

- The Kickstart boot parameter has been changed from ks to ks=cdrom:/ ks.cfg. This specifies the default Kickstart control file.

## HEADS UP!

It is possible to place more than one Kickstart control file on the CD-ROM. There must be one in the root directory of the CD-ROM called ks.cfg. Assuming there is also a file called samba-ks.cfg, it can be specified by entering the following at the command line:

```
append ks=cdrom:/samba-ks.cfg initrd.img ramdisk_size=8192
```

4. Now create the kickstart.msg message file that will be displayed onscreen when the system is booted from the CD-ROM that will soon be created. The following contents can be used as an example:

```
^L
^Xsplash.lss
 - This is a kickstart CDROM. Press the ^00f<ENTER>^007 key (default).

 - To effect a standard graphical installation, type:
            ^00flinux <ENTER>^007.
 - Use the function keys listed below for more information.

^)02[F1-Main] [F2-Options] [F3-General] [F4-Kernel] [F5-Rescue]^007
```

5.  The ks.cfg file can be created using any Unix text editor. A more convenient
    method is to use the GUI tool provided by Red Hat. To use the GUI tool,
    click the Red Hat icon, then select System Tools | Kickstart. Carefully edit
    the installation configuration control parameters. When the configuration is
    complete, save it to the directory that will become the root directory of the CD-
    ROM as a file named ks.cfg. In the example used above the fully qualified file
    location will be /export/RHEL3/ks.cfg. An example of this tool following
    configuration is shown in Figure 5-1.

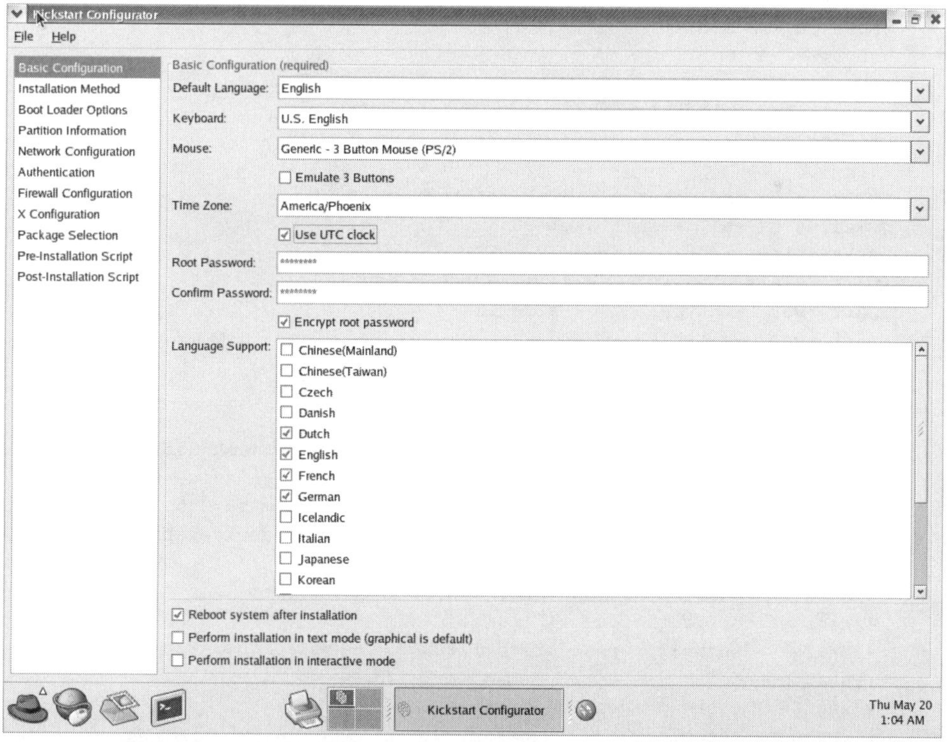

**Figure 5-1.** Red Hat Kickstart editor

The following listing was created using vi, the Unix system text editor. The file you have created will of course be different. Hopefully you will have selected just the software that is needed for your server.

```
#Kickstart control file manually created

#System language
lang en_US
#Language modules to install
langsupport --default=en_US
#System keyboard
keyboard us
#System mouse
mouse generic3ps/2
#System timezone
timezone --utc America/Phoenix
#Root password
rootpw not24get
#Reboot after installation
reboot
#Install or Upgrade Red Hat Linux
install
#Use CD-ROM media
cdrom
#System bootloader configuration
bootloader --location=mbr
#Clear master boot record
zerombr yes
#Partition and clear all disk information
clearpart --all --initlabel
#Partitions to be created
part / --fstype ext3 --size 1 --grow --asprimary
part /var --fstype ext3 --size 512
part swap --size 1024
#System authentication settings
auth --useshadow --enablemd5
#Network configuration
network --bootproto=static --ip=123.45.67.89 --netmask=255.255.255.192 \
--gateway=123.45.67.65 --nameserver=123.45.67.65 --device=eth0
network --bootproto=static --ip=192.168.1.1 --netmask=255.255.255.0 \
--gateway=192.168.1.1 --nameserver=192.168.1.1 --device=eth1
#Firewall settings
firewall --enabled --trust=eth1 --http --ssh --smtp
#XWindows configuration
xconfig --depth=32 --resolution=1280x1024 --defaultdesktop=GNOME \
--startxonboot
#Execute the setup agent on first boot
firstboot --enable
#Package installation details
%packages --resolvedeps
```

```
@ X Window System
@ GNOME Desktop Environment
@ Editors
@ Engineering and Scientific
@ Graphical Internet
@ Text-based Internet
@ Office Productivity
@ Authoring and Publishing
@ Server Configuration Tools
@ Web Server
@ Mail Server
@ Windows File Server
@ DNS Name Server
@ Network Servers
@ Administration Tools
@ System Tools
@ Printing Support
```

**6.** Add the ks.cfg file plus any additional Kickstart control files needed for your site to the root directory of the new CD-ROM.

**7.** Now that all the Kickstart configuration files are in place, place a blank CD-R into the drive. The final steps that will be used to create the CD-ROM disk are as follows:

```
[root@localhost /]# cd /export/RHEL3
[root@localhost RHEL3]# mkisofs -r -T -J \
-V "XYZ Corporation Custom Kickstart CD" \
-b isolinux/isolinux.bin \
-c isolinux/boot.cat \

-boot-emul-boot \

-boot-load-size 4 \

-boot-info-table \
-o /export/kickstart-cdrom-20040515.iso /export/RHEL3
[root@localhost RHEL3]# cd /export
[root@localhost /export]# cdrecord -v speed=4 dev=0,0,0 \
/export/kickstart-cdrom-20040515.iso
```

**8.** You may now boot from the newly created CD-ROM to test the new Kickstart facility.

When creating the Kickstart control file, you may have noticed the provision for executing pre-install and post-install scripts. These make it possible to automate the configuration of the server. The scripts can be stored on a network file system from which they may be executed. This combination permits considerable flexibility in the use of Kickstart once it has been mastered.

Kickstart was introduced by Red Hat before Red Hat Linux 5.0 was released. It is a mature facility that has stood the test of time. Kickstart GUI configuration tool was a welcome addition. It will be interesting to see the development path that Red Hat will follow with Kickstart. Just imagine how powerful this tool might be if the entire process of creating a Kickstart environment could be fully automated so that even a novice can use it.

Red Hat Linux lacks a facility like YaST2 that will back up all files, including those that are not part of the operating system or configuration files that have been altered since the system was installed, and then be able to restore them for recovery. The administrator should therefore do a complete backup using his own scripts or commercial software. Scripts or software can then be used to restage the system. A commercial solution should be considered as the most reliable solution for this approach since implementing backup scripts and performing a complete recovery of a server is a very delicate task.

### Using a Network-Based Kickstart Installation

Red Hat Linux can be installed over the network. Various methods can be used. The simplest method boots from a CD-ROM and simply obtains the Kickstart control file via NFS or FTP. It is also possible to use a boot floppy disk that has a Kickstart ks.cfg file that specifies a network source location for all installation files. Kickstart is a very flexible tool that can be used with Intel PXE or alternative DHCP-enabled means to provide a boot floppy image, thus doing away with the need even for a physical boot floppy disk. This way, the entire installation process can be automated. This is of particular interest to sites that want to roll out Linux to many thousands of systems.

Please refer to the network installation methods available for your version of Red Hat Linux, as documented in the administration guide.

## Using SUSE YaST Auto-installation Tools

SUSE has taken its time to develop its YaST toolset. (YaST is an acronym for Yet another Setup Tool.) YaST in SUSE SLES8 is in its second generation. Prior to YaST, SUSE had a tool called ALICE (Automated Linux Installation and Configuration Environment). ALICE was extensively used, but lacked some features demanded by administrators.

YaST is an entirely new, integrated system for Linux system management that has recently been released under the GPL license. YaST is an exceptionally ambitious project that is much too complicated to document in one short chapter. The SUSE Linux administrator really ought to spend time getting to know the capabilities of this incredibly powerful toolset. The instructions for creating a SUSE auto-installation image are provided in the following steps.

SUSE has substantially updated YaST2 in SLES9. Autoyast (the auto-installation configuration system) in SLES8 can be used to generate a full ISO (CD-ROM or DVD) image of the installed system, or may be used to generate auto-installation control files. In SLES9, these two very different requirements have been separated into two tools, both of which are much easier to use than the compound all-in-one tool present in SLES8.

In both SLES8 and SLES9 Autoyast versions, it is possible to import a configuration file that was generated using the SLES7 ALICE toolset. It is also possible to import a Red

Hat Kickstart control file. This capability adds flexibility and the ability to migrate from earlier versions as well as from Red Hat Linux to SUSE SLES without loss of previous effort. A personal preference of some administrators is to begin each new installation with a clean slate, thus the capacity to migrate using these backward-compatible tools is not of interest to all.

This is a good place to refocus on the objective of this chapter: to make it possible to rapidly recover from a major system breakdown. It's nice to have the ability to automatically roll out new servers, but that is not the primary focus here.

It is most helpful to provide an installation server to facilitate network based installations. Two NFS file systems are required. One will be used to store the installation files from the SUSE SLES8 install CD-ROMs, the other share will be used to store system backups.

You will create an NFS share point on the installation server (assumed hostname is pomeroy, IP address 10.0.0.95). In this case, it will be the file system under /export. The following steps complete the process:

- Create the SLES8 network installation shared directory tree.
- Include SLES8 SP3 in the NFS installation server share.
- Create an ISO image of the installed system.
- Create a recovery backup archive.

## Create the SLES8 Network Installation Shared Directory Tree

Log into the Linux system as the user root, and open a shell session by clicking the icon of the shell in front of a computer monitor.

1. Create the shared directory and load its contents as follows:

```
[root@localhost /]# mkdir -p /export/{SLES8/{UL/CD{1,2,3},SLES},Backups}
[root@localhost /]# echo "/export *(rw,no_root_squash,sync)" >> /etc/exports
[root@localhost /]# rcnfslock start
[root@localhost /]# rcnfsserver restart
[root@localhost /]# chkconfig nfslock on
[root@localhost /]# chkconfig nfsserver on
```

2. Insert the SLES8 install CD into the CD-ROM drive.

   The following steps permit the CD-ROM to be mounted so that the files on it may be copied to the hard disk:

```
[root@localhost /]# mount /dev/cdrom /mnt
[root@localhost /]# cd /export/SLES8/SLES
[root@localhost CD1]# cp -a /mnt/. .
[root@localhost CD1]# umount /mnt; eject cdrom
```

3. Insert the UnitedLinux CD1 into the CD-ROM drive.

   Now repeat the process of mounting the next CD-ROM so that its contents also may be copied to the hard drive as follows:

```
[root@localhost /]# mount /dev/cdrom /mnt
[root@localhost /]# cd /export/SLES8/UL/CD1
[root@localhost CD1]# cp -a /mnt/. .
[root@localhost CD1]# umount /mnt; eject cdrom
```

4. Insert the UnitedLinux CD2 into the CD-ROM drive.

Each CD-ROM must be copied to its respective directory, so just keep following the steps shown here:

```
[root@localhost /]# mount /dev/cdrom /mnt
[root@localhost /]# cd /export/SLES8/UL/CD2
[root@localhost CD2]# cp -a /mnt/. .
[root@localhost CD2]# umount /mnt; eject cdrom
```

5. Insert the UnitedLinux CD3 into the CD-ROM drive.

The following steps complete the process of copying the SLES8 product installation CD-ROMs to the hard drive:

```
[root@localhost /]# mount /dev/cdrom /mnt
[root@localhost /]# cd /export/SLES8/UL/CD3
[root@localhost CD3]# cp -a /mnt/. .
[root@localhost CD3]# umount /mnt; eject cdrom
```

6. Create the multi-source resource links and files so that the installer will find all necessary installation source files.

Just follow the next steps carefully. Pay close attention to ensure that the correct number of > characters are used in each command executed in the following steps:

```
[root@localhost /]# cd /export/SLES8
[root@localhost /]# mkdir yast
[root@localhost /]# echo -e "/SLES\t/SLES" > yast/order
[root@localhost /]# echo -e "/UL/CD1\t/UL/CD1" >> yast/order
[root@localhost /]# echo -e "/UL/CD1\t/UL/CD1" > yast/instorder
[root@localhost /]# echo -e "/SLES\t/SLES" >> yast/instorder

[root@localhost /]# ln -sf SLES/content
[root@localhost /]# ln -sf SLES/media.1
[root@localhost /]# cp -a SLES/boot .
```

7. Set the file system permissions on these two resources as follows:

```
[root@localhost /]# chmod ug+rwx,o-rwx /export/Backups
```

8. Click the gecko (KDE) icon, then click Run Command. Enter **yast2**. Click the Run button.

9. Select Software | Change Source Of Installation.

10. Delete the original entries that were created during installation from CD-ROM.

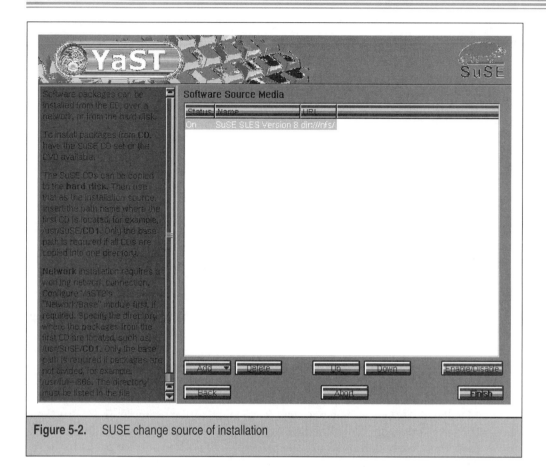

**Figure 5-2.**    SUSE change source of installation

11. Click the Add button, click Local Directory, enter the path to the SLES8 installation CD-ROM files (/export/SLES8), then click OK. Figure 5-2 shows the screen as it should appear after the new settings have been applied.

12. Click Finish.

Now log onto the server that is the subject of the backup and for which auto-installation facilities are being prepared.

**Including SLES8 SP3 in the NFS Installation Server Share**    According to the SUSE FAQ for auto-installation (see http://www.suse.de/~nashif/autoinstall/faq.html), service pack 3 sources may be added into the installation server SLES8 share as shown in the following example:

```
mkdir -p SLES
mkdir -p UL/{CD1,CD2,CD3}
mkdir -p SP3/{CD1,CD2}
```

```
mkdir -p yast
mount -o loop /iso/SLES-8-x86-64-CD1.iso SLES
mount -o loop /iso/UnitedLinux-1.0-x86-64-CD1.iso UL/CD1
mount -o loop /iso/UnitedLinux-1.0-x86-64-CD2.iso UL/CD2
mount -o loop /iso/UnitedLinux-1.0-x86-64-CD3.iso UL/CD3
mount -o loop /iso/UnitedLinux-1.0-SP-3-x86-64-CD1.iso SP3/CD1
mount -o loop /iso/UnitedLinux-1.0-SP-3-x86-64-CD2.iso SP3/CD2
ln -sf SLES/boot
ln -sf SLES/media.1
ln -sf SP3/CD1/driverupdate
ln -sf SP3/CD1/linux
ln -sf SLES/content
printf "/SP3/CD1\t/SP3/CD1\n" >  yast/order
printf "/SLES\t/SLES\n" >>  yast/order
printf "/UL/CD1\t/UL/CD1\n" >> yast/order
printf "/UL/CD1\n" > yast/instorder
printf "/SLES\n" >> yast/instorder
printf "/SP3/CD1\n" >>  yast/instorder
```

The ISO image files can be created from the official CDs by executing the following:

```
mkdir /iso
dd if=/dev/cdrom of=/iso/SLES8-CD-name.iso
```

The use of CD-ROM ISO images is not recommended for large scale use because mounted resources cannot be exported via NFS. It is a better proposition to copy each CD-ROM to the file system as shown in steps 2 to 5 in the earlier example. The instructions shown here were taken directly from the FAQ and are included purely for completeness. In any case, this clearly demonstrates the principles of adding service packs to the installation server exported files share.

When adding SP3 you will need the boot information from the SP3 CD-ROM, and the pointers to media.1 and content from the base SLES CD-ROM.

### Create an Auto-installation Control File

The first step toward production of a CD-ROM disk from which the system can be fully cloned (recovered) is to create the auto-installation control file. This file will contain a list of all packages that have been installed as well as disk partitioning instructions.

The following steps will create the master file needed for the ISO image creation step:

1. Click the gecko (KDE) icon, then click Run Command. Enter **yast2**. Click the Run button.

2. Select Software | Change Source Of Installation.

3. Delete the original entries that were created during installation from CD-ROM.

4. Click Add, click the NFS option, enter the IP address (10.0.0.95) into the Server Name box, then enter the path to the SLES8 installation CD-ROM files (/export/ SLES8). Click OK.

**5.** Click Finish.

**6.** Open a shell GUI by clicking on the icon of the shell on top of a monitor.

**7.** From a shell prompt, mount the installation server NFS file system (/export) as follows:

```
[root@localhost /]# mkdir /nfs
[root@localhost /]# mount -t nfs 10.0.0.95:/export/SLES8 /nfs
[root@localhost /]# exit
```

**8.** Click Misc I Autoinstallation.

**9.** In the Profile Management section, click the radio button beside Clone This Machine, then click Next.

**10.** Click the Preferences button. Enter the path **/nfs**, then click Next. Figure 5-3 shows the edited screen before clicking the Next button.

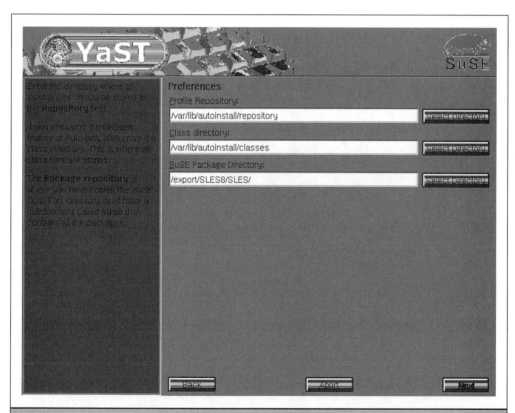

**Figure 5-3.**   SUSE Autoyast preference settings

11. Click the option to Save Result Into Repository. Set the name of the resulting profile to **clone.xml** as shown in Figure 5-4, then click Next. Be patient, this step can take a few minutes.

12. The File Management panel shows the current profile, clone.xml, as shown in Figure 5-5. Click Save, click OK, and then click Finish.

The auto-installation control file that is needed for the ISO image production is ready for use. Now follow the steps outlined to create ISO image of installed system.

# HEADS UP!

You should edit the clone.xml file using the auto-installation tool, carefully making certain that all options you want to create on the target system are correctly shown.

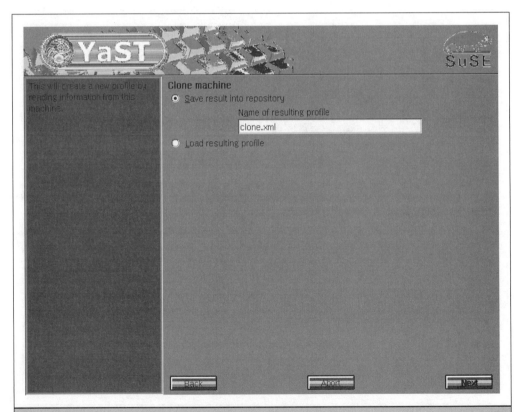

**Figure 5-4.**  SUSE Autoyast showing entry of the filename clone.xml

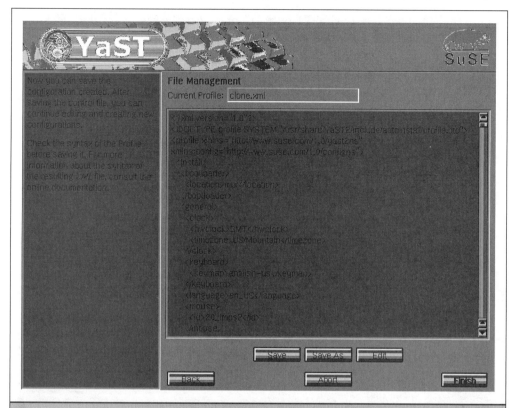

**Figure 5-5.** SUSE AutoYaST utility ready to save the clone.xml profile file

## Create an ISO Image of the Installed System

The following process will create an ISO (CD-ROM) image from which the system can be reinstalled at a future date. The resulting CD-ROM will create only a clone of the machine from which it is produced.

1. Mount the installation server shared resource under a directory called /nfs:

```
[root@localhost /]# mkdir /nfs
[root@localhost /]# mount -t nfs 10.0.0.95:/export /nfs
[root@localhost /]# mkdir /nfs/Backups/portofive
```

The hostname of the server being installed (and subject to backup) is portofive.

2. Click the gecko (KDE) icon, then click Run Command. Enter **yast2**. Click the Run button.

3. In the left panel of the YaST Control Center, click the Misc icon, then click the Autoinstallation icon.

4. Click the radio button in the Media Management section on the right panel to activate Create ISO Image, then click Next.

5. Select the control file clone.xml and click Next. See the example screen in Figure 5-6. The control file called mysystem.xml was generated to configure a different server. This was included to highlight the fact that in a large deployment there will likely be many server configurations. You can name the file that contains the control information that results from cloning your system by any name you choose, but if you use another name it must be used consistently throughout the remaining process of generating the auto-installation ISO file.

6. Enter the Destination as **/export/clone.iso**. Click Next. The action that results can take some time, so be patient even if nothing seems to happen for a few minutes. Figure 5-7 shows the screen we generated at the conclusion of this step and before the Next button was clicked.

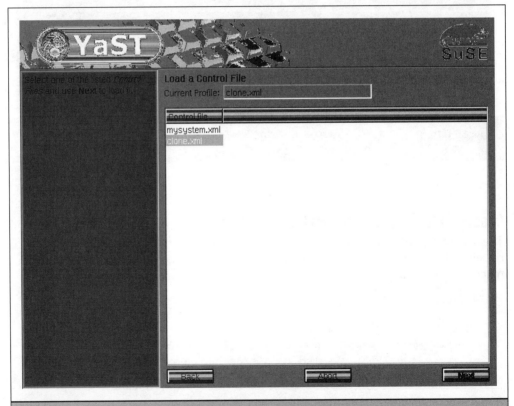

**Figure 5-6.**   SUSE Autoyast selection of the clone.xml profile

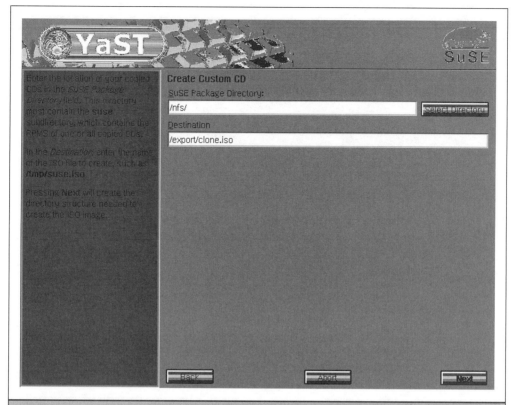

**Figure 5-7.** SUSE Autoyast Create Custom CD screen

7. At this time, the files that must be copied to the ISO image will be copied to a temporary disk area under the /tmp directory. This step will fail if there is insufficient space in the /tmp directory for approximately the volume of data that will be copied to the ISO image plus a margin of about 10 percent to cover intermediate operations.

Figure 5-8 shows the final state of this operation. Click Next to complete the building of the ISO file.

Figure 5-9 shows the final screen after the ISO file has been created. Note that when this screen is displayed there may still be considerable disk activity while the ISO image is being written to disk.

The ISO image must now be burned to CD-R or DVD-R media. The ISO image size will depend on the software that has been installed on the system. The image produced in this example was 968MB—obviously too large for a CD-R.

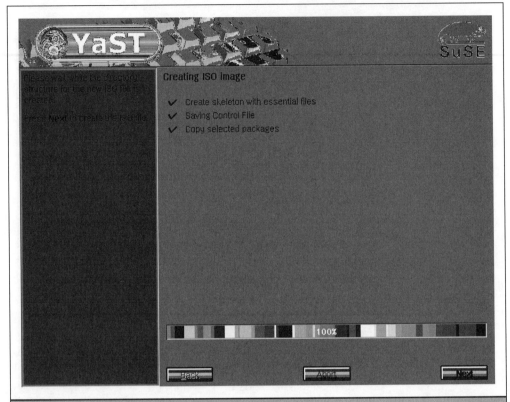

**Figure 5-8.** SUSE Autoyast ready to create the ISO image

If the ISO is larger than a CD-R can hold, the only choice is to burn it to DVD media. SUSE Linux products ship with a utility called **k3b** that can be used to burn ISO images to either CD-R or DVD-R media.

8. Click Close, then Back to exit autoyast.

### Create Recovery Backup Archive

YaST2 has a very useful backup and restore facility that can be used to back up all files that do not belong to system packages (see Figures 5-10 and 5-11). It can also be used to back up system configuration files that do belong to packages and that may have been modified during system configuration. The tar archive file that is generated by this process can be stored on a network file system from which it can be used to restore the server to its ready-to-run condition.

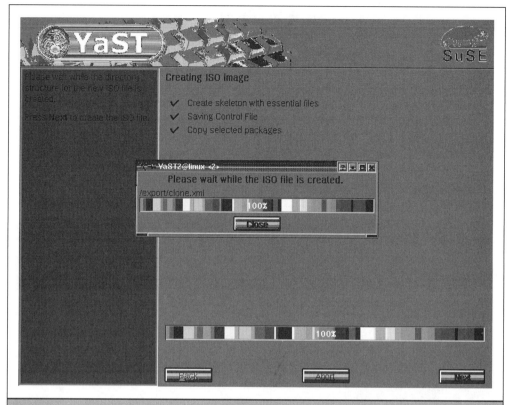

**Figure 5-9.** SUSE Autoyast ISO file has been created

This process should be completed when all software has been installed at the conclusion of system configuration. The resulting backup archive can be tailored to fit across CD-ROM–sized files that can be burned to CD-Rs for safekeeping.

The backup archive for this machine can be created as follows:

1. Mount the installation server shared resource under a directory called /nfs:

```
[root@localhost /]# mkdir /nfs
[root@localhost /]# mount -t nfs pomeroy:/export /nfs
```

If the directory for the machine portofive does not yet exist, create it using the following command:

```
[root@localhost /]# mkdir /nfs/Backups/portofive
```

2. Click the gecko (KDE) icon, then click on Run Command. Enter **yast2 backup**. Click the Run button.

3. In the Archive File Name box, enter **/nfs/portofive/Backup20040515.tar**.

4. Select archive type "tar with bzip2 subarchives." bzip2 is a more efficient compression tool than gzip. Click Next.

5. Select the options "Search files that do not belong to any package" and "Check MD5 sum instead of time or size." Click Next.

6. Click Add. Add the /nfs directory to the list of directories to be excluded from search. Click Next.

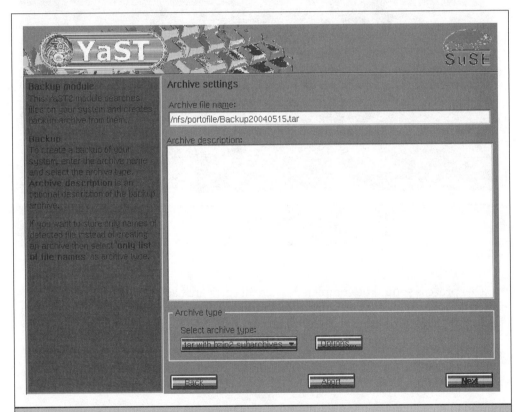

**Figure 5-10.** YaST2 backup showing selection of backup archive location and type

The backup archive will now be created. The resulting file can be used with the **yast2 restore** facility to reset all configuration settings to the original values at any time.

This backup file can also be integrated into an auto-installation process, but that is beyond the scope for this book. Consult the administration guide that was provided with your copy of SUSE SLES8 for details on how to effect further integration where this is required.

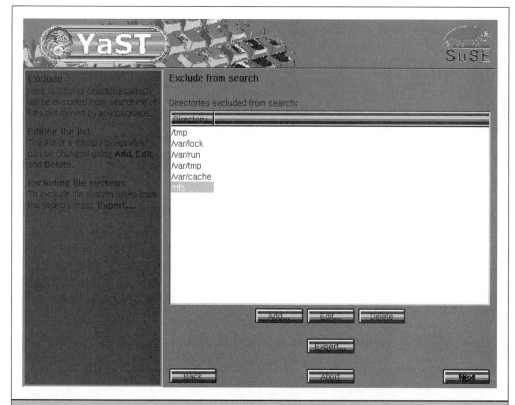

**Figure 5-11.** YaST2 backup showing exclusion of the /nfs mounted resources

# Chapter 6

# Hardening Access Controls

- Linux File Permissions and Ownership
- Review File and Directory Access Controls

**S**trong network access controls prevent unauthorized users from accessing a system. File access controls are important not only for preventing intruders from gaining too much access, but also to limit authorized users to their own data, and to maintain secure configuration and log files. This chapter provides an overview of the Linux file system access control capabilities and provides some quick techniques for auditing your system's files and directories to ensure they meet good security practice. Linux distributions have evolved enough that "out of the box" implies a file system that is already configured with proper restrictions. This means that all configuration files, log files, and programs are owned by the root user and exceptions are made only where necessary. Root ownership of a file or directory is more secure because it limits what other users of the system can access or modify. The trick is to maintain that integrity while adding users, permitting users to add their own files, and installing new applications.

# Linux File Permissions and Ownership

If you are comfortable with the Unix file system and understand the concept of users, groups, and access modes, this section may cover many familiar topics, but it's still important to understand the security capabilities of the file system in order to avoid mistakes. This section explains the permission modes and ownership that can be applied to files and directories in the Linux file system. These capabilities and limitations of the file system's permission structure influences the design and implementation of a secure configuration.

## Use POSIX Access Control Lists

The standard Linux file system follows the POSIX model of access control. A POSIX (Portable Operating System Interface) standard is intended to establish common behavior among operating system commands. The POSIX access control list (ACL) model did not reach official status as a standard and, in fact, further work on it has been abandoned. Yet it remains the de facto model by which Linux enforces file system security.

Linux files and directories have permission modes and user and group ownership. Valid modes are read (**r**), write (**w**), and execute (**x**). Each of these modes is defined as approved (**true** or one of **rwx**) or denied (**false** or **-**). The modes are applied to three categories of users: the mode for the user ID (UID) that owns the file, the mode for the members of the group ID (GID) that owns the file, and the mode for all other users whose UID and GID do not match the file's ownership. Thus, a file's permissions are defined by three groups of three modes as shown in Table 6-1.

Modes can be combined alphabetically, **rwx**, or numerically, **7 (4+2+1)**. Visually, these settings are clearly discernable with the **ls** command. The leftmost column of

| Mode | Alpha Shorthand | Numeric Shorthand |
|------|-----------------|-------------------|
| Read | r | 4 |
| Write | w | 2 |
| Execute (A directory must have execute privileges in order for users to **cd** into it and search the directory for information such as attributes of files.) | x | 1 |
| Example: Read, Write, Execute | rwz | 7 |
| Example: Read, Write | rw- | 6 |
| Example: Read, Execute | r-x | 5 |

**Table 6-1.**    Permission Mode Descriptions

10 characters indicates the file's permissions (the first character is used to describe the list member as a file, directory, or special device). A file with all permissions would have mode **rwxrwxrwx**. A file with no permissions would have mode --------- (nine hyphens).

```
# ls -l /etc/passwd
-rw-r--r--    1 root      root           1573 May  6 10:39 /etc/passwd
# ls -l /bin/login
-rwxr-xr-x    1 root      root          20092 Sep 25  2003 /bin/login
# ls -l /usr/bin/procmail
-rwxr-xr-x    1 root      mail          80064 Jan 24  2003 /usr/bin/procmail
```

The permissions for /etc/passwd are described in Table 6-2.

| Type of User | Mode | Description |
|--------------|------|-------------|
| User owns file (UID root) | rw- | Can read, can write, cannot execute |
| Group owns file (GID root) | r-- | Can read, cannot write, cannot execute |
| World (non-user, non-group) | r-- | Can read, cannot write, cannot execute |

**Table 6-2.**    File Permission Modes for /etc/passwd

The **chmod** command (change mode) is used to change file access permissions on a file or directory. This command sets and unsets permissions for the user (**u**), group (**g**), world (**o**), or all (**a**). Here is an example that shows how permissions change on a file:

```
# touch temp.txt
# ls -l temp.txt
-rw-r--r--    1 root      root             0 Jun 10 14:49 temp.txt
# chmod o-r temp.txt
# ls -l temp.txt
-rw-r-----    1 root      root             0 Jun 10 14:49 temp.txt
# chmod g+w temp.txt
# ls -l temp.txt
-rw-rw----    1 root      root             0 Jun 10 14:49 temp.txt
# chmod a-w temp.txt
# ls -l temp.txt
-r--r-----    1 root      root             0 Jun 10 14:49 temp.txt
```

The **chmod** command also supports numeric arguments for permissions. Note that this method requires you to set all modes at once: user, group, world.

```
# touch temp.txt
# ls -l temp.txt
-rw-r--r--    1 root      root             0 Jun 10 14:53 temp.txt
# chmod 0640 temp.txt
# ls -l temp.txt
-rw-r-----    1 root      root             0 Jun 10 14:53 temp.txt
# chmod 0660 temp.txt
# ls -l temp.txt
-rw-rw----    1 root      root             0 Jun 10 14:53 temp.txt
# chmod 0440 temp.txt
# ls -l temp.txt
-r--r-----    1 root      root             0 Jun 10 14:53 temp.txt
```

In this example, a leading zero (0) was added to the three digits used to define the user, group, and world permissions. This leading zero can be omitted. It was included because there is actually a fourth attribute group that is reserved for special permission modes.

## Special Permission Modes

The basic modes for all files and directories are read, write, and execute. There are three additional attributes that subtly affect how a file is executed or accessed: set user ID (SUID), set group ID (SGID), and sticky. These attributes work differently when applied to files and directories, as described in Tables 6-3 and 6-4.

| Attribute (Mode) | Effect When Applied to a File |
|---|---|
| SUID (4) | The file is executed in a process whose privilege matches the UID of the user *owner* of the file instead of the privilege of the user who executed the file. This is used to enable a user to execute a single program under a different set of privileges. Typically, a file will be SUID root (meaning that it executes with root privileges regardless of the UID of the user) in order to provide a root-level capability to a non-root user. This way users do not have to have a root password and log in to the root account in order to perform a simple task. It is always better to limit the number of persons who have access to the root password for a system. |
| SGID (2) | The file is executed in a process whose privilege matches the GID of the *group owner* of the file instead of the privilege of the user who executed the file. The uses of the SGID bit are identical to SUID. |
| Sticky (1) | None. |

**Table 6-3.**  Special File Permissions

| Attribute (Mode) | Effect When Applied to a Directory |
|---|---|
| SUID (4) | None. |
| SGID (2) | When a file is created in the SGID directory, the *group owner* is set to the *group owner* of the SGID directory, not the GID of the user who created the file. This can be used to ensure that all users within a particular group are able to access, modify, and delete files in a directory. Common scenarios are development environments, shared document repositories, or file shares. Take care to note that one user may affect any other users' files. A greater trust is placed in the users assigned to a group when this bit is used. |
| Sticky (1) | When a file is created in the sticky directory, only the *user owner* of the file or root can delete or rename the file. This overrides the implied permissions of the directory. For example, if a directory is world-readable and world-writable, then all users would be able to create, delete, and modify files created by any other user. This prevents other users with write permissions to a file from deleting the file. This is most commonly seen on the /tmp directory. |

**Table 6-4.**  Special Directory Permissions

These modes can be set with the **chmod** command using numeric arguments. The SUID bit is shown in the place normally reserved for the user's execute permission.

```
# touch temp.sh
# ls -l temp.sh
-rw-r--r--    1 root      root            0 Jun 10 17:24 temp.sh
# chmod 0755 temp.sh
# ls -l temp.sh
-rwxr-xr-x    1 root      root            0 Jun 10 17:24 temp.sh*
# chmod 4755 temp.sh
# ls -l temp.sh
-rwsr-xr-x    1 root      root            0 Jun 10 17:24 temp.sh*
```

The sticky bit is evident on the system's /tmp directory. The **t** replaces the execute bit for all other users.

```
# ls -ld /tmp
drwxrwxrwt    5 root      root         4096 Jun 10 17:24 tmp/
```

Further information about file permissions, ownership, and modes can be found with the **man chmod** command.

## Implement Extended Attributes

Linux file systems also support extended attributes. The attribute relevant to server hardening is the **immutable** attribute. When a file is immutable, it cannot be modified, deleted, renamed, or linked to by any user on the system—including root. It is most useful for protecting sensitive configuration files or other data files whose content is static.

---

**CAUTION** The **immutable** and other attributes depend on support from the kernel's file system driver. The attributes apply to ext2, ext3, ReiserFS file system types, as well as most other file system types available in the stock Linux kernel. If you are running a server that uses a different type of file system, there's a chance you might not have access to these capabilities. This will not be a problem for SUSE, Red Hat, or Mandrake users. Use the **mount** command to see what type of file system you have if you are unsure.

---

For files whose content continually changes, such as log files, the **append only** attribute can be used to enable the system to continue to write to the file, but not delete, overwrite, or rename the file.

The attributes cannot be viewed or modified with the **ls** or **chmod** command. Instead, use the **lsattr** (list attributes) and **chattr** (change attributes) commands.

```
# touch log
# chattr +a log
```

```
# lsattr
-----a------- ./log
# chattr -a log
# lsattr
------------ ./log
```

It is very important to point out that the root user was able to set and unset these flags. In practice, you will want to restrict even root from removing the **append only** or **immutable** attribute. The Linux kernel controls this access via capabilities defined at compile time and accessible via the **sysctl** interface. The **sysctl** interface is located in /proc/sys/kernel/cap-bound, but you need a special tool called **lcap** to easily access this interface.

By default, Red Hat only restricts a single capability that is unrelated to file system management. Use the **lcap** tool to change capabilities. The tarball (lcap-0.0.3.tar.bz2) is available at http://www.packetstormsecurity.org/. When you restrict access to a capability, the file attributes associated with that capability are recognized, but can no longer be changed. You need to have access to the **CAP_LINUX_IMMUTABLE** capability in order to set the **immutable** attribute for a file, but **CAP_LINUX_IMMUTABLE** is not necessary to enforce the **immutable** attribute once it has been set.

```
# ./lcap
Current capabilities: 0xFFFFFEFF
    0) *CAP_CHOWN                 1) *CAP_DAC_OVERRIDE
    2) *CAP_DAC_READ_SEARCH       3) *CAP_FOWNER
    4) *CAP_FSETID                5) *CAP_KILL
    6) *CAP_SETGID                7) *CAP_SETUID
    8)  CAP_SETPCAP               9) *CAP_LINUX_IMMUTABLE
   10) *CAP_NET_BIND_SERVICE     11) *CAP_NET_BROADCAST
   12) *CAP_NET_ADMIN            13) *CAP_NET_RAW
   14) *CAP_IPC_LOCK             15) *CAP_IPC_OWNER
   16) *CAP_SYS_MODULE           17) *CAP_SYS_RAWIO
   18) *CAP_SYS_CHROOT           19) *CAP_SYS_PTRACE
   20) *CAP_SYS_PACCT            21) *CAP_SYS_ADMIN
   22) *CAP_SYS_BOOT             23) *CAP_SYS_NICE
   24) *CAP_SYS_RESOURCE         25) *CAP_SYS_TIME
   26) *CAP_SYS_TTY_CONFIG
     * = Capabilities currently allowed
```

Simply use a capability name as an argument to **lcap** in order to disable it.

```
# ./lcap CAP_LINUX_IMMUTABLE
# ./lcap
Current capabilities: 0xFFFFFCFF
    0) *CAP_CHOWN                 1) *CAP_DAC_OVERRIDE
    2) *CAP_DAC_READ_SEARCH       3) *CAP_FOWNER
```

```
 4)  *CAP_FSETID                 5)  *CAP_KILL
 6)  *CAP_SETGID                 7)  *CAP_SETUID
 8)   CAP_SETPCAP                9)   CAP_LINUX_IMMUTABLE
10)  *CAP_NET_BIND_SERVICE      11)  *CAP_NET_BROADCAST
12)  *CAP_NET_ADMIN             13)  *CAP_NET_RAW
14)  *CAP_IPC_LOCK              15)  *CAP_IPC_OWNER
16)  *CAP_SYS_MODULE            17)  *CAP_SYS_RAWIO
18)  *CAP_SYS_CHROOT            19)  *CAP_SYS_PTRACE
20)  *CAP_SYS_PACCT             21)  *CAP_SYS_ADMIN
22)  *CAP_SYS_BOOT              23)  *CAP_SYS_NICE
24)  *CAP_SYS_RESOURCE          25)  *CAP_SYS_TIME
26)  *CAP_SYS_TTY_CONFIG
   * = Capabilities currently allowed
```

Now the **chattr** command is prohibited from setting **immutable** and **append** flags (**append** is assumed with **immutable**).

```
# lsattr
----i-------- log
# chattr -i log
chattr: Operation not permitted while setting flags on log
```

The idea is to boot the computer with full capabilities available to users, set the appropriate attributes for the desired files, remove the capabilities, and place the system in a production environment. Now an attacker cannot change an **immutable** file without gaining root access, rebooting the system, and then modifying the file. If all other security alarms fail, administrators should at least notice a system reboot.

---

**CAUTION**   Security measures that attempt "ultimate" security tend to have exceptions or hacking techniques that the root user can bypass. In the case of securelevel settings, it is possible for an attacker with root privileges to load a kernel module specifically designed to change the capabilities of a running system. Even non-modular kernels can be similarly attacked via manipulation of /dev/ mem and /dev/kmem. Securelevel 1 also tries to resolve this by restricting write access to /dev/ kmem and preventing modules from being loaded.

---

Be very careful when enabling and disabling capabilities on your system. Start with **CAP_LINUX_IMMUTABLE** and **CAP_SYS_RAWIO** disabled. This should provide protection for **immutable** and **append only** flags that you wish to set.

## Linux Standards Base (LSB) Implications

The LSB attempts to create a uniform behavior, naming, and expectations among diverse Linux distributions. Its standards for file system security are simple. New packages to be installed on a system should have these assumptions:

- Only the user's home, /tmp, /var/tmp, and /var/opt/*package* directories are expected to have write permissions even if the package does not own the directory (which it shouldn't). The directories should have the sticky bit set to protect files from only being manipulated by their creator. This limits the amount of world-writeable directories on the system.

- The package should not expect to have write privileges to any file not owned by the UID or GID of the user executing the process. This means that no files should be world-writeable.

- The package should not expect to have read or execute access to all files on the system.

- The package should not expect other files to have SUID or SGID permissions. The package may install a SUID/SGID file, but it should not expect other files not installed by the package to have those permissions. This lets administrators remove SUID/SGID files without breaking dependencies for future packages.

- The package should not modify the permission modes or ownership of any file not explicitly installed by the package. If it requires permission changes, then it should inform the user.

These are also good guidelines for creating a strong security policy for custom applications or modified applications that will be deployed on your system.

### Rely on Samba Tools for Windows File Controls

If your Linux system supports the Samba service, use the Samba tools and administration interfaces to manipulate permissions for files that are shared with Windows computers. The Samba code does an excellent job of mapping Windows access control lists (ACLs) to POSIX ACLs without introducing overhead for the user. Windows ACLs provide more granularity than the basic read/write/execute settings for a user/group/world associated with a file. Samba is able to replicate the philosophy of Windows ACLs while maintaining the actual files on a Samba-shared Linux file system. It does this through extended POSIX ACLs, much like the **immutable** and **append** attributes mentioned in the previous section. One of the biggest differences from a file-sharing standpoint is that permissions for a single file can be defined for multiple users. Several users can be assigned different permissions, such as read, write, or delete, while another group of users may be explicitly denied access.

# Review File and Directory Access Controls

Maintaining file and directory permissions on a server is very easy because the majority of the work can be automated with scripts and cron jobs. All of these techniques use the

**find** command to search for files with particular permission sets. Use the **-perm** option to match a particular mode and the **-type** option to look for files (**-type f**) or directories (**-type d**).

# Verify the Sticky Bit for Temporary Directories

The term "temporary directory" means a permanent directory that is used by applications and users to store temporary files or files that are only needed for a short period of time before they can be erased. These directories need the sticky bit set because multiple users write to the same directory, and it is important to prevent users from modifying someone else's files. Look for directories with the sticky bit set. The **-ls** option prints the equivalent of the **ls -dils** command (the first column is the inode number).

```
# find / -type d -perm -1000 -ls
    971    0 drwxrwxrwt   2 root    root      40 Jun 10 23:39 /dev/shm
 309473    4 drwxrwxrwt   2 root    root    4096 Jun 10 15:26 /var/tmp
1270606    4 drwxrwxrwt   2 root    root    4096 Aug 11  2003 /var/spool/vbox
  97875    4 drwx-----T   2 lp      sys     4096 Sep  1  2003 /var/spool/cups/tmp
1564241    4 drwxrwxrwt   2 root    root    4096 Sep 25  2003 /var/spool/samba
 211745    4 drwxrwxrwt   5 root    root    4096 Jun 10 23:40 /tmp
 440693    4 drwxrwxrwt   2 xfs     xfs     4096 Jun 10 23:40 /tmp/.font-unix
```

Instead of relying on the formatted output of the **-ls** option, you can use the **-printf** option to create a customized list that may be more script-friendly. The additional information you can access via **-printf** is of great use during forensic investigations as well. Here is the same command, but with different formatting of the output:

```
# find / -type d -perm -1000 \
> -printf "%p, %u(%U), %g(%G), %k, %m, %AY%Am%Ad-%AT%AZ\n"
/devshm, root(0), root(0), 0, 1777, 20040610-23:39:55PDT
/vartmp, root(0), root(0), 4, 1777, 20040611-00:58:38PDT
/var/spoolvbox, root(0), root(0), 4, 1777, 20040611-00:58:38PDT
/var/spool/cupstmp, lp(4), sys(3), 4, 1700, 20040611-00:58:38PDT
/var/spoolsamba, root(0), root(0), 4, 1777, 20040611-00:58:38PDT
/tmp, root(0), root(0), 4, 1777, 20040611-00:58:38PDT
/tmp.font-unix, xfs(43), xfs(43), 4, 1777, 20040611-00:58:38PDT
```

This creates a comma-delimited list with the full path and filename (**%p**), username (**%u**) and UID (**%U**), group name (**%g**) and GID (**%G**), size in 1K blocks (**%k**), permission modes (**%m**), and access time (**%AY%Am%Ad-%AT%AZ**). Delimited output is easier to parse with Perl, Python, the **cut** command, and other methods. To create a truly forensics-friendly list, include the last status change (**%CY%Cm%Cd-%CT%CZ**) and last modification (**%TY%Tm%Td-%TT%TZ**) times.

---

**NOTE** A file or directory's modification, access, and change times are immensely helpful for debugging problems as well as providing a detailed picture of the activity of an intruder. It's also a good idea to use **%s** instead of **%k** in order to report the exact file size in bytes.

---

Sticky bits should appear on /tmp, /var/tmp, and /var/spool/samba at the very least.

# Record SUID/SGID Files and Directories

Obtain a list of all current SUID and SGID files and directories once a system has been installed and configured. This list contains all of the special privileges files and directories that are necessary for the system to function properly. It is unlikely that you will add more files with SUID permissions. Periodically check the list for new files or files in directories that aren't expected to have binaries. If these are present, they may indicate an intrusion, a malicious user, or a user who does not understand the implications of SUID and SGID security requirements.

Use mode 4000 for SUID files and mode 2000 for SGID files or directories. This is the command to find SUID files:

```
# find / -type f -perm -4000 \
> -printf "%p, %u(%U), %g(%G), %k, %m, %AY%Am%Ad-%AT%AZ\n"
/usr/X11R6/bin/XFree86, root(0), root(0), 1908, 4711, 20040610-21:50:02PDT
/usr/sbin/usernetctl,  root(0), root(0), 16, 4755, 20030925-21:39:16PDT
/usr/sbin/userhelper,  root(0), root(0), 28, 4711, 20040610-22:41:12PDT
/usr/sbin/userisdnctl,  root(0), root(0), 8, 4755, 20030811-13:50:39PDT
/usr/sbin/suexec,  root(0), apache(48), 20, 4510, 20030925-06:31:52PDT
/usr/bin/chage,  root(0), root(0), 36, 4755, 20030604-12:18:20PDT
/usr/bin/gpasswd,  root(0), root(0), 36, 4755, 20030604-12:18:21PDT
/usr/bin/chfn,  root(0), root(0), 16, 4711, 20030925-06:10:33PDT
/usr/bin/chsh,  root(0), root(0), 12, 4711, 20030925-06:10:33PDT
/usr/bin/newgrp,  root(0), root(0), 8, 4711, 20030925-06:10:33PDT
/usr/bin/passwd,  root(0), root(0), 16, 4511, 20030213-13:19:55PST
...<snip>...
```

This is the command to find SGID files:

```
# find / -type f -perm -2000 \
> -printf "%p, %u(%U), %g(%G), %k, %m, %AY%Am%Ad-%AT%AZ\n"
/usr/sbin/lockdev, root(0), lock(54), 12, 2755, 20030908-14:01:28PDT
/usr/sbin/utempter, root(0), utmp(22), 36, 2755, 20030218-17:26:19PST
/usr/sbin/sendmail.sendmail, root(0), smmsp(51), 724, 2755, 20040610-
3:40:38PDT
```

```
/usr/bin/wall, root(0), tty(5), 8, 2555, 20030625-13:31:56PDT
/usr/bin/write, root(0), tty(5), 20, 2755, 20030925-06:10:25PDT
/usr/bin/lockfile, root(0), mail(12), 16, 2755, 20030124-22:39:17PST
/usr/bin/slocate, root(0), slocate(21), 28, 2755, 20040610-04:04:19PDT
...<snip>...
```

The following is the command to find SGID directories. It is unlikely that your system will have such directories, although /var/spool/mail is a possible match.

```
# find / -type d -perm -2000 \
> -printf "%p, %u(%U), %g(%G), %k, %m, %AY%Am%Ad-%AT%AZ\n"
/tmp/temp, root(0), root(0), 4, 2755, 20040611-01:13:55PDT
```

The following is the command to find world-writeable files. No such file should be on your system. If one is present, it may have been created by a poorly written application or the permission was set by accident. It should be removed or the world-writeable bit removed.

```
# find / -type f -perm -0002 \
> -printf "%p, %u(%U), %g(%G), %k, %m, %AY%Am%Ad-%AT%AZ\n"
/tmp/temp.txt, root(0), root(0), 0, 777, 20040611-01:17:27PDT
```

The following is the command to find world-writeable directories. Any such directory should also have the sticky bit set. All of the directories in this example adhere to this rule (the first mode is 1).

```
# find / -type d -perm -0002 \
> -printf "%p, %u(%U), %g(%G), %k, %m, %AY%Am%Ad-%AT%AZ\n"
/dev/shm, root(0), root(0), 0, 1777, 20040610-23:39:55PDT
/var/tmp, root(0), root(0), 4, 1777, 20040611-01:15:51PDT
/var/spool/vbox, root(0), root(0), 4, 1777, 20040611-01:15:51PDT
/var/spool/samba, root(0), root(0), 4, 1777, 20040611-01:15:51PDT
/tmp, root(0), root(0), 4, 1777, 20040611-01:15:51PDT
/tmp/.font-unix, xfs(43), xfs(43), 4, 1777, 20040611-01:15:51PDT
```

Each of these commands should be run just before the system is placed into production and the output stored in a secure location. Then the commands should be run on a periodic basis and their output compared with the known good copy. Any discrepancies should be investigated and resolved by the administrator.

# Chapter 7

# Hardening Data Storage

- Understand Legal and Ethical Issues with Cryptography
- Use Proper Procedures
- Use GnuPG to Encrypt Files
- Use OpenSSL for File Encryption
- Install and Use a Cryptographic File System

In this chapter, you will find directions for protecting your data beyond the boundaries of external measures and internal permissions. There is only so much that can be done to protect a system, and in the end, the protections a user gives a file may be the last bulwark of defense against unwanted breaches of privacy. Cryptographic software can help protect the information contained in files. Encryption can be used to secure data stored on disk, and encrypted files can be transmitted without fear that they can be read if intercepted. If data is considered sensitive enough to warrant internal protection, encryption can provide the extra security required.

If you are concerned enough about protecting your data to work to secure a machine to any degree beyond the very basics, this chapter may prove quite useful. If you are uncertain, you should at least consider whether using some form of encryption on your data has a place in your workflow.

# Understand Legal and Ethical Issues with Cryptography

When using encryption to protect data, it is important to use it correctly. You'll want to be able to recover data if original keys are lost, and there are a number of technical, legal, and ethical issues as well as procedural ones to consider.

---

### HEADS UP!

If you find yourself planning on doing a large amount of cryptography, you may want to consider using hardware accelerators. Hardware accelerators speed the encryption process by offloading the encryption from the CPU to a separate device.

---

## Comply with Legal Requirements

Data encryption software provides the extra security sensitive files require. Unfortunately, the use of cryptographic systems is not governed by strictly mechanical considerations alone. Most countries have some form of restrictions in place dealing with what you can and cannot do when using encryption. These restrictions apply to both hardware and software, and there are laws governing key size and usage that do not always seem to make much sense. Please do not set your key sizes based on the examples provided in this chapter. You must determine what adequate sizes are, and use keys large enough to provide protection. Larger keys are harder to break, but the downside is that they tend to take longer to process, thus your workflow or the load you're placing on your machines could be unreasonably impacted by the length of time it takes to encrypt or decrypt a file.

If you have questions about what the laws are and how to comply, doing a lookup in a search engine will bring you a plethora of links. Two useful web sites on compliance may be helpful:

- **U.S. Bureau of Industry and Security**   In general, inside the United States, the Department of Commerce's Bureau of Industry and Security currently handles cryptography matters. This web site can help you review any issues you may encounter when dealing with persons or companies in other countries. It's worth noting that there are no proscriptions against using strong cryptography inside the U.S., so you should feel confident in the use of strong keys and strong crypto when working strictly inside the U.S. http://www.bis.doc.gov/encryption/

- **Crypto Link Farm**   Outside the U.S., a good set of links can be found at the Crypto Link Farm. These pages deal specifically with law and policy. If the URL below becomes obsolete at some point, a search for "Crypto Link Farm" should bring up a mirror of it, as it is well distributed. In any case, inside the U.S. or the E.U., you should not worry too much about using encryption for personal use, as even though it's regulated, the laws are not likely to inhibit that sort of utility. Rather, it is sharing data across borders that can cause problems. http://www.cs.auckland.ac.nz/~pgut001/links/standards.html

## Understand Ethical Issues

Before we proceed to the nuts and bolts, it's worth saying something about the ethics of using cryptography. Since cryptography has many laws surrounding it—and given that there are places in the world where its use can get one imprisoned or even executed—there exists a lot of ethical confusion that inevitably crops up when considering using it at all. Many governments are at odds with themselves over its usage as well. They want data protected from bad guys, but do not want anyone whom they might consider a bad guy now or in the future to use it. So the opinions that spew forth surrounding cryptography do not always make much sense to someone trying to do the right thing. The simplest test is one of harm. If you're using cryptography to prevent harm from befalling your organization, it could prove beneficial. If you're using cryptography for activities that cause harm to others, suffice it to say that this chapter is not for you.

Situations often crop up where cryptography can help prevent harm to others, such as a company using it to encrypt medical test data on a shared system. In that circumstance, cryptography prevents unauthorized persons from accessing data they shouldn't have and helps protect the company against mistakes that could increase liability. Such a use of cryptography is obviously a laudable one and should be encouraged. Generally speaking, it's best not to get too bound up in the ethics surrounding cryptography. Simply determine if it can help secure your data, look at the circumstances you need to use it in, and make an effort to comply with any applicable laws. Undergoing the process of basic legal research needed to make sure you are following the law is not difficult. The most common hitch to using crypto in organizations is not mechanical, but rather fear, uncertainty, and doubt (FUD) surrounding the use of it. In nearly all cases, the level of

FUD is wholly unjustified. It is important to recognize that any questions you have about legal issues are fairly easy to answer. You will not need a barrage of lawyers to comply with the necessary laws, but you may need contract agreements between business partners. They are not the same thing, nor should they be lumped together when considering an implementation. To use cryptography as a personal tool, there's far less need to concern yourself with legal compliance. Generally if you have access to the software and aren't planning on traveling or sending your data elsewhere in the world, there's little to worry about. Even if you are planning on international travel or conveyance, the rules on such things are fairly straightforward and easy to find.

# Use Proper Procedures

It's not enough to merely encrypt data; you must provide and use appropriate procedures or risk invalidating your efforts. In particular, a full set of restoration procedures and thorough testing are required. Whatever method you use to encrypt archive media will create the need to integrate the archive's decryption as part of any effort to restore the archive. If not properly implemented, data encryption may just provide a false sense of security. If you use only data encryption alone, you have not provided a secure foundation for your system's data. Key management and access policy restrictions on both live and offline data are particularly important. Without some policy to control who can do what with backups, situations can occur where groups do not communicate well and data can be inadvertently destroyed. The same is true of key protected material, where problems may exist with the keys as well as with the data the keys are there to protect.

Use proper document retention policies in conjunction with backups. In many businesses, attention is given to document retention and association only in the matter of accounting data. While it is good to back up the databases associated with doing a monthly, quarterly, or year-end financial report, associated source documentation files should also be backed up. If you are the person responsible for scheduling backups, rotating tapes, and doing the retention scheduling on backup media, it's important to know if the data you are responsible for carries legal requirements that exceed the actual organizational use of that data.

Proper storage of media is an important part of any backup policy. Most media decays, and electronic media is vulnerable to the ravages of time. Currently, CD-ROM discs have the best shelf life, with DVDs a close second, but both are very quality-dependent. Some DVDs are quite fragile, and the layering technology that is used is where this will often manifest. If you are planning on using DVD media for long-term storage, check the media quality first. The more durable a disk seems, the more durable it probably is. CDs and DVDs should be stored in a cool, dark environment, away from ultraviolet light sources.

Magnetic media has gotten much more reliable than it was in the past, and for this reason it is important to look closely at a vendor's MTBF (mean time between failure) figures and whatever life cycle information they provide. The actual media itself can suffer from oxidation over time, although newer tape materials have drastically reduced this problem. Tape can also become brittle with age and break easily upon attempted use. There is another and far more common problem that comes into play with magnetic tape storage, however: inadvertent demagnetization. Often tapes that are being shuttled offsite or stored locally end up in aluminum cases or plastic tubs. Storing these cases near magnetic sources or placing tubs near computer monitors can play havoc with the contents. If the floor is regularly vacuumed near the containers, each time a strong electromagnetic motor is oscillating at a very high rate near the tape.

In addition to preserving data, it is inevitable that some data will also need to be safely and thoroughly destroyed. There are several ways to destroy a CD or DVD. They can be broken, but the shattered fragments can be sharp and dangerous. They can be scarred to the point of destruction, and removing portions of the silvered media on CDs will do a good job. There are CD/DVD "shredders" that may be a worthwhile option.

Destroying data stored on magnetic media is usually accomplished on an individual tape basis by erasing it in a drive. When there are too many tapes to be erased by tape drives, you should purchase a tape demagnetizing device. Some are portable hand units, others are tabletop devices. When tapes are ready for recycling, their disposal does not generally require specialized media destruction procedures.

The expiration of public and private keys associated with an archive should closely match that of the expected lifetime of the archive, or you could find yourself with files with no keys or keys with no files. This doesn't present a problem if complete destruction of the documents contained in the archive is your goal, as without keys decryption of your media becomes nearly impossible even with fairly weak encryption. However, the destruction of keys should be entirely within your control, and if you have created good procedures, should not happen due to misunderstanding.

## Store Data Securely

To secure backups, keep them offsite. This can mean anything from someone taking a few tapes back and forth from work every day to data storage in locked containers in a storage bunker. The primary goal is usually to secure copies of the data against disaster and theft. Properly handled, backups can help secure data against disaster, however, theft and mishandling cannot always be handled by storage placement decisions. If data is kept in a third-party archiving facility, the main concern will be one of mishandling, as it is easy for confusion to develop without prior agreement over how to handle the data stored offsite. If the other location is another company office, confusion over storage and usability of the media can come into play, so it is a good idea to develop shared procedures across facilities. If you have a small to medium sized business and are considering any sort of rented storeroom, or home storage, it is very important to consider the possibility of casual theft or fire. The best way to combat these is through the use of a fire safe. There are many vendors for these devices, and they can be found at many home improvement stores as well.

There are some handling procedures that are beyond transport. At a minimum you need to have two people in any organization know what the critical backups are and where they are stored, as well as the procedures for doing so, and preferably there should be more than two. If the backups contain data that is material to the conduct of day-to-day business by the directors and officers of the corporation, or has a direct impact on profit and loss activities, or is in some other way deemed mission-critical to business continuity, the people who know what to do with the backups should not travel together if at all possible.

## Remove Plaintext Copies of Data

It is a good idea to securely remove plaintext source files from any system you do not fully trust under all circumstances. Further, given that no system is 100 percent trustable, it may be a good idea to store the data encrypted, except when you're actually working with the data. This reduces your vulnerability to the latest bugs and exploits, and can leave you much less exposed to the mercies and whims of those responsible for patching and debugging potential problems.

When a file is encrypted, the process of encryption will leave the original, plaintext file in place unmodified. Some software allows the removal of source files as an option, but this is a non-cryptographic feature and is not always present. If a software package says that it removes a file, this will in most cases amount to a simple removal and not obliteration of the source data. Some packages will offer a choice to obliterate the data, and it is important to always do so. The normal file removal process leaves cleartext data intact, and it is quite common for old data to lurk on disks for a very long time. Overwriting a file thoroughly removes what information was there, and scrubs trace information from the disk while it is doing so. Since it is possible to look at data remnants even on a live system, using a separate server to stage files, overwriting, and controlling access to encryption keys are all critical steps.

To securely remove files, use the **shred** command. It is part of the GNU **fileutils** package, and thus is common to Red Hat and SUSE distributions. The program can be found as /usr/bin/shred and is far better than the simple **rm** command. Using **rm** does not erase the data that was contained in a file, it removes the linkage to the file and marks the space as being available to the operating system for reuse. Files that have been removed with **rm** are restorable using a variety of easily obtainable commercial and open source software. In many cases, even if the full file itself is not restorable, partial restoration is possible. In all cases, if the data is still on the disk in the clear, it can be viewed if the interested party has the necessary access. Viewing does not require complex machines, or even that a disk be removed from a system, although under some circumstances this is done as a common procedure to isolate the disk from further changes. While it is true that files deleted from a Unix system are not as easily restored nor is the data quite as easily accessed as those under other operating systems, it is not at all true that the data is "lost forever" or completely inaccessible. The structure of Unix file systems is harder to cope with than that of other products, but the basic rules of data still apply: until it's overwritten, the data is still there. Partialy this is due to market saturation, but it's also due to a level of complexity that exists in the designs. There are undelete utilities and such for most Unix file systems, but they are not common software. Mainly they end up being used by people who do forensic work or data recovery, but they are quite freely accessible, and they can be put to use in information gathering. It is therefore prudent to overwrite the cleartext of files to whatever degree is possible when they are destined for encryption.

**shred** is an accessible and easy-to-use command that serves well to obliviate information contained in cleartext to a reasonable degree, though it does have limitations. Logs or journaled file systems and file systems that use caches are cases where the information contained in a file that's been shredded will not be fully and immediately removed. However, using **shred** on files in these types of file systems does significantly raise the amount of effort that must be given to access any remaining fragments of data. Subsequent file system traffic will eventually remove all traces of removed files if such activity is sufficient, but you cannot count on this occurring unless you know the affected system receives adequate amounts of traffic to create these changes.

To use **shred** to remove and overwrite files, it should be invoked like this:

```
# /usr/bin/shred -u <filename>
```

The **-u** flag tells **shred** to remove the file after overwriting it. The default is to overwrite it 25 times without removing it. On particularly large files this may consume an excessive amount of time, and the number of times the file is overwritten can be reduced via the **-n$N$** switch, where $N$ is the number of times you wish to overwrite the file. To invoke it while removing files, use the following command:

```
# /usr/bin/shred -n10 -u <filename>
```

This would overwrite the file 10 times and then remove it entirely. If your file operations need a higher level of security than this, it is possible to do your encryption and decryption operations inside the /dev/shm directory. This is a shared memory file system, and thus is suitable for these sorts of traceless file operations, but this method comes with a cost of memory limitations. The main virtue of doing this is that there is a minimum of data remnants created during the encryption processing efforts. Such remnants, whether deleted but not overwritten files, partially overwritten segments of files, or remainders of filenames, can all be used to extract information that encryption is trying to protect.

# Use GnuPG to Encrypt Files

Both SUSE and Red Hat come with **gpg**, which is the command name for GnuPG (GNU Privacy Guard). It is a free and complete replacement for PGP, and does not contain any patent or licensing issues. It complies with the OpenPGP standard that can be found in RFC 2440. This is a quite commonly used utility, and it is useful when communicating with others who use **gpg** or some other PGP-oriented application. Your introduction to the program may well originate with a request from another user to use PGP-style encryption to securely convey data that you both consider sensitive. Or it may be that you are doing work on site at a customer's location and wish to keep proprietary data available for your own use in a manner that preserves necessary confidentiality. Obviously, the applications are numerous.

**gpg** uses a method of securing files commonly referred to as public key encryption. One of the most common terms associated with this type of usage is PKI, which stands for public key infrastructure. Companies that rely on public key encryption to keep financial, personal, and medical data secure often find themselves in the position of having to use a more coordinated approach with application and key management than the typical one-to-many approach that an individual will use. While a robust public key infrastructure in a company is often quite a good thing, it's a large topic that can only be touched upon here. Public and private PKIs have evolved as a means of doing business with an access management infrastructure to go with the encryption that parties agree to in a normal course of action. They allow buisnesses to quickly and easily set up trusted secure relationships with a minimum of technical negotiation and act as trust brokers as well. Internaly, they allow access management and controls to be policy driven and easily administered. In combination with directory services like LDAP, the management of access can be easily combined with security functionality to seamlessly manage information access and trust. Third-party organizations now have key banks available for public key storage, and the same technology can be used to manage sets of keys as part of an internal security process. Externaly they can allow buisnesses to rapidly share data among different parties on the same projects when a third party trust broker is not called for.

## Creating Keys in a Secure Manner

Before you even begin the key generation process, you should be logged on in a secure manner. This means being at a console you know you can trust, connected to your target machine either directly or via a connection that you are as certain as possible is secure. You should be using SSH or some other wholly encrypted connection if you must use a network to connect to the machine remotely. The use of Telnet, **rsh**, or any other unencrypted connection means is unacceptable during this step. Inevitably, someone somewhere along the line will say "Yes, but…" to this provision about key creation. There are few circumstances that meet the "Yes, but" criteria. Two machines that you have set up yourself, with a switch in between that you plugged in yourself that connects those two machines with one network cable for each machine and no others, in a locked room that no one has access to but you—in that circumstance alone, Telnet might be acceptable (until you turned it off). Multiple security breaches have resulted from people disregarding sensible precautions because the computing environment was trusted and the people they worked with were trusted.

One thing is certain: all those trust mechanisms in their myriad forms are only true until they are not. When that time comes, you do not want to be in the position of having relied on another trust method while you were creating a trust method such as encryption. Not taking the necessary steps to secure your connectivity during key creation and while using your passphrases, creates very high risks. It only takes one time to snoop your passphrase, and even a lackadaisical assailant, much less a determined attacker, can keep a sniffer running for months looking for that one mistake on your part without any effort to speak of.

It is important not to leave keying data on a potentially vulnerable file system. If an organization uses file encryption, the storage of the secret key data and any public keys that must be kept confidential should not occur on a system that might be subject to an attack. Instead, storage on some other, possibly removable media should occur.

# Creating Keys for Use with GnuPG

The first step in using **gpg** is to generate keys to be able to send others encrypted data. There are minimum sizes on the keys that we will use in this example, and you can decide if these are appropriate key sizes for your circumstances. You should make sure that your GnuPG version is up to date—new versions come out regularly in response to bug fixes and feature improvements. Before getting to a point where you can proceed, you'll need to run **gpg** either by itself or with any flag, such as the **--gen-key** flag that we are going to work with next. This will cause the .gnupg directory to be created in your home directory if it doesn't exist. Some versions of RedHat do this creation step inline, and do not require a separate initialization step.

Inside the .gnupg directory, the only file that exists currently is the options or gpg.conf file, which contains a set of default options that you can tweak if you wish. It is a standard #-commented file, so while some of the options may be arcane, the format is a familiar standard that makes it a bit easier to follow. After the above step, some new files will be created by what you do next in actually making the keys.

Now that everything is set up, the creation of new keys is pretty straightforward. To do so, invoke **gpg** with the **--gen-key** command. This will bring up an interactive menu that will prompt you for required information. What follows is an example of the interactive menu with brief explanations of what is occurring throughout:

```
# gpg --gen-key
gpg (GnuPG) 1.0.7; Copyright (C) 2002 Free Software Foundation, Inc.
This program comes with ABSOLUTELY NO WARRANTY.
This is free software, and you are welcome to redistribute it
under certain conditions. See the file COPYING for details.

gpg: Warning: using insecure memory!
gpg: please see http://www.gnupg.org/faq.html for more information
gpg: keyring '/home/budcobackup/.gnupg/secring.gpg' created
gpg: keyring '/home/budcobackup/.gnupg/pubring.gpg' created
Please select what kind of key you want:
   (1) DSA and ElGamal (default)
   (2) DSA (sign only)
   (4) ElGamal (sign and encrypt)
```

```
(5) RSA (sign only)
Your selection?
```

As you can see, there are four choices, with 1 being the default. At this point, you want to pick the default so that you can perform whatever encryption operations you need to. Picking option 1 will allow you to create encrypted and, if you wish, signed messages that are compatible with the OpenPGP standard.

Upon selecting option 1, a new set of choices will come up. At this point you will be selecting a key size. The menu looks like this:

```
Your selection? 1
DSA keypair will have 1024 bits.
About to generate a new ELG-E keypair.
              minimum keysize is  768 bits
              default keysize is 1024 bits
    highest suggested keysize is 2048 bits
What keysize do you want? (1024)
```

In this example, we've selected option 1, which brought up the next menu. Notice the default in this case is 1024. The minimum is listed as 768 bits. You need to pick numbers that are multiples of 8 since the size is in bits. Numbers like 1024, 2048, 4096, or 8192 fit within these parameters. We are not advocating any of these numbers; they are there to merely illustrate the program's sizing requirements. Larger key sizes can increase security by lengthening the time it takes to potentially break encryption, but the downside to large keys is that they increase the amount of time it takes to encrypt and decrypt a file. Depending on your hardware, something that might be easy for you to encrypt could take a lot more time to decrypt on a recipient's machine if their hardware is less powerful than yours. The other major factor that comes into play when you are choosing a key size is the size of the files you intend to encrypt or decrypt. With small files such as those created for e-mail purposes, often this means encrypting a page or two of text, which doesn't take much time. A typical file containing a full two pages of text may only be 4 or 5K in size, but just about every other type of file you might work with will be a great deal larger. For moderate-sized text-based files, such as spreadsheets, you still will probably be dealing with a relatively small file size, and your key size selection will not have much of an impact. However, if you are planning to use **gpg** to encrypt files that are too big to fit on a floppy disk, you should know that the amount of time it will take to encrypt a file can increase dramatically as you increase your key size.

A good rule of thumb is that if the file is not something you would consider too big for sending in e-mail, then you probably will not mind the time it takes to process it. However, if you are planning on encrypting larger files, things that fill substantial amounts of space on a CD or larger, it is a good idea to run some timing tests to see if the amount of time needed to encrypt or decrypt your intended file is acceptable. Since key exchange is the usual next step after creating keys, you want to avoid a situation where you discover after you've exchanged keys and are all ready to go that you have created an issue with the time it takes to process your files.

In our example, we're going to pick the smallest size possible. The number that's right for you will vary on your application, the size of the files you plan on encrypting, and importantly, who you are communicating with and where they are located.

After picking a key size, you will be prompted to potentially have your key expire after a date you set. If you have a need to expire your key at some point, it would be advisable to spend more time with the GnuPG documentation to examine the ramifications of doing so. For our example, we will create a key that does not expire:

```
What keysize do you want? (1024) 768
Requested keysize is 768 bits
Please specify how long the key should be valid.
         0 = key does not expire
      <n>  = key expires in n days
      <n>w = key expires in n weeks
      <n>m = key expires in n months
      <n>y = key expires in n years
Key is valid for? (0) 0
Key does not expire at all
Is this correct (y/n)?
```

Notice that the default is zero, and that the key will not expire. No matter what you type, the program will prompt you for an answer. We will answer **y** for yes. Next you will be prompted to enter your real name, e-mail address, and a comment to go with the key. An example is given as part of the menu as well in case you aren't sure about the format you want:

```
You need a User-ID to identify your key; the software constructs the user id
from Real Name, Comment and Email Address in this form:
    "Heinrich Heine (Der Dichter) <heinrichh@duesseldorf.de>"
Real name: Budco R&D Enterprise Backups
Email address: backups@budbigcorp.com
Comment: Budco R&D group enterprise backup key for 2004 - 2005
You selected this USER-ID:
    "Budco R&D Enterprise Backups (Budco R&D group enterprise backup key for 2004 -
2005) <backups@budbigcorp.com>"



Change (N)ame, (C)omment, (E)mail or (O)kay/(Q)uit?
```

As you can see, any of the fields can be edited to change them. You can also just bail out of the whole process if you are not happy with what you've picked thus far. Since GnuPG is often used in conjunction with the electronic identities of others, many people find it convenient to use the comment field for organization and affiliation information.

Next, you will be prompted to create a passphrase. You do not want to pick something that you will easily forget. This phrase is part of what forms your secret key, and you will not be giving this key phrase out to anyone else, unless you intend for others in your office to be able to use the keys you create to decrypt files collectively. Notice there is a difference in what is being asked for from the typical "create a new password" type of prompt that you may be familiar with from creating a Linux user account password. The program is asking for a passphrase, not a password. The difference is in the length of the string. Passphrases are much like passwords, in that they need to be unique, need to be something that you can easily remember, and need to be something that is secure. The security requirements are not quite as stringent as those associated with creating a password, however, due to the length. You may (but are not required to) use character substitution (such as using zero for the letter o, or a 1 for an I), or use special characters like ;%&* in your passphrase. It is good practice to do some of these things in the creation of a passphrase, but far more important is creating a phrase of adequate length, and one that you can remember.

Don't use common phrases like "the quick brown fox jumped." Combinations of personal data, like the model and year of your car, along with a random street you pass every day on the way to work, followed by the color of your pet's fur or feathers, and a portion of the title of your favorite book, all strung together with some randomized characters, would form a good passphrase. You can also use spaces between the words if you want. For some people, typing a sentence without using any spaces is much more difficult than doing it with spaces, and it may be easier to remember. An adequate passphrase might look like "99Bu1ckLightAtSm1thStreetBlu3DogL1ghtOfAsia." Being able to remember it is more important than length, as you will need to regurgitate it upon demand whenever someone sends you an encrypted file.

If it is a key you are planning on using with a group of people at work, it may end up being something that you have to refer to from a sheet of paper or from some other removable media. If you are planning on using a key under those circumstances, you should not store the unencrypted passphrases in a file on the same machines that you are using to encrypt the files, or especially, transmitting them from. To do so is to invite disaster in the event of a security breach. Even if you've been diligent about cleaning up the unencrypted versions of your files prior to transmission, anyone who gets hold of your keyring files and your passphrases can decrypt all of your encrypted files. It's particularly advisable to take basic steps to prevent this sort of disaster from occurring by separating the storage means for your passphrases. Having an "air gap," where there is no conceivable route over a network to the storage of a passphrase repository, is not just best practice, it's just plain common sense.

The prompt to create a passphrase looks like this:

```
Enter passphrase:
```

This text will be replaced with a prompt to

```
Repeat passphrase:
```

If you make a mistake it will warn you and prompt you to enter it again. It's a good idea to practice typing your passphrase a few times in an editor or via some other means that will not save it, to ensure you can correctly type it and recall it. Be sure to backspace over what you've typed to delete it or close without saving the file you were using to practice with.

Once you reenter your passphrase successfully, the program will continue, and you will see output that looks like the following:

```
We need to generate a lot of random bytes. It is a good idea to perform some
other action (type on the keyboard, move the mouse, utilize the disks) during
the prime generation; this gives the random number generator a better chance to
gain enough entropy.
+++++..++++++++++++++++++++++++++++++++++++++++++++++..++++++++++.+++++++++++++++++
++++++++++++++++++++++++++++++++++++.++++++++++.++++.+++++.+++++...>+++++.........
...................................................................................
....>++++....<+++++.........>+++++........<+++++....................................
..........................................+++++

Not enough random bytes available.  Please do some other work to give
the OS a chance to collect more entropy! (Need 265 more bytes)
We need to generate a lot of random bytes. It is a good idea to perform
some other action (type on the keyboard, move the mouse, utilize the
disks) during the prime generation; this gives the random number
generator a better chance to gain enough entropy.
..++++++++++.++++++++++++++++++++++++++++++++++++++++++++++++++++++++..+++++++++
+.++++++++++++++++++++..+++++++++++++++.++++++++++++++++++++.....................
.+++++^^^^^^^^^^
gpg: /home/budcobackup/.gnupg/trustdb.gpg: trustdb created
public and secret key created and signed.
key marked as ultimately trusted.

pub  1024D/D6FFA7FD 2004-06-04 Budco R&D Enterprise Backups (Budco R&D group
enterprise backup key for 2004 - 2005) <backups@budbigcorp.com>
    Key fingerprint = 1106 874F 4ADF FC00 8B64  0463 D17D DD8E D6FF A7FD
sub   768g/50608F06 2004-06-04
```

Notice in the above example that the program prompted us to be active on the system in some manner, and when enough activity was not taking place, it stopped and asked us to create enough random activity on the system for the process to continue. In this case we logged in another shell and ran the **sync** command to create a mix of CPU and disk activity sufficient to satisfy the program. More random bytes are better than less, so loading the system down a little bit during the process before this step begins is a good idea.

In short, the steps to take to create a key pair are

**1.** Enter the following on the command line:

```
gpg -key-gen
```

2. Enter a key type selection; here we picked **1**.

3. Enter in a key size of your choice, being careful to use a bit-friendly number.

4. Enter an expiration date; here we picked **0**.

5. Enter in your user ID information.

6. Enter a passphrase.

7. Make sure there is some good random activity going on.

That's all there is to the actual typing mechanics in key pair creation. Once you have completed these steps, two sets of keys will have been created. The first is your secret key, which you never reveal to anyone else. It is secured by the passphrase that only you know. The second key is the one you will give out to others so they can create encrypted files that you can then decrypt using your secret key. This is known as your public key. In the previous example, the public key is listed as "pub 1024D/D6FFA7FD 2004-06-04 Budco R&D Enterprise Backups." The parts of that key that other users will use to specify your identity are "D6FFA7FD" and the name portion, "Budco R&D Enterprise Backups." It is usually easiest to use the numeric portion to specify which key you want to use to encrypt files for a recipient. Once you start using GnuPG you can rapidly accumulate many keys for many different people, and commonly even more than one key for the same person. In a following section, you will see how to use these keys to prepare files for transmission.

Before you encrypt a file with someone else's public key, or have another person encrypt a file for your use with your public key, you have to be able to extract your public key to send to them, and be able to load in your "keyring" key files that they send you.

To extract a public key to send to other people, use the following command sequence:

```
# gpg --armor --export D6FFA7FD > budcobackups.key
```

This gives you a public key in a file that you have named budcobackups.key. The > shell command writes the key to a file rather than standard out, so without the > shell operator, the key would have just been written to the screen. Writing it to the screen is often ideal for a simple copy and paste operation into mail. The **--armor** switch tells **gpg** to output your command in ASCII format so that it will be compatible with e-mail transfer, and using this switch ensures there will not be strange conversion errors along the way when the mail is sent. It's suitable for just pasting into a mail program, so most mail clients will work, and you do not need the ability to send attachments to send the keys.

Output from the command should look something like this shortened example:

```
-----BEGIN PGP PUBLIC KEY BLOCK-----
Version: GnuPG v1.0.7 (GNU/Linux)

mQGiBECsQUwRBACVb2PQq/JdhoUadEgImxqicxhwpXhG3IUcxEH6E7zhZj7wgqdy
```

```
Eot3Fykdu3XGNohGBBgRAgAGBQJArEFOAAoJEHRFmISdWXYRKA4An1BKO3hncdPU
j1eSwLFVOs8f7kdEAKCBVfqTgJHlDdutsNvWCgQ/NB+thg==
=kZyF
```
```
-----END PGP PUBLIC KEY BLOCK-----
```

When you create a key for your own use, it is very likely that the key will be bigger, even if you chose the default, which is not much larger than the minimum permitted size that was used in the example.

The next thing to know is how to load up a key that you have been given by someone else. Once you have another person's key, you can encrypt files with it for their use. These are the keyring files that are used to encrypt or decrypt your files, and they are the key data that you need to be concerned about when creating secure backups. Only someone with their key files and passphrase can decrypt files meant for them. Possibly you have been given a public key block file with many keys in it. This is a file that contains multiple keys, and they could be individual or group-oriented keys. To give you a more ground-up view of these key files, here is an example of files that have appeared in the .gnupg directory since it was first created earlier. Earlier in the chapter we showed where the options file had been created inside the directory. Now there are more files. The list includes

```
-rw-r--r--    1 budcobackup       users        8129 2004-05-22 16:29 options
-rw-r--r--    1 budcobackup       users         858 2004-05-22 16:29 pubring.gpg
-rw-r--r--    1 budcobackup       users           0 2004-05-22 16:29 pubring.gpg~
-rw-------    1 budcobackup       users         600 2004-05-22 16:29 random_seed
-rw-------    1 budcobackup       users        1265 2004-05-22 16:29 secring.gpg
-rw-r--r--    1 budcobackup       users        1240 2004-05-22 16:29 trustdb.gpg
```

The pubring.gpg file is comparatively small at this point because it's only got one key in it. When we add new keys, it will grow. The first thing to do with keys that someone has given you is create a place to store them. It is not a good idea to leave key files randomly lying around, not only because of preservation reasons, but because keeping them organized helps facilitate their removal. In this case, we are going to use a directory named Keys, though you may wish to use something more discreet. Inside that directory we have a couple of keys from colleagues:

```
-rw-r--r--    1 budcobackup       users        1690 2004-05-22 16:38 bob.key
-rw-r--r--    1 budcobackup       users        1694 2004-05-22 16:47 john.key
```

To add them, we just run the command

```
# gpg --import john.key
```

which produces command output that looks like this:

```
gpg: Warning: using insecure memory!
gpg: please see http://www.gnupg.org/faq.html for more information
gpg: key E4F39AD7: public key imported
```

```
gpg: Total number processed: 1
gpg:                    imported: 1
```

Following that, the file john.key was loaded with a similar command:

```
gpg --import john.key
```

There is now a larger keyring to work with than just the main backups key. We will be able to see these keys if everything has worked right, and thereafter use them to encrypt files meant for John or Bob.

To first see their keys, run the GnuPG command **-kv** (for key view). Running it on our newly grown keyring results in this output:

```
# gpg -kv
gpg: Warning: using insecure memory!
gpg: please see http://www.gnupg.org/faq.html for more information
/home/budcobackup/.gnupg/pubring.gpg
---------------------------
pub  1024D/D6FFA7FD 2004-06-04 Budco R&D Enterprise Backups (Budco R&D
group enterprise backup key for 2004 - 2005) <backups@budbigcorp.com>
sub   768g/50608F06 2004-06-04

pub  1024D/E4F39AD7 2004-05-22 John Conner (John at Work)
<john@myexampledomain.com>
sub  2048g/6DF7E821 2004-05-22

pub  1024D/7DA701A0 2004-05-20 Bob Dobbs (Bob at Work)
<bob@myexampledomain.com>
sub  2048g/EFB1A2C9 2004-05-20
```

Notice that both Bob and John have keys associated with their common names. John's key is E4F39AD7, and Bob's key is 7DA701A0. Now that we have keys for them added to our keyring, we can see how the files have changed from the earlier output. Inside the .gnupg directory we can see

```
-rw-r--r--    1 budcobackup    users    8129 2004-05-22 16:29 options
-rw-r--r--    1 budcobackup    users    3204 2004-05-22 16:50 pubring.gpg
-rw-r--r--    1 budcobackup    users    2033 2004-05-22 16:50 pubring.gpg~
-rw-------    1 budcobackup    users     600 2004-05-22 16:29 random_seed
-rw-------    1 budcobackup    users    1265 2004-05-22 16:29 secring.gpg
-rw-r--r--    1 budcobackup    users    1240 2004-05-22 16:29 trustdb.gpg
```

The pubring file has grown in size at this point, and even the backup file that was automatically created is larger. That is because we added in Bob's and John's keys as separate files. The key data is contained in these files. The creation of a directory to store them in while processing does not mean they have to be kept at all, as they are stored in the pubring.pgp file and referenced from there as well.

We can now encrypt a file for archival purposes using the backups key we have created or use an individual or group key. During the key creation process, one of the commands was **--armor**, and this command comes into play when encrypting files. Because mail servers and clients can be somewhat incompatible when handling included files, the **--armor** switch is used quite often in those applications. It should not be used for files destined for archival storage, or during any backup process that involved the files being transferred via the Web, **scp**, or FTP, and should not be used in order to save disk or tape space. Any transfer mechanism you use that will do a binary transfer of the files you want to send will eliminate the need to **--armor** your files in ASCII mode. You will find that compression of the binary files will not gain you much, because one of the main goals of ciphering text is to have it be as random seeming as possible, and that makes for bad compression.

To encrypt files with **gpg** for inclusion in mail with John's key, use these commands:

```
# gpg -ea -r E4F39AD7 test.zip
gpg: Warning: using insecure memory!
gpg: please see http://www.gnupg.org/faq.html for more information
gpg: checking the trustdb
gpg: checking at depth 0 signed=0 ot(-/q/n/m/f/u)=0/0/0/0/0/1
gpg: 6DF7E821: There is no indication that this key really belongs to the owner
2048g/6DF7E821 2004-05-22 "John Conner (John at Work) <john@myexampledomain.com>"
          Fingerprint: 529F ACEA 2B05 6770 AA30  6BE1 B7DF 66EF 6DF7 E821

It is NOT certain that the key belongs to its owner.
If you *really* know what you are doing, you may answer
the next question with yes

Use this key anyway? yes
```

In the above example, we specified John's key with the **-r** (recipient) flag. For each **-r** flag, one recipient can be specified, and you can encrypt one file for multiple recipients with subsequent **-r** flags. The argument to the **-r** flag is a person's key, and if you have more than one key for a person, often the best way to identify the key you want to use is to use the number. Arguments like the person's full name, "Budco R&D Enterprise Backups" or "John Conner" in the above examples, can be used as well, and you may find this smoother to work with. The **-e** switch stands for encrypt, and the addition of the **-a** switch for **-ea** armors the output for mail. Since the trust attributes have not been updated, **gpg** prompts to ask if you wish to use the key despite this, and as long as you know you are using the right key, you can answer **yes**. Further examination of GnuPG commands will instruct you in updating the trust of keys in your keyring, at which point the program will no longer ask for this information.

GnuPG outputs a file with an extension of .asc. The above example resulted in two files in the directory, the first being the initial cleartext file, the second being the encrypted and armored file:

```
-rw-r--r--    1 budcobackup      users      72K 2004-05-22 17:18 test.zip
-rw-r--r--    1 budcobackup      users      99K 2004-05-22 17:33 test.zip.asc
```

As you can see, the armored file is larger. If we do not use the **-a** switch, and run a command like the following,

```
# gpg -e -r E4F39AD7 test.zip
```

the output yields a file with a different extension, in this case .gpg, that does not have ASCII character encoding and is subsequently smaller. A new directory listing looks like this:

```
-rw-r--r--    1 budcobackup      users         72K 2004-05-22 17:18 test.zip
-rw-r--r--    1 budcobackup      users         99K 2004-05-22 17:33 test.zip.asc
-rw-r--r--    1 budcobackup      users         73K 2004-05-22 17:37 test.zip.gpg
```

Notice the .gpg non-ASCII file is not a great deal larger in size than the original zip file is before encryption. On small files this doesn't make much difference, but on larger files, substantial disk or tape space can be taken up by files unnecessarily put in an ASCII format. It also increases the length of transfer time.

In the previous example, the original unencrypted file test.zip has been used as a source, but has not been removed. The next step should be to remove this source file in a secure manner, using **shred** if necessary.

The beginning of the output from the ASCII encoded command looks something like this:

```
-----BEGIN PGP MESSAGE-----
Version: GnuPG v1.0.7 (GNU/Linux)

hQIOA7ffZu9t9+ghEAgAtVZXRYu/CfXFRsRzwKaGjqRgSeRdJho9GerrNe3Vjv51
TtEeH1CKgDdp+r9S99BqSOEoJ6HHoLXWR1aBxPAcxy49wm5eJO8uYT7+kAlP09u4
```

That pattern of a big formatted list of ASCII only characters comprises the type of content found in the file until its end. Without armor, the .gpg file that is created is a data file filled with seemingly random binary content.

Either the .gpg file or the .asc file can now be sent to John for his decryption using whatever means you want.

If a file is needed for decryption later, the private key part of the public key pair used in the file's creation must be used to decrypt it. Other steps in encrypting a file for decryption look much the same as shown previously.

To decrypt files, we'll use a very simple process:

```
-rw-r--r--    1 budcobackup      users        769K 2004-05-22 19:44 budcoplan.zip.gpg
```

The command to use is

```
# gpg -o budcoplan.zip -d budcoplan.zip.gpg
```

In that statement, **-o** is short for the **-output** switch, and the **-d** switch is the abbreviation for the **-decrypt** switch. We could also do something like this:

```
# gpg   -d budcoplan.zip.gpg >budcoplan.zip
```

or use any other shell operators. When executed to decrypt something, **gpg** prompts for your passphrase, and it looks something like this:

```
# gpg -d budcoplan.zip.gpg > budcoplan.zip
gpg: Warning: using insecure memory!
gpg: please see http://www.gnupg.org/faq.html for more information

You need a passphrase to unlock the secret key for
user: " Budco R&D Enterprise Backups (Budco R&D group enterprise backup key for 2004 -
2005) <backups@budbigcorp.com>"
768-bit ELG-E key, ID 50608F06, created 2004-05-23 (main key ID D6FFA7FD)

Enter passphrase:
```

Upon being prompted for your passphrase, or the passphrase used to encrypt the files, you should enter it. Once you do, the files will be decrypted, and you can process them further with archival software or the appropriate applications.

GnuPG has many different options. The **-help** command and online documentation are extremely useful in dealing with a variety of circumstances from mail to automated batch processing. For further help, consult the man page or the online documentation at the URL found in the various examples above.

# Use OpenSSL for File Encryption

Another easy-to-use method of file encryption included with Red Hat and SUSE is one that's sure to be familiar to anyone who has set up or upgraded SSH. It is OpenSSL, and while people commonly use it as a component of other programs, like Apache or SSH, the package is more than just the libcrypto or libssl libraries whose misplacement occasionally causes grief for developers. Also included in the package is the **openssl** program, which permits fairly simple encryption operations on files using a wide variety of cryptographic algorithms. The following list is selectable for use:

- **bf, bf-cbc, bf-cfb, bf-ecb, bf-ofb**   Variations of the Blowfish cipher.
- **cast, cast-cbc**   A pair of encoding variations for the CAST cipher.
- **cast5-cbc, cast5-cfb, cast5-ecb, cast5-ofb**   A later version of the CAST cipher. As you can see, there are more encoding variations available to use with the CAST5 cipher.
- **des, des-cbc, des-cfb, des-ecb, des-ede, des-ede-cbc, des-ede-cfb, des-ede-ofb, des-ofb**   The many variations of encoding for the DES cipher, not all of which are what you would normally want to use. Additionally, DES is not the most secure of ciphers anymore.

- **des3, desx, des-ede3, des-ede3-cbc, des-ede3-cfb, des-ede3-ofb**   DES3 is the Triple-DES cipher, a more advanced and more secure variant of DES.

- **idea, idea-cbc, idea-cfb, idea-ecb, idea-ofb**   The IDEA cipher and variants.

- **rc2, rc2-cbc, rc2-cfb, rc2-ecb, rc2-ofb**   The RC2 cipher and its encoding variants.

- **rc4**   The RC4 cipher without encoding varieties.

- **rc5, rc5-cbc, rc5-cfb, rc5-ecb, rc5-ofb**   The RC5 cipher and encoding variants.

In using these ciphers to encrypt files, there isn't much need to worry about encoding variants, as these are mainly used for communications purposes. Using them for file encryption is fairly straightforward, and some of the options are used for similar purposes in GnuPG as well. The programs are remarkably different, however, and often are used differently as well. OpenSSL is often used as a research tool and as part of other programs to perform cryptography, whereas GnuPG is used more commonly in standalone mode as a primary application.

The use of **openssl** to encrypt or decrypt a file is a barebones affair compared to the steps that are necessary to use **gpg**. There are no elaborate keyring files, no options file to tweak default behavior, and no separate key generation tasks. Instead, keys are stored in your head, or barring that, in some other form of secure media. Keys can be fed to **openssl** on the command line or as a part of a program, but this is usually a bad idea as the keys get exposed to anyone who happens to look at the process table while the command is running.

The command sequence to encrypt a file with **openssl** using the Blowfish cipher can look something like the following example:

```
# openssl enc -bf -e -a -in example1.txt -out example1.bf
enter bf-cbc encryption password:
Verifying password - enter bf-cbc encryption password:
```

In this example, we end up with a file named example1.bf, and the file extension is one that was chosen for this example; there is no default. In fact, we could have specified the output filename to be anything at all.

In breaking down the switches in the previous example you will see some similarities in operations with what you might do while using **gpg**. The first command of the **openssl** program is **enc**, which tells the program you plan on encoding with ciphers. The second command is a cipher name, in this case the Blowfish cipher. Notice that it is specified with a hyphen (-) before the cipher name, resulting in **-bf**. This could easily have been **-des3** or some other cipher. The next flag is **-e**, which stands for encrypt. Conversely, the **-d** flag tells the program that you plan on decrypting a file. The next command is the **-a** switch, which tells **openssl** to use ASCII armoring suitable for use in e-mail programs. Without this, you end up with a data file that is smaller, but not suitable for mailing. Next is the **-in** command. This flag specifies the plaintext file that you are using for input and are planning on encrypting. This is followed by the **-out** command, which specifies a file to output your now encrypted text into. Running the command produces file contents that look something like this:

```
U2FsdGVkX1+XlRIc3C/xLRWLA97efV4ehZHa88vHGrll3OZQsHCkWWLCjhh1K3K1
ZcJ+d0cSERucUkweWULyh3EUqSnPXsfzkgFyed4SdQrO3kb7Ogi1RAPY5iRaTQx5
```

This is the beginning of the file, and the entire contents look much the same. You may notice there is no header information like that found in GnuPG or PGP files. There is nothing at all in the file to indicate what type of cipher was used to encrypt it, and had the output file example been named differently, there would be no hint whatsoever as to what cipher was used to encrypt the file. The result is that it becomes important to remember both your password and what cipher you used to encrypt a file, as neither is obvious afterward.

To decrypt the same file, the commands look like this:

```
# openssl enc -bf -d -a -in example1.bf -out example1.txt
enter bf-cbc decryption password:
```

Notice there is no prompt for any password verification. This is because if you make an error you can always try again to decrypt the file. You may notice that the filenames were reversed from the first example. After encrypting the file, we removed the plaintext, which left only the ciphertext file. This made output using the original filename a complete restoration, but any name would have served. They are reversed in order from the first example because in the above operation we are decrypting the ciphertext. The way this is indicated to **openssl** is via the **-d** switch, which tells the program to decrypt the ciphertext.

If you need quick and dirty encryption, **openssl** can be just the right tool to do it with. It leaves no obvious tracks if discretion is desired, and files created with it are indistinguishable from any other anonymous data files. The major difference is that files encrypted with **openssl** will have smaller key spaces than those in use with **gpg**.

# Install and Use a Cryptographic File System

Working with encryption can be onerous if it requires the constant encryption and decryption of files in an archive that you use on a regular basis. In these circumstances, you may want to consider the use of disk encryption. One of the easiest ways to do it is with the CFS package. This is a program originally written by Matt Blaze that has since promulgated into many variations and flavors. There is TCFS, which is an Italian variety, as well as others. Unfortunately, however, the Linux Crypto API documentation has been taken offline in protest over software patents in Europe by the people responsible for hosting it. Due to the endless nature of the protest, the Crypto API and many of the efforts to create Linux-specific cryptographic functionality have since grown moribund. For the following examples, the archive at http://sourceforge.net/projects/cfsnfs/ was used. Google will provide other possible archives of interest if you search with keywords of "cryptographic filesystem linux."

To install the package found on the site, run the following command:

```
rpm -vv -i cfs-1.4.1-5.i386.rpm
```

This will install a complete package for CFS. It is recommended that you take this approach, as it simplifies the creation of the various script files. Afterward, however, you will have to fix broken symbolic links if you are running SUSE. The package is installed in /etc/init.d and /etc/rc.d, and installs directories called rc0.d through rc5.d, with scripts in them that are named appropriately, but linked to "../init.d/cfsd," which will not work under SUSE. The broken links in SUSE are easy to spot, and this is not a problem for Red Hat. Do the following to correct them if you are running SUSE; skip these steps if you are using Red Hat:

1. Change to the first rc directory where there is an error:

   ```
   cd /etc/init.d/rc0.d
   ```

2. Remove the old file:

   ```
   rm K15cfsd
   ```

3. Then use the following command to relink to the script to files to shut the program down cleanly:

   ```
   ln -s ../cfsd K15cfsd
   ```

4. Repeat the above steps for /etc/init.d/rc1.d and /etc/init.d/rc2.d.

5. In /etc/init.d/rc3.d and /etc/init.d/rc5.d, use the following command to create the links to start the program:

   ```
   "rm S65cfsd ; ln -s ../cfsd S65cfsd"
   ```

6. Edit the /etc/init.d/cfsd script to make your mount points appropriate to your needs if you are changing from the default.

You can now restart the system and CFS will run normally. If you wish, you may change the mount points by modifying the /etc/exports file, and modifying the /etc/init.d/cfsd script to reflect the locations you prefer.

Since it is all too likely that you will have to build and install CFS for yourself, the steps to do so will be laid out for you here. There may be some differences among the flavors of CFS out there, but many of the essential elements will be the same. There are more steps in this method, but if you want to tweak things, this will get you started. If you have installed the RPM binary package, you can skip this section.

The following command will install the necessary sources in the /usr/src/packages/ SOURCES directory:

```
rpm -install cfs-1.4.1-5.src.rpm
```

From there it is a matter of unpacking the files and building the source trees. This version of CFS needs the RSAref2 package, which is included as a part of the RPM. Since it needs to be installed first, the following steps should be taken:

1. Set your umask to 022, and **cd** to the /usr/src/packages/SOURCES/ directory.

2. Unpack the gzipped tar file like this:

   ```
   gzip -dc rsaref2.tar.gz|tar -xvf -
   ```

3. **cd** into the resulting rsaref2 directory.

4. **cd** further into the install directory, then the unix directory.

5. Type **make** to build the software with default options. This will result in two programs and one library file. The programs are dhdemo and rdemo, demonstration programs for Diffie-Hellman extensions to the RSA reference package, and for the RSA cryptographic functions. The library file is named rsaref.a, and contains functions needed to compile CFS.

6. Copy dhdemo and rdemo into /usr/local/bin.

7. Copy rsaref.a into /usr/local/lib, then run **ranlib** on it to reset the libraries' contents manually, by executing the following command:

   ```
   ranlib /usr/local/lib/rsaref.a
   ```

8. Copy the header files from the rsaref2/sources directory into /usr/local/ include. You may want to specify the **-i** switch to avoid possibly overwriting similar header files if they exist. The command with full pathnames would look like this:

   ```
   # cp -i /usr/src/packages/SOURCES/rsaref2/sources/*.h /usr/local/include
   ```

   These locations will later be used in the CFS makefile to tell it where to look for the files.

That's all there is to that step. There is no install option in the makefile, so installation needs to be done by hand. In the next steps, building and installing CFS will be done:

1. Unpack the CFS software from the gzipped tar file with the following command:

   ```
   gzip -dc cfs-1.4.1.tar.gz|tar -xvf -
   ```

2. **cd** into the cfs-1.4.1 directory, and open the makefile in an editor of your choice.

3. On line 78, change the **COPT=-O2 -DPROTOTYPES=1** line to say **COPT=-O2 -DPROTOTYPES=0**.

4. On line 87, change the **RSALIB= variable** to say **/usr/local/lib/rsaref.a** instead of the default of /usr/mab/rsaref/install/rsaref.a, which will not exist on your system.

5. On line 88, change the **RSAINCLUDES= line** to read **/usr/local/include** instead of the original /usr/mab/rsaref/source.

6. Uncomment lines 128 to 131, and remove the **-traditional** flag from line 128 so that your text looks something like this:

```
CFLAGS=$(COPT) -U__OPTIMIZE__ -Dd_fileno=d_ino -I$(RINCLUDES)
LIBS=
COMPAT=
RPCOPTS= -k -b
```

7. Put a comment at the beginning of line 232 to make it look like this:

```
#CC=you_forgot_to_edit_the_makefile
```

8. Save the file and exit.

Following that, you will be ready to build CFS. This is straightforward; in the source directory, typing **make** alone will give you the potential targets:

```
make cfs, esm, install_cfs or install_esm
```

The first step is to make CFS, so to do so just type **make cfs**. Next type **make esm** to make the **esm** program. Once these builds have completed without errors, you can install the software by typing **make install_cfs** and **make install_esm**. You will then have to install the man pages by hand. You will do this from the CFS source directory as follows:

```
cp *.1 /usr/local/man/man1
cp *.8 /usr/local/man/man8
```

That is the last step to installing the software. Next you need to configure it for use. CFS has some uncommon requirements because it operates over the loopback network interface, and functions much like a normal NFS mount would.

To configure it for use, take the following steps:

1. Pick a bootstrap mount point. This will not get used for anything, but is necessary for everything to run. It's easiest to make a directory called /null to do this. Create the directory and remove unnecessary permissions as follows:

```
mkdir /null;chmod 0 /null
```

2. Add a line to your /etc/exports file that contains the words **/null localhost** on a single line.

3. Make a directory where you want your encrypted file system to be mounted. For example, **mkdir /crypt** will put it in the root directory on /.

4. Create an **rc** startup script that should be run by the system after the **mount** command is run. This should be put in /etc/init.d/rc2.d under SUSE, and /etc/rc2.d under Red Hat. The contents of the script should be something like this:

```
if [ -x /usr/local/etc/cfsd ]; then
    /usr/local/etc/cfsd && \
        /etc/mount -o port=3049,intr localhost:/null /crypt
fi
```

This contains the mount points that we specified earlier. If you want them located in different places, the file systems containing them must be mounted before **cfsd** starts in order for it to function correctly.

5. At this point you may either reboot or start CFS manually. To do so you will have to export the null mount that you created before, by executing **exportfs -a**. You may also have to start /usr/sbin/rpc.mountd. Once you have done that, you can run the following command to fire up the CFS daemon:

```
/usr/local/etc/cfsd &
```

6. Run the following command to set up the mount over the loopback:

```
mount -o port=3049,intr localhost:/null /crypt
```

7. If everything has happened correctly, you should be able to run an **ls** of the /crypt directory, and see the mount using **df**. It should look something like this:

```
#df -a
Filesystem              1K-blocks      Used Available Use% Mounted on
/dev/sda7                8385636   2020300   6365336  25% /
proc                           0         0         0   -  /proc
devpts                         0         0         0   -  /dev/pts
/dev/sda5                  15522      5734      8987  39% /boot
shmfs                     144144         0    144144   0% /dev/shm
usbdevfs                       0         0         0   -  /proc/bus/usb
localhost:/null                0         0         0   -  /crypt
```

Notice that the mount over the loopback device is visible as **localhost:/null** for a source export, and the subsequent mount is on /crypt.

To test and use CFS, the first command you will run will be **cmkdir** *exampledir* to create an encrypted directory. The command is straightforward, and will create a directory in the place of your choosing that is an empty CFS file system. In this example,

```
werewolf:/home/budcobackup/testcfs # cmkdir cfstest
Key:
Again:
```

you can see that **cmkdir** prompts twice for a password. Thereafter, this is the password you want to use to attach the encrypted directory for use.

This created a directory called cfstest relative to the location in which it was run. In this case it is a directory inside our home directory. Listing the contents of this directory yields output that looks like this:

```
werewolf:/home/budcobackup/testcfs/cfstest # ls -al
total 16
drwxr-xr-x    2 root      root          144 2004-05-24 18:21 .
drwxr-xr-x    4 root      root           96 2004-05-24 18:21 ..
-rw-r--r--    1 root      root            8 2004-05-24 18:21 ...
-rw-r--r--    1 root      root            1 2004-05-24 18:21 ..c
-rw-r--r--    1 root      root           32 2004-05-24 18:21 ..k
-rw-r--r--    1 root      root            7 2004-05-24 18:21 ..s
```

Next you want to run the **cattach** program to mount your encrypted directory and be able to use it like you would a normal file system. Use the following syntax,

```
cattach your-cmkdir-name
```

where the argument is the directory name you used when you ran the **cmkdir** command. In the following example, you can see that **cattach** prompted for your password and then exited:

```
werewolf:/home/budcobackup/testcfs # cattach cfstest
Key:
```

Now, however, looking in /crypt we can see a new directory,

```
# ls -l /crypt
total 1
drwxrwxrwx    4 root      root         8192 2004-05-24 18:23 .
drwxr-xr-x   24 root      root          552 2004-05-24 17:27 ..
drwx------    2 root      root          144 2004-05-24 18:21 cfstest
```

which shows that there is a new directory cfstest available for use. If you copy files into that /crypt/cfstest directory, you will be able to work with them as though they were in a normal directory. However, if the encrypted directory is not mounted or attached, you will not be able to see them. To unmount the CFS file system, use the **cdetach** command. The argument to it is the name of the encrypted directory that you want to detach from the /crypt mount point. In the following example, you can see that the cfstest directory is no longer visible:

```
werewolf:/ # cdetach cfstest
werewolf:/ # ls -l /crypt
total 1
```

```
drwxrwxrwx    4 root     root         8192 2004-05-24 18:39 .
drwxr-xr-x   24 root     root          552 2004-05-24 17:27 ..
```

The files are there, just encrypted and stored under the directory that was made when you ran the **cmkdir** command earlier.

With a little creativity, it is very easy to customize locations that are suitable for use with CFS. Care must be taken with mounting file systems, as the cleartext space inside the directories that you have attached are visible to anyone who has permissions to look at your files, and are otherwise unprotected as long as you have the crypto file system attached.

# Chapter 8

## Hardening Authentication and User Identity

- Use Pluggable Authentication Modules (PAM) to Provide Flexible Authentication
- Correctly Configure PAM to Avoid Compromise
- Name Switching Service (NSS)

**P**AM is an authentication mechanism that originated on Solaris, but is used on various systems, including Linux. The Linux PAM implementation allows a system administrator to choose how users authenticate to various services. New modules can be added by an administrator at any time, offering overall flexibility in how authentication happens.

# Use Pluggable Authentication Modules (PAM) to Provide Flexible Authentication

Traditionally, Linux and other Unix-like systems simply authenticated users against an entry in the file /etc/passwd. Everyone had read-only access to the password file, and the encrypted passwords were available to anyone with access to the system. This simple design made password files vulnerable to "dictionary attacks," an attack where the attacker would encrypt common words and compare his encrypted words with what was in the password file. If a match was found, the attacker then would know the password. As a countermeasure, Linux and other Unix-like systems changed from the standard password file to a "shadow" password file, where passwords were moved out of the traditional /etc/passwd file into a different file (typically /etc/shadow). Since the /etc/passwd file needs to be readable by any user on the system, moving sensitive password hashes out of the world-readable file limited the availability of the hashes to the root user only.

Many experts believe that having a single authentication mechanism for each service on the system (terminal logins, local logins, network logins, etc.) is too inflexible. Typically, each service needed its own authentication code or had to use the single mechanism available. PAM is the answer to inflexible single authentication mechanisms. PAM allows different modules to be added for authenticating new services and for adding new authentication mechanisms for old services. PAM can also be used to enable shadow file authentication for applications that don't natively support it. PAM module information can be found in the following places on the Internet:

- The Linux PAM resource page at kernel.org: http://www.kernel.org/pub /linux/libs/pam/modules.html

- The OpenWall PAM page, which is where pam_passwdqc and pam_mktemp live: http://www.openwall.com/pam/

- Freshmeat's PAM section: http://freshmeat.net/search/?q=pam&section= projects&x=0&y=0

Remember that PAM contains the keys to your system, so you should only run PAM modules that are from known sources and that you trust. Anything else may allow an attacker to access your system.

There are interesting modules for voice authentication, smart cards, tokens, and a host of other types. Make sure you either have a known good way to get in by experimenting on one service rather than a core function, or that you can boot to single user mode and recover the system if you decide to experiment.

## Use PAM Because...

PAM allows you to enable strong per-service authentication features, shadow passwords, stronger hashing functions, and change mechanisms due to changing system requirements. The flexibility comes with a small cost of increased complexity, outweighed by the benefits.

## Enforce Strict Password Requirements

You can use a PAM module to enforce strict password requirements. Many administrators don't want their users' passwords to be easy to guess, so they might require a strong password module to authenticate password changes.

Strong passwords are often difficult for users to remember. Their use should be weighed with the fact a user might write his password down and therefore accidentally make it available to a local attacker, balanced against remotely accessible services that may be open to common wordlist type "dictionary" attacks.

With PAM, you can require a user's password to contain a certain number of non-alphabetic and non-numeric characters, and adhere to a specific length requirement. On a standard ASCII keyboard, there are 26 letters, 10 digits, 32 symbols, and the space character. While a two-character password is hardly strong enough for most purposes, if it were two alphabetic characters, an attacker would only have to go through 32 different combinations before exhausting the possibilities. If the password is any keyboard character, then the attacker has to go through 138 potential combinations. With longer passwords the difference is even more pronounced.

By requiring a password to not include dictionary words, an administrator can further reduce the amount of success an attacker can have either on a blind attack against a user's account or even on "cracking" the password hash with a large dictionary program.

## Enable Wheel Group Access

BSD-style Unix systems use a special form of group access to decide which users can use the **su** command to gain root access. Users who are authorized to gain root access are added to a specific system group, and only those users can change to root to perform administrative functions. This group is typically named "wheel," and Linux administrators can add a PAM module to enable wheel group access to their machines.

Limiting access to only people who need to be able to perform functions that require root permissions makes it more difficult for an attacker to gain escalated privilege through a non-privileged account, such as that of a web server's process or a user who uses the same password on another compromised system.

## Enable the Use of a Centralized Authentication Server

Some administrators like to enable a central authentication server, so that users can authenticate with one password to multiple systems, and that password only has to be maintained in a single place. The most common of these is the Windows domain account through a domain controller or Active Directory. Another popular choice is a RADIUS server. RADIUS is supported by many dial-up systems used by ISPs, and it is also supported by RSA's SecureID ACE server protocol. An ACE server is a server that supports two-factor authentication using a hardware token that's time synchronized to the server and a PIN that the user knows. Large corporations often use ACE/SecureID to authenticate to important systems where security is an issue. By changing which PAM module is used to authenticate, an administrator may use one of these centralized services without any application changes.

# Correctly Configure PAM to Avoid Compromise

It is very important to test all changes carefully when changing a service's PAM configuration files.

## Remove Obsolete PAM Configuration File

Originally, PAM used /etc/pam.conf as its configuration file. This is no longer the case unless the PAM default configuration directory does not exist. Therefore, you should either remove pam.conf if it exists on your system, or ensure that its directives match your security requirements. These days, PAM has all of its configuration information in a directory called /etc/pam.d.

Removing the file will ensure that a misconfigured system won't allow unauthorized access. Simply changing the default file to match your security policy will ensure that if the /etc/pam.d directory is corrupted or accidentally removed, you'll still be able to access the system without having to reboot into single user mode.

Also, if you administer lots of similar systems where older PAM configuration files are necessary, it may be easier to keep them all the same; however, upgrading to recent versions of PAM is strongly recommended.

Each service has its own configuration file in /etc/pam.d, named after the program or service. For example, the login application (/bin/login) is configured in /etc/pam.d /login. Application programmers define the service names of their applications—each service should install its own configuration file when you install that service. The operating system installers normally do this for you.

# Configuration File Format

Each non-comment line of a PAM configuration file consists of four possible arguments: a module interface, control flag, module path, and module arguments. Comments begin with a # symbol and continue to the end of the line.

So each line has the structure

```
interface    control_flag    module_path        [module_arguments]
```

The module arguments field is optional and depends on the module and setup.

Here's an example line that has only the first three fields:

```
auth    required    pam_unix.so
```

## Module Interface

Module interface is the PAM jargon for the type of authorization a module does. A PAM module may do just one or all four possible interfaces. Those interfaces are **account**, **auth**, **password**, and **session**. Each interface will be specified in the configuration file for a service if it's appropriate for the module and the administrator wishes to use that interface.

- **account**   The **account** interface checks to see if an account is authorized to use the system, which could mean checking to see if it exists, has expired, or is allowed access at a particular time or via a particular service.

- **auth**   The **auth** interface authenticates a user. That can be by prompting for and then checking a password, a database, or another mechanism. **auth** modules are also allowed to set credentials such as group memberships or Kerberos tickets.

- **password**   The **password** interface is for checking and setting password authentication.

- **session**   The **session** interface configures and manages a user's session. This may include housekeeping tasks like mounting directories, creating files, and so on.

## Control Flags

For each interface, the configuration file specifies a control flag, which determines what PAM does next based upon the result of the check performed. There are four control flags: **optional**, **required**, **requisite**, and **sufficient**.

- **optional**   Optional modules do not affect the success or failure of the authentication unless there are no other modules for a particular interface.

- **required**   A successful result must be returned for the user to continue. User notification doesn't happen until all modules for an interface are satisfied.

- **requisite**   A successful result must be returned for the user to continue. User notification happens immediately for failure of the first **requisite** or **required** module for an interface.

- **sufficient**   A successful result combined with no failures of **required** or **requisite** modules allow for a good authentication, assuming no other modules follow. Failure of a **sufficient** module is ignored.

### Module Path

The module path tells PAM the location of the module. It is normally a full pathname, including the module name and extension, such as /lib/security/pam_unix.so. If no path is specified, PAM defaults to /lib/security to find the module. Please note that the module path may include the variable $ISA as shipped from the vendor. This variable is an artifact of Solaris PAM originally, where 32- and 64-bit modules would both be shipped, and it would be replaced at load time with the correct architecture value. Linux may use this value in the near future with the ia64 architecture machines, so if you remove it, document its removal. It is best to fully qualify the path to each module.

### Module Arguments

If a module requires arguments, this is where they will go, such as **db=/etc/login.db**. Invalid arguments do not affect the login process and are simply logged to **syslog**.

This information is important for understanding PAM, but fortunately you don't have to remember much of it once you've got things set up.

## Backing Up the Configuration Before Making Changes

If you have a pam.conf file, back it up by copying it to a new name. It's easier to figure out who did the changes and when if you include initials and a date in the new filename.

```
cp  -pr /etc/pam.conf /etc/pam.conf.040404.pdr
```

This will back up pam.conf to a file named pam.conf.040404.pdr. Copying the file back over the original will restore the original, which is accomplished like this:

```
cp -pr /etc/pam.conf.040404.pdr /etc/pam.conf
```

The same technique works for backing up the /etc/pam.d directory:

```
cp -pr /etc/pam.d /etc/pam.d.040404.pdr
```

For restoring the directory, if you've added additional service configuration files, you can copy individual files back to the original /etc/pam.d directory, copy all the files back over (which won't overwrite any new files), or simply move the entire backup directory to restore to the original configuration. The last option would simply require the following command:

```
mv /etc/pam.d.040404.pdr /etc/pam.d
```

# Recovering from Catastrophic Errors

If you accidentally delete your configuration files, you'll find out that you can't log on to your system anymore. If you don't have backup files, don't panic, simply boot into single user mode, and follow these steps:

```
cd /etc
mv pam.conf pam.conf.backup
mv pam.d pam.d.backup
mkdir pam.d
cd pam.d
vi other
```

Then type the following lines in insert mode (by pressing the **I** key):

```
auth       required      pam_unix.so
account    required      pam_unix.so
password   required      pam_unix.so
session    required      pam_unix.so
```

Then use the ESC key to get back to command mode, type **:wq**, and press the RETURN or ENTER key.

This is the simplest PAM configuration. You can save the file **other**, then reboot the system and log on normally. At that point, you can restore your configuration from backups or reinstall the PAM collection from your distribution to regain the default configuration. It's useful to back up the original settings prior to making changes, so that restoring a working configuration is easy.

Now we'll do three things: check the framework, harden the basic services that we expect to authenticate to, and look at new PAM modules that might make our systems more secure.

# PAM Framework

First make sure that /etc/pam.conf doesn't exist unless this is an old system running an older version of PAM.

Next, make sure that /etc/pam.d exists, and contains PAM configuration files.

The first user to log in at the console of a Linux box can get ownership of many hardware devices, depending on how PAM is configured. Traditionally, Unix systems let the superuser (root) own the hardware, but to make it easy for desktop users to access devices such as sound cards, CD drives, and the like, the first console user can be set up to have ownership of these devices. Ownership reverts to root when the console user logs out. The device list is in /etc/security/console.perms, and ownership is changed by the PAM module **pam_console.so**.

The console user is also allowed to access PAM-aware applications with their names in the /etc/security/console.apps directory. Halting and rebooting the machine are typically controlled by **pam_console.so**.

Ensure that the /etc/pam.d/other and /etc/pam.d/common-* or /etc/pam.d/system-* configuration files contain acceptable values. These are the files that are referenced for any PAM application where there isn't a specific configuration file, so they're like default settings for PAM services.

Different distributions may handle this differently, the /etc/pam.d/other file is the fallback name for PAM to use if it can't find a service name specifically. It may reference /etc/pam.d/common-* or /etc/pam.d/system-* a set of files for each interface, such as /etc/pam.d/common-auth, /etc/pam.d/system-auth, etc/pam.d/system-password, and so on.

Alternately, you can strengthen your Linux system to not allow unknown programs to authenticate. This is highly recommended. Here's a sample /etc/pam.d/other file that does not allow unknown services to authenticate a user:

```
auth        required        /lib/security/pam_deny.so
auth        required        /lib/security/pam_warn.so
account     required        /lib/security/pam_deny.so
account     required        /lib/security/pam_warn.so
password    required        /lib/security/pam_deny.so
password    required        /lib/security/pam_warn.so
session     required        /lib/security/pam_deny.so
session     required        /lib/security/pam_warn.so
```

This configuration allows you to follow the "default deny" rule of security for unknown services. As with all PAM changes, you'll want to ensure that /lib/security/pam_warn.so and /lib/security/pam_deny.so exist prior to implementing this configuration.

## Traditional Services

The /bin/login program is the traditional Unix console/terminal authentication mechanism. Linux's /bin/login uses PAM.

Here's the default /etc/pam.d/login from Red Hat Enterprise Linux AS 3.0:

```
#%PAM-1.0
auth        required        pam_securetty.so
auth        required        pam_stack.so service=system-auth
auth        required        pam_nologin.so
account     required        pam_stack.so service=system-auth
password    required        pam_stack.so service=system-auth
session     required        pam_stack.so service=system-auth
session     optional        pam_console.so
```

This configuration file calls four different modules: **pam_securetty.so**, **pam_stack.so**, **pam_nologin.so**, and **pam_console.so**. The **pam_stack.so** module is called for four different interfaces: **auth**, **account**, **password**, and **session**.

The authentication stack first checks to see if the user is logging on from a device listed in /etc/securetty. Next it uses the normal password authenticator, **pam_stack**. The **service** argument tells PAM to use the /etc/pam.d/system-auth configuration file, which looks like this:

```
#%PAM-1.0
# This file is auto-generated.
# User changes will be destroyed the next time authconfig is run.
auth        required       /lib/security/$ISA/pam_env.so
auth        sufficient     /lib/security/$ISA/pam_unix.so likeauth nullok
auth        required       /lib/security/$ISA/pam_deny.so
account     required       /lib/security/$ISA/pam_unix.so
password    required       /lib/security/$ISA/pam_cracklib.so retry=3
password    sufficient     /lib/security/$ISA/pam_unix.so nullok  use_authtok md5 +
password    required       /lib/security/$ISA/pam_deny.so
session     required       /lib/security/$ISA/pam_limits.so
session     required       /lib/security/$ISA/pam_unix.so
```

For **auth**, we can see that the first thing that is required is passing through **pam_env.so**, which sets up the user's environment using variables specified in /etc/security/pam_env.conf. Typically, it's not used, but could be used to have PAM set the **DISPLAY** environment variable, for instance. There are many commented-out examples in the default file. This module is required.

Next, we have a call to **pam_unix**, the PAM password authenticator. The first argument is **likeauth**, which makes the module return the same value for credential (password) changes as for authentication, ensuring equivalent security in both cases. The next argument, **nullok**, should be removed for a hardened system, as it allows null passwords to be set for accounts. This module is marked as **sufficient** so that the next module can be tested.

This brings us to **pam_deny.so**. This module disallows access, so this line is a "default deny" line unless the **sufficient pam_unix** passes success back.

Next, we have an **account** method, which uses the **pam_unix.so** module. This module checks to see if the user has a valid account and that the account hasn't expired. This module is required because we obviously don't want people authenticating who don't have accounts on the system.

Next, we have three **password** methods. The first, **pam_cracklib.so**, checks the password against common words and disallows them as passwords. We have it set to allow three attempts to find a non-dictionary password; this method is set to **required**. After checking the word, **pam_unix** is used with this method. For hardening a system, we'll want to remove **nullok**, which would allow a blank password. We're also set up for using an authentication token (already supplied password), md5, and shadow passwords. The **use_authtok** parameter tells the module to use the already supplied password instead of prompting for it. Since the user was already prompted for a password, this is obviously good behavior, and ensures that the password has been through **pam_cracklib.so**. The **md5** parameter says that the system should have the password using

the Message Digest 5 hashing function. This function is more secure than the traditional DES-based Unix password hashing method. Finally, the **shadow** parameter tells the module to store the password hash in the /etc/shadow file, which should only be accessible to the root user ID, rather than in the traditional /etc/password file, which
is world-readable. This module is marked as **sufficient**, because it's followed by the "default deny" of **pam_deny.so**.

Next, we have the session methods **pam_limits.so** and **pam_unix.so**. The **pam_limits** module sets resource limits based upon the file /etc/security/limits.conf. By default, all the entries in /etc/security/limits.conf are commented out for most distributions, but you can control things like the size of core files, memory used, CPU used, number of processes, and maximum number of logins by user, group, or default. Finally, we see the **pam_unix** module for this method. This method updates the lastlog file with the last login time, and provides last time the user logged in, which is printed by some programs like /bin/login. It is also set up to log the start and finish of a session at the INFO level in syslog. Common distributions set this to be /var/log/messages.

Now we're back to the original file again, but since the same **pam_stack** module was used for each method, we simply have to check out what **pam_console** does. As we discussed earlier, this module generally deals with device ownership for the user logged in at the physical console.

As you can see, there's a lot of complexity and intertwining dependencies when dealing with PAM. Before you modify your configuration, you should trace through the stack of modules to ensure you understand what happens normally for that service. Backing up the files before modification is also critical. I recommend changing only one configuration file at a time, and testing that change fully prior to making new changes. Testing should include testing a valid account with no password, an invalid password, and a correct password, and testing an invalid account with any password and no password. Whenever possible, testing should be done in a controlled network environment, or with ipchains or iptables filtering protecting the service if it's a network service.

You should examine **login**, **passwd**, **sshd**, **su**, and any other PAM modules you expect to use regularly to ensure they're set up correctly. In general, the distribution defaults are fine for the default modules, other than any special purpose modules you might want to add.

Now let's look at adding some PAM modules to enhance your system's security.

# A BSD-Like wheel Group

The module **pam_wheel.so** is included by default in the PAM package. It allows you to specify which users may **su** to root. Typically, on BSD systems, only users who are in the wheel group, typically group 0, are permitted to use the **su** command to gain root privileges. This means that even if a user knows the root password, they're not permitted to use it to gain root access from their account. Obviously, enforcement of this requires that root be not allowed to directly access the system's login methods. Typically, this means not allowing root to use SSH remotely.

To enable wheel group in Linux, insert the following line to the top of your PAM configuration for **su** (/etc/pam.d/su):

```
auth    required    pam_wheel.so use_uid group=wheel
```

If you want to use the default group that's set up for root, with a group ID of 0, you don't need to use **group=wheel**. Renaming the group ID 0 group in /etc/group to wheel will make your configuration easier to understand for administrators used to BSD systems.

## Per-User Temporary Directories

On multiuser systems, flaws in file handling are often exploited as race conditions. For systems where we expect multiple users, there's a PAM module, **pam_mktemp**, which makes a private per-user temporary directory and then assigns both the **TEMP** and **TEMPDIR** environment variables to that directory. Lack of a shared /tmp directory eliminates most of the exposure to symbolic link race conditions. Adding **pam_mktemp** to the module stack for interactive logins (**ssh**, **login**, **telnetd**, and so on) will help limit race condition exploitation for root-executed and user-executed processes.

## Require Strong Passwords

Many administrators like to require strong passwords. It's a tradeoff that should be considered carefully. Weak passwords are often easy for users to remember, but may be attackable. First of all, if a service is network available, such as the SSH daemon, an attacker can try to brute force or dictionary attack that service by using a program to try known user IDs and dictionary word passwords. If the administrator isn't paying attention to failed authentication in the logs, this may gain the attacker enough time to get into the system. Also, if an attacker can get the password hashes for the system, then a dictionary attacking program for passwords can match the hashes in a very short period of time, allowing the attacker access to the system. With enough fast computers, the attacker may be able to match even a relatively strong hash in minutes. The San Diego Supercomputer Center's Teracrack paper is worth reading for both the methodology and the surprisingly difficult passwords generated by their attempts: "Teracrack: Password cracking using TeraFLOP and Petabyte Resources" is available at http://security.sdsc.edu/publications/teracrack.pdf.

Adding strong passwords that require many different types of characters, or even passphrases, will help negate dictionary attacks. However, the tradeoff is that users will likely write down the passwords in a convenient place or will regularly forget their password. Note that just adding digits or special characters to a word will not make it less dictionary attackable, as most password cracking programs do a very good job of enumerating obvious modifications.

So the password "password" is obviously easily crackable, but so are "password123" and "123password." Both "pass" and "word" are dictionary words, so "pass123word" is also easily cracked. Besides English words, most dictionaries used by attackers contain foreign words, common computer terms, and even common transformations, such as substituting the number 4 for an *a* character, or zero for an *o* character, so "p4ssw0rd" is no safer than "password." The string "I^34WxV2" is not normally considered dictionary attackable, but is difficult to remember (and may be added to a common dictionary once someone reads this).

The criteria for deciding if you want to enforce strong passwords should include what your primary purpose is for the passwords. If it's local, physical access to a system where there aren't network services available, then having the password written down is probably worse than allowing weak passwords (other than those easily guessed, such as "password," "secret," and the ID itself). That's because an attacker is more likely to be local to the system. For remote authentication where the authentication mechanism is open to a wide range of systems, like SSH open to the Internet, stronger passwords make much more sense.

## Require Strong Passwords Using the pam_passwdqc Module

In any case, besides the **pam_cracklib** PAM module, there's a strong authentication module that allows you to require very strong non-guessable passwords from your users. That module is **pam_passwdqc**. This module is used for password changing programs like **passwd**, and it allows you to enforce strong passwords, and passphrases (a series of words, rather than just one), and can generate random passwords for users. This module is included in SUSE distributions, but must be added by the administrator for older Red Hat releases. Red Hat started including **pam_passwdqc** in Red Hat Enterprise Linux AS 3.0 in an update in May 2004.

Both **pam_cracklib** and **pam_passwdqc** should not be used in the same service configuration file. Therefore, **pam_passwdqc** should replace **pam_cracklib** in a configuration file if you want to use it.

The **pam_passwfqc** module should be inserted prior to **pam_unix** or **pam_pwdb** in the **password** method of a service's authentication stack. This module defines four character classes: digits, lowercase letters, uppercase letters, and all others. Non-ASCII characters are assumed to be non-digits. The module allows the administrator to set the minimum length limits for passwords made of each type of character, and disable completely a particular class. The parameter for minimum password length is **min= N0,N1,N2,N3,N4**, which defaults to **min=disabled, 24,12,8,7**.

- **N0**   By default, this group is disabled. This group represents a password that consists of one character class, such as all lowercase letters.

- **N1**   By default, this group requires 24 characters. This group represents a password that consists of two character classes and does not meet the requirements for a passphrase.

- **N2**   By default, this group requires 12 characters. It is reserved for passphrases, which must contain a minimum number or words (see the **passphrase** option).

- **N3**   By default, this group requires 8 characters. It represents a password that consists of three character classes.

- **N4**   By default, this group requires 7 characters. It represents a password that contains four different character classes.

Note that this module does not count uppercase initial characters or trailing digits when counting the number of character classes. So Apassword99 will count only as one class, while ApaSSword99 counts as two, and A99PassworD counts as three.

The next parameter the module accepts is **max=**, which is the maximum password size. The default is **max=40**. The value **8** has a special meaning, and passwords used will be truncated to 8 characters if that value is used to ensure compatibility with older Unix programs, which can't deal with longer passwords. This should only be used if absolutely necessary.

The next parameter is **passphrase**, which defaults to **passphrase=3**. This is the minimum number of words allowed in a passphrase. A value of **0** disables passphrase support.

Next, we have **match**, which defaults to **match=4**. This is a case and direction insensitive substring-matching function that is used to determine if a substring is common. Passwords aren't rejected for having common substrings, the substring value is just removed from consideration when calculating the number of different character classes, just as leading capitals and trailing digits are.

Next, we have **similar**, which can be either **similar=permit** or **similar=deny**. The default is **deny**, which means the new password isn't allowed to be similar to the old password. Passwords are subject to the common substring test from **match**, and rejected if they're too similar. This stops users from using passwords similar to ones that may have been compromised. So, if the user's previous password was "mypass1" they wouldn't be allowed to use "mypass2" as their next password.

Next, we have **random**, which defaults to **random=42**. This is the default length for randomly generated passwords. Random passwords are allowed no matter what other restrictions are in place. A **0** value will disable this feature, and the string **,only** appended to the length will disallow user-chosen passwords.

The next setting is **enforce**. This can have a value of **none**, **users**, or **everyone**. The default is **enforce=everyone**. **none** will warn of weak passwords only, but not enforce their rejection. **users** will enforce the restrictions for all non-root users on the system. **everyone** will enforce the restrictions for all users, including root.

Next, we have the **non-unix** option. This tells the module to not use the traditional **getpwnam** function call to get the user information. It's useful for services that don't use /etc/passwd for their authentication, such as some POP3 e-mail daemons. By default, this option is not specified.

The next parameter is **retry**, and defaults to **retry=3**. This is the number of chances the user gets to enter a sufficiently strong password.

The last four parameters all default to not being specified. This is because the module expects to normally be used in conjunction with the pre-existing configuration.

The **ask_oldauthok** parameter has the module prompt for the old password during the preliminary check. If it's specified as **ask_oldauthok=update**, then the old password is asked for during the update phase.

The **check_oldauthok** parameter has the module check that the old password is valid prior to performing the update. This is usually left to other modules, but something in the module stack should do this, otherwise anyone could walk up to an already logged-in account and change the password.

The next two options are mutually exclusive: **use_first_pass** and **use_authtok**. Both of these options tell the module to use the password provided by a prior module in the stack, instead of interacting with the user. The **use_first_pass** option is incompatible with **ask_oldauthok**, otherwise they're functionally the same.

Using this module, the default options are acceptable for everything other than randomly generated passwords. Long random passwords will almost require the user to write down the password, and should only be used in situations where they're necessary.

The following line before the **pam_unix.so** password line will add **pam_passwdqc** to a service:

```
password required pam_passwdqc.so enforce=users ask_oldauthok=update check_oldauthok
```

Modern distributions have lots of interdependencies for PAM, so for example, on Red Hat, the default **system-auth** service, which is referenced by many services through the **pam_stack** module, is auto-generated when the system is installed. Let's look at an example of replacing **pam_cracklib** with **pam_passwdqc**. Here's the original /etc/pam/d/system-auth file:

```
#%PAM-1.0
# This file is auto-generated.
# User changes will be destroyed the next time authconfig is run.
auth        required      /lib/security/$ISA/pam_env.so
auth        sufficient    /lib/security/$ISA/pam_unix.so likeauth nullok
auth        required      /lib/security/$ISA/pam_deny.so
account     required      /lib/security/$ISA/pam_unix.so
password    required      /lib/security/$ISA/pam_cracklib.so retry=3
password    sufficient    /lib/security/$ISA/pam_unix.so nullok use_authtok md5 +
password    required      /lib/security/$ISA/pam_deny.so
session     required      /lib/security/$ISA/pam_limits.so
session     required      /lib/security/$ISA/pam_unix.so
```

This is the replacement:

```
#%PAM-1.0
# This file is auto-generated.
# User changes will be destroyed the next time authconfig is run.
auth          required        /lib/security/$ISA/pam_env.so
auth          sufficient      /lib/security/$ISA/pam_unix.so likeauth nullok
auth          required        /lib/security/$ISA/pam_deny.so
account       required        /lib/security/$ISA/pam_unix.so

password required pam_passwdqc.so enforce=users ask_oldauthok=update check_oldauthok +
password      sufficient      /lib/security/$ISA/pam_unix.so nullok use_authtok md5 +
password      required        /lib/security/$ISA/pam_deny.so
session       required        /lib/security/$ISA/pam_limits.so
session       required        /lib/security/$ISA/pam_unix.so
```

# Name Switching Service (NSS)

The Name Switching Service (NSS) tells your system where to look to find the mapping of names to other information, such as machine addresses, service port numbers, and so on. This is handled by the file /etc/nsswitch.conf. This file consists of lines of text. The # symbol denotes a comment and is ignored. Entries consist of an entry name followed by a colon, then a space-separated list of places to find the information. Order is important, as the resources are checked in order.

Here are some sample entries from /etc/nsswitch.conf:

```
passwd:      files
shadow:      files
group:       files
hosts:       files dns
bootparams:  nisplus [NOTFOUND=return] files

ethers:      files
netmasks:    files
networks:    files
protocols:   files
rpc:         files
services:    files

netgroup:    nisplus

publickey:   nisplus

automount:   files nisplus
aliases:     files nisplus
```

If you're not running in an NIS/NIS+ environment, then the references to NIS should be removed. Probably the most commonly referenced entry is the **hosts** line. Our example line tells the system to look in files, then use the domain name service. So the system's resolver will first look in /etc/hosts, then use the name server listed in /etc/resolv.conf to find a host. Since we're not in an NIS+ environment, we wouldn't want the system to use a network information server to resolve hostnames (any NIS server on our network would be a hostile machine!). Files come before DNS because we want the ability to "force" a hostname to a particular IP address in /etc/hosts for several reasons. We can then "blackhole" a malicious machine by setting its address to loopback, make and test changes on a per-system basis, and override a DNS response if the DNS has been cache poisoned, compromised, or if the server is down. This requires keeping /etc/hosts up to date. If we switch the order, we can have DNS answers go first, then the /etc/hosts file, which would give us a fallback if DNS was down, but not protect from the other issues raised.

You can simply delete the word **nisplus** from every single entry where it's found to batten down the system. Removing NIS from the equation not only makes it more difficult for an attacker to redirect such services, but also removes a lot of potentially buggy library code from the execution path of the system.

If you are in an NIS/NIS+ environment, then you should decide which resources you want to get from the NIS server, and remove the dependencies from the other entries.

# Chapter 9

# Restricted Execution Environments

- Restrict Functionality
- Use chroot to Protect a Service
- Build the chroot Directory Structure
- Install the Service(s) to the chroot Directory
- Configure the Service to Log Activity
- Troubleshoot chroot Environment Problems
- Combine chroot and Your Distribution's Security Capabilities
- Maintain chroot

A strong network and system security policy implements redundant and complementary countermeasures to the threats faced by computers deployed on a network. Whether you want to consider an onion, a castle, or a domino theory as an appropriate metaphor for this strategy, the approach is a solid one that can reduce the scope of a compromise, help maintain service uptime, and enable administrators to take on a proactive security role rather than a continuous reaction to bug reports and security updates. This chapter details the steps necessary to create a restricted execution environment with the Linux **chroot** command. Other types of restricted environments are User Mode Linux and the BSD family's **jail** command. **chroot** is present by default on most Linux distributions, therefore we will focus on that command.

# Restrict Functionality

One of the ideal ways to improve the security for a network service is to provide as little extraneous functionality to the service as possible. The definition of what is extraneous will vary. In the following example, a web server is used. Customers may need access to an e-commerce web server or employees may need access to an internal HR web application. In each case, the service itself (a web server) has a specific collection of data and scripts necessary to support its users. The service does not need access to a C++ compiler, text editor, web browser, or dozens of the dynamic libraries installed on the host operating system. A service has a level of risk associated with its current patch level and configuration. While the presence of additional tools, programs, and libraries does not affect the web server's initial risk of compromise, their presence does contribute to the level of impact should a compromise occur. Without a strong host configuration and restrictive policies, a single attack can fully compromise the host or even place other hosts on the network in danger.

A major threat to network services is the buffer overflow exploit. A successful buffer overflow typically gives the attacker root access to the entire host. Since it is impossible to protect a service from a zero-day exploit for which no patch exists, the administrator must be able to design a configuration in which a successful buffer overflow–based attack dumps the attacker into a non-root, limited privilege environment. Otherwise, the attacker will have immediate access to sensitive information (passwords, e-mail, databases, file shares) or additional attack vectors, such as turning user nobody access into root access via a local buffer overflow exploit. If you remove the password file and delete the vulnerable library used to gain root, the web server will still run normally, but the attacker will have to spend a lot more time trying to escalate privilege.

The restricted environment may or may not make your web server more resistant to a buffer overflow or other attack, but if the system is compromised, your hardening work can reduce the amount of time you need to spend containing, analyzing, and cleaning an attack. For example, if you have removed the password file, you will not have to spend time changing passwords for all servers on a network or instructing users to change their passwords. You may not have to rebuild the host from scratch.

Any work that has to be done has a direct effect on the time—and money—that goes into managing your network.

# Use chroot to Protect a Service

**chroot** is available as a shell command as well as a system call for binary applications. We will focus on using the **chroot** command (**man 1 chroot**) since programming with **chroot** (**man 2 chroot**) introduces a different set of considerations. Also, our goal is to improve the security of an established service, not reinvent the wheel!

---

**NOTE**  The **chroot** command is native to most Linux distributions. It is currently part of the GNU coreutils package, http://www.gnu.org/software/coreutils/, although you may find references to its previous package, shellutils. **chroot** ("change root") enables the administrator to execute a shell in a specially restricted root directory.

---

## Understand What Is Protected...and What Isn't

Processes running inside a **chroot** environment are intended to be run with non-root privileges. Even though common services such as web, DNS, and SSH can be configured to run with non-root privileges, the process still has access to the entire file system. All of these services have also suffered from buffer overflow exploits. If the exploit provides shell access in the context of the process's owner (a non-root account), then you can strictly limit the scope of a compromise. Instead of allowing a buffer overflow to dump a root shell from a root-owned process, send the attacker into a non-root shell. Then isolate the service and its directory structure with chroot so that it doesn't even contain an /etc/shadow file. This way you expose less of the operating system while preserving the full functionality of the service.

**chroot** environments can also be placed on alternate partitions and closely monitored. Administrators have many areas to watch for potential security problems. By narrowing the focus to a specific portion of the operating system and its file system, the administrator's job becomes a little easier.

The **chroot** command shares a common attribute among security-related tools and techniques. If regarded as a panacea against attackers or relied upon as the sole defense, it is sure to cause the administrator headaches when a compromise occurs. A root process can escape a **chroot** environment, but this fact shouldn't lead you to unilaterally dismiss the command.

Remember that **chroot** environments only restrict access to the file system. This is an important distinction from restricting access to a process. One of prerequisites to running a service with **chroot** is that it is not a root-owned process. **chroot** tells the process only what it can access, not what types of processes it can spawn or—if it is root—how to escape the chroot directory. A detailed description of breaking **chroot** can be found at http://www.bpfh.net/simes/computing/chroot-break.html. A more detailed perspective can be found in *The Shellcoder's Handbook* (John Wiley & Sons), which has a two-line method of breaking **chroot** by a root process.

Yet just because **chroot** is not impenetrable does not mean it should be dismissed. This falls into a policy decision and careful consideration of the gains brought by implementing **chroot** versus the potential attacks that can still occur.

Automated hacks such as Internet worms will always be significantly impeded by **chroot** environments. These types of attacks rely on default configurations, known file locations, and the presence of specific files. A **chroot** environment will very often lack many of the resources exploited by the more dangerous aspects of a worm. Thus, even if a buffer overflow compromises an Apache, DNS, or SSH daemon, the worm's secondary attacks may be stopped. It is unlikely that the automated attack will include steps to identify and break out of a **chroot** environment.

Attacks that are manually executed pose more risk. If the service can be initially compromised (either by a buffer overflow or stolen user credentials), then the attacker will be limited to the **chroot** environment only until there is a desire to try and break out of the **chroot**. In some cases, the attacker may not be aware of **chroot** (thoroughly possible in the land of script kiddies) and leave the system because it does not offer any enticing items. More capable attackers may attempt to break the **chroot**, but the time spent on the machine in order to identify **chroot** and attack the system increases the chances that network or system monitoring will alert administrators to the attack.

# Build the chroot Directory Structure

The basic establishment of a **chroot** environment is simple. Create a directory that will server as the new root (in other words, the new / directory). Then assign ownership of that directory to a non-root user and group. Before we explain how to fully deploy a service within a **chroot** environment, let's take a look at how it works.

The following steps set up a simple chroot base directory and assign its ownership to min (our "minimum" access user).

```
# mkdir /opt/chroot
# ls -l /opt/chroot/
total 0
```

Now, compare the output of the **ls** command when run from the user's shell with the output of the **ls** command executed within a shell in the **chroot** environment.

First, use **ls** from the user shell:

```
# ls -l /
total 52
drwxr-xr-x   2 root     root         4096 Dec  5 10:22 bin/
```

```
drwxr-xr-x    3 root      root          4096 Apr 21 16:40 boot/
drwxr-xr-x    1 root      root             0 Dec 31  1969 dev/
drwxr-xr-x   67 root      root          4096 Apr 22 10:11 etc/
drwxr-xr-x    4 root      root          4096 Apr 22 10:11 home/
drwxr-xr-x    2 root      root          4096 Jun 21  2001 initrd/
drwxr-xr-x   10 root      root          4096 Dec  5 10:22 lib/
drwxr-xr-x    5 root      root          4096 May 23  2000 mnt/
drwxr-xr-x    3 root      root          4096 Apr 22 09:59 opt/
dr-xr-xr-x   92 root      root             0 Apr 21 12:39 proc/
drwx------   14 root      root          4096 Apr 22 10:17 root/
drwxr-xr-x    2 root      root          4096 Dec  5 10:23 sbin/
drwxrwxrwt    7 root      root          4096 Apr 22 10:01 tmp/
drwxr-xr-x   12 root      root          4096 Nov 17 10:54 usr/
drwxr-xr-x   21 root      root          4096 Aug 29  2003 var/
```

We need to copy some system libraries in order to make the **ls** command work correctly in /opt/chroot:

```
# chroot /opt/chroot/ /bin/ls -lR /
total 8
drwxr-xr-x    2 0         0             4096 Apr 22 14:35 bin
drwxr-xr-x    2 0         0             4096 Apr 22 14:35 lib

/bin:
total 80
-rwxr-xr-x    1 0         0            76620 Apr 22 14:24 ls

/lib:
total 1312
-rwxr-xr-x    1 0         0            80296 Apr 22 14:34 ld-linux.so.2
-rwxr-xr-x    1 0         0          1237568 Apr 22 14:29 libc.so.6
-rwxr-xr-x    1 0         0            12112 Apr 22 14:28 libtermcap.so.2
```

In this example, we executed **/bin/ls -lR /** to generate a recursive list of all subdirectories of the root (/). The root, of course, is really /opt/chroot, so we need to have a copy of **ls** and any libraries on which it relies. If we had omitted these libraries and assumed that **ls** would execute, the result of the **chroot** command would have been a less-than-helpful error:

```
# chroot /opt/chroot/ ls -l
chroot: ls: No such file or directory
```

The error does not mean that there is no such file as **ls**. The error actually means that **ls** could not find a dynamic library that it needed in order to execute. Unfortunately,

**chroot** does not have the ability to perform a robust error analysis. If you see an error like "No such file or directory," you may have an incomplete directory structure.

The deceptively simple command line usage of **chroot** actually requires some behind-the-scenes preparation in order for commands to execute smoothly. In the subsequent sections we'll cover some tricks for preparing the new environment and setting up common services with **chroot**.

## Resolve Dynamic Library Dependencies

Usually, the biggest challenge when establishing a **chroot** environment is determining the libraries required by a binary. This was highlighted in the previous section when we had to copy three system libraries in order for the **ls** command to work. The natural follow-up question is, "How does one figure out which libraries a binary uses?" There are a few system utilities that help an administrator identify the libraries and system calls made by a program. One of the simplest is **strace**.

The **strace** command has many capabilities, most of which aid users trying to debug a binary or kernel. We need only be concerned with the basic use of **strace**, which traces the system calls and signals used by a command. Let's return to our /opt/chroot example where we tried to execute **/bin/ls**. Watch what happens when we use **strace** to list the system calls used by the command:

---

**NOTE** **strace** is not installed by default for most desktop and server installation profiles. It is likely that you will need to install the **strace** RPM before continuing this section. **strace** is a standard package in the Development Tools category for Red Hat.

---

```
# strace /bin/ls
execve("/bin/ls", ["/bin/ls"], [/* 45 vars */]) = 0
uname({sys="Linux", node="worm", ...})   = 0
brk(0)                                    = 0x805ba2c
old_mmap(NULL, 4096, PROT_READ|PROT_WRITE, MAP_PRIVATE|MAP_ANONYMOUS,
        -1, 0) = 0x40014000
open("/etc/ld.so.preload", O_RDONLY)     = -1 ENOENT (No such file
        or directory)
open("/etc/ld.so.cache", O_RDONLY)       = 3
fstat64(3, {st_mode=S_IFREG|0644, st_size=39641, ...}) = 0
old_mmap(NULL, 39641, PROT_READ, MAP_PRIVATE, 3, 0) = 0x40015000
close(3)                                  = 0
open("/lib/libtermcap.so.2", O_RDONLY)   = 3
```

The first line, with **execve**, represents the command and any of its arguments. **strace** produces a lot of output. The easiest way to capture these data is to use the **-o** option to save the information to a file:

```
strace -o info.txt /bin/ls
```

We're looking for **open** calls because those are used to access libraries (among other things). In the previous example, the output was truncated at the first reference to a library, /lib/libtermcap.so.2. Thus, we have our first system library that must be copied from its current location to the new one:

```
# cd /opt/chroot
# mkdir lib
# cp -p /lib/libtermcap.so.2 /opt/chroot/lib/libtermcap.so.2
```

---

**TIP**  Use the **-p** option for the **cp** command to preserve the file's attributes, including mode, ownership, timestamps, and links

---

Those of you familiar with Unix know there's always more than one way to do something. You can use the **-e** option with **strace** to only print **open** calls. For example, here is the complete output of **strace** used with **ls**:

```
# cd /opt
# strace -eopens /bin/ls
open("/etc/ld.so.preload", O_RDONLY)    = -1 ENOENT (No such file or
    directory)
open("/etc/ld.so.cache", O_RDONLY)      = 3
open("/lib/libtermcap.so.2", O_RDONLY)  = 3
open("/lib/i686/libc.so.6", O_RDONLY)   = 3
open("/usr/share/locale/locale-archive", O_RDONLY|O_LARGEFILE) = -1
    ENOENT No such file or directory)
open("/usr/share/locale/locale.alias", O_RDONLY) = 3
open("/usr/share/locale/en_US/LC_IDENTIFICATION", O_RDONLY) = 3
open("/usr/share/locale/en_US/LC_MEASUREMENT", O_RDONLY) = 3
open("/usr/share/locale/en_US/LC_TELEPHONE", O_RDONLY) = 3
open("/usr/share/locale/en_US/LC_ADDRESS", O_RDONLY) = 3
open("/usr/share/locale/en_US/LC_NAME", O_RDONLY) = 3
open("/usr/share/locale/en_US/LC_PAPER", O_RDONLY) = 3
open("/usr/share/locale/en_US/LC_MESSAGES", O_RDONLY) = 3
open("/usr/share/locale/en_US/LC_MESSAGES/SYS_LC_MESSAGES", O_RDONLY)
    = 3
open("/usr/share/locale/en_US/LC_MONETARY", O_RDONLY) = 3
open("/usr/share/locale/en_US/LC_COLLATE", O_RDONLY) = 3
open("/usr/share/locale/en_US/LC_TIME", O_RDONLY) = 3
open("/usr/share/locale/en_US/LC_NUMERIC", O_RDONLY) = 3
open("/usr/share/locale/en_US/LC_CTYPE", O_RDONLY) = 3
open(".", O_RDONLY|O_NONBLOCK|O_LARGEFILE|O_DIRECTORY) = 3
chroot/
```

In the preceding example, the **-eopen** option instructs **strace** to only print **open** calls. The final line with the **chroot/** entry is the output of the **ls** command.

Finally, copy the /lib/ld-linux.so.2 library into the chroot directory. Binaries use this file to determine its library dependencies. It is the dynamic loader used by all programs, even though you may have noticed that there was no reference to the ld-linux.so.2 library in any of the **open** calls. It is required in the **chroot** environment if any dynamic libraries are present. Since binaries use ld-linux.so.2 to find their own dependencies, you can simply execute this file with the **--list** option to manually list all library dependencies of a command. This produces a clearer and complete list of libraries to be copied.

```
# ./ld-linux.so.2 --list /bin/ls
        libtermcap.so.2 => /lib/libtermcap.so.2 (0x4000b000)
        libc.so.6 => /lib/i686/libc.so.6 (0x4000f000)
        /lib/ld-linux.so.2 => ./ld-linux.so.2 (0x80000000)
```

Another system tool, **ldd**, performs the same function.

```
# ldd /bin/ls
        libtermcap.so.2 => /lib/libtermcap.so.2 (0x4001f000)
        libc.so.6 => /lib/i686/libc.so.6 (0x40023000)
        /lib/ld-linux.so.2 => /lib/ld-linux.so.2 (0x40000000)
```

On Red Hat Enterprise Linux AS 3.0, the list of dynamic libraries for **/bin/ls** is longer:

```
# ldd /bin/ls
        libacl.so.1 => /lib/libacl.so.1 (0xb75d9000)
        libtermcap.so.2 => /lib/libtermcap.so.2 (0xb75d5000)
        libc.so.6 => /lib/tls/libc.so.6 (0xb749e000)
        libattr.so.1 => /lib/libattr.so.1 (0xb749b000)
        /lib/ld-linux.so.2 => /lib/ld-linux.so.2 (0xb75eb000)
```

Both **libacl** and **libattr** provide interfaces to extended file permission settings.

## Determine File Dependencies

At this point, you may be wondering why we introduced the more complicated **strace** at all. Well, more complex programs have file dependencies other than dynamic libraries. The most common examples are configuration files that reside in the /etc/ directory, such as passwd, group, hosts, and nsswitch.

Without getting too far ahead of ourselves, let's take a look at Apache on Red Hat Enterprise Linux AS 3.0:

```
$ cp /usr/sbin/httpd .
$ strace -f -o info.txt ./httpd -k start
$ less info.txt
21154 execve("./httpd", ["./httpd", "-k", "start"], [/* 46 vars */])=0
21154 uname({sys="Linux", node="GeidiPrime", ...}) = 0
21154 brk(0)                                = 0x80a8dd4
21154 old_mmap(NULL, 4096, PROT_READ|PROT_WRITE, MAP_PRIVATE|
      MAP_ANONYMOUS, -1, 0) = 0x40014000
21154 open("/etc/ld.so.preload", O_RDONLY) = -1 ENOENT (No such
      file or directory)
21154 open("/etc/ld.so.cache", O_RDONLY) = 3
21154 fstat64(3, {st_mode=S_IFREG|0644, st_size=49684, ...}) = 0
21154 old_mmap(NULL, 49684, PROT_READ, MAP_PRIVATE, 3, 0)=0x40015000
21154 close(3)                              = 0
21154 open("/lib/i686/libm.so.6", O_RDONLY) = 3
21154 read(3, "\177ELF\1\1\1\0\0\0\0\0\0\0\0\0\3\0\3\0\1\0\0\0\0005
      \0"..., 512) = 512
```

After you've tracked down library dependencies, the next major file group relates to the /etc/directory. Again, take a look at some selected lines from the **strace** output of Apache:

```
$ grep "open(" info.txt | less
21154 open("/etc/group", O_RDONLY)      = 4
21154 open("/etc/host.conf", O_RDONLY)  = 3
21154 open("/etc/hosts", O_RDONLY)      = 3
21154 open("/etc/ld.so.cache", O_RDONLY) = 3
21154 open("/etc/nsswitch.conf", O_RDONLY) = 4
21154 open("/etc/passwd", O_RDONLY)     = 4
21154 open("/etc/resolv.conf", O_RDONLY) = 3
```

These files are referenced during the startup process. Consequently, it will be necessary to recreate the files or at least their relevant content in the **chroot** environment. Notice that the /etc/group and /etc/passwd files are accessed by Apache. These files contain the user and group information (UID, GID) defined by the User and Group directives in the httpd .conf file. Apache starts with root privileges, but drops to these lower privileges once the daemon binds to a listening TCP port. The account's password is not necessary, which we confirm by noticing that no calls are made to the /etc/shadow file. We'll address Apache in more detail later in this chapter. For now, it is just important to understand the benefit of **strace**.

## Create Devices in the chroot Directory

If an application requires an interface to the device file system, you must create the device in the chroot directory. Unlike adding dynamic libraries and file dependencies, devices cannot be copied with the **cp** command. Devices are often necessary when dealing with hardware (USB devices, CD-ROM drives, floppy drives, the hard drive) and remote access (console devices). If you know that any of these will be accessed by the service, you must create the /dev file system. If you are unsure, you can still create the /dev file system without introducing a security risk to the **chroot** environment.

First, create the /opt/chroot/dev directory. For Red Hat Enterprise Linux AS 3.0, use your system's **/dev/MAKEDEV** script to populate the new directory defined with the **-d** option:

```
# mkdir /opt/chroot/dev
# /dev/MAKEDEV -d /opt/chroot/dev/ generic
```

---

**NOTE**   The Red Hat **MAKEDEV** script interprets the **-d** argument as a target directory. SUSE interprets **-d** as an instruction to delete a device. Double-check the man page for **MAKEDEV** before you execute this command.

---

For SUSE, change to the target dev directory and omit the **-d** option.

```
# mkdir /opt/chroot/dev
# cd /opt/chroot/dev
# /sbin/MAKEDEV generic
```

The **generic** argument instructs **MAKEDEV** to create a generic, default set of devices. Red Hat defines the devices for **generic** in the /etc/makedev.d/generic file. There are several other options available in this same directory. SUSE does not have this directory, but provides **generic**, **std**, and **local** device creation options.

```
# ls /etc/makedev.d/
00macros   cciss    console   ftape           ia64   ida      ipfilter   linux1394
mouse      raid     sound     undocumented    v4l    ataraid  cdrom
dac960     generic  ibcs      ide             isdn   linux-2.4.x         qic
redhat     std      usb
```

The **generic** choice will probably create many devices unnecessary to the application. Simply create a new file in the /etc/makedev.d/ directory. For example, these are generic devices:

```
# cat /etc/makedev.d/generic
# Support for the older "generic" devices.
a generic std
```

```
a generic fd
a generic had
a generic hdb
a generic hdc
a generic hdd
a generic tty
a generic ptyp
a generic mouse
a generic lp
a generic parport
a generic sound
```

Any application that requires pseudo-terminals needs a special device. Such applications typically provide console access to the server. The /dev/pts device is created like this:

```
# mkdir -p /opt/chroot/dev/pts
# mount -t devpts devpts /opt/chroot/dev/pts
```

The man page for **MAKEDEV** provides detailed information for specific types of devices and alternate command line options.

## Establish Shells and User Environments

This step is often unnecessary for most services that do not provide an interactive shell.

A **chroot** environment works best as a combination of a restricted file system and a service running with non-root privileges. When you execute **chroot** with root privileges, you want to be sure that the daemon assigned to the **chroot** executes with some other account ID. Apache is a good example of a service that is executed as root, but switches to a low-privilege account once the server is bound to a port. The account must be defined in the **chroot** environment when the service does this type of "privilege dropping" action.

When a service only switches from root to another account, you just need to provide an /etc/passwd and /etc/group entry for the service. No shadow file is necessary. The steps necessary for this are simple; just copy the relevant lines from each file into their **chroot** equivalent:

```
# touch /opt/chroot/etc/passwd
# grep apache /etc/passwd
apache:x:48:48:Apache:/var/www:/sbin/nologin
# grep apache /etc/passwd >> /opt/chroot/etc/passwd
```

Red Hat Enterprise Linux AS 3.0 provides configuration options for setting up **chroot** environments for users who authenticate via SSH. Check out the pam_chroot section later in this chapter.

## Use BusyBox to Manage Shells and Command Line Tools

An alternative to copying a large number of shells, system tools, and dynamic libraries is to use the BusyBox (http://www.busybox.net/) suite of utilities. This is a collection of GNU utilities (coreutils, fileutils, and others) that have been placed into a monolithic package. Still, BusyBox enables you to compile only a particular subset of tools or tool options, which lets you create a customized toolset and maintain a minimal environment. This is the quickest way to add command line utilities to a **chroot** environment that is intended for a service that will provide users with remote shell access.

Once you've downloaded BusyBox, **untar** the file and set your desired configuration options. Use the **make menuconfig** command to access a curses-based configuration menu. If you've ever compiled a custom Linux kernel, then you'll be at home with this menu system. Figure 9-1 shows the top-level menu.

You should build the static library version, so make sure to install the **glibc-static-devel** RPM for your system. Otherwise, you'll receive the error "Cannot find -lc." The **static** option is under the Build Options menu. Also, set the **chroot** target in the Installation Options menu and check the option for "Don't use /usr." Figure 9-2 shows this menu.

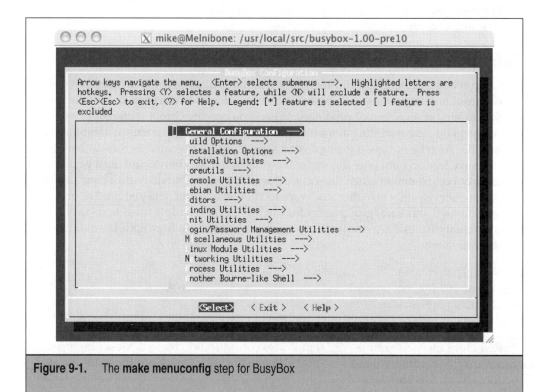

**Figure 9-1.**    The **make menuconfig** step for BusyBox

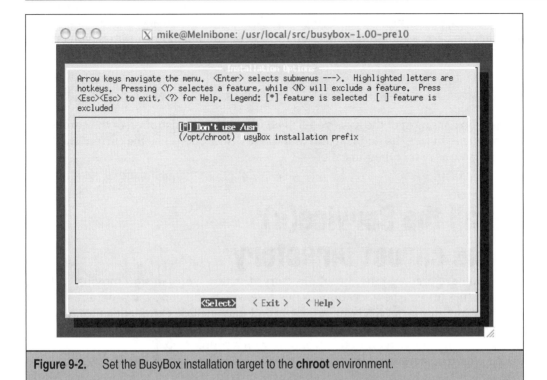

**Figure 9-2.**   Set the BusyBox installation target to the **chroot** environment.

The steps to install and use BusyBox are easy. Start with a fresh /opt/chroot directory in which nothing has been copied or installed:

```
# mkdir /opt/chroot
# cd /usr/local/src/busybox-src
# make menuconfig
# make dep
# make
# make install
```

Now, give the **ls** command a try in the new **chroot** environment:

```
# chroot /opt/chroot /bin/ls
bin      linuxrc   sbin
```

It works! The tools have been compiled statically, so you don't even need to worry about finding dynamic libraries. There's another advantage. Take a look at how the **ls** command is created:

```
# ls -l /opt/chroot/bin/ls
lrwxrwxrwx  1 root root 7 Apr 22 13:45 /opt/chroot/bin/ls -> busybox*
```

Each BusyBox command is actually a soft-link to a single binary. Instead of trying to match file permissions and ownership for several command line utilities, you only need to modify and monitor the **busybox** binary:

```
# ls -l /opt/chroot/bin/busybox
-rwxr-xr-x  1 root root 784888 Apr 22 13:45 /opt/chroot/bin/busybox*
```

BusyBox has most of the tools you'll need for daily administration of the **chroot** environment. In fact, the Red Hat and Mandrake distributions use the current stable branch (0.60) as part of their installer.

# Install the Service(s) to the chroot Directory

Once you have prepared the chroot directory structure, you can start moving each service's files into the new location. In this case, you could copy the program's root directory, but this is not likely to be simple and may include extraneous files, which goes against one of the reasons for creating a restricted environment. The easiest method is probably to rebuild the program from a source tarball.

An administrator may want to use RPM packages for services to be deployed because there are certain advantages to using packages instead of compiling from source. RPMs are provided by the Linux distribution, which implies that they have been patched and tested for the specific OS. They are easy to install, upgrade, and remove, which saves time when maintaining large numbers of hosts. Also, RPMs have specific configurations and build settings. This final point straddles the line between benefits and drawbacks. On the one hand, the administrator can be sure that new services installed by an RPM will be identical (including any policy for post-installation steps). On the other hand, many RPMs are designed to be as useful as possible "out of the box" and may contain configurations or components that administrators would rather remove. Source RPMs provide the best combination of configurability and maintainability. Binary RPMs can be used in **chroot** environments, but they often pose significant hurdles to creating a working service.

## Install from Source

Most Linux source code employs the **autoconf** utility for configuring the program's settings. The typical install procedure for these types of programs is

```
./configure make, make install

./configure
make
make install
```

This installs the program into a default location, which is most often /usr/local. To compile a program for a **chroot** environment, all you need to do is change the **--prefix** option to **configure**. For example, this is how to install Apache 2.0 to /opt/chroot/apache2 instead of the default /usr/local/apache2:

```
# cd /usr/local/src/httpd-2.0.49
# ./configure --prefix /opt/chroot/apache2
# make
# ldd ./httpd
not a dynamic executable
```

Installing the service from source provides the most benefits for creating a customized binary with a specific configuration. Common configuration steps include removing unnecessary functionality and building statically linked versions of the binary. For example, if a binary has IPv6 support that you don't need, remove that support when you build the program. It isn't necessary to the core function of the program even though there might not be any known security risk to including it. By building a static version of the program, you reduce the number of dynamic libraries that must be copied into the chroot directory structure. This reduces the amount of administration overhead and stays in line with the **chroot** philosophy of creating a minimal environment.

Most software provides a detailed list of configuration options if you type

```
./configure --help
```

This will help you determine if you can build static or shared versions, disable unnecessary options, and other build steps.

## Install from a Source RPM

If establishing an install order and fighting not-uncommon-enough circular dependencies is too difficult, then considering rolling your own RPM. This combines the ease of package management with the customization afforded by building from source code. Additionally, you can create an RPM that can be installed into a chroot directory, but is recorded in the host system's RPM database. To do this properly requires careful editing of the source RPM's spec file. This can turn into a daunting task; but the reward for creating an RPM ready for deployment into a **chroot** environment surpasses the pain.

First, take a look at the spec file snippet in Figure 9-3. This file has already been modified to build a binary RPM that installs *every related file* into a **chroot** environment. In the case of OpenSSH, this not only includes the **sshd** daemon, but configuration information typically stored in the /etc/ directory such as host keys and startup scripts.

The RPM's attributes can be verified with the **-qip** options:

```
# rpm -qip openssh-chroot-3.6.1p2-8mdk.i586.rpm
Name       : openssh-chroot          Relocations: /opt/chroot
Version    : 3.6.1p2                 Vendor: (none)
```

```
Release        : 8mdk                    Build Date: Fri 23 Apr 2004
                                          1:11:57 AM EDT
Install Date: (not installed)            Build Host: Melnibone
Group          : Networking/Remote access Source RPM: openssh-chroot-
                                          3.6.1p2-8mdk.src.rpm
Size           : 356180                   License: BSD
Signature      : (none)
URL            : http://www.openssh.com/
Summary        : OpenSSH free Secure Shell (SSH) implementation
Description :
Modified the original spec file with a customized build that
deploys to /opt/chroot.
```

To get to this point we needed to modify three components of the spec file: tags, macros, and instructions. Tags provide summary information about the package. The most important tag for **chroot**-related packages is the Prefix value. Macros define file paths, compile options, and package options. The instructions control the flow of building the source RPM and creating the final binary package.

The specific steps to modify a source RPM vary among packages, but mostly relate to where the final files are installed and what supporting files must be included. The most important aspect of the RPM is that the Relocations tag must report a directory. It doesn't matter if the directory is /opt/chroot and we want to install to /var/chroot. All that matters is that the RPM is relocatable. Once that is set, it is trivial to install to an alternate location.

**Figure 9-3.** Example spec file

| spec Tag | Notes |
|----------|-------|
| Name | The name of the RPM. Append a value such as **-chroot** to create a unique name. |
| Version | Version information. |
| Release | Release information. |
| Prefix | This is rarely present in a source RPM, but it is the most important tag when building a package for a **chroot** environment. This tag enables a package to be relocatable with the command<br><br>`rpm --relocate /old/path=/new/path` |
| Source[n] | Source file archive(s). |
| Patch[n] | Patch file(s). Patch files are important because they either apply architecture-specific fixes for the package or apply security fixes. |

**Table 9-1.** Important spec Tags

Table 9-1 lists the most relevant tags of the spec file. Tag values are assigned on the same line as the tag. The value can be a string or a macro. This example uses a string for Summary and a macro for Name.

```
Summary:        OpenSSH free Secure Shell (SSH) implementation
Name:           %{name}
```

If a spec tag's value is set by a macro, the macro can either be defined by the environment or within the file. Macros are set in the spec file with the **%define** instruction. For example, the previous Name tag's value is defined this way:

```
%define name    openssh-chroot
Name:           %{name}
```

Table 9-2 lists most of the important macros used to build and modify a binary RPM. This list is not complete, but you should know at least these macros if you want to modify an existing source RPM. Table 9-3 lists spec file instructions.

The complete list of macros can be found in the /usr/lib/rpm/macros file. Use the ~/.rpmmacros file to set macro values specific to your user account. These will be used during the **rpmbuild** process and applied to any packages you create from a spec file.

## Example spec File: openssh

Here is an example of how to modify a spec file so that it can be installed with the relocatable option. OpenSSH is a good example because it relies on system files (/etc /passwd, /etc/shadow) that must also be considered when changing **%build**, **%install**,

| spec Macro | Notes |
|---|---|
| %{_prefix} | Default: /usr |
| %{_exec_prefix} | Default: %{_prefix} |
| %{_lib} | Default: lib |
| %{_libdir} | Default: %{_exec_prefix}/%{_lib} |
| %{_libexecdir} | Default: %{_exec_prefix}/libexec |
| %_unpackaged_files_ terminate_build | Default: 1<br>Set this value to 0 if the final RPM will not include some of the files created during the staging install process. For example, you may want to exclude all of the man pages or documentation.<br>Otherwise, **rpmbuild** generates an error like "Warning: Installed (but unpackaged) file(s) found" and terminates the build even though everything has compiled correctly. |

**Table 9-2.**    Important spec File Macro Definitions

| spec Instruction | Notes |
|---|---|
| %define | Define a macro and its value. Reference the value with this format:<br><br>`%{macro_name}`<br>`%define foo bar`<br>`Name: %{foo}` |
| %prep | The steps to prepare the source for configuration. |
| %build | The command line to configure and compile the source code. |
| %description | Default: <text><br>This entry is required. At the very least, provide information specific to the **chroot** environment. |
| %doc | Remove. |
| %files | This is important! These files are placed in the package. Include each file required by the program. You can add other files, such as /etc/passwd or /etc/group to ensure that every dependency is met.<br>Another useful trick is to remove the documentation and man files. Such files do not need to be included in a deployed environment. |
| %changelog | Describe the modifications made. |

**Table 9-3.**    Important spec File Instructions

and **%files** steps. The **%{chroot}** macro was prepended to several options to the **configure** command.

```
%build
%serverbuild
CFLAGS="$RPM_OPT_FLAGS" ./configure \
  --prefix=%{chroot}%{_prefix} \
  --sysconfdir=%{chroot}%{_sysconfdir}/ssh \
  --mandir=%{chroot}%{_mandir} \
  --libdir=%{chroot}%{_libdir} \
  --libexecdir=%{chroot}%{_libdir}/ssh \
  --datadir=%{chroot}%{_datadir}/ssh \
  --disable-largefile \
  --with-pam \
  --with-default-path=/bin:/usr/bin \
  --with-privsep-path=/var/empty \
  --with-superuser-path=/sbin:/bin:/usr/sbin:/usr/bin \
  --with-md5-passwords \
  --without-4in6 \
  --without-sectok \
  --without-skey \
  --without-tcp-wrappers
make
```

It is very important to notice that the installation files are all prefixed with the **%{chroot}** macro. If this were not the case, files would be installed to directories without a common root (other than /). There are three configuration directives that do not have the **%{chroot}** prefix:

```
--with-default-path
```

```
--with-privsep
--with-superuser-path
```

Each of these configuration options are specific to OpenSSH and affect how the installed binary operates. Consequently, each of these paths is relative to the **chroot** base path. For example, **--with-default-path** defines the default file path given to users when they authenticate. When the **sshd** daemon is running inside the **chroot** environment, /opt/chroot/bin and /opt/chroot/usr/bin appear to the daemon as /bin and /usr /bin. It would be incorrect to give the daemon /opt/chroot/bin as a default path because that would really imply /opt/chroot/opt/chroot/bin to the daemon.

A customized spec file that creates a relocatable RPM means that you can install and manage the RPM normally, without supplying additional command line options or creating a secondary RPM database in the chroot directory. Use the **--relocate** option to install a **chroot**-capable RPM into an alternate directory:

```
# rpm --relocate /old/path=/new/path ...
```

The /old/path value cannot be the root (/) and will be the new prefix for all files installed by the package. This is why it is necessary to massage the spec file to support relocation.

## Install a Binary RPM to an Alternate Location

The **rpm** command provides a command line switch to set an alternate root directory into which the package will be installed. By default, the root directory is /, as one expects. If you want to install into the **chroot** environment, /opt/chroot, you'll have to prep the environment before installing any packages. Otherwise, you'll receive an error similar to the following:

```
# rpm --install --root /opt/chroot openssh-3.6.1p2-8mdk.i586.rpm
error: cannot open lock file /opt/chroot/var/lib/rpm/RPMLOCK in
       shared mode
error: cannot open Packages database in /opt/chroot/var/lib/rpm
```

It is easy to establish the new RPM root and database structure in the **chroot** environment:

```
# mkdir -p /opt/chroot/var/lib/rpm
# rpm --initdb --root /opt/chroot
# ls -l /opt/chroot/var/lib/rpm/
total 8
-rw-r--r--    1 root     root        12288 Apr 22 14:23 Packages
-rw-r--r--    1 root     root            0 Apr 22 14:23 RPMLOCK
```

You're not out of the woods yet, because library dependencies will need to be met for each of the packages to be installed. Luckily, RPM errors are friendly enough to tell you what's missing:

```
# rpm --install --root /opt/chroot openssh-3.6.1p2-8mdk.i586.rpm
warning: /mnt/iso/Mandrake/RPMS/openssh-3.6.1p2-8mdk.i586.rpm:
        V3 DSA signature: NOKEY, key ID 70771ff3
error: Failed dependencies:
        openssl >= 0.9.7 is needed by openssh-3.6.1p2-8mdk
        libc.so.6 is needed by openssh-3.6.1p2-8mdk
        libc.so.6(GLIBC_2.0) is needed by openssh-3.6.1p2-8mdk
        libc.so.6(GLIBC_2.1) is needed by openssh-3.6.1p2-8mdk
        libc.so.6(GLIBC_2.2) is needed by openssh-3.6.1p2-8mdk
```

```
libc.so.6(GLIBC_2.3) is needed by openssh-3.6.1p2-8mdk
libcrypto.so.0.9.7 is needed by openssh-3.6.1p2-8mdk
libnsl.so.1 is needed by openssh-3.6.1p2-8mdk
libutil.so.1 is needed by openssh-3.6.1p2-8mdk
libz.so.1 is needed by openssh-3.6.1p2-8mdk
```

It is possible to set up a skeleton chroot directory structure and step through the RPMs in their required order. However, such a kludge leads to an inelegant procedure for most binary packages and often leads to the undesirable necessity of using the **--nodeps** option during install. The **--nodeps** option ignores dependencies and, even if the RPM installs successfully, a critical error may be silently suppressed by this method.

The **rpm** command has an option called **--relocate** that will change the directory location for a base path common to all files in the package. Refer to the previous section for more information on this option.

There is a legitimate argument that a complex procedure only needs to be performed once and can then be automated by some creative scripting. The real disadvantage of using binary RPMs is that each RPM adds more and more items that the administrator probably doesn't want in the **chroot** environment. Consequently, it might be a better idea to build a custom package or just use a source tarball.

# Configure the Service to Log Activity

The information to be logged from a service in a **chroot** environment does not differ from when the service executes from the normal root. In fact, part of the build policy related to the **chroot** configuration should explicitly state the logging requirements. Nevertheless, disk space is a major consideration for this scenario. One of the reasons to create a **chroot** environment is to minimize the disk space available to attackers in the event of a compromise. Once again, you have several options for logging the service.

Even though the service may be writing to a file in the /var/log directory, this directory is within the **chroot** environment. However, other processes on the system with the correct privileges can freely access the files in /opt/chroot/var/log. A simple cron job can periodically move logs from the **chroot** environment to a location that is more secure and has more disk space available. This also helps the administrator centralize and parse logs.

A basic log directory would appear as such:

```
/var/
    log/
        lastlog
        messages
        secure
        wtmp
    run/
```

The other option is to forgo writing logs in the **chroot** environment altogether and send the log messages to a **syslog** server. This has the benefit that you can further restrict the size of the partition assigned to **chroot**. You must create an /etc/syslog.conf file in the **chroot** environment to do this.

Additionally, be aware that commands such as **w** or **who** only apply to their current environment by default. This is the desired result for the **chroot** environment (users in **chroot** cannot observe if non-**chroot** users are logged in). As an administrator, you should still monitor when users log in, what commands they execute, and when they log out. In fact, this is easy to do. Typing **who** on the host system only displays users who are not authenticated within a **chroot** environment (via **pam_chroot**, for example).

```
# who
root      pts/0       May  7 09:08 (10.0.1.3)
root      pts/1       May  7 09:08 (10.0.1.3)
```

To observe the users logged into a **chroot** environment, query the appropriate wtmp file:

```
# who /opt/chroot/var/log/wtmp
mike                  May  7 09:40 (10.0.1.3)
```

Logfiles provide useful information not only if a compromise occurs, but for monitoring the status and problems that might occur in a **chroot** environment.

# Troubleshoot chroot Environment Problems

If a service within a **chroot** environment is not working correctly, the first thing to do is carefully review the **strace** output and make sure every required file is present. Very often, a few common, non-sensitive files in the /etc directory, such as resolv.conf and nsswitch.conf, have been forgotten.

Many programs will write error messages to **syslog** or to /var/log/messages by default. Remember, this is the /var/log/messages in the chroot directory (/opt/chroot /var/log/messages) and not the /var/log/messages file of the root file system.

Be aware of incorrect file permissions. Many services are sensitive to file ownership and modes. Whenever possible, use **cp -p** to preserve the original file permissions when copying files from their original location to the **chroot** environment. The **tar** command also uses **-p**, or you can specify **--preserve** as a long option.

If you have placed the chroot directory structure on its own partition or set disk quotas, make sure that sufficient disk space remains for the program to execute, write to temporary files, write logfiles, and otherwise be able to access some free disk space.

You can reduce the logging overhead by using **syslog** to send events to another server rather than write to the chroot directory.

Mounting **chroot** systems over NFS is not a good idea. NFS will squash root privileges on files by default and silently map them to the nobody user. So, aside from the possible performance impact, NFS may wreak havoc on the file permissions you expect for the environment.

# Combine chroot and Your Distribution's Security Capabilities

Secure shell access on a system with many users may seem like a prime candidate for a **chroot** execution, but in this case the administrator may want to simply rely on the privilege separation capabilities inherent to OpenSSH. Privilege separation was established as part of the default configuration starting with version OpenSSH-3.3p1. Privilege separation follows a similar concept of Apache's reduced privilege execution once the server has been bound to a port. In the case of OpenSSH, the daemon uses an unprivileged account (UID > 0) to perform network and user request processing. Thus, the result of an exploit in the key exchange, authentication, or shell interaction will be limited to a restricted, non-root environment.

Of course, there are other reasons for establishing a **chroot** environment. The administrator may want to provide users with an interactive shell, but limit access to the full resources and utilities of the operating system. While privilege separation provides a defense against compromise, it does not impose restrictions on the shell and resources available to users.

## pam_chroot and Red Hat Enterprise Linux AS 3.0

Red Hat Enterprise Linux AS 3.0 contains a pluggable authentication module (PAM) that enables administrators to set up **chroot** environments for users who remotely log in to the system. This plug-in, **pam_chroot**, uses the system's core files (such as /etc/passwd and /etc/shadow) to authenticate users, but then hands off the user into a restricted portion of the file system. This has the significant advantage that users' passwords can be stored outside of the **chroot** environment.

Select the service you want to **chroot** from the /etc/pam.d/ directory. We will use SSH in this example. Each file in the /etc/pam.d/ directory contains PAM directives to authenticate (identify the user and check a password) and define actions for the session (logging, quotas, **chroot**, and so on). All PAM plug-ins are located in the /lib/security/ directory. Add a new session entry in the PAM file that applies **pam_chroot** to the user's login procedure. This line is shown in bold:

```
# cat /etc/pam.d/sshd
#%PAM-1.0
auth        required      pam_stack.so service=system-auth
```

```
auth         required       pam_nologin.so
account      required       pam_stack.so service=system-auth
password     required       pam_stack.so service=system-auth
session      required       pam_stack.so service=system-auth
session      required       pam_limits.so
session      required       pam_chroot.so onerr=fail debug
session      optional       pam_console.so
```

There are two arguments passed to this module. The **onerr=fail** argument instructs PAM to explicitly fail if it encounters any errors while processing the **chroot** switch. The **debug** argument provides additional information to **syslog** if you have difficulty setting up the environment. Even though this module is **required**, it will not be applied to a user unless that user's name is defined in the /etc/security/chroot.conf file. Thus, user authentication still occurs normally for all users (including root) until further configuration steps are taken.

The format of the /etc/security/chroot.conf is simple. Each row contains two columns. The first column contains a specific username or regular expression that matches multiple usernames. The second column contains the root directory used for the **chroot** switch. Here is an example:

```
# /etc/security/chroot.conf
# format:
# username_regex        chroot_dir
mike                    /opt/chroot
```

There is an important caveat when combining **pam_chroot** and SSH. Nearly all current OpenSSH installations use **PrivilegeSeparation** by default. The **pam_chroot** plug-in requires root privileges to establish a restricted environment via SSH. This means that you cannot use **PrivilegeSeparation** without significant configuration changes, because the listening process runs as the **sshd** user instead of root. If the SSH daemon is using privilege separation, you will see an error in /var/log/secure similar to this:

```
pam_chroot[pid]: chroot(/opt/chroot) failed: Operation not permitted
```

Therefore, ensure that **PrivilegeSeparation** is disabled in /etc/ssh/sshd_config:

```
UsePrivilegeSeparation no
```

This presents a policy decision in which you must weigh the pros and cons of running SSH processes with root privileges and restricted user environments or running SSH listening processes with reduced privileges and restricted user environments. **PrivilegeSeparation** is designed to reduce the impact of a zero-day exploit against the daemon and underlying system. **pam_chroot** is designed to reduce the impact of a compromise against a user account and the underlying system.

The only remaining step to complete the implementation of **pam_chroot** is to establish a proper user environment in /opt/chroot. Place the binaries and dynamic libraries within /opt/chroot as described previously in this chapter. Also, remember to create a /dev/pts entry, otherwise users will not be able to log in. The /dev/pts handles the pseudo-terminals assigned to users when they log in to a system.

```
# mkdir -p /opt/chroot/dev/pts
# mount -t devpts devpts /opt/chroot/dev/pts
```

Of course, a more complete device structure can be built with the **MAKEDEV** command, but this will not create the necessary /dev/pts entry:

```
# /dev/MAKEDEV -d /opt/chroot/dev/ generic
```

The remainder of the user environment must still be created. Remember that the /etc/passwd and /etc/group files are necessary, but /etc/shadow is not.

## Monitor File Mode and Permission Settings

Mandrake's **msec** utility is a collection of Python scripts and cron jobs that continuously monitor security settings. With regard to **chroot**, **msec** comes in handy for ensuring that the file permissions and modes do not change.

Although **msec** does not exist on Red Hat or SUSE, its concept can be adopted and implemented with cron jobs and scripts that just focus on the chroot directory. In fact, this step is merely an extension of the policy you use to monitor sensitive files on the base file system. If a tool like **msec** or **tripwire** is used for the base operating system, then it should be adopted for the **chroot** service as well.

**msec** is executed by the host operating system. Define the settings in the /etc/security /msec/perm.local file (this file might not be present by default). If you're unsure of how to set up this file, refer to the default settings for each perm.* file in the /usr/share/msec directory. Each perm.* file corresponds to an **msec** security level (0–5). The settings in /etc/security/msec/perm.local supersede the perm.* value for the current level.

```
# Some msec file permission entries.
# File or Directory              owner.group              mode
/opt/chroot/                     root.root                 711
/opt/chroot/bin/                 root.root                 711
/opt/chroot/etc/                 root.root                 711
/opt/chroot/etc/ftpaccess        root.root                 600
/opt/chroot/etc/ftpconversions   root.root                 600
/opt/chroot/etc/ftpgroups        root.root                 600
/opt/chroot/etc/ftphosts         root.root                 600
/opt/chroot/etc/ftpusers         root.root                 600
/opt/chroot/etc/hosts.allow      root.daemon               644
/opt/chroot/etc/hosts.deny       root.daemon               644
```

| | | |
|---|---|---|
| /opt/chroot/etc/hosts.equiv | root.daemon | 640 |
| /opt/chroot/etc/ld.so.conf | root.root | 600 |

The /etc/security/msec/level.local file toggles specific **msec** checks. These will be less useful for the **chroot** environment. For example, password and shadow file checks are performed on the host, not the **chroot** environment. Still, it's a good idea to be aware of additional security options you can set for the host system.

# Maintain chroot

A compromised **chroot** environment is much easier to recover than a compromised host. A tarball of the directory is all that is necessary to rebuild the **chroot** structure. Make sure to use the **--preserve** option when creating the initial tarball. This is perhaps the easiest way to back up and recover the chroot directory.

```
# tar czvfp chroot.tar.gz /opt/chroot
```

**chroot** also lowers the number of logs, users, and processes that must be monitored. Although the initial creation of a **chroot** environment requires a lot of effort, ongoing administration is actually improved.

The administration of a **chroot** environment is no different from that of a service installed normally. As you define policies for the configuration, logging, and patching of services on the operating system, make sure to include specific policies for the **chroot** services.

# Chapter 10

## Hardening Communications

- Secure Protocols
- IPSec

ommunications can be the bane of any security administrator. They are required for business purposes in most cases, but can be the weak point in the security schema if not employed properly. To secure your network, you should

- Use SSH in lieu of unencrypted protocols
- Set up password-free logins as required
- Replace **r** services and FTP with SSH equivalents
- Implement SSH port forwarding
- Secure X connections with SSH
- User virtual private networks

# Secure Protocols

In the time before general public use of the Internet, communications between machines were not regularly encrypted because most communications didn't take place over public networks, only a few machines were connected to the Internet and most people knew the other machines on the network, and there were few publicized cases of data theft, destruction, or monitoring. This all changed as the Internet grew into what we know of it today. In order to provide more security to your network, and to protect information traversing your network, you should implement the use of secure protocols that encrypt the information contained within the payload. Using unencrypted protocols can allow attackers to gather sensitive information such as account names and passwords (as shown in Chapter 14) or gather information during transit.

SUSE SLES8 and Red Hat Enterprise Linux AS 3.0, the examples used in this book, do not have some of the more dangerous protocols enabled (as discussed in Chapter 2). This does not preclude someone from using the service to connect to an outside entity, though, unless you remove or restrict the binary files as discussed in Chapter 4. The following are the most commonly used insecure services:

- **r** tools such as **rsh**, **rcp**, and **rlogin**
- Telnet
- FTP
- TFTP

These protocols have alternatives that encrypt the session as described in Table 10-1.

The services in the first column of Table 10-1, in addition to others, are unencrypted and care should be taken when using them with sensitive information. If at all possible within your environment, utilize encrypted protocols for all transmissions.

| Insecure Protocol | Encrypted Replacement |
|---|---|
| Telnet | SSH |
| rsh | SSH |
| rlogin | SSH |
| TFTP | sftp |
| FTP | sftp |
| rcp | scp |

**Table 10-1.**    Protocol Comparison

# Use SSH

SSH and its accompanying tools are included by default with most major Linux distributions, as they are the de facto standard. SSH provides many benefits, including

- Encrypted communications
- Prevention of host spoofing (host authentication)
- Data integrity
- User authentication
- Secure file transfer

There are two versions of SSH available, protocols 1 and 2. Protocol 1 had a couple of issues that were of concern, primarily because of patent issues with RSA (RSA was patented, but that patent has run out) and security concerns, such as the vulnerability for insertion attacks. Protocol 2 is rewritten with security in mind and used a non-patented algorithm (DSA).While protocol 2 is the more secure of the two protocols, some environments require protocol 1 use, so you may have to allow both to run for maximum compatibility. This is wholly dependent on your environment, and if at all possible, you should use protocol 2 for all SSH connections due to its enhanced security.

Before you can use SSH for network communications, you need to ensure that both the host and server have SSH installed (and a server available for the client to connect to) as well as allowing TCP port 22 through your firewall (as discussed in Chapter 3). If you are using TCP wrappers, you will need to allow SSHD access in /etc/hosts.allow. RHEL AS 3.0 and SUSE SLES8 have SSH installed and enabled by default, but if you are running a Linux distribution that doesn't have it installed, you can visit http://www .openssh.org/ to download and install the latest version.

## Use SSH in Lieu of Unencrypted Protocols

To use these tools, you can use the **ssh** command just like you would the **telnet** command. You have to provide the hostname as an argument to the command, so if you were trying to connect to a machine called linux2, you would type

```
ssh linux2
```

If this were the first time you were connecting to the machine via SSH, you would see output similar to that shown in Figure 10-1.

Lines 2, 3, and 4 show a feature of SSH that prevents "spoofing" of a trusted machine, meaning that it prevents one machine from presenting itself as another, so you can be generally assured that you are connected to the correct machine. To determine the hostkey fingerprint for the server you are connecting to, use the **ssh-keygen -l** command. When asked for the file the key is in, use /etc/ssh/ssh_host_rsa_key or /etc/ssh/ssh_host_dsa_key, with /etc/ssh/ssh_host_rsa_key as the default. Figure 10-2 shows the output of the command run from the machine locally. Note there are two ways to run the command, with the **-l** option and with the **-lf** option, both of which produce the same results.

## HEADS UP!

Don't run **ssh-keygen** from the initial **ssh** connection, as you are only verifying the machine you are connected to, not necessarily the one you think it is. You will want to separately run it on the remote machine locally (via console or trusted network connection) to ensure you are getting the fingerprint of the machine you want.

Your key fingerprint should match what the remote machine shows as the key fingerprint. If you have connected to the machine in the past and you see a message similar to that in Figure 10-3, you should terminate your connection if the system doesn't do so automatically and contact the system administrator of the remote machine.

This indicates that there is a difference between the hostkey you have and the hostkey the server presents. This could be as innocuous as a simple key regeneration on the distant end or reinstallation of software, or it could be that someone is trying to intercept your traffic. Always err on the side of caution and investigate the cause behind the change.

A habit you should get into, especially if you are logging in as another user from time to time, is to specify the user you want to connect to the remote machine as. This alleviates the problem of trying to connect to the remote server as the user you are logged in as, which may not be the same user you want to connect as. To do this, you only need to specify on the command line as follows:

```
ssh jdoe@linux2
```

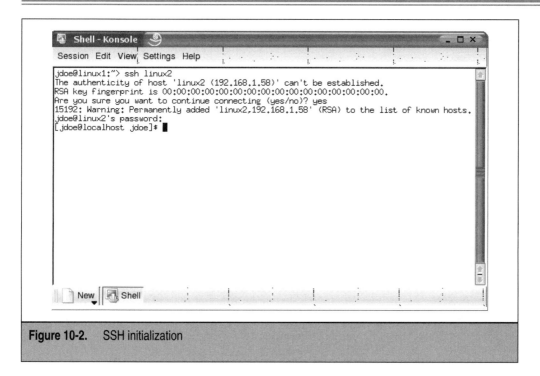

**Figure 10-2.**    SSH initialization

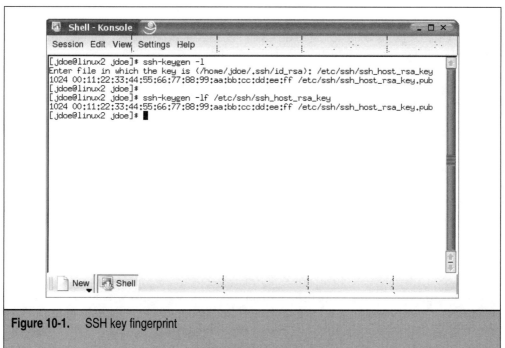

**Figure 10-1.**    SSH key fingerprint

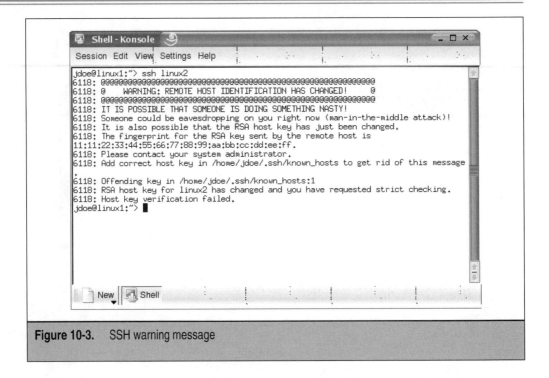

**Figure 10-3.** SSH warning message

This tells SSH you want to log in as jdoe even if you are currently logged in as root on the machine you are connecting from. If you don't specify the user, SSH will try to log onto the remote machine as the user you are currently logged on as. This is because it will pass the username of the account you are logged in if you don't specify it, which could be a problem when accounts are local to the machine and possibly different.

## Set Up Secure Automatic Logins with SSH

In some environments, you will have legacy applications that might require running remote commands on another system via scripts. This was often done in the past using **rsh** and **rlogin**, which are unencrypted protocols. SSH allows for the same functionality, with much more security. Password-free logins allow you to use the public key infrastructure to allow machines to log in using public keys instead of using a simple username/password combination. There are multiple ways to use SSH for password-free logins, including host-based authentication, using trust relationships between systems, **rhosts** authentication, which can be set up to allow password-free logins via a file, and the version we will be talking about, identity-based authentication. The steps outlined for password-free logins will seem attractive for everyday use, but you should only use this when required and if at all possible avoid using it on the root account. If you aren't using **ssh-agent** and someone breaks into your system and gains access to an account on one system, you have handed them access to multiple other systems as well.

The steps involved in setting up password-free logins are shown next and described in the rest of this section.

1. Set up keys using **ssh-keygen**.
2. Ensure files are created in your home directory's .ssh directory.
3. Put a copy of the local machine's public key to the remote server.
4. Modify permissions on the remote server's .ssh directory and public key files.

You will need to set up the keys first by running one of the following commands in your home directory:

```
ssh-keygen -t dsa
ssh-keygen -t rsa
```

As shown in Figure 10-4, the tilde (~) represents the home directory, which in this case is /home/jdoe. If you choose not to enter a passphrase, you are removing some of the security functionality of SSH and it is therefore highly discouraged. We will assume you are going to enter a passphrase and use **ssh-agent**. Depending on your requirements, you may decide that you cannot run **ssh-agent** and not enter a passphrase.

## HEADS UP!

With **ssh-agent**, you will be required to enter a passphrase at least once, which may present a problem if your machine is rebooted or another issue causes **ssh-agent** to lose the password. You may be tempted to not use a password because of this, but this creates tremendous security vulnerabilities if an unauthorized or malicious entity gains access to the account with ssh-agent enabled. With no password the attacker can then potentially access other systems on the network that have SSH logins enabled with no password.

After generating the keys, you will see that you have two new files in your home directory, an .ssh directory called id_rsa and id_rsa.pub as shown in Figure 10-4 (you can also create dsa keys using the **-t dsa** command in addition to or in place of the **-t rsa** command). Your private key is id_rsa and id_rsa.pub is your public key, or if you're using dsa, your files will be id_dsa and id_dsa.pub for your private and public key, respectively. You will now need to put a copy of your public key on the server you want to connect to, using the **sftp** or **scp** command. If we wanted to put jdoe's public key on linux2, so that he could log in without a password on linux2, we would run the **sftp** command (as noted later in this chapter in the section "Replace r services and FTP with SSH Equivalents") to connect to the remote server, create a .ssh directory in the

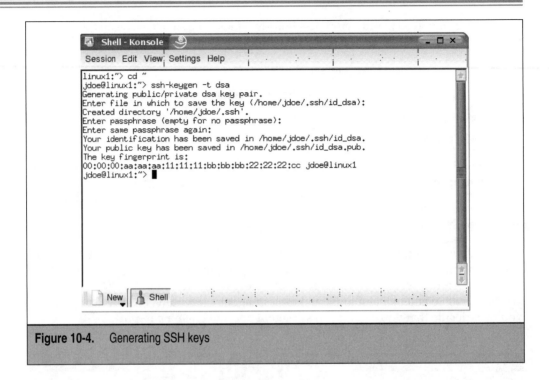

**Figure 10-4.** Generating SSH keys

login directory if it doesn't already exist, and then copy the id_rsa.pub (or id_dsa.pub) file from the local home directory to the remote directory. An example of this process is shown in Figure 10-5.

SSH requires a strict permission set on the files for security reasons. You will need to modify your .ssh directory to have read/write/execute for the owner only permissions, using the following command:

```
chmod 700 ~/.ssh
```

The authorized keys file will need read-only permissions for the owner, as follows:

```
chmod 400 ~/.ssh/authorized_keys
```

For maximum protection you should also provide read-only permission for the owner on your private key on the host. Since you entered in a passphrase when you generated your key, you need to have a way to pass those keys to the programs that will use SSH. To do this, you need to run **ssh-agent**, which passes your passphrase to other processes spawned from the original. Run the **ssh-agent** and **ssh-add** commands as shown in Figure 10-6, and then you will only have to enter your password the one time for any processes spawned from that shell window.

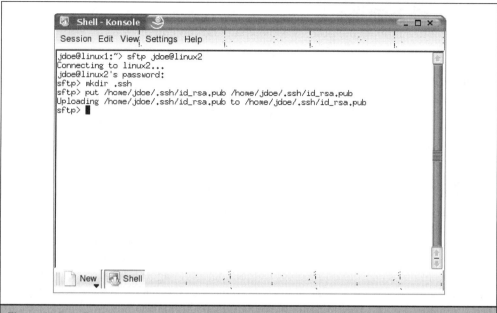

**Figure 10-5.**    Putting a public key on remote server

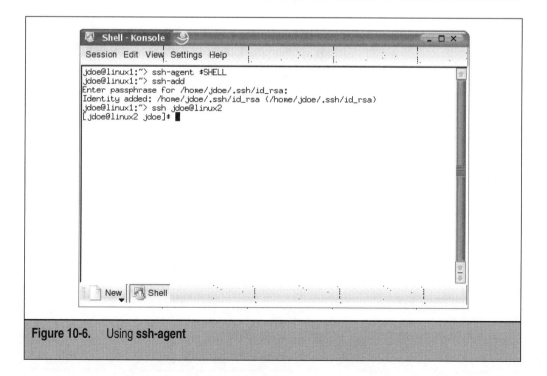

**Figure 10-6.**    Using **ssh-agent**

## Automate ssh-agent Use

If you want to automate the process somewhat, you can add an entry to your .bashrc (or other initialization file) to run **ssh-agent** automatically upon login, and you will be asked your password at login or bootup, which makes it available for the entire session. If you didn't enter a passphrase during key generation, by pressing RETURN only, you would not need to add the **ssh-agent** portion of this as there is no passphrase required. We only mention it because it is required for some environments due to operating constraints, but again, this is highly discouraged as you weaken the built-in security that SSH provides and open a path for intrusion to other systems if the main server is compromised.

## Replace r services and FTP with SSH Equivalents

The functionality that **rsh** and **rlogin** provide can be easily replaced by SSH using the password-free login mentioned before, while providing encryption for the session. The **rsh** and **rlogin** commands are usually used in environments that permit password-free logins between machines for scripting or ease of use. Another function that is provided by **rsh** is that users can run commands without actually logging in to an interactive session. The benefit of using SSH instead of **rsh** or **rlogin** is that the session is encrypted and the authentication mechanisms are more secure. To do this with SSH, you need to provide the command you run after the login information within quotation (") or tick (") marks as shown in Figure 10-7.

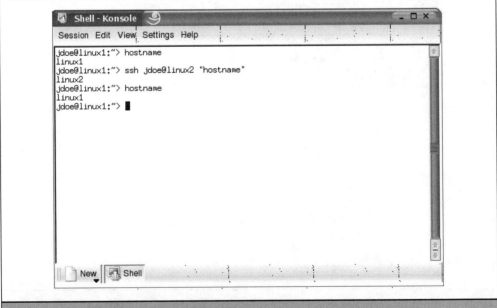

**Figure 10-7.** Remote command execution

Note that in this example the user is still on the original machine after the command completes. This allows you to script commands to run on different machines without an interactive session, similar to the functionality provided by **rsh**. Some programs run interactively and these will require that you use the **-t** option in order to set up a pseudo-terminal so that you may run the application interactively (such as pine, links, and so on).

**sftp** provides the same functionality as provided by FTP, with the same command structure as well. To use **sftp** you need only type the command as you would **ftp**, such as

```
sftp linux1
```

although a better way is to specify the user you will be **sftp**-ing as, similar to

```
sftp jdoe@linux1
```

Most commands are similar to the **ftp** command as well as having some added features that can be found by using pressing **?** and pressing RETURN at the **sftp>** prompt. One particularly interesting option is **-b** (for batch), which allows you to script commands to **sftp**. This works with non-interactive authentication (password-free login as described previously in this chapter). One benefit of this is if you consistently run a set series of commands with the **sftp** command, you can put those commands in a file and run them in the order listed in the file. For instance, you have a process that you run every hour of every weekday where you download a file called production_file with **get**, upload a different file to the server called put_file with **put**, and then remove the original production_file using the **rm** command. Every hour a new version of all these files is put on the system from another program, so every time the data is new. Instead of running these commands every time interactively, you can put the three commands in a file and use the **-b** option to run them. In our example, we could put the following commands in a text file called hourly_process, which would contain the following lines:

```
get production file
put put_file
rm production_file
```

We could now run the following command to replace three interactive commands that would have been required without the **-b** option (assuming the file is in /home/jdoe):

```
sftp -b /home/jdoe/hourly_process jdoe@linux1
```

**rcp** provides the ability to copy files to a remote system without an interactive session, making the transmission of files via script or one-line commands extremely easy. This functionality is provided by the **scp** command that comes with SSH (which is encrypted). To use this command you need to provide the name of the file you want to copy, the machine you want to copy it to, and the new filename. The format for this command is

```
scp <filename> <username>@<remote machine hostname or IP>:<filename to save as>
```

Figure 10-8 shows jdoe copying a file in his current directory from linux1 to linux2 and an **ls** of jdoe's home directory after the copy.

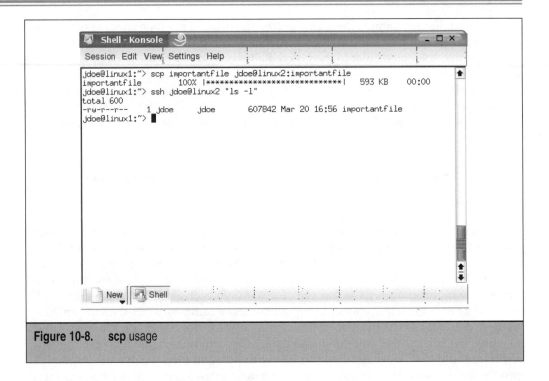

**Figure 10-8.** scp usage

One of strong points of **scp** is that it can easily be inserted into a shell script when used in conjunction with password-free logins for non-interactive scripting. These tools allow you to replace most of the more insecure, unencrypted protocols that may exist on your network, increasing your overall security posture.

## Implement SSH Port Forwarding

SSH provides the ability to encrypt other TCP/IP protocols via a technique called port forwarding or tunneling. You need to have SSH installed on the local and remote machines you are trying to port forward to, but other than that, there are no special requirements for implementation of this. SSH port forwarding allows your users to encrypt traffic that would otherwise be unencrypted and hence not as secure. When using these techniques you are only encrypting the connections specified and not all your communications, which is something that a virtual private network (VPN) does. SSH port forwarding could be set up to allow an external host that is not within your network to a border host (externally exposed server with firewall protections) for instance. An example of this is that you have a Linux mail server on your network. Using SSH port forwarding, you can set up your Windows client to check e-mail via an encrypted session. SSH port forwarding is not limited to this specific example, but can be used for any protocol the administrator needs. To enable this, you only need to provide an argument to the standard

**ssh** command. The syntax for running port forwarding from the local host to a remote host is as follows:

```
ssh -L <local port to forward>:<hostname (usually localhost)>:<remote port> <username
to forward as>@<hostname to forward packets to>
```

To allow remote connections to connect to the local port, use this syntax:

```
ssh -R <remote port>:<hostname (usually localhost)>:<local port to forward)> <username
to forward as>@<hostname>
```

To better understand the process, the following example is one where it is necessary to allow FTP connections, but you do not want to allow unencrypted FTP traffic. Your FTP server is linux2. Your users will be connecting to linux2 while connected to linux1. To set up a connection on the local host, you would type the following at a command prompt on linux1:

```
ssh -L 9001:localhost:21 jdoe@linux2
```

You can now open another terminal on linux1 and run this command:

```
ftp localhost 9001
```

You can only forward ports below 1024 as root for security reasons, but all other ports can be forwarded as any valid user (the first port before the hostname). When running the command you are connecting to the local host (127.0.0.1), which is another name for the local machine, on port 9001. This request is forwarded over the encrypted path to port 21 on the remote computer (via SSH).

Another scenario might be that you want to check your e-mail on a remote server that also supports SSH from your local computer named linux1. Your mail server is linux2, which uses port 25 (SMTP) for sending your mail and port 110 (POP3) to receive your mail. Your login is jdoe and you want to check your mail over an encrypted transmission. You can run the following command on your local computer:

```
ssh -L 9090:localhost:25 -L 9091:localhost:110 jdoe@linux2 -N
```

This forwards ports 9090 and 9091 to 25 and 110 on linux2, respectively, without running a command (**-N**). In your mail client, you would configure your mail to use localhost (or 127.0.0.1) as the mail server for send and receive, port 9090 for sending mail, and port 9091 for receiving mail. When you check your mail, it will be encrypted and carried over the SSH transmission.

If you have Windows clients that have a mail client such as Outlook or Eudora, you can set up your users to use SSH port forwarding as well. Using an SSH client that supports port forwarding, you can give your Windows users the same functionality for encryption that your Linux users enjoy. PuTTY (http://www.chiark.greenend.org.uk /~sgtatham/putty/) is a Windows SSH client that supports SSH port forwarding and includes documentation on using these features.

Remote forwarding works in the same manner as local forwarding with some minor adjustments as noted previously. Using the **-g** option allows other machines to use your remote tunnel as well, although you should be careful in using this as it does give you the ability to encrypt partial points of a transmission if you can't encrypt an entire session.

Using **-N** at the end of the forwarded command will tell SSH to not execute any commands so you don't get a shell on the remote machine you are forwarding to. If you set up your keys and are using **ssh-agent**, you won't be prompted for your password after the first time you enter it, making port forwarding very unobtrusive. You can identify what connections are currently open by pressing ~# in the terminal you started your forward in. You should also note that SSH port forwarding is good for as long as your SSH session is open. When you close it, you will lose the port forwarding that you had. This can be easily scripted and added to your initialization or startup files in conjunction with **ssh-agent**.

You can make this a little easier for users and yourself by adding the port forwarding capabilities to the ssh_config file. Edit your /etc/ssh/ssh_config file and use LocalForward or RemoteForward as appropriate to the type of forward you are doing. For the command

```
ssh -L 9001:localhost:21 jdoe@linux2
```

we can add the following to the /etc/ssh/ssh_config:

```
Host linux2ftp
Hostname linux2
LocalForward 9001 localhost:21
```

The first Host line specifies the alias we are going to use to call the directive. Hostname is the host the forward is going to, and the LocalForward line is the local port to forward, the hostname of the local forward (usually localhost), and the remote port to use. To use the command to start port forwarding, you would type

```
ssh linux2ftp
```

Your local forward is run from that point. The same format applies to the RemoteForward directive.

Before using SSH forwarding, you should determine if it violates your company's security policy, as it could be seen (and is sometimes used) to subvert firewall rules that have been put in place for the protection of the network. Attackers can also use these techniques to mask their activities through encryption and by subverting firewall restrictions on ports other than SSH.

## Secure X Connections with SSH

SSH allows you to secure your X Window communications between an X server and a client. This allows you to run graphical programs from one machine onto another machine, with full encryption and the protection of SSH. This could be useful if you want to run a graphical configuration utility, check packages via a package manager on another machine, or just run any other type of graphical applications off a server without having to log in locally.

The first step in configuring X11 forwarding is to edit the /etc/ssh/sshd_config file and set the X11Forwarding directive to yes. Restart **sshd** as follows:

```
[root@linux1 ssh]# /etc/init.d/sshd restart
Stopping sshd:                                          [  OK  ]
Starting sshd:                                          [  OK  ]
[root@linux1 ssh]#
```

To use the graphical programs, you only need to **ssh** with the **-X** option and after logging in, run the command you normally would on the remote system. The graphical program will come onscreen on your local machine. For instance, if you wanted to run **xeyes** graphically on your local machine (linux1) from a remote connection (linux2), you would run these commands:

```
ssh -X linux2
xeyes
```

This would show an **xeyes** initiation on your local machine served from the remote machine. This should be used with caution, as it could be used for nefarious purposes as described in the man pages.

## Use Virtual Private Networks

A virtual private network (VPN) is a private, encrypted network that traverses a public network. This offers the VPN user security and network resources without the added costs of a dedicated network line. Most companies use VPNs today to allow remote users or different offices to communicate with one another over the Internet, at a significantly reduced cost than previously required. VPNs can be set up over any type of network connection, such as a leased line, but the standard use is over public networks. VPNs should be configured and planned carefully, and should be implemented with care. Most medium to large organizations will implement dedicated VPN solutions, managed by trained network staff. There are many VPN programs available, and this chapter will briefly cover one of the easier to install programs. Note that there are other more complicated, but equally robust packages available such as FreeS/WAN (http://www.freeswan.org/).

CIPE (Crypto IP Encapsulation) is a relatively easy to use VPN implementation that operates on the network level and is available on the CDs that come with SUSE SLES8 and Red Hat Enterprise Linux AS 3.0. To set up CIPE you need to install it from your distribution CDs or you can download it from the CIPE homepage at http://sourceforge .net/projects/cipe-linux (click on the homepage section to see the latest files), which is the recommended route.

To use CIPE, you need to configure a few parameters in a file called options. Copy the options template file located in either /usr/share/doc/cipe<VERSION>/samples /options or /etc/cipe/samples.options to /etc/cipe/options. There you need to configure the /etc/cipe/options file and configure your local area network addresses and the publicly routable addresses of your firewall. Here a sample:

```
# Surprise, this file allows comments (but only on a line by themselves)
# This is probably the minimal set of options that has to be set
# Without a "device" line, the device is picked dynamically
# the peer's IP address
ptpaddr         <My IP Address for this virtual link>
# our CIPE device's IP address
ipaddr          <Remote IP Address for this virtual link>
# my UDP address. Note: if you set port 0 here, the system will pick
# one and tell it to you via the ip-up script. Same holds for IP
0.0.0.0.
me              <My Routeable IP>:<a port that I choose>
# ...and the UDP address we connect to. Of course no wildcards here.
peer            <The Remote Routeable IP>:<a port that I choose>
# The static key. Keep this file secret!
# The key is 128 bits in hexadecimal notation.
key             1234567890abcdefghijklmnopqrstuv
```

This file will need to be configured on both endpoints and the comments above apply to the machine you are one. So <my routable IP> is the routable IP of the machine you are configuring the options file on. Here's an example CIPE options file for the local machine:

```
# Surprise, this file allows comments (but only on a line by themselves)
# This is probably the minimal set of options that has to be set
# Without a "device" line, the device is picked dynamically
# the peer's IP address
ptpaddr         192.168.10.1
# our CIPE device's IP address
ipaddr          192.168.20.1
# my UDP address. Note: if you set port 0 here, the system will pick
# one and tell it to you via the ip-up script. Same holds for IP
0.0.0.0.
me              10.0.0.1:8080
# ...and the UDP address we connect to. Of course no wildcards here.
peer            10.0.0.2:8080
# The static key. Keep this file secret!
# The key is 128 bits in hexadecimal notation.
key             1234567890abcdefghijklmnopqrstuv
```

Here's an example CIPE options file for the remote machine:

```
# Surprise, this file allows comments (but only on a line by themselves)
# This is probably the minimal set of options that has to be set
# Without a "device" line, the device is picked dynamically
# the peer's IP address
ptpaddr          192.168.20.1
# our CIPE device's IP address
ipaddr           192.168.10.1
# my UDP address. Note: if you set port 0 here, the system will pick
# one and tell it to you via the ip-up script. Same holds for IP
0.0.0.0.
me               10.0.0.2:8080
# ...and the UDP address we connect to. Of course no wildcards here.
peer             10.0.0.1:8080
 # The static key. Keep this file secret!
# The key is 128 bits in hexadecimal notation.
key              1234567890abcdefghijklmnopqrstuv
```

---

**NOTE**   Your firewalls will need to allow the traffic on the ports you indicate on the UDP address lines (in the previous example, port 8080 would need to be allowed incoming and outgoing traffic, as that is the port that is in use).

---

The 10.0.0.0 network is not really routable, but in this example we are using it in place of where you would put your real, routable IP. The shared secret key must be the same in both configuration files. You can create a quick key with a command such as

```
#cat /var/log/messages | md5sum
1234567890abcdefghijklmnopqrstuv  -
```

The shared secret key (or static link keys) is a reference key for the different CIPE networks to pass information to each other. It is absolutely imperative if you use a shared secret key that you keep the keys secure and private. You should set appropriate file permissions on the /etc/cipe/options file as discussed in Chapter 6 to prevent unauthorized users from viewing the shared keys.

---

**NOTE**   Set the permissions to remove read, write, and execute permissions for group and others on the /etc/cipe/options file before running **cipe-cb**, use

```
chmod go-rwx /etc/cipe/options
```

---

CIPE also supports the use of public keys with PKCIPE if you do not want to use shared secret keys. Now that your configuration files are set up, you can start CIPE by running the **ciped-cb** command. To add network routes, you can edit the /etc/cipe/ip-up and /etc/cipe/ip-down scripts for additional interfaces for your environment. You are ready to use the VPN.

For more information on CIPE and some of its many uses, see the CIPE homepage at http://sites.inka.de/bigred/devel/cipe.html or the Red Hat documentation at http://www.redhat.com/docs/manuals/linux/ (specifically look at the security guide for information on CIPE).

# IPSec

IPSec has been an Internet standard for encrypted network transmissions since 1998 and is covered in RFC 2401, RFC 2402, RFC 2406, and RFC 2407, which can be found at http://www.ietf.org/rfc.html. IPSec is an extension to the ubiquitous IPv4 protocol, which adds authentication and confidentiality mechanisms to this protocol. In the next generation IP protocol, IPv6, IPSec has been incorporated into the protocol standard, and its support is mandatory. In contrast to many other networking protocols, IPSec is a suite of protocols rather than a single protocol specification. While an in-depth study of different IPSec protocols is beyond the scope of this book, this chapter will cover the most important aspects of this protocol and provide a sample use of IPSec. For further information, refer to the RFCs previously noted.

The two main protocols of IPSec are the authentication header (AH) and the encapsulating security payload (ESP). AH is an IPSec protocol that provides data integrity, data origin authentication, and anti-replay services to IP. ESP is a protocol header inserted into an IP packet to provide confidentiality, data origin authentication, anti-replay, and data integrity services to IP.

It is important that you understand the functionality provided by each of these protocols in order to be able to use them correctly. AH ensures that the IP packet has not been altered or tampered with on its way to the destination, but it does not provide any confidentiality regarding the content of the message. An eavesdropper can still read the IP packet. ESP addresses the encryption of the traffic preventing eavesdropping by third parties on the IP packets. Therefore, according to your needs, whether you want to protect your data from eavesdropping or protect your traffic from alteration by a third party, you should use ESP or AH.

IPSec provides two modes: transport and tunnel mode. Each mode can be used with AH, ESP, or both. (A detailed explanation of these modes can be found in *IPSec: The New Security Standard for the Internet, Intranets, and Virtual Private Networks*, by N. Doraswamy and D. Harkins.) To simplify, transport mode is used for host-to-host connections, while tunnel mode is used to include the whole IP packet into a new IP packet to be sent. The transport mode is useful when you need to protect the traffic between two individual nodes. The tunnel mode is used when the ultimate destination of traffic can be different from your end security point. This is very often the case when you want to establish a VPN between two gateways through an untrusted network to protect traffic between two subnetworks against eavesdropping and alteration. Whenever either end of the IPSec connection is a gateway, the tunnel mode is most frequently used.

The variety of functionality provided by IPSec allows its use in different scenarios. We have chosen to illustrate its use in the case of setting up a VPN connection between two gateways in tunnel mode.

One of the major software packages that implement IPSec for Linux is FreeS/WAN (http://www.freeswan.org/). There are two things to note concerning IPSec support in Linux. First, there is a new native implementation of IPSec in the new 2.6.X Linux kernels. As this implementation is new, and this kernel is not yet used in many Linux distributions, we will concentrate on FreeS/WAN in this chapter, as it is the most widely used implementation. Another thing to note is that FreeS/WAN is no longer in active development although, as is the custom in open source development, there has been a codefork to allow for continued development of the FreeS/WAN codebase in the form of Openswan (http://www.openswan.org/). In this chapter, we will use a standard configuration of FreeS/WAN to set up a virtual private network (VPN) tunnel between two gateways.

## Set Up a VPN with FreeS/WAN

In the example scenario, we will show the setup of an IPSec tunnel between two gateways called Linux1 and Linux2 as shown in Figure 10-9. The goal is to provide a secure connection (encrypted tunnel) between two gateways for the IP traffic exchanged between the subnetworks A and B.

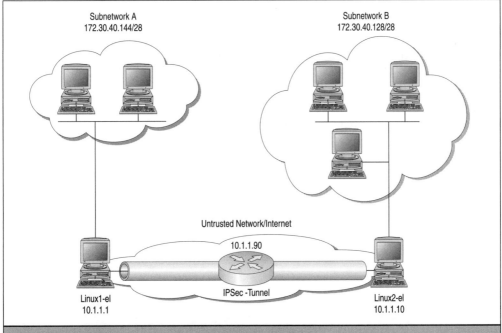

**Figure 10-9.**    IPSec tunnel set up between two subnetworks

In this example, Linux1 protects the subnetwork A, while Linux2 protects subnetwork B. Each gateway has one network interface in the public IP domain (10.1.1.10 for Linux1 and 10.1.1.1 for Linux2) and another one in the private domain (subnetwork A for Linux1 and subnetwork B for Linux2). FreeS/WAN uses the keyword "next hop" to designate the default router for each gateway. In our scenario, the two gateways both forward IP traffic to the external nodes to the main router with IP address 10.1.1.90 (note that the next hop address can be different for each gateway).

This router can be your main switch in your company network or any other IP address defined by your ISP provider.

## Install FreeS/WAN

If you use SLES8, the FreeS/WAN packages are already installed. On Red Hat Enterprise Linux AS 3.0, you need to install it using RPMs. You can download the RPMs from the FreeS/WAN web site on ftp://ftp.xs4all.nl/pub/crypto/freeswan/binaries/RedHat-RPMs. Do not forget to download both the freeswan-module RPM and the user land tools freeswan-userland RPM.

Install RPMs by typing the following:

```
$rpm -ivh freeswan-*
```

### HEADS UP!

Be sure to pick up the right RPM corresponding to the Linux kernel running on your system, otherwise FreeS/WAN will not work. You can find out the Linux kernel version of your system by using **$uname -a**.

In this example, FreeS/WAN 2.0.5 on a Red Hat machine was used, but the behavior of FreeS/WAN is identical among distributions.

The next step is to activate the **ipsec** daemon. To do this on a RHEL AS 3.0 machine, run the following:

```
$service ipsec start
```

On SLES8, do the following:

```
$/etc/init.d/ipsec start
```

## HEADS UP!

Be careful: upon initialization the **ipsec** daemon filters all connections not defined in the IPSec configuration policy (explained below). This means that if you work on your system through a remote session, you can lose connectivity when you start the **ipsec** daemon. To avoid this problem, you should be on the local console when activating the **ipsec** daemon.

## Generate Authentication Keys for Your Gateways

After you installed FreeS/WAN, you need to run **ipsec newhostkey** on both gateways to generate the authentication keys. This creates a pair of RSA public/private keys and stores them in /etc/ipsec.secrets file. This file contains the secrets necessary to protect your IPSec installation. You should not disclose this file to any untrusted party. Remove read and write permissions for other than root by doing the following:

```
$chmod go-rwx ipsec.secrets
```

## Configure FreeS/WAN

The most convenient way of configuring FreeS/WAN is through the ipsec.conf file located in the /etc directory. In the following listing, we modified the default FreeS/WAN configuration file to implement the scenario described previously:

```
# /etc/ipsec.conf - FreeS/WAN IPsec configuration file
# RCSID $Id: ipsec.conf.in,v 1.11 2003/06/13 23:28:41 sam Exp $
# This file:  /usr/local/share/doc/freeswan/ipsec.conf-sample
#
# Manual:     ipsec.conf.5
#
# Help:
# http://www.freeswan.org/freeswan_trees/freeswan-2.05/doc/quickstart.html
# http://www.freeswan.org/freeswan_trees/freeswan-2.05/doc/config.html
# http://www.freeswan.org/freeswan_trees/freeswan-2.05/doc/adv_config.html
#
# Policy groups are enabled by default. See:
# http://www.freeswan.org/freeswan_trees/freeswan-2.05/doc/policygroups.html
```

```
#
# Examples:
# http://www.freeswan.org/freeswan_trees/freeswan-2.05/doc/examples
version    2.0    # conforms to second version of ipsec.conf specification
# basic configuration
config setup
     # Debug-logging controls:  "none" for (almost) none, "all" for lots.
     # klipsdebug=all
     # plutodebug=dns
# Add connections here.
# sample VPN connection
conn grumm
     # Left security gateway, subnet behind it, next hop toward right.
     left=10.1.1.1 # Gateway Linux1
     leftsubnet=172.30.40.144/28  # sub-network protected by Linux2
     leftnexthop=10.1.1.90 # next hop to the right from left
     # RSA 3584 bits   Linux1 Wed Apr 21 13:31:33 2004
     leftrsasigkey=0sAQNrBIuTQuDXGlw….. # left RSA public key for Linux2
     # Right security gateway, subnet behind it, next hop toward left.
     right=10.1.1.10 # Gateway Linux2
     rightsubnet=172.30.40.128/28 # sub-network protected by Linux1
     rightnexthop=10.1.1.90 # next hop to the left from right
     # RSA 2064 bits   Linux2   Wed Apr 21 11:59:07 2004
     rightrsasigkey=0sAQNfhF2pEN7…. # right RSA public key for Linux1
     # To authorize this connection, but not actually start it, at startup,
     # uncomment this.
     auto=start
```

For this example, we defined our tunnel in the section starting with **conn grumm** and ending with **auto=start**. **grumm** is the name of the only VPN tunnel we define in this configuration file. Be careful when entering extra spaces or characters as indentation is important in this file.

To define your own tunnel, you should replace **grumm** with the name you would like to use. Then you need to define the specifications for either end of your tunnel, designated as left and right in the configuration file. The designation of which network is right and left is arbitrary and not dependent on IP address or other factors. In the example used in this chapter, the left is Linux1 as it was on the left side of the figure. The important part of the selection of subnetworks is to be consistent with the definition in both IPSec configuration files on both gateways: subnetwork A is defined as the left subnetwork, and subnetwork B is defined as the right subnetwork. You should now define different network specifications for each subnetwork:

- **left**   The gateway for the left subnetwork (here Linux1).
- **leftsubnet**   The subnetwork protected by the gateway (here subnetwork A).

- **leftnexthop** The first hop on the untrusted public IP network, to which the left gateway forwards external IP traffic (here 10.1.1.90).

- **leftrsasigky** The public part of your RSA key on the left gateway. To obtain it, go to the left gateway and run **ipsec showhostkey -left**, then copy and paste the result in the ipsec.conf file.

For the right network, you would follow the same steps previously listed.

The **auto=start** line in /etc/ipsec.conf authorizes the connection to be established automatically and is determined by the needs of your connection.

After the /etc/ipsec.conf file has been configured on one of your gateways, you will need to securely copy the file to the other gateway so that both configuration files match.

## Establish the VPN

Before trying to establish the connection, check whether the IP forwarding is enabled on both gateways, as discussed in Chapter 3. You can enable the IP forwarding by running the following command:

```
$echo "1" > /proc/sys/net/ipv4/ip_forward
```

Also, be sure that the ports UDP 500 (used for IPSec for management) and ESP (IP protocol 50) are allowed through your firewall (also discussed in Chapter 3).

## HEADS UP!

FreeS/WAN does not support Network Address Translation and masquerading for the tunneled traffic. Therefore, you should disable NAT and masquerading on your gateways for the traffic you want to tunnel between gateways.

To set up the VPN connection, start by logging into your gateways and running the following command:

```
$ipsec auto - -up grumm
```

A successfully established connection will have output similar to

```
112 "grumm" #6: STATE_QUICK_I1: initiate
004 "grumm" #6: STATE_QUICK_I2: sent QI2, IPsec SA established {ESP=>0x9ac0b107 <0x8bfd214e}
```

The previous lines of output indicate that the VPN connection named **grumm** using an ESP type connection has been successfully established. Now all IP traffic between subnetworks A and B, exchanged between the gateways Linux2 and Linux1, will be encrypted.

To be sure that the traffic is really encrypted, you can use tcpdump or Ethereal to monitor the traffic (as discussed in Chapter 11). All traffic between the nodes in subnetworks A and B must be of type ESP now (encrypted). The following output is generated by tcpdump on one of the gateways, which shows the traffic generated from a node on subnetwork A going to a node on subnetwork B. As you can see, the traffic is of type ESP between the two nodes (and therefore encrypted).

```
16:31:02.691787 Linux2 > Linux1: ESP(spi=0xa7f12200,seq=0x1a)
.........
16:31:03.691674 Linux2 > Linux1: ESP(spi=0xa7f12200,seq=0x1b)
16:31:03.691976 Linux1 > Linux2: ESP(spi=0x5319a0bb,seq=0x15)
16:31:04.691511 Linux2 > Linux1: ESP(spi=0xa7f12200,seq=0x1c)
16:31:04.691811 Linux1 > Linux2: ESP(spi=0x5319a0bb,seq=0x16)
.........
```

If you need to take down your VPN connection , you can disable IPSec using the following command on RHEL AS 3.0:

```
$service ipsec stop
```

On SLES8, do the following to disable IPSec:

```
$/etc/init.d/ipsec stop
```

This command can be very useful when debugging your setup.
Some other VPN software products available for Linux are

- **Openswan**  http://www.openswan.org/
- **VPN with SSH and PPP**  http://tldp.org/HOWTO/VPN-HOWTO/
- **Virtual Tunnel**  http://vtun.sourceforge.net/

*Building Linux Virtual Private Networks*, by Oleg Kolesnikov and Brian Hatch, is a highly regarded book dedicated to the subject of Linux VPNs.

## Verify the Connection

Double-check your setup by verifying your access paths between two subnetworks. Trace the route between the gateways and nodes on different subnetworks A and B, using the **ping -R** command (or **traceroute**). This command not only verifies the connectivity of the other node, but also shows the access path between two nodes. Verify if this path corroborates your view of the network defined in /etc /ipsec.conf file.

Setting up your own VPN server should not be taken lightly. It requires knowledge of your network and the requirements of your users, as you will often have to reconfigure your firewalls to allow for VPN traffic to pass through, as well as configuring end-client machines. With that said, Linux offers some easy-to-use and full-featured VPN products for free that will fit most needs.

Securing communications within Linux is not a difficult task, and there are many choices for securing your systems. We have covered a few of the more popular tools for hardening communications on your Linux machine, and we recommend reviewing the resources listed in the appendix of this book to find more resources on hardening network communications.

# Part III

# Once Is Never Enough!

# Chapter 11

## Install Network Monitoring Software

- Install a Network Analyzer
- Utilize a Network Intrusion Detection System
- Honeypots/Honeynets
- Other Tools

**K**now thy network. This is the mantra of network security advocates, with good reason. In order to determine if you have been or are being attacked by malicious entities, you must know what normal traffic looks like. If you don't know what normal network behavior is, it is very difficult to pick out unusual traffic that should be investigated. To determine what normal traffic is, you should use these tools for a period of time under normal conditions to baseline your network and the normal activity on it. After you baseline your network, you can begin to tweak the tools to fit your needs and exclude what is normal. Security professionals will sometimes make the mistake of thinking they understand their networks and modify their tools to reduce the amount of information presented. This can lead to the tools' effectiveness being significantly reduced, because attackers or unusual traffic can be missed due to overzealous filtering.

All the tools mentioned in this chapter will allow you to identify certain types of traffic, but it does require a level of knowledge of your network in order to properly identify if the information you are seeing is a problem. In this chapter, we will be discussing some of the common open source tools used for monitoring network activity.

Before embarking on this chapter, please note that you need to understand the basics of TCP/IP to get full use of this chapter and the tools described. There are many online tutorials available on the Internet, and a good start is RFC 1180, available at http://www.ietf.org/rfc/rfc1180.txt, as well as RFC 793, available at http://www.ietf.org/rfc/rfc793/. A good pocket reference for tcpdump and TCP/IP is located at http://www.sans.org/resources/tcpip.pdf. You should also be familiar with UDP and ICMP. To find more information on UDP and ICMP, visit http://www.ietf.org/rfc/rfc0768.txt and http://www.ietf.org/rfc/rfc0792.txt, respectively, or use your favorite search engine to find out more information.

## HEADS UP!

Be aware that the tools presented in this chapter can be used by attackers if they gain access to your system, so know what programs are installed on your system and who has access to the tools.

If you are building or managing a sensitive production machine or other truly hardened machine, do not install these programs. Instead, install them on a machine built for the purposes of monitoring the network. If in doubt, install on a separate machine for maximum security or at a minimum, lock the permissions down on the executables to prevent unauthorized use. To gain full functionality of these tools, most require that you be logged in as the superuser or root as well, so if you find you don't have all the functionality mentioned in this chapter, log in as root during these operations only.

# Install a Network Analyzer

A network analyzer, sometimes generically called a sniffer (when capitalized, Sniffer is a registered trademark of Network Associates and refers to a specific product), is a program that collects and gathers all network traffic it has access to. These programs can be invaluable for discovering causes of network issues, determining the health of a network, and determining whether a malicious entity is attacking or has attacked your network. When a machine is set in promiscuous mode, the normal Ethernet hardware filtering is removed and the network interface collects all traffic on the network segment, allowing it to monitor all network traffic that passes the network interface. Network analyzers can be used both for good purposes, such as detecting network intrusions or troubleshooting the network, or for more nefarious purposes, such as obtaining user passwords or mapping network for attack. Remember that installing the software on your system can create vulnerability for you in that an attacker can gain access and use the tools against your network. Use these tools only on hardened hosts and if at all possible on non-production, network monitoring dedicated machines.

In this section, we discuss some of the more common network analyzer programs. The open source community is famous for its diverse set of applications that have similar functions, but offer different ways of doing those things. You will have to choose what program meets your needs and which you are comfortable with. For most of these programs you will need **libpcap**, which is a tool for capturing packets on your network interface. You may already have **libpcap** on your system, so determine if you do have it installed by running

```
rpm -q libpcap
```

If you have **libpcap** installed already, you will see a message similar to "libpcap-0.7.1-56," otherwise you will receive an informational message stating "package libpcap is not installed." If you do not have **libpcap** installed or you want to download the latest version, visit http://www.rpmfind.net to get the latest rpm for your platform or use the support site for your distribution to get the latest version, or visit http://www.sourceforge.net/projects/libpcap/ for the latest release of libpcap directly from the maintainers. Once you have downloaded the rpm, install it with the following code (replace libpcap-0.7.1-56.i586.rpm with the rpm name):

```
rpm -Uvh libpcap-0.7.1-56.i586.rpm
```

## Install and Use ngrep to Monitor the Network

**ngrep** (network grep) is a tool that mimics the functionality of the standard GNU **grep** command, but on a network level. This tool allows you to watch your network in real time, and separate packets based on specific parameters that you define in an easy-to-use format. You can install **ngrep** from CD if you are using SUSE, or you can find the **rpm** version of **ngrep** for your distribution at http://www.rpmfind.net. If you can't find or use the **rpm** version of **ngrep**, you can download the source at sourceforge.net/projects/ngrep/. After downloading **ngrep**, use the **rpm** command as follows to install the package:

```
rpm -Uvh ngrep-1.40-241.i586.rpm
```

**ngrep** has many different functions. The most common ones are shown in Table 11-1.

There are also some important qualifiers to assist getting more specific requests as shown in Table 11-2.

If you simply want to watch traffic as it goes through your network, just use this command:

```
ngrep
```

The output for someone going to a web site on the network followed by a ping command, for instance, would be similar to the following statements:

```
linux1:/ # ngrep
interface: eth0 (192.168.1.0/255.255.255.0)
###
T 192.168.1.1:32945 -> 192.168.1.100:80 [AP]
  GET / HTTP/1.1..Host: linux1..User-Agent: Mozilla/5.0 (X11; U; Linu
  x i686; en-US; rv:1.0.1) Gecko/20020903..
######
I 192.168.1.1 -> 192.168.1.100 8:0
  ......J@........................... !"#$%&'()*+,-./01234567
```

Let's dissect the output of **ngrep** in Table 11-3.

| Options | Meaning |
|---------|---------|
| **-d** | Use other device (not default device) |
| **-h** | Display help information on command use |
| **-i** | Ignore case, useful if you want to ignore the case of your ngrep |
| **-q** | Run quietly |
| **-v** | Don't match regex |
| **-w** | Word regular expressions (regex) |
| **-x** | Dump packet contents in hexadecimal and ASCII format |
| **-X** | Treat the expression as a hexadecimal string |

**Table 11-1.** **ngrep** Options

| Qualifier | Available Options | Examples |
|---|---|---|
| type | host, net, and port | host linux1, net 192.168.1, port 80 |
| dir | src, dst, or combination of both | src linux1, src or dst linux1, src and dest 192.168.1.1 |
| proto | tcp, udp, icmp | tcp port 23 |

**Table 11-2.    ngrep** Qualifiers

Let's try a more complex **ngrep** command using some of the options described previously. We want to watch traffic from machine192.168.1.1 (source) going to 192.168.1.100 (destination) with a destination port of 80. We are specifically looking for traffic similar to the first output shown previously.

```
linux1:/ # ngrep port 80 and src host 192.168.1.1 and dst host 192.168.1.100
interface: eth0 (192.168.1.0/255.255.255.0)
###
T 192.168.1.1:32945 -> 192.168.1.100:80 [AP]
  GET / HTTP/1.1..Host: linux1..User-Agent: Mozilla/5.0 (X11; U; Linux i686;
en-US; rv:1.0.1) Gecko/20020903..
```

**Line Analyzed:** T 192.168.1.1:32945 -> 192.168.1.100:80 [AP]

| Section of Line | Explanation |
|---|---|
| T | Shows the protocol in use, TCP = t, ICMP=I, UDP=U |
| 192.168.1.6 | Source IP |
| :32945 | Source port used |
| 192.168.1.101 | Destination IP |
| :80 | Destination port |
| [AP] | In this instance Ack Push |

**Line Analyzed:** I 192.168.1.1 -> 192.168.1.100 8:0

| Section of Line | Explanation |
|---|---|
| I | ICMP protocol |
| Source IP | 192.168.1.6 |
| Destination IP | 192.168.1.101 |
| 8:0 | Type 8 Code 0 (a ping request) |

**Table 11-3.    Analysis of ngrep** Output

Make sure to use "and" between qualifiers to include them as the command will fail if you were to type **ngrep port 80 src host 192.168.1.1 dst host 192.168.1.100**.

For easier-to-read output, try using **ngrep -x** as shown in the following output:

```
ngrep -x
interface: eth0 (192.168.1.0/255.255.255.0)
####
T 192.168.1.1:32967 -> 192.168.1.100:80 [AP]

47 45 54 20 2F 20 48 54    54 50 2F 31 2E 31 2E 2E    GET / HTTP/1.1..
48 6F 73 74 3A 20 6C 69    6E 75 78 31 2E 2E 55 73    Host: linux1..Us
65 72 2D 41 67 65 6E 74    3A 20 4D 6F 7A 69 6C 6C    er-Agent:Mozill
61 2F 35 2E 30 20 28 58    31 31 3B 20 55 3B 20 4C    a/5.0 (X11; U; L
69 6E 20 20 78 20 69 36    38 36 3B 20 65 6E 2D 55    in  x i686; en-U
53 3B 20 72 76 3A 31 2E    30 2E 31 29 20 47 65 63    S;rv:1.0.1) Gec
6B 6F 2F 32 30 30 32 30    39 30 33 2E 2E D0 A0 00    ko/20020903..
```

When dealing with a large amount of output, this might be easier to read in real time, as the output in a columnar format. The first two columns of output are hexadecimal representation of the text and can be ignored unless needed. The third column is the actual ASCII information (packet) going through.

Here are a couple of other sample **ngrep** commands to show some of the usage of **ngrep**. The following searches for all telnet traffic (port 23):

```
ngrep port 23
```

The following searches for the login prompt on port 23 (telnet) from 192.168.1.1:

```
ngrep -q -t  "ogin" port 23 and src host 192.168.1.1
```

---

**NOTE**   The **ngrep** is only looking for "ogin" as opposed to "Login." This is to ensure that a match happens for all instances, even if the initial L is dropped in transmission or whether the system is using an upper or lowercase L initially.

---

There are multiple options when using **ngrep** and initially you will probably want to just watch some traffic or dump it to a file for review later. You can use many types of filters, including filters based on host, type, protocol, or direction of packet, or even exclude based on the same. To have the output of your **ngrep** command go to a file, use the following:

```
ngrep port 23 > /tmp/ngrep_logfile
```

Note that you will need to keep an eye on the logfile you send your output to, as it can get very large and take up significant amount of disk space if not monitored closely.

# Install and Use tcpdump

**tcpdump** is simply a program that "dumps" all traffic headers passing along the network, as opposed to the entire packet. Most major distributions (including SUSE and Red Hat) have **rpms** available at http://www.rpmfind.net or on the distribution CD. If downloading the **rpm**, simply install by doing the following (depending on the filename):

```
rpm -Uvh tcpdump.3.8.1.1.i386.rpm
```

If rpm doesn't work for you or you prefer to build it yourself, you can download the source files from sourceforge.net/projects/tcpdump/ (currently tcpdump-3.8.1). If you take this route, you will need to install gcc, which is available at http://www.rpmfind.net as well. After downloading, install the source files with the following:

```
tar -zxf tcpdump-3.8.1.tar.gz
cd tcpdump-3.8.1
./configure
make
make install
```

**tcpdump**, as any other open source tool, has a multitude of options that it can be run with. Table 11-4 lists some of the more common options.

As with **ngrep**, **tcpdump** has qualifiers, as identified in Table 11-5.

**tcpdump** can create a lot of output if no options are passed, but we should look at the standard output for a better understanding of what is available (telnet session).

| Options | Meaning |
| --- | --- |
| -a | Convert network and broadcast addresses to an FQDN |
| -c | Stop after receiving a specific number of packets |
| -e | Print link-level header on every line |
| -i | Listen on specified interface |
| -l | Make stdout line buffered, so you can pipe the output to **grep** or **tee** (for example, **tcpdump -l I grep ssh**) |
| -N | Only print hostname instead of FQDN |
| -q | Print less detailed information (good for just identifying connections with a small amount of information output on the command line or file) |
| -v | More verbose output |
| -vv | Even more verbose output |
| -vvv | Extremely verbose output |
| -w | Write raw packets to file |

**Table 11-4.**   **tcpdump** Command Line Options

| Qualifier | Available Options | Examples |
|-----------|-------------------|----------|
| type | host, net, and port | host linux1, net 192.168.1, port 80 |
| dir | src, dst, or combination of both | src linux1, src or dst linux1, src, and dest 192.168.1.1 |
| proto | ether, fddi, tr, ip, ip6, arp, rarp, decent, tcp, udp | tcp port 23 |

**Table 11-5.    tcpdump** Qualifiers

**NOTE**  Due to space constraints, some of the command output lines have to be adjusted with five spaces of indention throughout the rest of the chapter. This is not how the output will look when you run the command; the lines will simply wrap to the next line.

```
linux1:/ #tcpdump
tcpdump: verbose output suppressed, use -v or -vv for full protocol decode
listening on eth0
09:03:35.842102 IP 192.168.1.1.32868 > 192.168.1.100.23: P 28:137(109)
     ack 52 win 5840 <nop,nop,timestamp 123456 1876543210>
09:03:35.919887 IP 192.168.1.100.23 > 192.168.1.1.32868: . ack 137 win
     5792 <nop,nop,timestamp 1876543218 123456>
09:03:35.919902 IP 192.168.1.100.23 > 192.168.1.1.32868: P 52:55(3)
     ack 137 win 5792 <nop,nop,timestamp 1876543218 123456>
09:03:35.922717 IP 192.168.1.1.32868 > 192.168.1.100.23: P 137:140(3)
     ack 55 win 5840 <nop,nop,timestamp 123464 1876543218>
09:03:36.005509 IP 192.168.1.100.:S23 > 192.168.1.1.32868: P 55:85(30)
     ack 140 win 5792 <nop,nop,timestamp 1876543227 123464>
09:03:36.008526 IP 192.168.1.1.32868 > 192.168.1.100.23: P 140:143(3)
     ack 85 win 5840 <nop,nop,timestamp 123473 1876543227>
09:03:36.083412 IP 192.168.1.100.23 > 192.168.1.1.32868: P 85:92(7)
     ack 143 win 5792 <nop,nop,timestamp 1876543225 123473>
09:03:36.123182 IP 192.168.1.1.32868 > 192.168.1.100.23: . ack 92 win
     5840 <nop,nop,timestamp 123493 1876543225>
09:03:42.790047 IP 192.168.1.1.32868 > 192.168.1.100.23: F 143:143(0)
     ack 92 win 5840 <nop,nop,timestamp 124125 1876543225>
09:03:42.863202 IP 192.168.1.100.23 > 192.168.1.1.32868: F 92:92(0)
     ack 144 win 5792 <nop,nop,timestamp 1876543907 124125>
09:03:42.863547 IP 192.168.1.1.32868 > 192.168.1.100.23: . ack 93 win
     5840 <nop,nop,timestamp 541733 1876543907>
```

The standard output format of a line from tcp protocol is *source > destination: flags data-seqno ack window urgent options*. The single line of output that follows is dissected in Table 11-6:

```
09:03:35.842102 IP 192.168.1.1.32868 > 192.168.1.100.23: P 28:137(109)
     ack 52 win 5840 <nop,nop,timestamp 541031 152328860>
```

| Section of Line | Explanation |
|---|---|
| 09:03:35.842102 | Timestamp |
| IP | Internet Protocol |
| 192.168.1.1 | Source IP |
| .32868 | Source port |
| 192.168.1.100 | Destination IP |
| .23 | Destination port |
| P | TCP flag set |
| 28:137(109) | Sequence number (first:last) and amount of data in bytes |
| ack 52 | Ack tcp flag |
| win 5840 | Window size (5840 in this case) |
| <nop,nop,timestamp 541031 152328860> | Miscellaneous tcp options |

**Table 11-6.** tcpdump Output Dissected

Again, familiarity of TCP/IP is crucial to understand what you are seeing, but having previous knowledge of the protocols and a knowledge of your network allows you to get a better understanding of what is occurring on your network.

If you just want to use **tcpdump** to get some quick output, try using **tcpdump** with the **-q** option. The results of not using the **-q** option and using it are shown next. As usual, the command precedes the output. Here is the difference in output on a simple ping command:

```
linux1:/ # tcpdump
09:58:04.932897 IP 192.168.1.100 > 192.168.1.1: icmp 64: echo request
    seq 256
09:58:04.934294 IP 192.168.1.1 > 192.168.1.100: icmp 64: echo reply
    seq 256
09:58:04.949401 IP 192.168.1.100.32787 > 192.168.1.200.53:  19937+ PTR?
    1.1.168.192.in-addr.arpa. (42)
09:58:04.962599 IP 192.168.1.200.53 > 192.168.1.100.32787:  19937
    NXDomain 0/1/0 (129)
09:58:04.965071 IP 192.168.1.100.32787 > 192.168.1.200.53:  19938+
    PTR? 200.1.168.192.in-addr.arpa. (42)
09:58:04.983159 IP 192.168.1.200.53 > 192.168.1.100.32787:  19938
    1/2/2 PTR[|domain]

linux1:/tmp # tcpdump -q
tcpdump: verbose output suppressed, use -v or -vv for full protocol decode
listening on eth0
09:59:06.054203 IP 192.168.1.100 > 192.168.1.1: icmp 64: echo request seq 256
09:59:06.057390 IP 192.168.1.1 > 192.168.1.100: icmp 64: echo reply seq 256
```

```
09:59:06.105772 IP 192.168.1.100.32787 > 192.168.1.200.53: UDP, length: 42
09:59:06.122104 IP 192.168.1.200.53 > 192.168.1.100.32787: UDP, length: 129
09:59:06.142766 IP 192.168.1.100.32787 > 192.168.1.200.53: UDP, length: 42
09:59:06.157319 IP 192.168.1.200.53 > 192.168.1.100.32787: UDP, length: 165
```

The **-q** option simply provides less information, but is much easier to read when dealing with a large amount of data.

You might find that initially using the **-q** option will make it easier to get a very general overview of what is happening on your network as well as for gaining a better understanding of networking.

```
man tcpdump
```

---

**TIP**   This program has an extremely well written and informative man page that should be referenced if you are looking to get more familiar with this tool. To see the man page, simply type **man tcpdump**.

---

There are other tools to make the standard **tcpdump** command display easier to read, available at http://www.freshmeat.net using the search function with the keyword of **tcpdump**. **tcpdump** is a powerful tool, but it requires a high level of knowledge in networking concepts and protocols. If used properly, this tool can create a deeper understanding of the network and its effect on your Linux machine.

Okay, so this might seem like a lot of work for watching some pings, but the real value of **tcpdump** lies in the ability of the security administrator to audit the network. Let's look at an FTP session to see what information is passed. Using the **-X** option, we run **tcpdump** and monitor our FTP connection. Here is the output:

```
linux1:~ # tcpdump -X
tcpdump: verbose output suppressed, use -v or -vv for full protocol decode
listening on eth0, link-type EN10MB (Ethernet), capture size 96 bytes
15:19:38.495492 IP 192.168.1.1.32781 > 192.168.1.200.domain:  21882+ PTR?
100.1.168.192.in-addr.arpa. (44)
0x0000    4500 0048 0000 4000 4011 74c3 c0a8 0106        E..H..@.@.t.....
0x0010    442e c005 800d 0035 0034 a53b 557a 0100        D......5.4.;Uz..
0x0020    0001 0000 0000 0000 0331 3030 0131 0331        .........100.1.1
0x0030    3638 0331 3932 0769 6e2d 6164 6472 0461        68.192.in-addr.a
0x0040    7270 6100 000c 0001                            rpa.....
15:19:38.506474 IP 192.168.1.200.domain > 192.168.1.1.32781:  21882
        NXDomain 0/1/0 (131)
0x0000    4500 009f 5af7 4000 fd11 5c74 442e c005        E...Z.@...\tD...
0x0010    c0a8 0106 0035 800d 008b 9a91 557a 8183        .....5......Uz..
0x0020    0001 0000 0001 0000 0331 3030 0131 0331        .........100.1.1
0x0030    3638 0331 3932 0769 6e2d 6164 6472 0461        68.192.in-addr.a
0x0040    7270 6100 000c 0001 c012 0006 0001 0000        rpa............
0x0050    128c                                           ..
15:19:38.508051 IP 192.168.1.1.32966 > 192.168.1.100.ftp: S
```

```
        890269150:890269150(0) win 5840 <mss 1460,sackOK,timestamp 387786
        0,nop,wscale 1>
0x0000    4500 003c 0000 4000 4006 b701 c0a8 0106        E..<..@.@.......
0x0010    c0a8 0164 80c6 0015 3510 6dde 0000 0000        ...d....5.m.....
0x0020    a002 16d0 9ee1 0000 0204 05b4 0402 080a        ...............
0x0030    0005 eaca 0000 0000 0103 0301                  ...........
15:19:38.516858 IP 192.168.1.100.ftp > 192.168.1.1.32966: S
        852782868:852782868(0) ack 890269151 win 5792 <mss
        1460,sackOK,timestamp 3027262 387786,nop,wscale 0>
0x0000    4500 003c 0000 4000 4006 b701 c0a8 0164        E..<..@.@......d
0x0010    c0a8 0106 0015 80c6 32d4 6f14 3510 6ddf        ........2.o.5.m.
0x0020    a012 16a0 cbac 0000 0204 05b4 0402 080a        ...............
0x0030    002e 313e 0005 eaca 0103 0300                  ..1>........
15:19:38.517185 IP 192.168.1.1.32966 > 192.168.1.100.ftp: . ack 1 win
        2920 <nop,nop,timestamp 387787 3027262>
0x0000    4500 0034 0000 4000 4006 b709 c0a8 0106        E..4..@.@.......
0x0010    c0a8 0164 80c6 0015 3510 6ddf 32d4 6f15        ...d....5.m.2.o.
0x0020    8010 0b68 05a9 0000 0101 080a 0005 eacb        ...h...........
0x0030    002e 313e                                      ..1>
15:19:38.526500 IP 192.168.1.100.ftp > 192.168.1.1.32966: P 1:21(20)
        ack 1 win 5792 <nop,nop,timestamp 3027263 387787>
0x0000    4500 0048 5e2a 4000 4006 58cb c0a8 0164        E..H^*@.@.X....d
0x0010    c0a8 0106 0015 80c6 32d4 6f15 3510 6ddf        ........2.o.5.m.
0x0020    8018 16a0 a344 0000 0101 080a 002e 313f        .....D........1?
0x0030    0005 eacb 3232 3020 2876 7346 5450 6420        ....220.(vsFTPd.
0x0040    312e 322e 3029 0d0a                            1.2.0)..
15:19:38.526841 IP 192.168.1.1.32966 > 192.168.1.100.ftp: . ack 21
        win 2920 <nop,nop,timestamp 387788 3027263>
0x0000    4510 0034 0000 4000 4006 b6f9 c0a8 0106        E..4..@.@.......
0x0010    c0a8 0164 80c6 0015 3510 6ddf 32d4 6f29        ...d....5.m.2.o)
0x0020    8010 0b68 0593 0000 0101 080a 0005 eacc        ...h...........
0x0030    002e 313f                                      ..1?
15:19:38.542083 IP 192.168.1.200.domain > 192.168.1.1.32782:  45715
        NXDomain 0/1/0 (131)
0x0000    4500 009f 5af9 4000 fd11 5c72 442e c005        E...Z.@...\rD...
0x0010    c0a8 0106 0035 800e 008b 3d77 b293 8183        .....5....=w....
0x0020    0001 0000 0001 0000 0331 3030 0131 0331        .........100.1.1
0x0030    3638 0331 3932 0769 6e2d 6164 6472 0461        68.192.in-addr.a
0x0040    7270 6100 000c 0001 c012 0006 0001 0000        rpa.............
0x0050    128c                                           ..
15:19:42.017006 IP 192.168.1.1.32966 > 192.168.1.100.ftp: P 1:17(16)
        ack 21 win 2920 <nop,nop,timestamp 388137 3027263>
0x0000    4510 0044 0000 4000 4006 b6e9 c0a8 0106        E..D..@.@.......
0x0010    c0a8 0164 80c6 0015 3510 6ddf 32d4 6f29        ...d....5.m.2.o)
0x0020    8018 0b68 7c41 0000 0101 080a 0005 ec29        ...h|A.........)
0x0030    002e 313f 5553 4552 2061 6e6f 6e79 6d6f        ..1?USER.anonymo
0x0040    7573 0d0a                                      us..
15:19:42.026889 IP 192.168.1.100.ftp > 192.168.1.1.32966: . ack 17 win
        5792 <nop,nop,timestamp 3027614 388137>
```

```
0x0000    4500 0034 5e2b 4000 4006 58de c0a8 0164    E..4^+@.@.X....d
0x0010    c0a8 0106 0015 80c6 32d4 6f29 3510 6def    ........2.o)5.m.
0x0020    8010 16a0 f78e 0000 0101 080a 002e 329e    ..............2.
0x0030    0005 ec29                                   ...)
15:19:42.026912 IP 192.168.1.100.ftp > 192.168.1.1.32966: P 21:55(34)
     ack 17 win 5792 <nop,nop,timestamp 3027614 388137>
0x0000    4500 0056 5e2c 4000 4006 58bb c0a8 0164    E..V^,@.@.X....d
0x0010    c0a8 0106 0015 80c6 32d4 6f29 3510 6def    ........2.o)5.m.
0x0020    8018 16a0 b043 0000 0101 080a 002e 329e    .....C........2.
0x0030    0005 ec29 3333 3120 506c 6561 7365 2073    ...)331.Please.s
0x0040    7065 6369 6679 2074 6865 2070 6173 7377    pecify.the.passw
0x0050    6f72                                        or
15:19:42.027281 IP 192.168.1.1.32966 > 192.168.1.100.ftp: . ack 55
     win 2920 <nop,nop,timestamp 388138 3027614>
0x0000    4510 0034 0000 4000 4006 b6f9 c0a8 0106    E..4..@.@.......
0x0010    c0a8 0164 80c6 0015 3510 6def 32d4 6f4b    ...d....5.m.2.oK
0x0020    8010 0b68 02a4 0000 0101 080a 0005 ec2a    ...h...........*
0x0030    002e 329e                                   ..2.
15:19:43.486412 arp who-has 192.168.1.1 tell 192.168.1.1
0x0000    0001 0800 0604 0001 0003 ff32 5e38 c0a8    ...........2^8..
0x0010    0106 0000 0000 0000 c0a8 0101              ............
5:19:43.489420 IP 192.168.1.1.32782 > 192.168.1.200.domain:  45716+
     PTR? 1.1.168.192.in-addr.arpa. (42)
0x0000    4500 0046 0000 4000 4011 74c5 c0a8 0106    E..F..@.@.t.....
0x0010    442e c005 800e 0035 0032 7a54 b294 0100    D......5.2zT....
0x0020    0001 0000 0000 0000 0131 0131 0331 3638    .........1.1.168
0x0030    0331 3932 0769 6e2d 6164 6472 0461 7270    .192.in-addr.arp
0x0040    6100 000c 0001                              a.....
15:19:43.490284 arp reply 192.168.1.1 is-at 00:0c:41:45:9a:18
0x0000    0001 0800 0604 0002 000c 4145 9a18 c0a8    ..........AE....
0x0010    0101 0003 ff32 5e38 c0a8 0106 0000 0000    .....2^8........
0x0020    0000 0000 0000 0000 0000 0000 0000         ..............
15:19:43.505854 IP 192.168.1.200.domain > 192.168.1.1.32782:  45716
     NXDomain 0/1/0 (129)
0x0000    4500 009d 5afa 4000 fd11 5c73 442e c005    E...Z.@...\sD...
0x0010    c0a8 0106 0035 800e 0089 7395 b294 8183    .....5....s.....
0x0020    0001 0000 0001 0000 0131 0131 0331 3638    .........1.1.168
0x0030    0331 3932 0769 6e2d 6164 6472 0461 7270    .192.in-addr.arp
0x0040    6100 000c 0001 c010 0006 0001 0000 0ea3    a.............
0x0050    004b                                        .K
15:19:46.351612 IP 192.168.1.1.32966 > 192.168.1.100.ftp: P 17:32(15)
     ack 55 win 2920 <nop,nop,timestamp 388570 3027614>
0x0000    4510 0043 0000 4000 4006 b6ea c0a8 0106    E..C..@.@.......
0x0010    c0a8 0164 80c6 0015 3510 6def 32d4 6f4b    ...d....5.m.2.oK
0x0020    8018 0b68 8a6d 0000 0101 080a 0005 edda    ...h.m.........
0x0030    002e 329e 5041 5353 2070 6173 7377 6f72    ..2.PASS.passwor
0x0040    640d 0a                                     d..
15:19:46.358216 IP 192.168.1.100.ftp > 192.168.1.1.32966: P 55:78(23)
     ack 32 win 5792 <nop,nop,timestamp 3028050 388570>
```

```
05 800e 0035 0032 7a54 b294 0100          D......5.2zT....
0x0020    0001 0000 0000 0000 0131 0131 0331 3638       .........1.1.168
0x0030    0331 3932 0769 6e2d 6164 6472 0461 7270       .192.in-addr.arp
0x0040    6100 000c 0001                                a.....
15:19:43.490284 arp reply 192.168.1.1 is-at 00:0c:41:45:9a:18
0x0000    0001 0800 0604 0002 000c 4145 9a18 c0a8       ..........AE....
0x0010    0101 0003 ff32 5e38 c0a8 0106 0000 0000       .....2^8........
0x0020    0000 0000 0000 0000 0000 0000 0000            ..............
15:19:43.505854 IP 192.168.1.200.domain > 192.168.1.1.32782:  45716
      NXDomain 0/1/0 (129)
0x0000    4500 009d 5afa 4000 fd11 5c73 442e c005       E...Z.@...\sD...
0x0010    c0a8 0106 0035 800e 0089 7395 b294 8183       .....5....s.....
0x0020    0001 0000 0001 0000 0131 0131 0331 3638       .........1.1.168
0x0030    0331 3932 0769 6e2d 6164 6472 0461 7270       .192.in-addr.arp
0x0040    6100 000c 0001 c010 0006 0001 0000 0ea3       a...............
0x0050    004b                                          .K
15:19:46.351612 IP 192.168.1.1.32966 > 192.168.1.100.ftp: P 17:32(15)
      ack 55 win 2920 <nop,nop,timestamp 388570 3027614>
0x0000    4510 0043 0000 4000 4006 b6ea c0a8 0106       E..C..@.@.......
0x0010    c0a8 0164 80c6 0015 3510 6def 32d4 6f4b       ...d....5.m.2.oK
0x0020    8018 0b68 8a6d 0000 0101 080a 0005 edda       ...h.m..........
0x0030    002e 329e 5041 5353 2070 6173 7377 6f72       ..2.PASS.passwor
0x0040    640d 0a                                       d..
15:19:46.358216 IP 192.168.1.100.ftp > 192.168.1.1.32966: P 55:78(23)
      ack 32 win 5792 <nop,nop,timestamp 3028050 388570>
0x0000    4500 004b 5e2d 4000 4006 58c5 c0a8 0164       E..K^-@.@.X....d
0x0010    c0a8 0106 0015 80c6 32d4 6f4b 3510 6dfe       ........2.oK5.m.
0x0020    8018 16a0 1261 0000 0101 080a 002e 3452       .....a........4R
0x0030    0005 edda 3233 3020 4c6f 6769 6e20 7375       ....230.Login.su
0x0040    6363 6573 7366 756c 2e0d 0a                   ccessful...
```

The tcpdump -X shows a sample FTP connection login and then **tcpdump** was exited. Granted, that is a lot of output, but this is what occurs when you do an FTP. If you peruse the entire output, you might notice a few interesting tidbits of information. Recall that we were using FTP, which is not encrypted. Now take a look at three sets of packets taken from the previous output:

```
15:19:38.526500 IP 192.168.1.100.ftp > 192.168.1.1.32966: P 1:21(20)
      ack 1 win 5792 <nop,nop,timestamp 3027263 387787>
0x0000    4500 0048 5e2a 4000 4006 58cb c0a8 0164       E..H^*@.@.X....d
0x0010    c0a8 0106 0015 80c6 32d4 6f15 3510 6ddf       ........2.o.5.m.
0x0020    8018 16a0 a344 0000 0101 080a 002e 313f       .....D........1?
0x0030    0005 eacb 3232 3020 2876 7346 5450 6420       ....220.(vsFTPd.
0x0040    312e 322e 3029 0d0a                           1.2.0)..
```

This shows that our ftp server (192.168.1.100) is running vsftpd 1.2.0 (look at line 0x0030 and 0x0040). This is not anything really private, as it is advertised whenever anyone FTPs to the server, but it should be removed to make it just a little harder for an attacker.

```
15:19:42.017006 IP 192.168.1.1.32966 > 192.168.1.100.ftp: P 1:17(16)
     ack 21 win 2920 <nop,nop,timestamp 388137 3027263>
0x0000   4510 0044 0000 4000 4006 b6e9 c0a8 0106     E..D..@.@.......
0x0010   c0a8 0164 80c6 0015 3510 6ddf 32d4 6f29     ...d....5.m.2.o)
0x0020   8018 0b68 7c41 0000 0101 080a 0005 ec29     ...h|A.........)
0x0030   002e 313f 5553 4552 2061 6e6f 6e79 6d6f     ..1?USER.anonymo
0x0040   7573 0d0a                                   us..
```

This shows that we passed anonymous as the username (look at line 0x0030).

```
15:19:46.351612 IP 192.168.1.1.32966 > 192.168.1.100.ftp: P 17:32(15)
     ack 55 win 2920 <nop,nop,timestamp 388570 3027614>
0x0000   4510 0043 0000 4000 4006 b6ea c0a8 0106     E..C..@.@.......
0x0010   c0a8 0164 80c6 0015 3510 6def 32d4 6f4b     ...d....5.m.2.oK
0x0020   8018 0b68 8a6d 0000 0101 080a 0005 edda     ...h.m.........
0x0030   002e 329e 5041 5353 2070 6173 7377 6f72     ..2.PASS.passwor
0x0040   640d 0a                                     d..
```

Now we can see the password is "password" (look at lines 0x0030 and 0x0040). From this **tcpdump**, an attacker would be able to gain a user's login name and password and the version of FTP server they were using (you could get this by simply FTP-ing, though, as it is the header information). Imagine if this were a real user account and password and what the implications of that would be. An encrypted session (SSH, SCP, SFTP, and so on) would show garbled text and would be unrecognizable.

## Install Ethereal

Ethereal (the Ethereal Network Analyzer) is a more user-friendly, graphical version of **tcpdump** with the same functionality. Ethereal is the de facto standard network analyzer in the open source community today, and with good reason. It supports many, many protocols, different output formats as well as other interesting options.

Ethereal is available on most Linux distributions, but if needed, you can find the **rpms** available at http://www.rpmfind.net and install with the **rpm -Uvh** command, or get it directly from http://www.ethereal.com. After installation, type the following to run Ethereal in the background:

```
ethereal &
```

After typing **ethereal**, you will see a screen similar to Figure 11-1.

In this section on Ethereal, we will not be covering the full gamut of options that are available, so we recommend that you visit http://www.ethereal.com/docs/user-guide/ for a full tutorial on the usage and capabilities of Ethereal.

To see a real-time capture of packets as they cross your network, you need to go to the Capture menu and click Start. You will be presented with the next screen of options related to packet captures, shown in Figure 11-2.

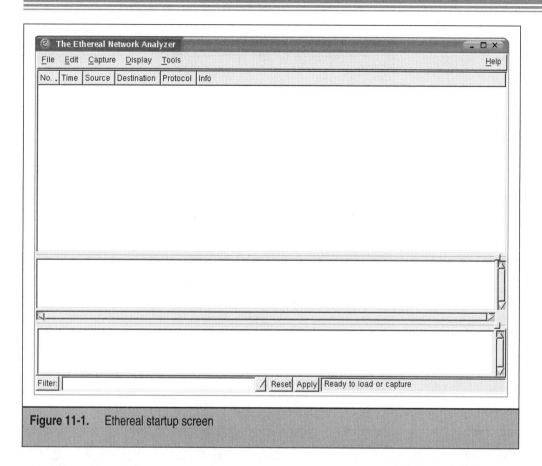

**Figure 11-1.** Ethereal startup screen

For real-time captures, select Update List Of Packets In Real Time. You can select Automatic Scrolling In Live Capture if you want scrolling enabled. After selecting any other options you require, click OK to start capturing packets. A new window showing statistics on packet capture will appear similar to Figure 11-3.

As packets start being collected, you will see the information displayed in the packet list pane. Figure 11-4 shows a ping request and reply.

Ethereal supports filtering similar to that described in **tcpdump** as well as many other options for displaying packets in an easier-to-read format, name resolution, multiple save options, and analysis options. You can import reports generated by other programs such as **tcpdump** into the graphical interface provided by Ethereal for easier analysis. Ethereal also has the ability to filter traffic with the Display Filters mechanism, allowing you to see only the traffic you want. This feature is accessible from the Edit menu under Display Filters. More documentation on this functionality is available at www.ethereal.com/docs/man-pages/ethereal-filter.4.html and http://www.ethereal.com/docs/dfref/.

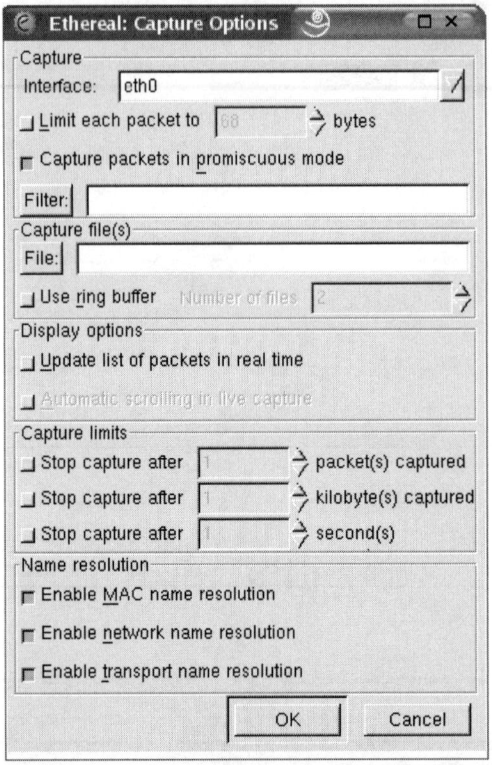

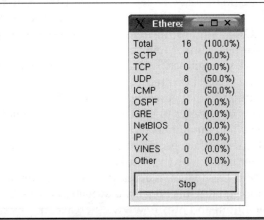

**Figure 11-2.** Ethereal Capture options

**Figure 11-3.** Ethereal protocol statistics

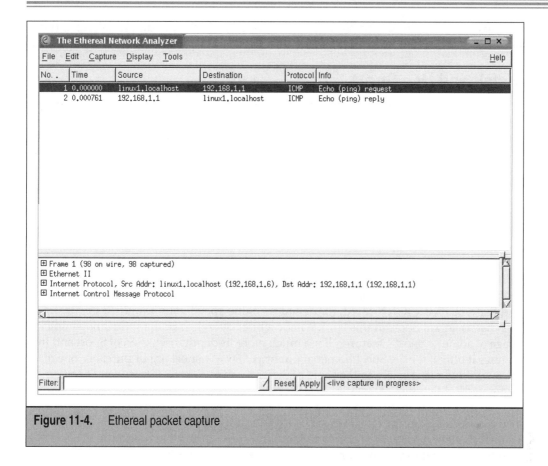

**Figure 11-4.**    Ethereal packet capture

Before using Ethereal, you should become familiar with the command line tools, as you will not always have access to a graphical user interface in times of need. Knowing and understanding the command line network analyzers will allow you to immediately determine if a situation exists or if there are anomalies on the network.

# Utilize a Network Intrusion Detection System

A network intrusion detection system is a machine or software that monitors network connections for signs of intrusion, denial of service, policy violations, or other unusual or user-specified activity. The network intrusion detection system (commonly referred to as NIDS) will watch a network or group of machines. It can be installed on a machine or be a completely separate component from the machines it is monitoring. This is in contrast to a host-based intrusion detection system, which typically monitors and is installed on a machine such as Tripwire, discussed in Chapter 14.

## Install and Use Snort

Snort is the ubiquitous network intrusion detection system in the open source community today. It can be a network analyzer (or sniffer), network intrusion detection system, or packet logger depending on the setup. Snort has a very large following and is growing every day—in fact, Snort has been so popular that it has spawned a commercial product. Before installing, you need to determine if you are going to have a database backend. There are a few benefits to having a database, such as searchable events as well as better performance. We won't be discussing setting up a database backend to Snort, as this is beyond the scope of this book. If you really want a database backend, see the excellent Snort documentation available at http://www.snort.org/docs/. You might want to consider the placement or whether you even want to run a network intrusion detection system on a production machine. A NIDS might be the first target of an attacker (internal or external) either through a denial of service or direct access to the machine. It is highly recommended that you do not run the NIDS on your production systems and that you create a dedicated, hardened machine specifically for NIDS purposes. The discussion of Snort in this book will be a brief overview of the setup and simple usage of some of Snort's features. For a much more in-depth discussion of Snort and the features it offers, see the Snort homepage at http://www.snort.org or purchase one of the books dedicated solely to the topic of Snort, such as *Snort 2.0 Intrusion Detection* (Syngress Publishing, 2003; ISBN 1931836744).

The first step is to download and install Snort from http://www.snort.org/dl/. You can install from **rpm** or from **src**. If installing from **rpm**, you can simply type **rpm -Uvh** *snort.x.x.x.rpm* at the command line substituting *x.x.x* with the version numbers. If installing from source, you will need to do the following:

```
tar -zxf snort.2.1.1.tar.gz
cd snort.2.1.1
./configure
make
make install
```

## Use Snort in Sniffing Mode

To use Snort in a sniffing mode, simply type **snort -v** and you will see output similar to the following (showing ping packets):

```
linux1:/ # snort -v
Running in packet dump mode
Log directory = /var/log/snort

Initializing Network Interface eth0
```

```
        --== Initializing Snort ==--
Initializing Output Plugins!
Decoding Ethernet on interface eth0

        --== Initialization Complete ==--

-*> Snort! <*-
Version 2.1.1 (Build 24)
By Martin Roesch (roesch@sourcefire.com, www.snort.org)
03/07-12:31:23.035680 ARP who-has 192.168.1.1 tell 192.168.1.100

03/07-12:31:23.038639 ARP reply 192.168.1.1 is-at 0:0:0:0:0:0

03/07-12:31:23.044477 192.168.1.100 -> 192.168.1.1
ICMP TTL:64 TOS:0x0 ID:0 IpLen:20 DgmLen:84 DF
Type:8  Code:0  ID:32790  Seq:256  ECHO
=+=+=+=+=+=+=+=+=+=+=+=+=+=+=+=+=+=+=+=+=+=+=+=+=+=+=+=+=+=+=+=+

03/07-12:31:23.045126 192.168.1.1 -> 192.168.1.100
ICMP TTL:150 TOS:0x0 ID:0 IpLen:20 DgmLen:84
Type:0  Code:0  ID:32790  Seq:256  ECHO REPLY
=+=+=+=+=+=+=+=+=+=+=+=+=+=+=+=+=+=+=+=+=+=+=+=+=+=+=+=+=+=+=+=+
-*> Snort! <*-
======================================================================
Snort analyzed 46 out of 46 packets, dropping 0(0.000%) packets

Breakdown by protocol:                  Action Stats:
        TCP: 0          (0.000%)        ALERTS: 0
        UDP: 0          (0.000%)        LOGGED: 0
       ICMP: 2          (50.00%)        PASSED: 0
        ARP: 2          (50.00%)
      EAPOL: 0          (0.000%)
       IPv6: 0          (0.000%)
        IPX: 0          (0.000%)
      OTHER: 0          (0.000%)
    DISCARD: 0          (0.000%)
======================================================================
Wireless Stats:
Breakdown by type:
    Management Packets: 0          (0.000%)
    Control Packets:    0          (0.000%)
    Data Packets:       0          (0.000%)
======================================================================
Fragmentation Stats:
Fragmented IP Packets: 0          (0.000%)
```

```
       Fragment Trackers: 0
     Rebuilt IP Packets: 0
      Frag elements used: 0
 Discarded(incomplete): 0
     Discarded(timeout): 0
   Frag2 memory faults: 0
======================================================================
TCP Stream Reassembly Stats:
        TCP Packets Used: 0            (0.000%)
        Stream Trackers: 0
         Stream flushes: 0
          Segments used: 0
   Stream4 Memory Faults: 0
======================================================================
Snort exiting
```

To stop Snort, press CRTL-C and you will see the latter part with statistics on your session. This is very basic information and you will probably want to see more packet information, which can be done with the command **snort -dev**. To have the packet information logged to a file, use the **-l** option such as **snort -dev -l /var/log/snort** (make sure the /var/log/snort directory or whichever directory you choose exists). The files that are created in the log directory you choose are very obvious, so peruse them as needed.

## Use Snort in Packet Capture Mode

Let's look at another interesting session as captured by Snort in packet capture mode (snort -dev):

```
=+=+=+=+=+=+=+=+=+=+=+=+=+=+=+=+=+=+=+=+=+=+=+=+=+=+=+=+=+=+=+=+=+=+=+

03/07-16:26:17.923667 0:AA:11:BB:22:CC -> 01:01:01:01:01:01 type:0x800 len:0xA2
192.168.1.100:21 -> 192.168.1.1:33003 TCP TTL:64 TOS:0x0 ID:51120
     IpLen:20 DgmLen:148 DF
***AP*** Seq: 0x2EEF469F  Ack: 0x30CDB4A5  Win: 0x16A0  TcpLen: 32
TCP Options (3) => NOP NOP TS: 3440943 787726
32 32 30 20 55 6E 61 75 74 68 6F 72 69 7A 65 64   220 Unauthorized
20 61 63 63 65 73 73 20 70 72 6F 68 69 62 69 74    access prohibit
65 64 2E 20 41 6C 6C 20 75 73 65 20 69 73 20 6D   ed. All use is m
6F 6E 69 74 6F 72 65 64 20 61 6E 64 20 75 6E 6C   onitored and unl
61 77 66 75 6C 20 61 63 63 65 73 73 20 77 69 6C   awful access wil
6C 20 62 65 20 72 65 70 6F 72 74 65 64 2E 0D 0A   l be reported...


=+=+=+=+=+=+=+=+=+=+=+=+=+=+=+=+=+=+=+=+=+=+=+=+=+=+=+=+=+=+=+=+=+=+=+

03/07-16:26:17.923965 01:01:01:01:01:01 -> 0:AA:11:BB:22:CC type:0x800
     len:0x42
```

```
192.168.1.1:33003 -> 192.168.1.100:21 TCP TTL:64 TOS:0x0 ID:0 IpLen:20
    DgmLen:52 DF
***A**** Seq: 0x30CDB4A5  Ack: 0x2EEF46FF  Win: 0xB68  TcpLen: 32
TCP Options (3) => NOP NOP TS: 787727 3440943

=+=+=+=+=+=+=+=+=+=+=+=+=+=+=+=+=+=+=+=+=+=+=+=+=+=+=+=+=+=+=+=+

03/07-16:26:20.280752 01:01:01:01:01:01 -> 0:AA:11:BB:22:CC type:0x800 len:0x4D
192.168.1.1:33003 -> 192.168.1.100:21 TCP TTL:64 TOS:0x10 ID:0 IpLen:20
      DgmLen:63 DF
***AP*** Seq: 0x30CDB4A5  Ack: 0x2EEF46FF  Win: 0xB68  TcpLen: 32
TCP Options (3) => NOP NOP TS: 787963 3440943
55 53 45 52 20 6A 64 6F 65 0D 0A                USER jdoe..

=+=+=+=+=+=+=+=+=+=+=+=+=+=+=+=+=+=+=+=+=+=+=+=+=+=+=+=+=+=+=+=+

03/07-16:26:20.281611 0:AA:11:BB:22:CC -> 01:01:01:01:01:01 type:0x800 len:0x42
192.168.1.100:21 -> 192.168.1.1:33003 TCP TTL:64 TOS:0x0 ID:51121 IpLen:20
    DgmLen:52 DF
***A**** Seq: 0x2EEF46FF  Ack: 0x30CDB4B0  Win: 0x16A0  TcpLen: 32
TCP Options (3) => NOP NOP TS: 3441182 787963

=+=+=+=+=+=+=+=+=+=+=+=+=+=+=+=+=+=+=+=+=+=+=+=+=+=+=+=+=+=+=+=+

03/07-16:26:20.281626 0:AA:11:BB:22:CC -> 01:01:01:01:01:01 type:0x800 len:0x64
192.168.1.100:21 -> 192.168.1.1:33003 TCP TTL:64 TOS:0x0 ID:51122 IpLen:20
    DgmLen:86 DF
***AP*** Seq: 0x2EEF46FF  Ack: 0x30CDB4B0  Win: 0x16A0  TcpLen: 32
TCP Options (3) => NOP NOP TS: 3441183 787963
33 33 31 20 50 6C 65 61 73 65 20 73 70 65 63 69  331 Please speci
66 79 20 74 68 65 20 70 61 73 73 77 6F 72 64 2E  fy the password.
0D 0A                                            ..

=+=+=+=+=+=+=+=+=+=+=+=+=+=+=+=+=+=+=+=+=+=+=+=+=+=+=+=+=+=+=+=+

03/07-16:26:20.281910 01:01:01:01:01:01 -> 0:AA:11:BB:22:CC type:0x800 len:0x42
192.168.1.1:33003 -> 192.168.1.100:21 TCP TTL:64 TOS:0x10 ID:0 IpLen:20
      DgmLen:52 DF
***A**** Seq: 0x30CDB4B0  Ack: 0x2EEF4721  Win: 0xB68  TcpLen: 32
TCP Options (3) => NOP NOP TS: 787963 3441183

=+=+=+=+=+=+=+=+=+=+=+=+=+=+=+=+=+=+=+=+=+=+=+=+=+=+=+=+=+=+=+=+

03/07-16:26:22.876297 ARP who-has 192.168.1.1 tell 192.168.1.1

03/07-16:26:22.879121 ARP reply 192.168.1.1 is-at 0:AA:11:BB:22:CC

03/07-16:26:24.851111 01:01:01:01:01:01 -> 0:AA:11:BB:22:CC type:0x800 len:0x51
192.168.1.1:33003 -> 192.168.1.100:21 TCP TTL:64 TOS:0x10 ID:0 IpLen:20
    DgmLen:67 DF
```

```
***AP*** Seq: 0x30CDB4B0  Ack: 0x2EEF4721  Win: 0xB68  TcpLen: 32
TCP Options (3) => NOP NOP TS: 788420 3441183
50 41 53 53 20 73 65 6D 70 65 72 66 69 0D 0A       PASS semperfi..
```

```
=+=+=+=+=+=+=+=+=+=+=+=+=+=+=+=+=+=+=+=+=+=+=+=+=+=+=+=+=+=+=+=+=+
```

Let's separate each section by the =+=+=+=+ line and view each packet. The first packet shows the FTP banner "220 Unauthorized access prohibited. All use is monitored and unlawful access will be reported." The third packet shows the user who is logging in, USER jdoe. The seventh packet shows our user's password, PASS semperfi.

Now, let's analyze a packet dump and figure out what everything means. For our example we will use the following packet:

```
03/07-16:26:24.851111 01:01:01:01:01:01 -> 0:AA:11:BB:22:CC type:0x800 len:0x51
192.168.1.1:33003 -> 192.168.1.100:21 TCP TTL:64 TOS:0x10 ID:0 IpLen:20
    DgmLen:67 DF
***AP*** Seq: 0x30CDB4B0  Ack: 0x2EEF4721  Win: 0xB68  TcpLen: 32
    TCP Options (3) => NOP NOP TS: 788420 3441183
50 41 53 53 20 73 65 6D 70 65 72 66 69 0D 0A       PASS semperfi..
```

Table 11-7 shows the analysis.

| Packet Segment | Description |
| --- | --- |
| 03/07-16:26:24.851111 | Date and timestamp |
| 01:01:01:01:01 | Source hardware address (not always present) |
| 0:AA:11:BB:22:CC | Destination hardware address (not always present) |
| type:0x800 | Type (not always present) |
| len:0x51 | Length (not always present) |
| 192.168.1.1 | Source IP address |
| :33003 | Port |
| 192.168.1.100 | Destination IP address |
| :21 | Destination port |
| TCP | Protocol |
| TTL:64 | Time to live |
| TOS:0x10 | Type of service |
| ID:0 | IP ID |
| IpLen:20 | Header length |
| DgmLen:67 | Datagram length |
| Frag Bits | DF |
| ***AP*** | TCP flags |
| Seq: 0x30CDB4B0 | TCP sequence |

**Table 11-7.**  Snort Packet Dump Overview

| Packet Segment | Description |
|---|---|
| Ack: 0x2EEF4721 | TCP Ack |
| Win: 0xB68 | TCP window size |
| TcpLen: 32 | TCP header length |
| TCP Options (3) => NOP NOP TS: 788420 3441183 | TCP options |
| 50 41 53 53 20 73 65 6D 70 65 72 66 69 0D 0A  PASS semperfi.. | Hex dump  ASCII dump (PAYLOAD) |

**Table 11-7.** Snort Packet Dump Overview *(continued)*

To use Snort in intrusion detection mode, you will need to configure a file for full use. You will need to edit the /etc/snort/snort.conf file (it might be located in /etc/snort.conf). If you don't have a /etc/snort/snort.conf file, you will need to **cd** to the directory where you untarred your snort download file and run the following commands:

```
cd snort.2.1.1/etc
cp snort.conf to /etc/snort/snort.conf
```

## Use Snort in NIDS Mode

Snort in network intrusion detection system (NIDS) mode runs the packets collected against the preprocessors and plug-ins and runs it against the rule sets (signatures) for matches. You may also need to move your rules directory to a more central location. To do this, run the following command (substitute the destination to your preference):

```
cd /etc/snort/rules
mkdir /usr/local/snort_rules
mv * /usr/local/snort_rules/
```

Now edit your snort.conf file using your favorite editor and modify the variables listed in Table 11-8.

Now that we have everything set up, we are ready to run Snort in NIDS mode, which will log any packets that match the rules specified in /var/log/snort. You need to identify the home network or the network that Snort is protecting with the **-h** option. If your home network were 192.168.1.0, you would type **-h 192.168.1.0/24**. If you wanted to run IDS mode, you would type this command to run Snort:

```
snort -dev -l /var/log/snort -h 192.168.1.0/24 -c /etc/snort.conf
```

This command will show all output to screen. If you plan on running Snort in IDS mode for a long period, you can just use **-d** without the **ev** options and then run it as a daemon with the **-D** option, which is far better for long-term operations. For the purposes of this chapter, we will leave the option as **-dev**.

| Variable | Default | Description |
|---|---|---|
| HOME_NET | var HOME_NET any | Specify the internal network or network you are protecting in different formats as described in the file |
| EXTERNAL_NET | var EXTERNAL_NET any | Specify the external network |
| DNS_SERVERS | var DNS_SERVERS $HOME_NET | Specify your DNS servers |
| Server lists | Miscellaneous | Specify as fits your requirements |
| Service ports | Miscellaneous | Specify as fits your requirements |
| RULE_PATH | ../rules | Point them to your rules directory (in this case, /usr/local/snort_rules, but usually /etc/snort/rules) |
| Rulesets | Miscellaneous | Edit which rules you want to include by removing or placing the # sign |

**Table 11-8.**   Snort.conf configuration variables

Now that we have Snort running, let's take a look at some sample logs. From our previous command line, we told Snort to log to /var/log/snort. Our log directory of /var/log/snort has a couple of directories and files. The first set of subdirectories are IP addresses of the packet being locked and then divided by transport layer protocol and the source and destination ports from the connection. As shown in Figure 11-5, our

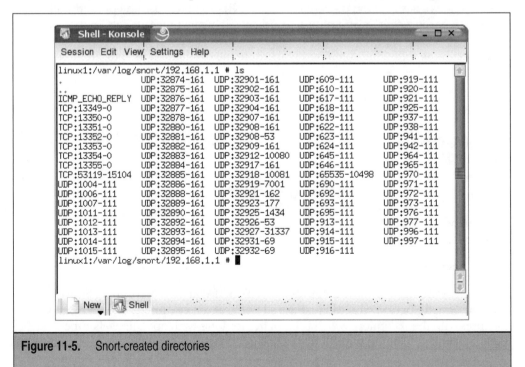

**Figure 11-5.**   Snort-created directories

second file is TCP:36016-15104, which shows this is the transport layer protocol (TCP), the source port (36016), and the destination port (15104).

The initial log we will probably look at is the alert log located in the /var/log/snort directory. This gives you a quick glance at what is going on. Here is a sample from the alert file:

```
[**] [1:1616:4] DNS named version attempt [**]
[Classification: Attempted Information Leak] [Priority: 2]
03/07-16:05:58.936992 01:01:01:01:01:01 -> 0:AA:11:BB:22:CC type:0x800 len:0x48
192.168.1.1:32908 -> 192.168.1.100:53 UDP TTL:64 TOS:0x0 ID:0 IpLen:20
    DgmLen:58 DF
Len: 30
[Xref => http://www.whitehats.com/info/IDS278]
[Xref => http://cgi.nessus.org/plugins/dump.php3?id=10028]

[**] [1:236:3] DDOS Stacheldraht client check gag [**]
[Classification: Attempted Denial of Service] [Priority: 2]
03/07-16:05:59.073262 01:01:01:01:01:01 -> 0:AA:11:BB:22:CC type:0x800 len:0x3C
192.168.1.1 -> 192.168.1.100 ICMP TTL:64 TOS:0x0 ID:4660 IpLen:20 DgmLen:39
Type:0  Code:0  ID:668  Seq:0  ECHO REPLY
[Xref => http://www.whitehats.com/info/IDS194]

[**] [1:577:10] RPC portmap bootparam request UDP [**]
[Classification: Decode of an RPC Query] [Priority: 2]
03/07-16:06:00.844683 01:01:01:01:01:01 -> 0:AA:11:BB:22:CC type:0x800 len:0x62
192.168.1.1:920 -> 192.168.1.100:111 UDP TTL:64 TOS:0x0 ID:0 IpLen:20
    DgmLen:84 DF
Len: 56
[Xref => http://www.whitehats.com/info/IDS16][Xref =>
    http://cve.mitre.org/cgi-bin/cvename.cgi?name=CAN-1999-0647]

[**] [1:584:8] RPC portmap rusers request UDP [**]
[Classification: Decode of an RPC Query] [Priority: 2]
03/07-16:06:01.110363 01:01:01:01:01:01 -> 0:AA:11:BB:22:CC type:0x800 len:0x62
192.168.1.1:920 -> 192.168.1.100:111 UDP TTL:64 TOS:0x0 ID:0 IpLen:20
    DgmLen:84 DF
Len: 56
[Xref => http://www.whitehats.com/info/IDS133][Xref =>
    http://cve.mitre.org/cgi-bin/cvename.cgi?name=CVE-1999-0626]

[**] [1:249:3] DDOS mstream client to handler [**]
[Classification: Attempted Denial of Service] [Priority: 2]
03/07-16:06:02.775998 01:01:01:01:01:01 -> 0:AA:11:BB:22:CC type:0x800 len:0x4A
192.168.1.1:53119 -> 192.168.1.100:15104 TCP TTL:64 TOS:0x0 ID:0 IpLen:20
    DgmLen:60 DF
******S* Seq: 0xCB1D88BF  Ack: 0x0  Win: 0x16D0  TcpLen: 40
TCP Options (5) => MSS: 1460 SackOK TS: 6321317 0 NOP WS: 0
[Xref => http://cve.mitre.org/cgi-bin/cvename.cgi?name=CAN-2000-0138]
    [Xref => http://www.whitehats.com/info/IDS111]
 [**] [1:237:2] DDOS Trin00 Master to Daemon default password attempt [**]
[Classification: Attempted Denial of Service] [Priority: 2]
```

```
03/07-16:06:30.232819 01:01:01:01:01:01 -> 0:AA:11:BB:22:CC  type:0x800 len:0x3C
192.168.1.1:1024 -> 192.168.1.100:27444 UDP TTL:255 TOS:0x0 ID:9 IpLen:20
     DgmLen:39
Len: 11
[Xref => http://www.whitehats.com/info/IDS197]
```

If you wanted to view the payload of the packet, you could use the information contained in the packet and traverse to the more detailed information. Let's use the following packet and get more information (packet is from /var/log/snort/alert):

```
[**] [1:249:3] DDOS mstream client to handler [**]
[Classification: Attempted Denial of Service] [Priority: 2]
03/07-16:06:02.775998 01:01:01:01:01:01 -> 0:AA:11:BB:22:CC type:0x800 len:0x4A
192.168.1.1:53119 -> 192.168.1.100:15104 TCP TTL:64 TOS:0x0 ID:0 IpLen:20
     DgmLen:60 DF
******S* Seq: 0xCB1D88BF  Ack: 0x0  Win: 0x16D0  TcpLen: 40
TCP Options (5) => MSS: 1460 SackOK TS: 6321317 0 NOP WS: 0
[Xref => http://cve.mitre.org/cgi-bin/cvename.cgi?name=CAN-2000-0138]
     [Xref => http://www.whitehats.com/info/IDS111]
```

If you want to view the payload of the file, you need to identify the source IP address, which is 192.168.1.1. This is a TCP packet and the source port and destination port are 53119 and 15104, respectively. So we know that the file that contains the detailed information about the packet would be located at /var/log/snort/192.168.1.1/TCP:53119-15104. Use the same logic when researching any file—for instance, this file shows us the following:

```
[**] DDOS mstream client to handler [**]
03/07-16:06:02.775998 01:01:01:01:01:01 -> 0:AA:11:BB:22:CC type:0x800 len:0x4A
192.168.1.1:53119 -> 192.168.1.100:15104 TCP TTL:64 TOS:0x0 ID:0 IpLen:20
        DgmLen:60 DF
******S* Seq: 0xCB1D88BF  Ack: 0x0  Win: 0x16D0  TcpLen: 40
TCP Options (5) => MSS: 1460 SackOK TS: 6321317 0 NOP WS: 0

=+=+=+=+=+=+=+=+=+=+=+=+=+=+=+=+=+=+=+=+=+=+=+=+=+=+=+=+=+=+=+=+=+=+
```

If you wanted more information on the packet, you could visit the Common Vulnerabilities and Exposure database link shown at the bottom of the alert. For the alert we were just watching, you would visit cve.mitre.org/cgi-bin/cvename.cgi?name= CAN-2000-0138 or http://www.whitehats.com/info/IDS111/ for further information.

If you use the initial set of rules and run Snort out of the box, you are likely to see a lot of false alarms. You need to modify your rules as appropriate. In your /etc/snort/ snort.conf file, you will see a section at the end containing a series of rule sets prefaced by "include $RULE_PATH." You can disable a series of rules by commenting out or putting a # sign as the first character of the line of rules that you want disabled. If you don't want to disable an entire rule set, but only individual rules, you can go to the $RULE_PATH directory, which on our default system is in /etc/snort/rules, and open the file that corresponds to the rule set you want to edit. If you have an Oracle rule that keeps triggering and you know it is a false alarm, you can edit the /etc/snort/rules/ oracle.rules. In that file you can find the specific rule you want to disable and place a # sign as the first character of the rule you want to disable. After adjusting the rules, you will need to restart Snort. Before removing or adding any rules, you should view the Snort documentation available at http://www.snort.org/docs/writing_rules/ to determine how to write and decipher rules.

## Use Snort Add-ons

There are many add-ons to Snort, including web-based graphical front ends such as ACID and other tools to make the output of Snort easier to read. You can find all the Snort add-ons at http://www.snort.org/dl/ as well as very good documentation with step-by-step instructions at http://www.snort.org/docs/. If you are running a dedicated Snort machine, we recommend that you specifically check out a Snort+Apache+PHP+ACID+MySQL combination, which gives an outstanding graphical interface in a fast, easy to use setting. More information on the Snort, ACID, and MySQL setup is available at http://www.snort.org/docs/ in the Setup Guides section. One of the great strengths of Snort is the vast array of signature files created by volunteers. When an exploit is available, Snort signature writers usually have a signature to identify the packet almost immediately. To view the rule sets or to update your rules, visit http://www.snort.org/cgi-bin/done.cgi. You should read the documentation on network intrusion detection systems before deploying them, as they should not be installed haphazardly or without proper forethought. With a properly deployed and utilized network intrusion detection system, you increase your ability to detect attacks.

# Honeypots/Honeynets

Another new, but controversial, network monitoring software tool available is what is called a honeypot or honeynet. These programs are available to allow you to monitor your system for attacks by presenting a target machine that is intended to lure attackers in. The attacker will spend time trying to break into the decoy system, which has been set up to monitor the attacker's activity and then block their access at a specific time. The benefit of honeypots is that they are designed to look like real servers and will often include files or databases set up to appear to be sensitive information. These machines can also provide early identification that your system is being probed or your network enumerated because no one should ever legitimately try to access the system since it won't have production data or services set up—only the illusion of them.

We will not go into honeypots or honeynets in this book, as there are some legal liabilities you assume when running these systems. This type of software should never be run on real production systems and shouldn't be arbitrarily set up. These machines are meant to be attacked, and improper setup could have very negative effects. More information on these programs is available at http://www.tracking-hackers.com/papers/ honeypots.html.

# Other Tools

There are several tools you can use for network monitoring that will enhance the monitoring of your system:

- **linux-mon (http://sourceforge.net/projects/linux-mon)**  Allows for monitoring of remote services for availability

- **Nagios (http://sourceforge.net/projects/nagios)**  Full featured program that provides the capability to monitor services, hosts, and networks via a web browser

- **ippl (http://www.pltplp.net/ippl/)**  Program that logs incoming IP packets

- **scanlogd (http://www.openwall.com/scanlogd/)**  Lightweight program that detects TCP port scans

- **argus (http://www.qosient.com/argus/)**  Network transaction monitor

The importance of monitoring your network for unusual activity cannot be overstated. If you do not know your network and if you are not monitoring your network for suspicious activity, you are essentially allowing an attacker to attack your systems unabated. Using the tools in this chapter, you can ensure your network is running in a normal manner, and you will be aware of any malicious activities proactively, rather than waiting for an attack to occur.

# Chapter 12

# Automatic Logfile Scanning

This chapter is about logfiles and logfile scanning, another critical facet in your total security architecture. It is important to create a policy and business strategy for dealing with system and application logfiles, because logs are vital company information that can be overlooked or undervalued. Logfiles are useful for three main reasons. First, logfiles help with troubleshooting system problems and understanding what is happening on the system. Second, logs serve as an early warning for both system and security events. Third, logs can be indispensable in reconstructing events, whether you have determined an intrusion has occurred and are performing the follow-up forensic investigation or just profiling normal activity. This chapter will start out discussing the importance of logfiles for yourself and your company. Then, there will be an explanation of the importance of centralized logging and the steps in establishing a centralized log server. After you see how to set up centralized logging, there will be instructions how to take it up a notch with encrypted centralized logging. We will look at how to search logfiles for different types of activity either manually or with searching tools. Last, we will look at a couple of examples of what hacker activities look like in the logs and how to make changes to compensate.

# Logfiles at a Personal Level

At a personal level, logfiles can give you an idea about what the different parts of your system are doing. As you work more and more with Linux, you will discover that the best way to get in touch with what is going on with the software you are running is by looking at logfiles. Logs can show you what is going right and what is going wrong. When you see errors reported, you should take steps to remedy the situation before the situation escalates, whether it's hardware failure, failed access attempts, or worse.

At a professional level, logfiles can provide a useful profile of activity. It is much easier to determine something is wrong if you are familiar with what the normal business routine looks like. From a security standpoint, it is crucial to be able to distinguish normal activity from the activity of someone attacking your server or network. It is not enough to merely gather logs, you need to protect and process them too. This chapter will recommend a process for log protection and for log processing. After becoming familiar with best logging practices, you should be able to detect intruders before they penetrate your defenses or take steps to prevent recurrence if the worst has happened. Good security is only possible through good logging.

You might need to make some configuration modifications to get the right amount of logging. Many applications can be made to log activity at different levels. Sometimes you want only critical things logged, while other times you may want to increase the verbosity of an application to a debug level. After a few weeks of gathering logs, you will have a useful archive that profiles the activity of your system and your network. An archive of logs can be useful when you notice a certain type of activity for the first time. You can immediately refer to the past logs to see if the activity looks familiar in some way. You might discover an activity that happens rarely but regularly, like once a month. You won't notice the regularity of these types of events until you have months of activity to profile.

Profiles of activity can also be extremely useful in capacity planning. When determining how much to invest in new equipment, you need to know how often certain activities have happened in the past. On the Web, people are concerned with the number of "hits" a certain web page has received. Other important metrics such as knowing the number of logins, e-mail messages, or transactions are crucial in determining the correct amount of resources to meet your future needs. Logs also provide statistics to back up the recommendations you make to management.

Everyone hopes that they will never need to provide proof of abuse to law enforcement. If the worst case scenario becomes a reality and you need to substantiate your claims or provide information to law enforcement, it will be a lot easier if you have prepared in advance for the situation. If you intend to take some legal action, officials will ask for logs validating your claims. If you don't have any documentation, you won't have a leg to stand on, so it's important to design and implement policy for dealing with logs from a legal basis.

## Use Centralized Logging

While working as a senior consultant for a major government agency's web site, a junior staff asked for help changing to root using the **su** command. He couldn't change into the root user, and he thought the root password had been changed. Investigations revealed that the root password had not been changed and that anyone could log in as root normally, they just couldn't become root with **su**. Further investigation showed that modifications had been made to the **su** binary. These changes were sophisticated enough that it was unlikely the staff had made them. Management was alerted, but disregarded security's recommendation to take the site down as being too disruptive and too conservative. Since there were not any logs collected or archived, it was impossible to determine what had occurred or when. Over the next several days, the hacker continued the rampage until they made their presence known by overtly changing the agency's homepage. The system needed to be taken offline and reinstalled. Again, had there been any logs showing what was done to break in, changes could have been made to prevent a recurrence. Management then again disregarded recommendations about restoring the system entirely from distribution instead of backups, and the hacker came back and wreaked havoc again. A comprehensive log policy would have prevented this from happening. If the policy had not been sufficient to prevent the occurrence in the first place by log searching, it certainly would have been sufficient to prevent its recurrence. Knowing what normal activity looks like is crucial. Otherwise, it is difficult—if not impossible—to distinguish appropriate activity from inappropriate.

Logs record what happens and when it happens. If unauthorized personnel are trying to access your computer, they will undoubtedly make many attempts before they succeed. If they do get in on their first attempt, it is because they have inside information and logging their activity is equally important. If your computer is compromised, and you are logging activity, you will have some record of what happened before the breach and what happened that permitted the breach.

If logfiles are only stored locally on your system, it is extremely likely that the person who breaks into your system will attempt to eradicate any evidence of what happened. The information on what IP(s) the attacker came from and what was done to break into your system may be altered or the files may be entirely deleted. Without logging information, it is unlikely that you will prevent hackers from penetrating your system's defenses repeatedly. However, if logs are stored somewhere else, the person needs to break into yet another system before he can delete the logs. In most organizations, the solution to the fragility of local log storage is a centralized log collection system.

Another reason for centralized logfile collection is the ease of administration it provides. When all logged information is centralized, it is easier to use the logs to obtain information about activity on the network. Searches can pinpoint suspicious activity across multiple systems, and the onerous task of visiting many systems and examining the logs is not necessary.

# Create a Logfile Policy

If you are in the position to make recommendations for best practices, you should recommend creating company policies for dealing with logfiles. Logfiles will protect you and your business, while providing support for your decisions as an administrator. Include in the policy:

- **Requirements for and management of centralized logging**   Centralized logs are easier to use and protect critical data from being accidentally lost or purposefully deleted or altered.

- **Provisions for logfile backup**   Logfiles are crucial company data that needs to be backed up and archived. If your backup jobs are large enough that you have defined groups, you should define a specific group that covers application and operating system logfiles.

- **Protection of logfiles**   Operating system logfiles should have restricted access since they can sometimes include passwords or other sensitive information.

- **Logfile retention period**   Archiving logfiles forever is not an unreasonable approach. A compressed logfile takes up much less space than an uncompressed one; there is no reason not to compress your offline storage.

# Configure the syslog Daemon

**syslog** is the Linux system's default logging daemon. The default location for **syslog**'s configuration file is /etc/syslog.conf. The **syslog** daemon is configurable and allows you to specify exactly where you want each type of system message to go. First, we will look at a format for a single line of syslog.conf since they all follow the same formatting. Then we will look at the whole **syslog** configuration file. A **syslog** configuration line looks like this:

```
mail.*                                    /var/log/mail
```

This line consists of two parts. First there is a selector or selectors, which in this case is **mail**. The selector section is followed by some white space and then an activity section, which in this case is

```
/var/log/mail
```

## The Selector Component

The selector component itself is broken into two parts separated by a period. The first piece is a facility and the second is a priority.

The selector is really a category for the message type. This helps you separate the kinds of messages into different places. **syslog**'s configuration supports more than one selector on a line as long as they are separated by a semicolon. In our example there is only the one selector **mail**. In the next section, we show the whole **syslog** configuration and there are several examples of lines with multiple selectors. Table 12-1 lists the selectors recognized in most flavors of the Linux operating system.

### Priorities

Priorities are the second part of a selector. Priorities are urgency rankings for the message. The programmer of an application decides in advance what the level of urgency is for any application message, so you must live with the priority any given message has unless you want to start recompiling your system applications. Table 12-2 shows the possible priorities in increasing level of severity.

Priorities are different from facilities because they are on a continuum. When an unmodified selector is used, it really means the minimum threshold and all increasingly urgent message types. So, if the priority **warning** is used in a selector it actually includes **warning**, **err**, **crit**, **alert**, and **emerg**.

### Priority Modifiers

**syslog**'s configuration permits you to modify priorities through the use of the three specifiers: the asterisk (**\***), the equal sign (**=**), and the exclamation mark (**!**). If you understand regular expressions, these modifiers will be familiar and intuitive.

| Facility | Description | Symbol in sys/syslog.h | syslog Number |
|---|---|---|---|
| kern | Kernel messages | LOG_KERN | 0 |
| user | User processes | LOG_USER | 1 |
| mail | Mail | LOG_MAIL | 2 |
| daemon | Background processes | LOG_DAEMON | 3 |
| authpriv | Authorization | LOG_AUTH | 4 |
| syslog | System logging | LOG_SYSLOG | 5 |
| lpr | Printing messages | LOG_LPR | 6 |
| news | Usenet news | LOG_NEWS | 7 |
| uucp | Unix-to-Unix copy program | LOG_UUCP | 8 |
| cron | Cron scheduled tasks | LOG_CRON | 9 |
| local0-local7 | Local use | LOG_LOCALn | 16–23 |
| * | Wildcard for any facility | | |

**Table 12-1.** Selector Components

The asterisk (*) means that all messages for the facility are sent to the activity component. Just like when it's used in a regular expression, the asterisk means "everything." In the example line **mail.*** this is exactly what is happening—all possible priorities are sent to the action. Using a specifier of * is exactly the same as using a specifier of **debug**, because a specifier means the minimum plus the rest.

| Priority | Meaning | Symbol in syslog.h | syslog Number |
|---|---|---|---|
| debug | Debug level – verbose | LOG_DEBUG | 7 |
| info | Informational messages | LOG_INFO | 6 |
| none | Log none of the messages | Not Defined | |
| notice | Normal yet important messages | LOG_NOTICE | 5 |
| warning | Warning messages | LOG_WARNING | 4 |
| err | Error messages | LOG_ERR | 3 |
| crit | Important messages | LOG_CRIT | 2 |
| alert | Urgent messages | LOG_ALERT | 1 |
| emerg | Emergency messages | LOG_EMERG | 0 |

**Table 12-2.** Priorities

The equal sign (=) limits only the specified priority to be sent to the activity. You might use this to send only debug messages without sending the increasingly urgent messages, which is a decent approach with production applications. The equal sign is used to single out an individual message priority. As in its use in programming, the equal sign means equivalence.

The exclamation mark (!) is another way to limit the priorities sent to the activity using an exception. It is a form of negation. For instance, this syslog line

```
mail.*;mail.!info          /var/adm/mail
```

would send all mail messages *except* the **info** ones to the logfile /var/adm/mail. This is because **mail.*** sends all the messages, but **mail.!info** blocks the **info** ones. As in its use in programming, the exclamation mark means "not."

# The Activity Component

Logged information can be divided among multiple files, sent to named pipes, to programs, and even to other machines, as explained in the next section. The **syslog** configuration file is straightforward and easy to read and work with. The information in the comments is useful and you should be sure to read it. This next code listing shows the default syslog.conf from SUSE. The default syslog.conf from Red Hat is very similar and a little shorter. (Comment lines start with #.)

```
# /etc/syslog.conf - Configuration file for syslogd(8)
#
# For info about the format of this file, see "man syslog.conf".
#
# print most on tty10 and on the xconsole pipe
#
kern.warn;*.err;authpriv.none      /dev/tty10
kern.warn;*.err;authpriv.none     |/dev/xconsole
*.emerg                           *
# enable this, if you want that root is informed
# immediately, e.g. of logins
#*.alert                    root
#
# all email-messages in one file
#
mail.*                   -/var/log/mail
#
# all news-messages
#
# these files are rotated and examined by "news.daily"
news.crit              -/var/log/news/news.crit
news.err               -/var/log/news/news.err
```

```
news.notice                -/var/log/news/news.notice
# enable this, if you want to keep all news messages
# in one file
#news.*                    -/var/log/news.all
#
# Warnings in one file
#
*.=warn;*.=err             -/var/log/warn
*.crit                     /var/log/warn
#
# save the rest in one file
#
*.*;mail.none;news.none    -/var/log/messages
#
# enable this, if you want to keep all messages
# in one file
#*.*                       -/var/log/allmessages
#
# Some foreign boot scripts require local7
#
local0,local1.*            -/var/log/localmessages
local2,local3.*            -/var/log/localmessages
local4,local5.*            -/var/log/localmessages
local6,local7.*            -/var/log/localmessages
```

## HEADS UP!

If the **syslog** daemon needs to write to a logfile it can often have implications on performance. A hyphen (-) in front of a logfile name as shown in the previous example tells **syslogd** not to sync the file system for the messages written to that particular logfile. This will reduce the load on the server, but it reduces the integrity of the system logging.

The downside of waiting to sync the logfiles is that if the system crashes, some log messages may be lost. When you want to know exactly what is going on at all times, you need everything to be written to log as soon as it happens. Of course this depends on the amount of activity on your system and may not be practical if there are several activities per second or many thousand activities per day. You need to determine what is reasonable for yourself since the way things are set up will alter how syncing affects your situation. The way to have immediate logging influence your server the least is to have the logs on a partition serviced by a separate controller and hard drive from the controller and hard drive running the applications and operating system.

# Set Up a Centralized Server

Creating a central server for system logs makes sense for a couple of reasons. First, any systems that are directly exposed to the Internet are on the front lines, so to speak. If a machine gets compromised, it is important to know what happened. It is likely that the intruder will erase evidence if they can. Keeping logs on a second system will make it more difficult for them to cover their tracks. Second, a centralized server with logs from all networked machines allows administrative staff to keep watch from a single location rather than having to log into all the servers all the time.

## Ensure Centralized Logging Dependencies Are Met

Correctly configured network services (DNS and NTP) are helpful in accurate logging. By default a centralized log server will try to resolve the fully qualified domain name (FQDN) of the machines that are sending it information. (You can disable this requirement by adding **-x** in the configuration.) If the **syslog** daemon is unable to resolve the address, it will continue to try, which will create unnecessary load and slow logging down dramatically. Likewise, if your systems' times are not synced, the centralized log server will put timestamps on events that do not match the timestamps on the machine sending them. This will make sorting events out more confusing than it needs to be, so synchronized time can be helpful in maintaining consistency across the network. By editing /etc/ntp.conf to point at a centralized time source, and by turning on **ntpd** to run at boot time, you will alleviate timestamp confusion for yourself.

## Configure the Centralized Server

**syslog** can easily accommodate centralized logging. Any server running the **syslog** daemon can be configured to receive messages from another machine, but by default this option is off. Unless otherwise noted, the following steps will work identically on either SUSE or Red Hat and many other distributions of Linux as well. To enable a server to accept incoming log messages:

   1. Edit the file /etc/sysconfig/syslog. On the line with **syslog** options, add **-r** to permit incoming messages, and consider adding **-x** if you do not have DNS entries for all the machines you want to log. You may also want to change the default mark message to something sensible like 240, which means to make a timestamp every 240 minutes, or 4 times a day. The **-- MARK --** message line is an indication that the daemon is running, When you are done the line should look like this:

      ```
      SYSLOGD_OPTIONS="-r -x -m 240"
      ```

2. Restart the **syslog** daemon. The changes will not take effect until the **syslog** daemon is restarted. To restart the daemon without restarting the system, you can execute one of the following two choices in Red Hat:

```
/etc/rc.d/init.d/syslog stop; /etc/rc.d/init.d/syslog start
/etc/rc.d/init.d/syslog restart
```

In SUSE, use one of the following three choices:

```
/etc/init.d/syslog stop; /etc/init.d/syslog start
/etc/init.d/syslog restart
rcsyslog restart
```

3. If **ipchains** or TCP wrappers are used, ensure that connections are permitted to port 514. Port 514 is used by the **syslog** daemon.

## HEADS UP!

If the network interface security restrictions like **iptables** or TCP wrappers do not permit connections to port 514, data cannot be logged. Once the network interface will permit connections to port 514, the server is ready to receive incoming messages.

## Configure Clients for the Centralized Server

It isn't very hard to set up client machines to a log central location. Edit the /etc/syslog.conf configuration file so that the activity portion uses an @ to point at the logging server, like this:

```
authpriv.*                                    @192.168.1.40
```

Alternatively, you can define a machine in DNS called loghost, which permits you to move the logging to another machine without changing every client machine's **syslog** configuration. The loghost line would look like this:

```
authpriv.*                                    @loghost
```

Again, you will need to restart the **syslog** daemon before the changes will take effect. It makes sense to continue to log messages locally to help you debug problems with the server. If you are centralizing logfiles, you can feel free to delete these logfiles as explained in the "Manage Logfiles" section.

# Create a Centralized Server with syslog-ng and stunnel

To take your security to the next level, you should consider installing a more powerful version of **syslog** called **syslog-ng**. When the **syslog** daemon sends its log messages to a centralized server, it does so using the UDP protocol and in plaintext. This is not a good idea, as logs can contain sensitive information such as passwords. Also, the UDP protocol doesn't ensure that the information makes it to its destination. In the next section, there will be detailed instructions about adding additional software to your system.

## SUSE: Download and Install stunnel 4.04

SUSE ships with **stunnel** 3.14. It is recommended but not essential that you download a newer version of **stunnel** such as 4.04 or newer. One quick way to get newer source code for **stunnel** is with **wget**:

```
wget http://www.stunnel.org/download/stunnel/src/stunnel-4.04.tar.gz
```

The next steps are the same as installing most source code, and are the same steps as the ones for compiling **syslog-ng** in the next section:

```
tar -xzvf stunnel-4.04.tar.gz
cd  stunnel-4.04/
./configure
make
make install
```

## Download and Install syslog-ng

These instructions have been tested for setting up a centralized server on Red Hat Enterprise Linux AS 3.0, Red Hat 9.0, and SUSE SLES8. The first step in installing **syslog-ng** is to get the distribution. At the time of this printing, there are no widely disseminated RPM packages, so we will step you through building **syslog-ng** and its dependencies from source. Acquire the archive for **syslog-ng** and the dependency that is outside the standard distribution for the operating systems listed above. We will be working with syslog-ng-1.6.tar.gz and libol-0.3.13.tar.gz since they both are easy to build in these environments.

First, go through the steps for **libol** and then repeat the steps with **syslog-ng**.

1. Unpack the archive and **cd** into the directory that was created:

   ```
   # tar -zxf filename
   # cd directory
   ```

2. Run **configure**, **make**, and **make check**. You should not see any errors produced by **make check**. If you do, you need to fix them.

```
# ./configure; make; make check
```

3. Now install the program:

```
# make install
```

Great! You have installed the software you need, now all that is left is to configure it.

---

## HEADS UP!

Adding software that is not provided by your vendor may void support. You should make your decision regarding addition of software after discussing your needs with your vendor.

---

## Create Certificates for Your Machines.

In Red Hat, you can do the following:

```
# cd /usr/share/ssl/certs
# make syslog-ng-server.pem
# make syslog-ng-client.pem
```

The SUSE distribution does not include the same makefile to create certificates that Red Hat does. You can make a script with the following commands and execute it to make your server and client certificates:

```
#!/bin/bash
###
### A quick script for making certificates for use with STUNNEL
###
umask 77 ; \
PEM1='/bin/mktemp /tmp/openssl.XXXXXX' ; \
PEM2='/bin/mktemp /tmp/openssl.XXXXXX' ; \
PEM3='/bin/mktemp /tmp/openssl.XXXXXX' ; \
PEM4='/bin/mktemp /tmp/openssl.XXXXXX' ; \
/usr/bin/openssl req -newkey rsa:1024 -keyout $$PEM1 -nodes -x509 -days 365 -out $$PEM2 ; \
cat $$PEM1 > syslog-ng-server.pem ; \
echo ""     >> syslog-ng-server.pem; \
cat $$PEM2 >> syslog-ng-server.pem ; \
echo "Done Making Server Certificate.";
/usr/bin/openssl req -newkey rsa:1024 -keyout $$PEM3 -nodes -x509 -days 365 -out $$PEM4 ; \
cat $$PEM3 > syslog-ng-client.pem ; \
```

```
echo ""    >> syslog-ng-client.pem; \
cat $$PEM4 >> syslog-ng-client.pem ; \
rm  $$PEM1 $$PEM2 $$PEM3 $$PEM4
rm /tmp/openssl.*
echo "Done Making Client Certificate.";
```

## Copy Certificates to /etc/stunnel

The server and client machines have different certificate requirements. The clients only need the certificate section of syslog-ng-server.pem. Remove the private key section from syslog-ng-server.pem. Next, copy the file syslog-ng-server.pem to each client machine and put it in the /etc/stunnel directory. You will know the private key section because it starts with

```
-----BEGIN RSA PRIVATE KEY-----
```

and ends with

```
-----END RSA PRIVATE KEY-----
```

On the server, copy the entire file into /etc/stunnel. Also, place the client's syslog-ng-client.pem in /etc/stunnel. For the server, create a special syslog-ng-client.pem containing the certificate sections for all the clients. You should remove the private key sections from all syslog-ng-client.pem files and concatenate what is left to create the server's special syslog-ng-client.pem.

## Check Certificate Permissions

Make sure the server certificates are owned by root and have read and write permissions. These commands will ensure that:

```
chown  root:root  syslog-ng-server.pem
chown  root:root  syslog-ng-client.pem
chmod 700 syslog-ng-server.pem
chmod 700 syslog-ng-client.pem
```

## Create stunnel Configuration on the Server

This code listing shows a possible server configuration for **stunnel** that would belong in file /etc/stunnel/stunnel.conf:

```
cert = /etc/stunnel/syslog-ng-server.pem
CAfile = /etc/stunnel/syslog-ng-client.pem
[5140]
       accept = server IP address:5140
       connect = 127.0.0.1:514
```

## Create stunnel Configuration on the Client

This code listing shows a possible client configuration for **stunnel** that would belong in file /etc/stunnel/stunnel.conf:

```
client = yes
   cert = /etc/stunnel/syslog-ng-client.pem
   CAfile = /etc/stunnel/syslog-ng-server.pem
   verify = 3
   [5140]
       accept = 127.0.0.1:514
       connect = server IP address:5140
```

## Create syslog-ng Configuration on the Server

This code listing shows a possible server configuration for **syslog-ng** that would belong in file /etc/syslog-ng.conf:

```
options {  long_hostnames(off);
              sync(0);
              keep_hostname(yes);
              chain_hostnames(no);   };
   source src {unix-stream("/dev/log");
               pipe("/proc/kmsg");
               internal();};
   source stunnel {tcp(ip("127.0.0.1")
                  port(514)
                  max-connections(1));};
   destination remoteclient {file("/var/log/remoteclient");};
   destination dest {file("/var/log/messages");};
   log {source(src); destination(dest);};
   log {source(stunnel); destination(remoteclient);};
```

## Create syslog-ng Configuration File on the Client Machines

This code listing shows a possible client configuration for **syslog-ng** that would belong in file /etc/syslog-ng.conf:

```
options {long_hostnames(off);
            sync(0);};
   source src {unix-stream("/dev/log"); pipe("/proc/kmsg");
               internal();};
   destination dest {file("/var/log/messages");};
   destination stunnel {tcp("127.0.0.1" port(514));};
   log {source(src);destination(dest);};
   log {source(src);destination(stunnel);};
```

# Start stunnel and syslog-ng Manually

These are two commands that need to be executed to start **stunnel** and **syslog-ng** manually:

```
# stunnel
# syslog-ng -f /etc/syslog-ng.conf
```

# Check for Activity on the Server

The command **tail -f** *filename* is an excellent way to watch logfile activity. Log into the server and watch the file for activity in real time. To create activity, type **su -** on a client machine and press RETURN a couple of times to simulate a failed password.

```
# tail -f  /var/log/remoteclient
```

If you should see some activity like this, everything is working:

```
Apr 1 12:34:56 chim su(pam_unix)[8451]: authentication failure;
logname=rreck uid=2112 euid=0 tty= ruser=rreck rhost=  user=root
```

If everything is not working as you expect, you can try running **stunnel** with increased debugging. In SUSE (**stunnel** version 3.14) you can type:

```
# stunnel -D 7
```

In **stunnel** version 4.04, which is default with Red Hat, you can add a line like this to /etc/stunnel/stunnel.conf for maximum verbosity:

```
debug = 7
```

Carefully read the messages and try to determine what is failing. It can be something as simple as a typo in one of the configuration files. Once things are working you can use these scripts to start and stop **stunnel** and **syslog-ng** and put them in /etc/init.d (Red Hat) or /etc/rc.d/ (SUSE). This code listing shows a sample startup script for **stunnel**, complete with LSB-compliant comment conventions:

```
#!/bin/sh
### BEGIN INIT INFO
# Provides: stunnel
# Description: A stunnel version 4.04 startup script
# with  LSB Comment Conventions.
# Adapted from an example script by martti.kuparinen@ericsson.com
# Further Adapted by Ronald P. Reck <rreck@iama.rrecktek.com>
### BEGIN INIT INFO
# Provides: stunnel
# Required-Start: $network
# Default-Start: 3 4 5
```

```
# Default-Stop: 0 1 2 6
# Short-Description: Start / Stop stunnel
### END INIT INFO
# Source function library.
. /lib/lsb/init-functions
[ -f /usr/sbin/stunnel ] || exit 0
# Where is the stunnel program
STUNNEL="/usr/sbin/stunnel"
case "$1" in
    start)
        ${STUNNEL} /etc/stunnel/stunnel.conf
        ;;
    stop)
        killall 'basename ${STUNNEL}'
        ;;
    *)
        echo ""
        echo "Usage: basename $0 { start | stop }"
        echo ""
        ;;
esac
exit 0;
```

This code listing shows a sample startup script for **syslog-ng**:

```
#!/bin/sh
#
# syslog-ng         Starts/Stops syslog-ng
#
# chkconfig: 345 11 70
# description: syslog-ng is a enhanced system and kernel logging daemon
# Original Author:     Georg Funke, <georg.funke@netcologne.de>
# Modifed by       Ronald P. Reck <rreck@iama.rrecktek.com>
# /etc/init.d/syslog-ng

# LSB 1.1.0 header information
### BEGIN INIT INFO
# Provides: syslog-ng
# Required-Start: network
# Required-Stop:  network
# Default-Start:  2 3 5
# Default-Stop:
# Description:     Start/Stop the syslog-ng logging daemon
### END INIT INFO
# Source LSB initscript functions.
. /lib/lsb/init-functions
```

```
# this is default place syslog-ng is installed to
[ -f /usr/local/sbin/syslog-ng ] || exit 0
# See how we were called.
case "$1" in
  start)
    echo -n "Starting system logger syslog-ng: "
    daemon syslog-ng -f /etc/syslog-ng/syslog-ng.conf
    echo
    touch /var/lock/subsys/syslog-ng
    ;;
  stop)
    echo -n "Shutting down system logger syslog-ng: "
    killproc syslog-ng
    echo
    rm -f /var/lock/subsys/syslog-ng
    ;;
  restart)
    $0 stop
    $0 start
    ;;
  reload)
    echo -n "Reloading syslog-ng: "
    killproc syslog-ng -HUP
    echo
    ;;
  *)
    echo "Usage: syslog-ng {start|stop|restart|reload}"
    exit 1
esac
exit 0
```

# Use the logger Command to Send Messages Directly to the syslog Daemon

You might want to log some piece of activity directly to the **syslog** daemon. The **logger** command can help you do it and it is easy to use. If you wanted to keep track of what the load was or how many users were logged in when someone new logged in, you could gather this information by editing the /etc/bashrc file and adding a line like

```
logger -p info "user $USER starting a shell at 'w | head -1'"
```

This would make entries into /var/log/messages like

```
Apr  1 06:34:46 chim rreck: user rreck starting a shell at  06:34:46
up 53 min,  3 users,  load average: 0.06, 0.03, 0:
```

## Use Perl's Sys:Syslog to Send Messages to the syslog Daemon

You can easily send messages to **syslog** using the standard libraries that accompany
Perl. This brief example shows how you can use a program to send messages to **syslog**
using a subroutine call:

```perl
#!/usr/bin/perl
###
### An example that sends a message to syslog using Perl
###
# a required library
use Sys::Syslog qw ( :DEFAULT setlogsock);
# a default message and priority
$user = $ENV{'USER'};
$msg='w |grep $user |wc -l';
$msg="$user is logged in $msg times";
$priority="info";
# call the subroutine
&log_message($priority,$msg);
sub log_message{
my ($priority, $msg) = @_;
setlogsock('unix');
openlog($0,'pid,cons','user');
syslog($priority, $msg);
closelog();
return 1;
}
```

Save this example in a file, and make it executable by typing **chmod +x** *filename*.
When you execute it, you will get a message sent to **syslog** that looks like:

```
May  1 00:16:29 chim ./syslogmessage.pl[20659]: root is logged in  7  times
```

## Manage Logfiles

Logfiles can get large fast, depending on the amount of activity you have on your network
and the verbosity of the applications being logged. Eventually, it will be necessary to
rotate your logfiles. There is a very useful and highly configurable tool for rotating logs
called  **logrotate**. **logrotate** has been around for many years and is scheduled in root's
crontab to run on a daily basis by default on most current versions of Linux. **logrotate**
has too many options to cover them all here, but we will cover the basics. The first thing
to know is that **logrotate** supports automatic rotation, compression, removal, and mailing
of system or application logfiles. The second thing to know is **logrotate** has a default

configuration file located in /etc/logrotate.conf. **logrotate** supports multiple configuration files and it's important to note that local definitions override global ones and later definitions override earlier ones. Any number of configuration files can be given to **logrotate** on the command line. Alternatively, the **include** directive allows one configuration file to point at many others. Since order can influence configuration precedence, this should be taken into account when planning things out. Application-specific configuration files are in the /etc/logrotate.d/ directory.

---

**TIP**   If you are centralizing your logs, you can tell **logrotate** to delete logs locally instead of rotating them by using a **maxage** setting equal to the **rotate** time. Make sure you confirm that the logs are going to the centralized log server before enabling this option.

---

Since **logrotate** usually runs as a daily cron job it will not modify a log multiple times in one day unless the log's size meets the size criteria and **logrotate** is invoked more than once a day. To force **logrotate** to perform an activity like when you are testing use **logrotate -f** or **logrotate --force**.

## Finding Logfiles

In general, most of the system logfiles live in /var/ as specified by the syslog.conf. If there are other applications running on the server, they may have other logfiles in other places. To make all the applications put their logs under /var/ you will need to edit each application's configuration file(s). Having logs under /var/ is a good idea because it means that all logs are in a single place when you need to check them, restrict access, or back them up. Second, /var/ is often in a file system independent from slash (/), which is important in case your logs get out of hand and fill up all the available space. If logfiles are written anywhere below the slash (/) file system, a hacker can crash your machine by causing enough logged activity that it fills the entire hard drive. You can find logfiles you didn't know about using the **find** command. Change to the slash directory and run the following command as root to locate files that were recently modified.

```
find . -type f -mtime -5 -print | grep -v proc | grep -v lock
```

# Other System Logfiles

There are two other system logfiles that have nothing to do with the **syslog** daemon: /var/run/utmp and /var/log/wtmp. These logfiles keep track of information about logins. The first file, utmp, tracks the current system state and is used by commands like **finger**, **write**, or **who**. The man page for utmp warns that many system programs "foolishly depend on its integrity" if utmp is writable to any user.

The second file, /var/log/wtmp/, archives login information. It can be a valuable way to see who logs in and with what regularity. Since the file is a binary format you need something besides a text editor to get at the information it contains. To see the contents of the wtmp file, type **last | more**. This shows who has logged in and from where. If the file is mysteriously empty or nulled, this is a sign that you have been hacked. Truncating these files is a common practice to cover one's tracks.

# Search Logfiles

There are dozens of different tools that can search logfiles and locate activities of interest. This section will help you search logfiles. First, we will explain the overall strategy to adopt when searching logfiles. Next, we will look at examples of how to check a logfile manually using the **grep** command. Then we will look at **logwatch**, a tool that is available as part of Red Hat Enterprise Linux AS 3.0, and **logsurfer**, a tool found in SUSE SLES8. Last, we will look at tools you can download and install, such as **swatch**.

There are several web sites that provide useful information to help you. One great resource that has links to useful programs, settings, log samples, and configuration samples is http://loganalysis.org/. A second site to check out is http://www.iss.net/. They have useful downloads and white papers.

## Strategy for Searching Logfiles

The challenge inherent in logfile analysis is to sort the exception activity from normal activity. This presupposes that you know what regular activity on your system and network looks like. Without experience to draw upon it is difficult to know how regular occurrences are represented in the logfiles. It is likely that it will take some time before normal logfile activity is familiar. Clearly, this cannot be done at one sitting, and it needs to be part of a process that is developed over time. Also, as applications and users are added or changed on the network, it is likely the logs will change too.

The next step after isolating an exception circumstance is to correctly identify when the exception constitutes an alarm condition. This can only be determined through understanding your business requirements. There needs to be a balance between system availability and risk. If it is imperative that the system is protected because it contains crucial company information like credit card numbers, then there will be a decrease in availability. This is because sometimes you may need to take the system off the network to protect it. There are circumstances where activity in the logs is so important that the machine should be shut down or immediately removed from the network.

If you need to have a server up as much as possible, you will need to be more tolerant of exceptions while keeping a watchful eye. If administrative staff carry pagers, when some activity requires immediate corrective action they can be interrupted with a page. An example of activity that warrants immediate concern includes evidence of port spoofing where the logged src port does not match the FQDN. If staff cannot respond immediately the best course of action might be to shut the machine down immediately with the **shutdown** command:

```
shutdown -h -t now 0
```

You can shut down a remote machine with an **expect** script that logs into the affected box and executes a **shutdown** command. An **expect** script that executes a remote shutdown looks something like this code listing:

```
#!/usr/bin/expect -f
# Perform a remote shutdown
set inet_host "192.168.1.10"
spawn ssh "$inet_host"
# give it a second to connect
sleep 1
expect "ssword:"
send "password_of_uid_searching_logs\n"
sleep 2
send "su -\n"
expect "ssword:"
send "remote_machines_root_password\n"
sleep 1
send " shutdown -h -t now 0\n"
sleep 10
```

The drawback in this type of remote shutdown is that the root password is in the script, which is less than desirable. Also, if the root password is changed, the script needs to be edited.

## Searching Logfiles Manually

**grep** is one of the most powerful Unix shell commands. An excellent use of this text file search command is to use **grep** to search for patterns inside logfiles. Using **grep** is easy—on the command line, type

```
grep "what to look for" file to look in
```

For example:

```
grep "failed" /var/log/messages.
```

When you run this command you receive a list of every line in the file with the word "failed" in it. By default the **grep** command is case sensitive, so depending on the context you may want to use **grep** with the **-i** flag to make searches case insensitive. One challenging aspect of searching logfiles is that you need to know what you are looking for before you can find it. There are a couple of ways to approach this dilemma. If there is an activity you know you want to catch, such as users trying to **su** to root, you could simply perform the activity and look for it in the logs. For instance, an unsuccessful **su** would look something like this in SUSE:

```
Apr  1 11:15:54 chim su: FAILED SU (to root) rreck on /dev/pts/1
```

Therefore, to find all such activities you would type

```
grep "FAILED SU" /var/log/messages
```

Similarly if you wanted to find failed remote access attempts, you might try logging in and failing to get the password right. The line for failing to log in to SSH would look something like:

```
Apr  1 11:24:17 chim sshd[1934]: Failed password for rreck from
::ffff:192.168.1.99 port 32942 ssh2
```

Then, to find a similar case you could type

```
grep "Failed password" /var/log/messages
```

These are both reasonable activities to be concerned with as they are indicative of hacking. If **grep** shows only a couple of instances of failed attempts, it's probably because someone forgot their password or mistyped. On the other hand, if **grep** highlights dozens of failed access attempts, someone is probably trying to break in and you should take steps to deny them access at the network level.

## Search Logfiles with logwatch

One commonly used tool, named **logwatch**, was written by Kirk Bauer using the Perl programming language. **logwatch** has been part of the standard Red Hat distribution for quite a while. **logwatch**'s configuration file can be found at /etc/log.d/conf/logwatch.conf. There are several other directories used by **logwatch** under /etc/log.d/. You probably won't need to change anything since it runs well without configuration modification, but it might be helpful to know where to look for files if you do.

The configurable options include the level of detail to include, whether to e-mail the results or print them to the screen, and a limited date range choice of Today, Yesterday, or All.

If you are running Red Hat Enterprise Linux AS 3.0, **logwatch** 4.3.2 is scheduled to run daily by default, because of a softlink in /etc/cron.daily/logwatch. The default configuration checks yesterday's system logs in /var/log/ and mails the results to the root user. You can see a sample of the report by typing

```
/etc/cron.daily/00-logwatch -print -range all
```

The report starts with a header that shows the settings that **logwatch** ran with. Next, there are sections for PAM activity, connections, SSH, and disk space. One nice thing about the report format is that it condenses and tallies the results for the day's activity.

# Search Logfiles with logsurfer

The program **logsurfer** comes with SUSE SLES 8.1 and 9.0. **logsurfer** was written to allow more precise decisions than other log searching programs like **swatch**, which we will look at in the next section. Much like other log searching programs, **logsurfer** compares each line in a logfile against regular expressions and if there is a match it performs an action. The actions are expressed as "rules." **logsurfer** goes further than **swatch** in a few ways. First, **logsurfer** matches lines using two regular expressions; the logfile's line needs to match the first expression, but must not match the optional second expression. This can be useful because it allows you to express exceptions. Another huge strength of **logsurfer** is that it works on contexts instead of single lines. This is handy because a single line in a logfile does not always contain enough information to make a decision.

On the downside, **logsurfer** can be hard to configure since you need to really understand regular expressions, and there are not many configuration examples included.

### Configuring logsurfer

The best place to find information about **logsurfer** is from the man page. The man pages that you see when you type **man logsurfer** or **man logsurfer.conf** are not the only man pages. A more detailed man page is available when you type **man 4 logsurfer.conf**. This tells the **man** command that you want the man page from section 4.

The details in Table 12-3 can be found in the man pages. Each line in the **logsurfer** configuration file is one of three things: if the line starts with # it's a comment, if it starts with white space it is a continuation of a previous rule, or otherwise it's the start of a new rule. Each new rule has six mandatory fields and one optional field. Table 12-3 explains the functions of each of the seven fields.

The last field of any **logsurfer** rule is the action field. The actions are useful in opening or deleting contexts and creating new rules. Table 12-4 lists the possible actions and what they do.

**logsurfer** does not need to run as the root user and a user could be made specifically to run **logsurfer**. If the logs **logsurfer** needs to read are restricted, it is recommended that a group be created for system administration and that **logsurfer** is added to that group. For this to work, the logs themselves will need to permit group level read access. Use the **chmod** command:

```
chmod +gr logfile
```

| Field Number | Optional | Field Name | Field Explanation |
|---|---|---|---|
| 1 | Required | match_regex | If the line matches this regular expression, the rest of the rule is parsed, otherwise **logsurfer** continues to find rules to match the line against, and the rest of the fields are skipped. |
| 2 | Required or - | not_match_regex | As long as there is something besides a hyphen (-), it is treated as a regex to contrast with the first regex. The line says match the first regex but not the second one. |
| 3 | Required or - | stop_regex | As long as there is something besides a hyphen (-), this regex is matched, then the rule is deleted from the list of active rules. |
| 4 | Required or - | not_stop_regex | As long as there is something besides a hyphen (-), it is treated as a regex not to match against. Only delete this rule if there is a stop_regex and the first stop_regex matches and this regex does not. |
| 5 | Required or 0 | timeout | This allows you to specify a number of seconds that a rule is good for. Set this to 0 to never time out. |
| 6 | Optional | Continue | If the word "continue" occurs, **logsurfer** continues to try to match rules against the line of the logfile. If there is no "continue," the rest of the rules are skipped. |
| 7 | Required | Action | One of the following actions: **ignore**, **exec**, **pipe**, **open**, **delete**, **report**, **rule**. |

**Table 12-3.**   **logsurfer** Fields

| Action | Purpose |
|---|---|
| ignore | This action means to do nothing and ignore the line. This is useful when you know the line you are working with is not important. |
| exec | The argument following this action is the program to execute. |
| pipe | This is similar to **exec** except that the invoked program gets the actual logline from **stdin**. |
| open | This means to open a new context, unless a context already exists for the **match_regex**. |
| delete | If an existing **match_regex** is used as an argument, the specified context is closed and deleted without applying the **default_action**. |
| report | The first argument specifies the external program (including options) that should be invoked. All further arguments specify context definitions that are summarized and fed as standard input to the invoked program. |
| rule | This allows the creation of new rules. Following the keyword rule must be an indication of what order the rule is to be applied: **before**, **behind**, **top**, or **bottom**. |

**Table 12-4.**   **logsurfer** Actions

# Search Logfiles with swatch

**swatch** is not part of the standard distribution for Red Hat Enterprise Linux AS 3.0 or SUSE SLES. Since **swatch** is easy to install, configure, and work with, you should consider downloading and installing it. On the command line, type

```
mkdir swatch-install; cd swatch-install
```

**swatch** requires the addition of some Perl libraries. The ones you need depend on how many of the operating system's packages you have installed. You might need

```
wget http://www.cpan.org/authors/id/J/JH/JHI/Time-HiRes-1.59.tar.gz
```

You will need

```
wget http://www.cpan.org/authors/id/M/MG/MGRABNAR/File-Tail-0.98.tar.gz
wget http://www.cpan.org/authors/id/S/ST/STBEY/Date-Calc-5.3.tar.gz
wget http://www.cpan.org/authors/id/S/ST/STBEY/Bit-Vector-6.3.tar.gz
wget http://unc.dl.sourceforge.net/sourceforge/swatch/swatch-3.1.tar.gz
```

Installing **swatch** in Red Hat Enterprise Linux AS 3.0 only requires one more library than in SUSE SLES. Install this as the fourth step, before installing **swatch** itself:

```
wget http://www.cpan.org/authors/id/G/GB/GBARR/TimeDate-1.16.tar.gz
```

Then for each of the files do these steps, in the same order you got them:

```
tar -xzf filename.tar.gz
cd filename
perl Makefile.PL
make
make test
```

Check for errors, but there shouldn't be any.

```
make install
```

**swatch** should now be installed, but to start working with it you need a configuration file. By default **swatch** looks for the file .swatchrc in the home directory of the user who invoked it, for instance /home/rreck/.swatchrc. You can specify a different configuration file by using the **-f** flag:

```
swatch -f /etc/.swatchrc
```

Let's look at how some hacker activities could be found by **swatch** and what to do when they are found.

## Modify swatch Configuration to Detect an Apache Exploit

Let's see an example of a real-life exploit, the logged information, and how to properly react and change system configurations. In the past, Apache's HTTP server has been the target of an exploit because of problems with **mod_userdir** (a default Apache module) and its default configuration. Hackers use a tool that scans remote hosts to find out disclosure information about user accounts. Their tool first checks for Apache and that the Apache version is a vulnerable one. Next, the exploit cycles through checking your system for many well-known user accounts. It is very fast and can check quicker than one account per second depending on the speed of your network connection and server. This user information is then used to target other system services, such as FTP, because the hackers know that the user account exists.

During the attack, there is a flurry of activity in Apache's access log. There will be a lot of messages indicating 404 errors when the hacker does not find a directory for the user accounts he is probing and 403 errors because the access to the existing directory is forbidden. These conditions are also returned to the attacker. Herein lies the exposure. These 403 errors are the ones the exploit is looking for, and the users' accounts that generated those error codes are likely to be targeted for further attack.

These few lines added to the .swatchrc file used on your Apache logs will let you know by e-mail which accounts are likely to be targeted:

```
# Apache 403 errors
watchfor    / 403 /
       echo
       bell
     mail
```

One error does not mean trouble is brewing, but if there are several 403 errors in the span of a few seconds you know to take action. Since error 403 is not a common error, you could search on a regular basis, such as every night at five minutes past midnight, by adding a line like this to root's crontab:

```
5 0 * * *  --config-file=swatchrc.apache swatch --examine-file=/var/log/httpd/access_log
```

The best security plan would be to run **swatch** as a daemon or in tail mode so you can find out immediately after the attempt happens, with a line like this:

```
swatch --config-file=swatchrc.apache --tail-file=/var/log/httpd/access_log
```

Once you realize this is happening, you should immediately try to remedy the situation by adding and altering a few configuration directives in Apache's configuration file /etc /httpd/httpd.conf (SUSE) and restart the daemon /etc/rc.d/apache restart (SUSE). One possible remedy is to disable the **UserDir** directive globally and then enable it on a user-by-user basis by adding these lines:

```
UserDir disabled
UserDir enabled user1 user2 user3
```

Alternatively, you might allow **UserDir** globally, but disable it for accounts that you don't want the world to know about, with lines like these:

```
UserDir enabled
UserDir disabled user4 user5 user6
```

You need to stay aware and understand what the log activity indicates. There is no perfect recipe for security other than to remain diligent. This is merely an example of how monitoring logs can reveal information that you need to react to by making configuration changes. Now let's look at the activity that would be logged by another exploit.

## Modify swatch Configuration to Detect an Attack on the SSH Daemon

Now let's look at an example involving the SSH daemon (**sshd**). Even when your services are tightened and minimized because you are running only the essentials, it is important to scan logs to keep an eye on things. Logging is only useful when something is done with the information. Someone could easily try to brute force their way into shell access by **ssh**-ing to your server and trying thousands of passwords against a known user's account. The downside for them would be that their attempts would look like this in the SUSE system's logs:

```
Apr  1 15:17:52 linux sshd[3950]: Failed password for rreck from
::ffff:192.168.1.99 port 33113 ssh2
Apr  1 15:17:53 linux last message repeated 2 times
```

The same activity would look something like this in the Red Hat system's logs:

```
Jun  6 13:01:56 chim sshd(pam_unix)[17331]: authentication failure; logname= uid=0
euid=0 tty=NODEVssh ruser= rhost=192.168.1.199  user=rreck
Jun  6 13:02:01 chim sshd[17331]: Failed password for rreck from 192.168.1.199 port
33181 ssh2
Jun  6 13:02:03 chim sshd[17331]: Failed password for rreck from 192.168.1.199 port
33181 ssh2
Jun  6 13:02:03 chim sshd(pam_unix)[17331]: 2 more authentication failures; logname=
uid=0 euid=0 tty=NODEVssh ruser= rhost=192.168.1.199
 user=rreck
```

The security strategy is to notice this is happening as soon as possible. Add a **swatch** configuration snippet to the system swatchrc that looks like this:

```
# Failed password
watchfor   / Failed password for /
      echo
      bell
   mail
```

Then when **swatch** runs, whether from cron or from a tail, you will get an e-mail alert. This e-mail notification is a call to action. Depending on your requirements you might need to let rreck log in from a multitude of hosts, but want to thwart this hacker's attempts. Edit /etc/ssh/sshd_config to explicitly deny access for rreck's user account from the site that has multiple failed access attempts, and at the same time permit rreck to log in from elsewhere.

```
# Prevent access for hacker even if they guess the password !
DenyUsers rreck@192.168.1.99
AllowUsers rreck@*
```

Then send **sshd** a SIGHUP signal or restart it with

```
/etc/rc.d/sshd restart
```

You know that the changes are working when you see messages in /var/log/messages from **sshd** indicating that the hacker's attempts are now being thwarted by **sshd**:

```
Apr  1 17:42:55 linux sshd[5864]: User rreck not allowed because listed in DenyUsers
```

This log message means that even if the correct password is guessed, the user will not gain access. From the hacker's side there is nothing to tell them you have changed the configs and that their efforts are futile.

The point is to understand that security is never done; it's an ongoing effort. The best way to mitigate risks is to be diligent and stay aware of what is going on. Pay attention to the logs and aberrations from normal activity.

# Respond to Attacks and Abnormalities

In the end, it is important to realize the best security posture involves process. It is helpful to consider all your options before something happens so that you don't waste any time before taking action. It also helps to think things out when emotion isn't involved, and you can be sure you are reacting the best way possible.

You can look at it like a decision tree—as you discover activities of interest you should ask yourself some questions. Is this a critical issue or maybe something lesser like your ISP doing a security audit, or just someone snooping around? If it is critical, is there some sort of attack going on or is something misconfigured somewhere? The best decision might be to shut the server down immediately or at least remove it from the network.

If you have determined that an attack is occurring, should you notify an administrator at the source end of the attack? Should you notify law enforcement? What service is being attacked? Is this a service your business requires? Has your system's security been penetrated? If so, what kind of damage was done? If not, what part of your defensive barrier has proven successful? Preparing yourself for these decisions in advance will allow you to act quickly when it matters most. When things are going wrong in the middle of the night, you will be reluctant to wake people up unless you have decided in advance that you need to. Proper planning and solid documentation through logfiles are the best strategy to hardening your system's auditing capabilities.

# Chapter 13

## Patch Management and Monitoring

- Apply Updates
- Patch Monitoring and Management

**P**atching your systems is absolutely crucial in this day of complex software. Patching allows distribution vendors and open source contributors to correct deficiencies found in software or to update software with the latest features. In this chapter, we will discuss how to patch your software both with a graphical user interface and at the command line, the basics of creating a change management process, and monitoring your patch process.

# Apply Updates

Updating your software is a basic, yet important phase of your security program. A vast majority of successful attacks occur on systems that have not been properly patched or updated. The simple act of patching your systems can significantly increase your security posture or at a minimum prevent unskilled attackers or those looking to compromise easily attacked machines. The distributions used in this book let you update your software in a more convenient way than was the norm previously. Many distributions provide a means of updating software in a centralized, easy-to-use manner, including the two distributions of focus for this book, Red Hat Enterprise Linux Advanced Server 3 and SUSE SLES8.

## Update and Patch SUSE Software

SUSE provides Yet Another Setup Tool (YaST), which contains a module for updating software called YOU (YaST Online Update). This tool can be used both from the command line and from a graphical user interface. The graphical tool is extremely easy to use, but may not be an option for those who want to run updates from a cronjob, who only have shell access, or for those who do not have X installed. We will discuss both the graphical and nongraphical versions in this section.

### Graphical Interface Patch Installation

To start online update in graphical mode, select Start | System | YaST2 If you are not logged in as root, you will be asked for your root password as shown in Figure 13-1.

To get to the online update module, select the Online Update icon as shown in Figure 13-2. After selecting Online Update, you will see the main YaST Online Update screen as shown in Figure 13-3.

On this screen, you have a few options to choose from. In the choice of update mode, you can choose Automatic Update, which downloads and installs all patches and installs them with no user intervention. The other option is to choose Manual Update, which allows you to view the updates you are installing to determine dependencies and relevance to your system. The next section of this screen allows you to choose your installation source, which by default is the SUSE servers. If you have another source for your updates, you can select it here. Later in this chapter we will discuss setting

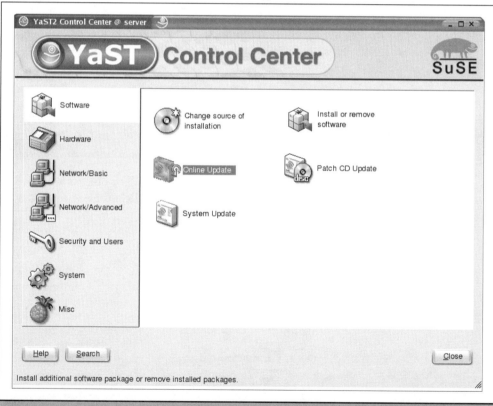

**Figure 13-1.**   Root password prompt

**Figure 13-2.**   Select Online Update

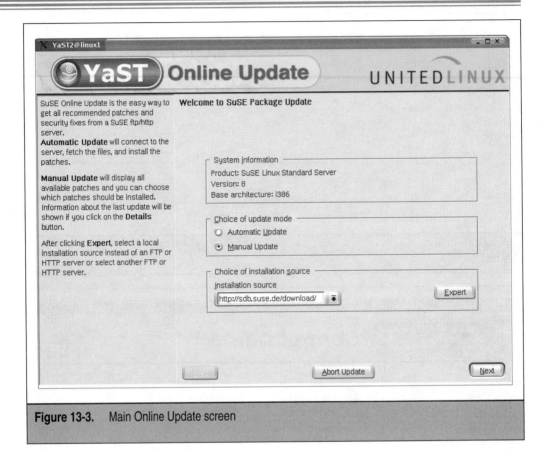

**Figure 13-3.** Main Online Update screen

up a local patch server, where this section would come into use. For our example, we chose Manual Update, left the default installation source, and clicked Next, at which point you will see the screen shown here:

This information can be obtained using your SUSE registration web site. Go to https://portal.SUSE.com/. You need to create a login name and password. Then you will be taken to the SUSE portal homepage. On the left side of the page, you will see a Manage Registrations link under the My SUSE link. Click that and then click on Activate Product, where you can enter your registration code. You then enter the user login and password you entered at the portal (don't use the registration code, as is implied, use your registration user ID). You will also want to unselect the Keep Registration Data checkbox. This is a security weakness, as your user ID and password will show up in plaintext the next time they come up (giving your login credentials to anyone with access to the machine). After entering your login data, you will see that the server is gathering information, as shown here, after which you will see the screen shown in Figure 13-4.

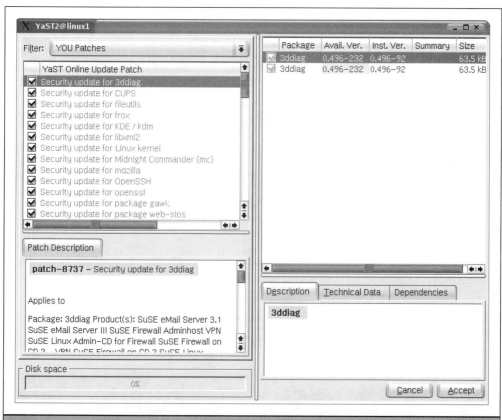

**Figure 13-4.** Patch selection

You can now select the packages you want to install after you view the description to determine if it will work in your environment. After selecting the updates you want to install, click Next and you will see a screen similar to that shown in Figure 13-5 showing the packages you selected are being retrieved (but not yet installed).

After the packages have been retrieved, the installation procedures begin as shown in Figure 13-6. During installation of some packages, you may receive instructions on procedures to follow after the patch is installed, as shown here. Make note of any instructions and follow the instructions after you have completed the total patch procedure.

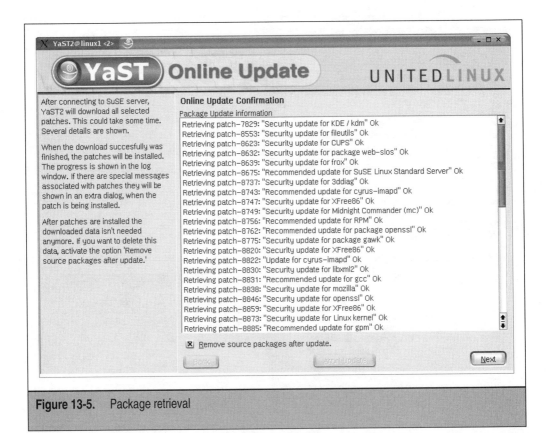

**Figure 13-5.**   Package retrieval

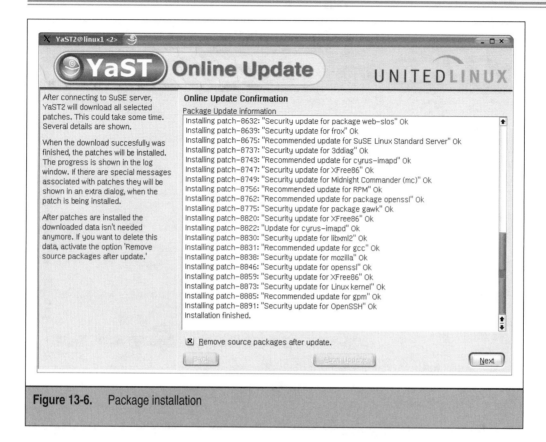

**Figure 13-6.**    Package installation

When the installation has completed, you will see the Installation Successful window as shown here. Click OK to finish installing patches. After clicking OK you will see the installation wrap-up screen as shown in Figure 13-7.

When this is complete, you can click Finish to end the update. To be absolutely certain that all the patches have installed and that there are no new patches to install, run through the process one more time.

## Command Line Interface Patch Installation

There will be instances when you cannot update a machine due to not having a GUI installed on the system or when you want to update automatically via a cronjob. To download patches from the first system listed in your /etc/suseservers file (YaST2 uses this file to indicate where to get the updates from) use the following command:

```
/sbin/yast2 online_update .auto.get
```

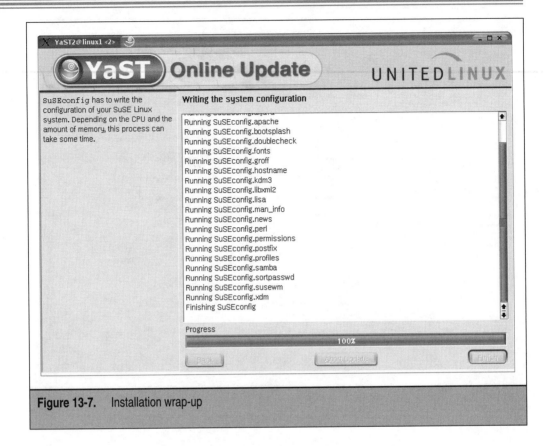

**Figure 13-7.**     Installation wrap-up

You can also specify patch groups as shown in Table 13-1.

| Patch Groups | Description |
| --- | --- |
| Document | Information about servers or patches |
| Optional | Minor patches |
| Recommended | SUSE recommended patches |
| Security | Security-related patches |
| yast2 | YaST2-related patches |

**Table 13-1.**     YaST2 Patch Groups

If you want to download security patches for later installation, use the following command:

```
/sbin/yast2 online_update .auto.get security
```

To research the patch and what it does, you can go to /var/lib/YaST2/you/i386 /update/SUSE-SLES/8/patches and open the files contained in this directory in your favorite text editor. Up to this point you have only downloaded the patches.

To install the patches, use the .auto.install option:

```
/sbin/yast2 online_update .auto.install
```

The preceding command installs all available patches. You can use the same options as **.auto.update**. Also note that you can use **.auto.get** alone to download all relevant patches and then use **.auto.install** to install only the security patches. The logfiles for these updates are located in /var/log/YaST2/ for later viewing. These commands can be added to a cronjob to be automated if appropriate with a crontab entry similar to this:

```
* 2 * * * /sbin/yast2 online_update .auto.get security
* 3 * * * /sbin/yast2 online_update .auto.install security
```

# Update and Patch Red Hat Software

Red Hat provides an easy-to-use update tool with its distribution, called **up2date**. With this tool you can automatically patch and install the latest software available. An additional added benefit of Red Hat's software management tools is the ability to manage many servers from the Red Hat network web site. This is one online update tool that is very robust, allowing management of many servers from one location.

## Graphical Interface Patch Installation

The easiest way to start the Red Hat Update Agent is to double-click on the exclamation mark in the lower-right side of the screen, or you can open a console window and type **up2date**.

Click Forward, where you will see the terms of service that you must read and accept before continuing, as shown in Figure 13-8.

If you need to configure the RHN update tool for proxy use, you will see a screen for you to put in proxy information as shown in Figure 13-9.

After the proxy configuration screen, you will see a Configuration Complete window, at which point you can click Apply.

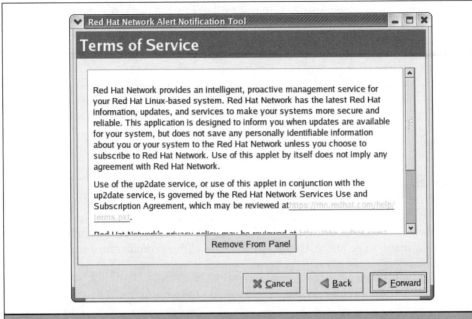

**Figure 13-8.**   Terms of Service

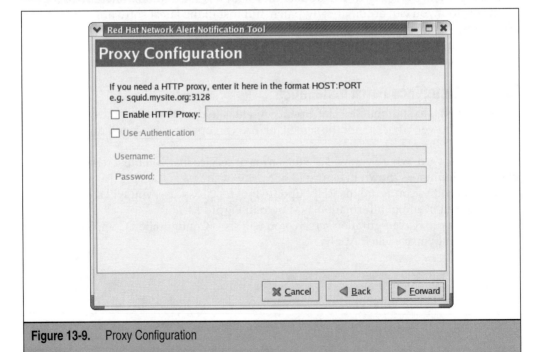

**Figure 13-9.**   Proxy Configuration

If your system has not been registered yet, you will receive the warning shown in Figure 13-10 (you may have to double-click the RHN Tool indicator or type **up2date** in a shell window).

At this point, you need to provide the root login, as patching and installing software using this tool requires root privileges.

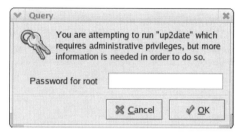

Now you are taken to a configuration screen, where you may enter any special configuration options your organization requires (see Figure 13-11). The defaults should be fine in the majority of instances.

Red Hat provides a GPG key to validate that the files you download and install are truly coming from Red Hat and not another untrusted source. The screen you will be presented with to approve importing Red Hat's public key is shown here. Click Yes to import and continue.

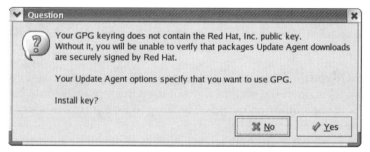

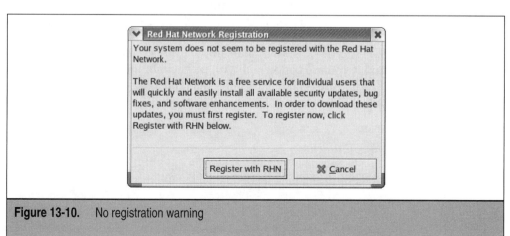

**Figure 13-10.** No registration warning

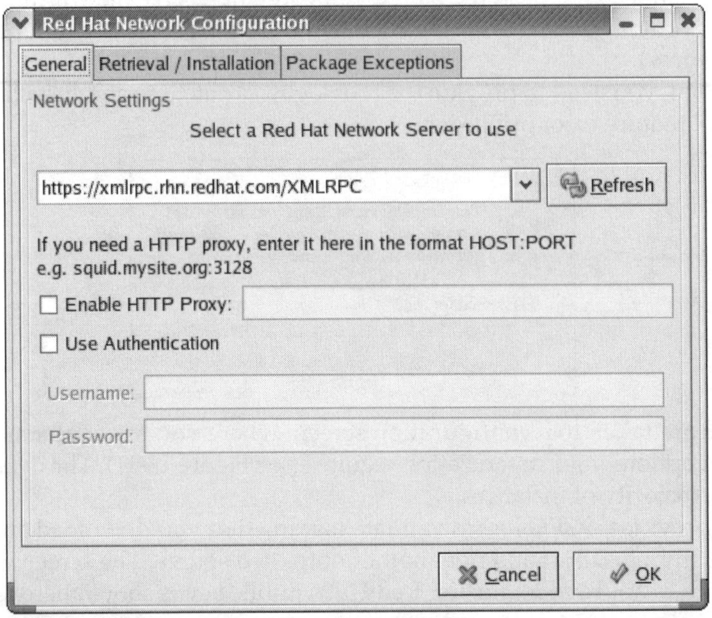

**Figure 13-11.** Red Hat Network Configuration

Next you will see the Red Hat Update Agent welcome screen. You may have to double-click the icon in the bottom right of the screen (which could be either an exclamation point or a question mark) or type **up2date** to bring this screen up if it doesn't show by itself.

Select Forward to go the screen shown in Figure 13-12. If you have a previous account with Red Hat, you can use the http://rhn.red hat.com/ account information in the Use Existing Account segment. If you don't, fill in the information to create a new account.

The final step in the initial update configuration is to register your system with the Red Hat Network. Figure 13-13 shows an example of this screen. Note that you can exclude information if you are concerned with privacy. In the screen shown, no information about the hardware is sent except the Red Hat Linux version and the hostname (profile name).

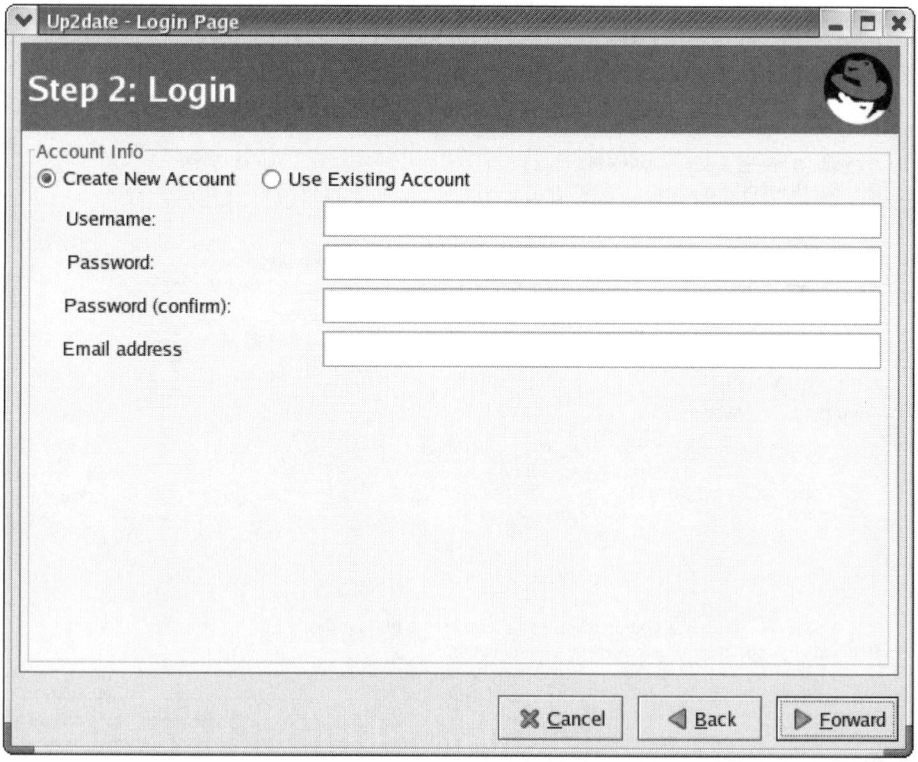

**Figure 13-12.** Red Hat Network login

To send the information to Red Hat, click Forward in the Send Profile Information to Red Hat Network screen.

At this point, your system is ready to collect specific information about the software installed (see Figure 13-14). This information allows Red Hat to customize the list of updates that are presented to the user for updating.

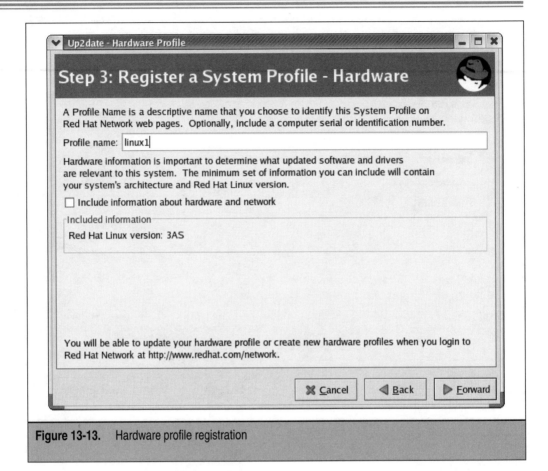

**Figure 13-13.** Hardware profile registration

After the registration is complete, you can now begin updating your system. The screen shown in Figure 13-15 is the one you see in all future occurrences of double-clicking the RHN Update icon or when you type **up2date** on the command line. Click Forward.

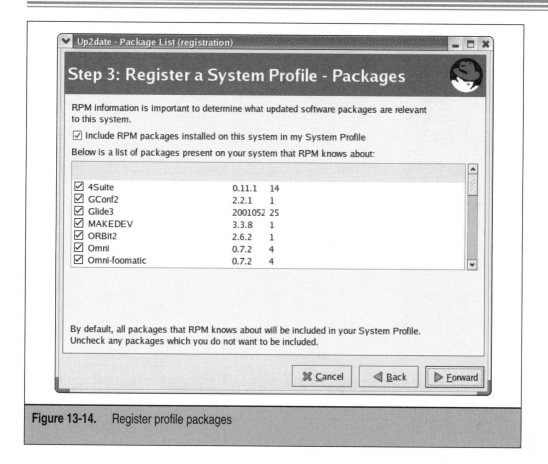

**Figure 13-14.**    Register profile packages

You are presented with a listing of the channels your system is subscribed to as well as checkboxes to select which channels you are updating, as shown in Figure 13-16.

The next screen is a listing of the available packages you can update via the Red Hat Network. In Figure 13-17 you can see that there are many packages that need to be updated. In the Package Information window you can determine what the package is for,

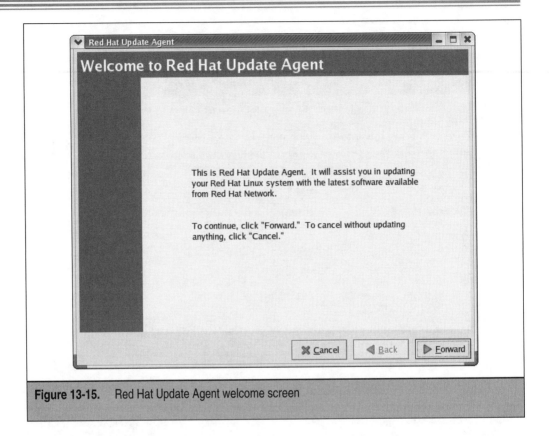

**Figure 13-15.** Red Hat Update Agent welcome screen

and the View Advisory button will provide further information on the update. Click Forward after you have determined the patches you want to apply to your system. The system will solve any interdependencies or conflicts.

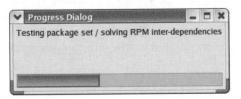

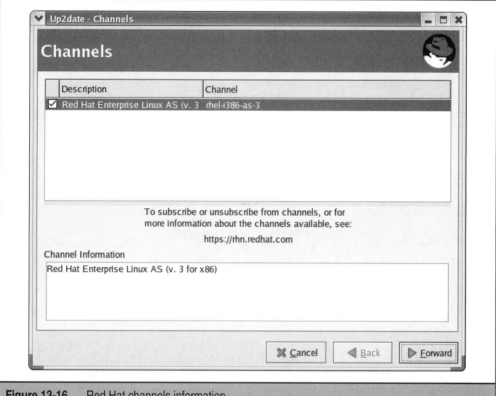

**Figure 13-16.** Red Hat channels information

# HEADS UP!

In Linux, there are many packages that depend upon each other to work properly, and removing them can cause many problems, as discussed in Chapter 4. If any problems are discovered, a screen similar to Figure 13-18 will pop up. If no package issues are found, you will not see this screen.

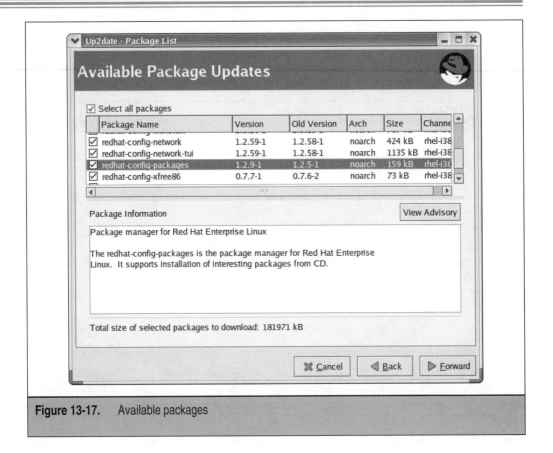

**Figure 13-17.** Available packages

At this point, all packages that were selected will be retrieved from Red Hat (see Figure 13-19). This may take a significant amount of time depending on how many updates are being installed and the speed of your Internet connection.

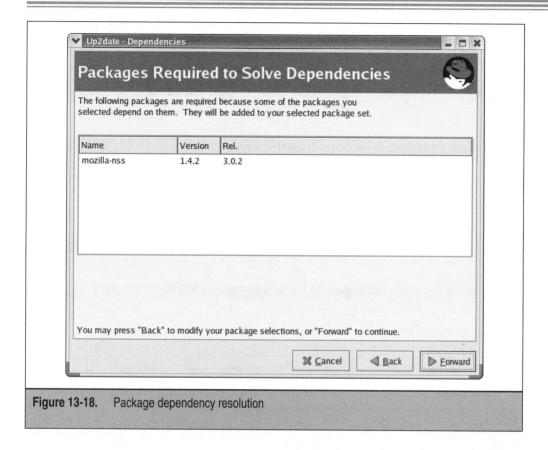

**Figure 13-18.**    Package dependency resolution

After the packages have been retrieved, the installation process will begin, as shown in Figure 13-20.

After all packages have been successfully installed, you will be shown an overview of what changes occurred, as shown in Figure 13-21.

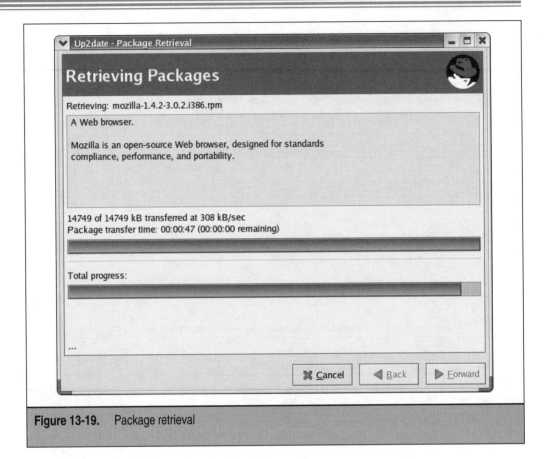

**Figure 13-19.** Package retrieval

## Command Line Interface Patch Installation

You will not always be able to use the graphical interface or you may want to automate the process of patching. To do this in Red Hat Linux, you can use **up2date** from the command line. One of the great benefits of this is you can update software, resolve dependencies, and install new software with a tool that is easy to use and administer. The more interesting options are listed in Table 13-2.

To have **up2date** update the system from the command line, type the following command (**--nox** is not always required, but it is better to be safe and add it):

```
up2date -u --nox
```

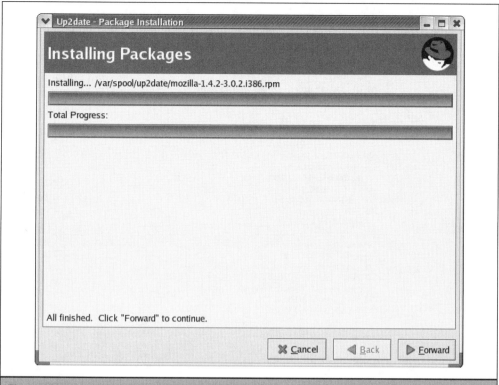

**Figure 13-20.** Package installation

| Option | Description |
|---|---|
| --configure | Use this option to configure the **up2date** agent. |
| --d | Download packages only (for later installation). |
| --dry-run | Show the packages available and dependencies. |
| -f | Force package installation, overriding all previous instructions. |
| -i | Install. |
| -l | List packages updated or for download and/or installation. |
| --nox | Do not try to display the GUI. |
| --showall | Show all packages available from currently subscribed channels (including those not installed). |
| -u | Update all currently installed packages. |

**Table 13-2.** **up2date** Options

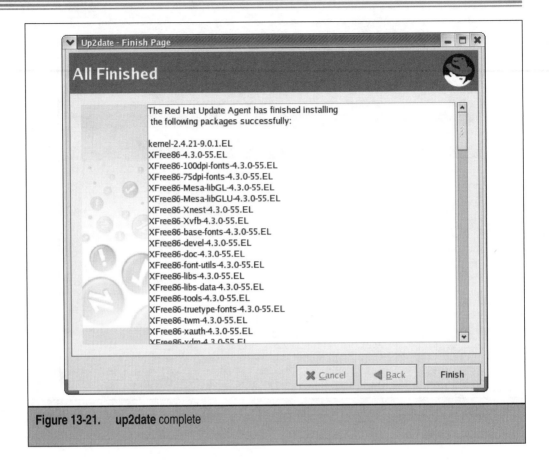

**Figure 13-21.** up2date complete

The output is as follows:

```
[root@linux2 root]# up2date -u --nox

Fetching package list for channel: rhel-i386-as-3...
########################################

Fetching Obsoletes list for channel: rhel-i386-as-3...

Fetching rpm headers...
########################################

Name                    Version        Rel
--------------------------------------------------
```

```
mozilla                        1.4.2        3.0.2              i386

mozilla-nspr                   1.4.2        3.0.2              i386


Testing package set / solving RPM inter-dependencies...
#########################################
mozilla-1.4.2-3.0.2.i386.rp ####################### Done.
mozilla-nspr-1.4.2-3.0.2.i3 ####################### Done.
mozilla-nss-1.4.2-3.0.2.i38 ####################### Done.
Preparing              ######################################### [100%]

Installing...
   1:mozilla-nspr        ######################################## [100%]
   2:mozilla-nss         ######################################## [100%]
   3:mozilla             ######################################## [100%]
The following packages were added to your selection to satisfy dependencies:

Name                          Version      Release
-----------------------------------------------------------
mozilla-nss                   1.4.2        3.0.2
```

This shows that mozilla was updated and some software that wasn't installed was installed to solve a dependency problem (last four lines). The information shown in the text output is similar to that shown in the graphical version, just in a more condensed, automated format.

If you only want to download patches or packages, but not install them, you can use **--download**. This allows you to determine what patches you want to apply in order to maintain maximum availability.

To have automatic updates run via a cronjob, you can put an entry in your crontab similar to

```
* 2 * * * /usr/sbin/up2date -u --nox
```

To view what changes were made to the system by **up2date**, you can view the logfile at /var/log/up2date, which provides any information you need.

---

Using the **--download** option allows you to test your patches individually instead of doing a group install. This facilitates testing and incremental patching over a period of time, preventing loss of availability due to software incompatibilities and dependency conflicts.

## Use a Central Patch Server

A central patch server allows you to consolidate all the patches for your systems onto one system that will directly connect to the external (vendor) patch server and allow the other client machines. By creating a central patch server, you can deploy security patches across your organization's systems in a fast, reliable manner, with minimal interaction with individual machines. Red Hat Enterprise Linux AS 3.0 and SLES8 provide commercial offerings that can provide a vendor supported means of patching your server. Red Hat Enterprise Linux AS 3.0 provides both RHN Satellite Server or RHN Proxy Server. The RHN Proxy Server collects all the configuration information from the managed machines and allows caching of updates to a local server (reducing bandwidth costs). The RHN Proxy Server model is recommended for small Red Hat server deployments. RHN Satellite Server retains all server information on the local network and allows for greater granularity in configuration options, and this model is preferred for larger or more security-minded organizations. More information from Red Hat on these two options is available at http://www.redhat.com/software/rhn/architecture/. SUSE provides a commercial central patch module for their products, although information on SUSE's web site is difficult to obtain. You will need to consult your salesperson for further information on the product and features. The desktop products provided by the distributions have easy central patch servers that can be modified to support server products. Since these alternative methods of patching are not necessarily supported, we won't go into great detail, but we can lead you in the right direction.

One nonsupported method is to create an NFS mount on a server that will download the patches and maintain them. Export the directory that holds the patches as read-only to the specific machines that are allowed to access the server. Note that you will have to enable the "download and save patches" on Red Hat and SUSE in the patch utilities provided by the distributions. You can then point your client machines to be patched to the NFS server and directory that holds the patches. Allowing NFS creates security issues of its own and is not the most desirable method of patching.

There are also a few packages available that allow you to patch systems with simple scripts. Here are a few of the programs that can assist in creating your central patch server:

- **http://susefaq.sourceforge.net/howto/you_local.html**  Discusses creating a central SUSE YOU server as well as patch CD-ROMs.

- **http://linux.duke.edu/projects/yum/**  YellowDog Updater Modified, discusses how to create a Red Hat central patch server. Primarily geared toward Fedora and workstation-level machines.

- **http://current.tigris.org/**  Red Hat Network central patch management replacement.

Note that these are not supported and require some adjusting of the default configurations of the operating system, which could lead to problems or failed patch installations. Be sure to consult your vendor for more information on their central patch management offerings.

Before deploying your Linux servers, you must consider the patching requirements and costs associated with the commercial products, as patching has become a crucial requirement for all Linux deployments.

# Patch Monitoring and Management

There is one absolute in our world: there will always be change. How we manage change determines the success or failure of our endeavors. There is a German proverb that states, "To change and to change for the better are two different things." If changes aren't managed properly, they can often have negative consequences, even if the changes were meant to improve things and are completely well intentioned. This is especially true in the IT world, where there is a delicate balance between a properly run system and a chaotic one.

You now know how to update your systems via the mechanisms provided by the distributions, but that is only half the battle. The reasons to implement a change management system are numerous and directly relate to the security and availability of a system. When your hardening steps have been completed, all the improvements you made could be wiped out by a single improperly planned change. Patching can be a destructive process if not managed properly or sensibly. As with any operating system, patches can help repair your systems and decrease the vulnerabilities, but they can also create denial of service or downtime if not properly tested and managed. Let's look at a real-life scenario that demonstrates the points of change management and testing of patches before deployment.

Jane, a webmaster for all internal and external web sites at her company, recently completed a hardening project of her internal web site (no access from the WAN) where all the steps in this book were taken. Joe, a junior system administrator, sees that there is a new vulnerability in the Apache packages on his favorite security site and decides to patch all the servers immediately to prevent someone from exploiting this vulnerability. He doesn't realize that there are some applications depending on the specific version of Apache and its feature set on the system that Jane administers. On Friday, Joe installs the patches on all systems without testing and leaves for the day, not to return until Monday. Jane gets a call on the weekend that the internal web site is down and the weekend staff needs access. Jane logs in via VPN and tries to figure out why the web applications won't work. After many hours of troubleshooting, she determines that the version of Apache is different from the one she needs for the applications. After more time spent reverting to the old version of Apache, she is finally able to get the web server up and running.

This scenario could have been completely avoided by using simple patch management and change management procedures. If Joe had contacted Jane, or at a minimum documented the change, many hours of downtime and problem resolution would have been averted. If the change had gone through a change control board, the problem may have never occurred at all. Even though the patch was needed, the urgency level was not as high since this was only an internal server with no connections to the outside. One interesting thing about this whole scenario is that there was a change management process in place, but it wasn't followed due to some underlying problems. Change management is the solution to this dilemma.

## Create a Change Process

Many companies have realized that change management is crucial for their business to run effectively. Companies often institute monolithic change management processes with multiple layers of control and overly complicated procedures. The processes are usually followed closely at first, but over time degrade to the point where the process isn't followed or is followed with the minimum requirements. If your organization has a change management process that isn't working, determine the cause of the failure. You should keep the following in mind when creating your change management program:

- Is it overly complicated?
- Does it impede normal operations in a manner that isn't consistent with the level of change (such as too much documentation for minor changes)?
- Is there management support and enforcement of the policy?
- Is the company culture resistant to change management?
- Is the change management policy properly documented in a way that users can understand?

These five questions may have surprising answers, and can often point out common causal factors in the failure of a change management process. When creating a change management process, you don't need to start with a large scope that includes all processes within your organization. You can start with a small log of all changes that occur to a server kept offline and progress from there. Creating a change management process is beyond the scope of this book, but a simple process can be implemented using the policy creation guidelines discussed in Chapter 16. Knowing you need a change management process is the first step in the creation of the process.

One other thing to note is the monitoring of your change management process, because the best laid plans can be thwarted if there is no supervision. An example of this is a company that had implemented a change management process that was thought to be successful in managing change. The change management process had been put in place to document every change that occurred on the system, regardless of the type of change, because of significant system outages or disruptions of service caused by improperly managed change. In fact, the manager in charge of the business segment commented that the systems ran better on the weekends when no one was around to "tweak" or otherwise modify them. The process had been in place for almost a year, but there were still problems, because it turned out that the users were not following the change management policy.

Some things to consider when creating a change management process are to ensure that patches and updates are planned and tested on a nonproduction server. Users and management must be informed of changes. Unplanned outages due to patches can create a hostile or apprehensive environment. Another important consideration is to ensure that the changes align to business goals. In our example of the Apache web server, the patching of the system didn't align to business goals, because the changes caused problems and were not critical enough to justify the change and expenditure of resources. These are only some of the things you should consider when creating a change management process.

## Monitor the Patch Process

After installing all your patches, you need to monitor them to ensure there are no unintended consequences. Patches may not immediately cause problems, but problems may show up days later when the patch was forgotten. You could minimize the impact of changes by using a test environment that mirrors your production environment, but realistically, most companies don't have the funding to run a mirror image of their production environments, so monitoring is crucial.

Patching is a critical but necessary evolution in the maintenance and security of modern operating systems. Keep your patching as timely as feasible and use your established change management and monitoring procedures to ensure maximum availability.

# Chapter 14

## Self-Monitoring Tools

- Install and Run a Host-Based Intrusion Detection System
- Install and Run a Password Checker
- Set Up Network Monitoring

**Y**ou now have your systems reasonably secured, so it's time to relax, right? Wrong. You must be constantly vigilant in order to keep your systems in a secure state. If a system is in use, there is potential for weakness and vulnerability to be introduced into the configuration. Knowing when your machine is attacked or vulnerable is paramount to a good security posture. In this chapter, we will discuss some of the many self-monitoring tools you can use on your system to ensure that you keep a consistent and secure server. Here are the steps you need to take immediately to ensure your systems are properly monitored:

- Install and run a host-based intrusion detection system
- Install and run password auditing programs
- Set up network monitoring

# Install and Run a Host-Based Intrusion Detection System

Intrusion detection systems have become more popular as of late due to the immense value they provide a security team in the detection of malicious and unusual events on a network or system. In this section, we will be discussing a host-based intrusion detection system (HIDS), which is based on the machine to be protected. There are many types of HIDS, from those that detect malicious connections or watch programs to detect anomalous events, to the ubiquitous file integrity checkers. At a minimum, you should run a host-based intrusion detection system on your most critical servers. But the better the coverage, the more protection you afford yourself. In this chapter, we will discuss some of the most popular versions.

## Install and Use Tripwire

Tripwire works by creating a baseline snapshot of the files identified in the policy file. It uses the baseline for comparison of files at scheduled intervals and, if changes are detected, alerts are processed based on the configuration. If changes are approved, the baseline is updated with the new information. If the changes are not authorized, you can investigate further based on the changes indicated by Tripwire.

There are two versions of Tripwire that we will discuss in this chapter, the commercial version and the open source version. The open source version of Tripwire is available at http://www.tripwire.org/. A 30-day evaluation copy of the commercial version of Tripwire software is available at http://www.tripwire.com/downloads/tmtfs/ and you will receive a download link or CD and an evaluation license. For management of multiple servers and for the feature set included with the commercial version of Tripwire, it is well worth the costs associated with the product. We recommend that you evaluate the

## HEADS UP!

Ideally, Tripwire should be installed on a machine that has just had the operating system installed and never on a network. This is not always a possibility, so you should install it on a known good machine. This is because Tripwire doesn't inspect the file in the way an antivirus program might. It only checks specific attributes of the file, not the contents of the file for malicious code. If you have a file that has been maliciously modified, and you install Tripwire, you are simply checking the integrity of the altered file, which does you no good. You also need to copy the initial Tripwire database that contains the file attributes to a read-only medium so that you will have an original, known good copy. The database for the commercial version is located in *TWROOT*/db/database.twd (/usr/local/db/database.twd in our example). In the open source version, it is located at /var/lib/tripwire/*hostname*.twd (/var/lib/tripwire/linux1.twd in our example).

commercial version and purchase it if it meets your needs, as you gain support and an excellent management interface for managing all aspects of Tripwire for multiple machines running Tripwire. The commercial version's management interface also allows you to manage Linux and non-Linux Tripwire installations from one central location as well as many more enhancements and improvements over the open source version. Besides offering host-based intrusion detection capabilities, Tripwire offers change management capabilities and significantly enhances any security and change management program.

### Commercial Version Pre-installation Preparation

To begin the installation, you will need to get the media or download file and traverse to where the install.cfg file is located (on the CD-ROM, it is in linux-x86). Review the install.cfg file to see if there are any special requirements for your system. Some things to watch out for in the install.cfg file are

- **TWROOT=/usr/local/tripwire/tfs**    This is where you want your Tripwire binaries, configuration files, and so on to be located. Depending on your system setup, you may need to change this.

- **TWSYSLOG=FALSE**    In most instances, you will want to set this to **TRUE**. You can then set up your syslog to log these messages to the remote syslog server for later analysis (or you can set up **TWSYSLOGHOST** directly to log remotely as discussed later in this chapter and in Chapter 12).

- **TWIPADDRESS=127.0.0.1**    Leave this parameter as is if you only have one network interface. If you have dual homed computers (multiple network interfaces), set this IP address to the trusted network interface.

- **INSTALL_INIT_SCRIPT=FALSE**   Set this parameter if you want to use Tripwire's default initialization (startup) script, which is used for starting Tripwire when the machine reboots or for easy startup.

- **MAILNOVIOLATIONS =TRUE**   This will send an e-mail whenever a check is run, whether or not a violation was found. While this is good, it can be overwhelming, especially if you have a very large number of machines running Tripwire and have the checks run frequently, such as every hour. Use with caution—if you get too many e-mails, you may begin to disregard them.

- **#MAILFROMADDRESS=**   This is commented out initially. You should remove the # sign and set a valid e-mail address, otherwise your e-mails will show up as coming from whatever user the program is run as, which can create problems with e-mail routing.

If you determine you need to alter the install.cfg file, you will need to copy the entire linux-x86 directory to a directory mounted on your system (such as /tmp) as the CD-ROM is a read-only file system.

## Open Source Version Pre-installation Preparation

Download the latest version (currently 2.3-47) of the open source Tripwire source files at http://www.tripwire.org. Next, you should ungzip and untar the file using the following command:

```
tar -zxvf tripwire-2.3-47.bin.tar.gz
```

You will find there are some documentation files and install.sh and install.cfg files. You will need to edit the install.cfg file before installing Tripwire to set it up for your system. In the file, you should edit the parameters as appropriate for your organization, but pay special attention to the following entries:

- **TWSYSLOG=FALSE**   In most instances, you will want to set this to **TRUE**. You can then set up your syslog to log these messages to the remote syslog server for later analysis (or you can set up **TWSYSLOGHOST** directly to log remotely as discussed later in this chapter and in Chapter 12).

- **TWMAILNOVIOLATIONS =TRUE**   This will send an e-mail whenever a check is run, whether or not a violation was found. While this is good, it can be overwhelming, especially if you have a very large number of machines running Tripwire and have the checks run frequently, such as every hour. Use with caution—if you get too many e-mails, you may begin to disregard them.

- **TWMAILMETHOD=SENDMAIL or TWMAILMETHOD=SMTP**
Determine if you are running sendmail (if you aren't running a mail server on the machine, use SMTP). If using sendmail, leave the sections alone. If you use SMTP, comment out the two **SENDMAIL** lines by putting # as the first entry of the line and removing the # from the first character of the 3 **SENDMAIL** entries (make sure to put in the proper information as well).

## Commercial Version Installation

After you have configured the install.cfg file as needed, you can then install the software. Begin the install process by typing

```
./install.sh
```

Read the license agreement, and at the end, press **q** to exit from the license file and if you accept, type **accept**. If you read the license and determine you don't want to accept at that time, the installation procedure will exit. The installation will begin from there and you will be asked a series of questions that should be self-explanatory. Answer as appropriate for your situation. Figure 14-1 shows a sample of what you should see when installing Tripwire.

**Figure 14-1.** Tripwire installation

Note that you will need to enter two passphrases, the local and site passphrases. These passphrases are used to protect the site and local keys by cryptographically signing files. The requirements for these two passphrases are that they must be at least eight characters, and contain one digit and one non-digit. The local key is used to sign database and report files, while the site key is used to sign the configuration and policy files. Make sure to pick two good passphrases as the loss of these can result in the loss of data.

**Adjust Tripwire Configuration Files**   Now that you have Tripwire installed, you need to set up your configuration files to fit the needs of your site. If you have Tripwire Manager installed, use the graphical interface to configure the schedule, policy, and configuration on all the servers you have already set up. For the purposes of this chapter, we will assume you are using the standalone Tripwire for Servers (TFS) product without the Tripwire Manager (TWM) product.

The first step in configuring Tripwire for Servers is to create a meaningful configuration file. Navigate to *TWROOT*/tfs/bin, which by default is /usr/local/bin/ tripwire/tfs/bin. There are two files related to the configuration in the directory: tw.cfg (signed configuration file) and twcfg.txt. The twcfg.txt file is the readable file that can be updated and configured by the user. Open twcfg.txt with your text editor and edit your configurations as needed, although most will pertain to your specific environment (view *TWROOT*/tfs/docs for further clarification on the different parameters) such as the TWIP setting for multi-IP machines, *TWROOT* for the root directory for your Tripwire installation, and so on. If you make any changes to the configuration file, you will need to sign the document using the following command while in the *TWROOT* directory (typically /usr/local/tripwire/tfs on a default installation. Signing prevents tampering on the system and confirms the authenticity of the file to Tripwire.

```
./twadmin -m F -s ../key/site.key twcfg.txt
```

You will be asked the passphrases you entered when installing Tripwire after entering the command.

## Open Source Version Installation

To install the open source version, you need to go to the untarred Tripwire directory, which in our case is tripwire-2.3. You now need to run the installation script with the following command:

```
./install.sh
```

You will be prompted to press ENTER to view the license file. After reading the entire file, type **q** to exit. You will be asked to type **accept** if you accept the license agreement (if you press just RETURN without typing **accept** or if you do not accept the license, the program will be terminated). After accepting the license, the installation will start and you will see information similar to

```
license agreement. [do not accept] accept
Using configuration file install.cfg
Checking for programs specified in install configuration file....
/usr/lib/sendmail exists.  Continuing installation.
/bin/vi exists.  Continuing installation.
---------------------------------------------
Verifying existence of binaries...
./bin/i686-pc-linux_r/siggen found
./bin/i686-pc-linux_r/tripwire found
./bin/i686-pc-linux_r/twprint found
./bin/i686-pc-linux_r/twadmin found
This program will copy Tripwire files to the following directories:
          TWBIN: /usr/sbin
          TWMAN: /usr/man
       TWPOLICY: /etc/tripwire
       TWREPORT: /var/lib/tripwire/report
           TWDB: /var/lib/tripwire
  TWSITEKEYDIR: /etc/tripwire
 TWLOCALKEYDIR: /etc/tripwire


CLOBBER is false.
Continue with installation? [y/n]
```

If the default locations look fine, type **y**. Your next set of prompts are related to the site and local passphrases and should be unique passwords that follow the guidelines noted in the prompts as discussed in the Commercial Version Installation. Here is what you will see in reference to the site and local passphrases:

```
---------------------------------------------
The Tripwire site and local passphrases are used to
sign a variety of files, such as the configuration,
policy, and database files.

Passphrases should be at least 8 characters in length
and contain both letters and numbers.

See the Tripwire manual for more information.

---------------------------------------------
Creating key files...

(When selecting a passphrase, keep in mind that good passphrases typically
have upper and lower case letters, digits and punctuation marks, and are
at least 8 characters in length.)

Enter the site keyfile passphrase:
Verify the site keyfile passphrase:
```

At this point you enter your site passphrase and verify it, at which point your keys will be generated as shown here:

```
Generating key (this may take several minutes)...Key generation complete.

(When selecting a passphrase, keep in mind that good passphrases typically
have upper and lower case letters, digits and punctuation marks, and are
at least 8 characters in length.)

Enter the local keyfile passphrase:
Verify the local keyfile passphrase:
```

At this point you enter your local keyfile passphrase and verify it, at which point your keys will be generated as shown here:

```
Generating key (this may take several minutes)...Key generation
complete.


----------------------------------------------
Generating Tripwire configuration file...


----------------------------------------------
Creating signed configuration file...
Please enter your site passphrase:
```

You will need to enter your site passphrase as entered previously:

```
Wrote configuration file: /etc/tripwire/tw.cfg

A clear-text version of the Tripwire configuration file
/etc/tripwire/twcfg.txt
has been preserved for your inspection.  It is recommended
that you delete this file manually after you have examined it.



----------------------------------------------
Customizing default policy file...


----------------------------------------------
Creating signed policy file...
Please enter your site passphrase:
```

You will need to enter your site passphrase as entered previously:

```
Wrote policy file: /etc/tripwire/tw.pol

A clear-text version of the Tripwire policy file
/etc/tripwire/twpol.txt
has been preserved for your inspection.  This implements
a minimal policy, intended only to test essential
Tripwire functionality.  You should edit the policy file
to describe your system, and then use twadmin to generate
a new signed copy of the Tripwire policy.
---------------------------------------------
The installation succeeded.

Please refer to /usr/doc/tripwire/Release_Notes
for release information and to the printed user documentation
for further instructions on using Tripwire 2.3 Open Source for LINUX.
```

## Create the Policy File

The next step is to create the policy file. The policy file identifies what files are to be watched and with what options. You will need to plan ahead and determine what files and directories you want Tripwire to watch. As you refine your settings or as new files or directories need to be added or removed you can adjust the policy files as shown in the next paragraph and reinitialize your database to keep your Tripwire policy up to date. Your selection should be based on what files or objects are not typically changed, or files that are sensitive. This policy file is very important and will take some time to configure properly.

To view the policy file, navigate to *TWROOT*/policy for the commercial version or /etc/tripwire for the open source version. There you will see two files: tw.pol is your signed file and twpol.txt is the editable file. For more information on writing the policy file and sample policy files, visit http://www.tripwire.com/resources/policy_center/index.cfm?cat=3#unix_policy_files or view the included documentation located in *TWROOT*/docs/tfs_unix_refcard.pdf for the commercial version or /usr/doc/tripwire in the open source version. Edit the file and add the files you want to watch. Now save the file and name it something meaningful; for our file we will name it new_twpol_feb04.txt. After you have configured your policy file, you will need to sign it for use by Tripwire with the command **twadmin**. For the sample policy file that was named new_twpol_feb04.txt, we would use the following command in either version of Tripwire:

```
./twadmin -m P /usr/local/tripwire/tfs/policy/new_twpol_feb04.txt
```

Or for the open source version we would use

```
/usr/sbin/twadmin -m P /etc/tripwire/new_twpol_feb04.txt
```

After you have signed your new file (by entering your site passphrase), you need to notify Tripwire what files to add to its baseline. This is called initializing the database in Tripwire terminology and must be completed for the policy file to be recognized by Tripwire. To initialize the database, run the following command in either version of Tripwire:

```
./tripwire -m i
```

## HEADS UP!

You should remove the unsigned or plaintext versions of your policy file and configuration file from your servers and store them off the machine. These files contain a roadmap to your protected systems and how notification is done, which can give an attacker deep insight to your systems or at a minimum a guideline for which file systems to avoid to get around integrity checking.

### Run an Integrity Check (Commercial Version)

After you have initialized the database, it is time to run the first integrity check. The integrity check compares Tripwire's baseline against the current state of the objects in the file system identified in the policy file. To initiate an integrity check, run the following command (in either version):

```
./tripwire -m c
```

Your output will be similar to the Tripwire report shown in Figure 14-2.

If you need your report for later use, you can run the **twprint** command to get the report to a file (called /tmp/integritycheck.txt for our example) for easier viewing (assuming our report name to update is linux1-20040228-115521.twr). For the commercial version, run

```
./twprint -m r -r ../report/linux1-20040228-115521.twr -o \
/tmp/integritycheck.txt
```

Or in the open source version, you can use

```
./twprint -m r -r /var/lib/tripwire/report/linux1-20040228-115521.twr > \
/tmp/integritycheck.txt
```

Note that the report above was created by Tripwire from the tripwire **-m c** command. The files will be located in your *TWROOT* directory under the report subdirectory in the commercial version, while in the open source version the reports are located in /var/

```
linux1:/usr/local/tripwire/tfs/bin # ./tripwire -m c
Parsing policy file: /usr/local/tripwire/tfs/policy/tw.pol
*** Processing Unix File System ***
Performing integrity check...
Wrote report file: /usr/local/tripwire/tfs/report/linux1-20040228-115521.twr


Tripwire Integrity Check Report version 4.0.0
Tripwire for Servers version 4.0.0.255

Report generated by:        root
Report created on:          Sat Feb 28 11:55:21 2004
Database last updated on:   Never

===============================================================================
Report Summary:
===============================================================================

Host name:                  linux1
Host IP address:            127.0.0.1
Host ID:
Policy file used:           /usr/local/tripwire/tfs/policy/tw.pol
Configuration file used:    /usr/local/tripwire/tfs/bin/tw.cfg
Database file used:         /usr/local/tripwire/tfs/db/database.twd
Command line used:          ./tripwire -m c


===============================================================================
Rule Summary:
===============================================================================

-------------------------------------------------------------------------------
  Section: Unix File System
-------------------------------------------------------------------------------

  Rule Name                 Severity Level   Added   Removed  Modified
  ---------                 --------------   -----   -------  --------
* Tripwire Data Files       100              1       0        0
  System Processes          100              0       0        0
  (/proc)
  System Devices            35               0       0        0
  Root's home directory     35               0       0        0
  (/root)
  Misc Files                15               0       0        0
  (/misc)
  Temporary directory       35               0       0        0
  (/tmp)
  Variable System Files     100              0       0        0
  Tripwire Binaries         100              0       0        0
```

**Figure 14-2.**    Sample Tripwire report

lib/tripwire/report (fully configurable if desired). The reports will have a format of *hostname-YYYYMMDD-hhmmss*.twr with *YYYY* representing year, *MM* representing month, *DD* representing day, *hh* representing hour, *mm* representing minutes, and finally *ss* representing seconds. So our sample report was created on February 28, 2004, at 11:55:21 local time. Whew!

## Update Tripwire Baseline

As changes are approved and made to your server, you will need to update your Tripwire baseline. For instance, someone adds a new user, so /etc/password will have changed and Tripwire notifies you about it. It was a planned change, so you want to update your baseline to take into account that this is an accepted change. If all your violations were expected changes, you can update the entire database by updating your baseline database. To do this you need to run the **tripwire** command (assuming our report name to update is linux1-20040228-115521.twr). In the commercial version the syntax would be

```
./tripwire -m u -r ../report/linux1-20040228-115521.twr \
--accept-all
```

while in the open source the syntax is

```
/usr/sbin/tripwire -m u -r \
/var/lib/tripwire/report/linux1-20040228 115521.twr --accept-all
```

If you don't want to accept all the changes, because some are not expected, you can run the update interactively. This will allow you to remove an "x" value from a box to prevent files you don't want updating with new values. To run the update in interactive mode in the commercial version, type

```
./tripwire -m u -r ../report/linux1-20040228-115521.twr
```

Or in the open source version run

```
/usr/sbin/tripwire -m u -r \
/var/lib/tripwire/report/linux1-20040228-115521.twr
```

an example of the output you will receive is shown here:

```
-------------------------------------------------------------------
Rule Name: Tripwire Data Files (/usr/local/tripwire/tfs/db)
Severity Level: 100
-------------------------------------------------------------------


Remove the "x" from the adjacent box to prevent updating the database
with the new values for this object.

Added:
[x] "/usr/local/tripwire/tfs/db/database.twd.bak"


-------------------------------------------------------------------
Rule Name: System configuration files (/etc)
Severity Level: 100
-------------------------------------------------------------------


Remove the "x" from the adjacent box to prevent updating the database
with the new values for this object.

Modified:
[x] "/etc/passwd"
```

## Run Scheduled Tripwire Checks

Now that Tripwire is properly installed on the system, you will want to run scheduled checks. You can put the Tripwire command for integrity checks into a cronjob for the open source version or you can schedule as appropriate in the Tripwire Manager that is available for the commercial version of Tripwire. A sample cron entry to run every hour would be (run **crontab -e** as root to edit root's crontab)

```
10 * * * * /usr/sbin/tripwire -m c 2&>1
```

# Use RPM for File Integrity Checking

If there is no money in the budget to purchase a full host-based intrusion detection system or if you want a very quick security check, you can use the **rpm** command as a basic system checker included with most distributions of Linux. Even if you do purchase commercial software or use open source products for integrity checking, it is always in good form to have multiple layers of defense and run this and other integrity checks periodically. Red Hat Package Manager (RPM) manages software packages for the system and can be used to check the integrity of system files. When using certain switches, it will check to see if aspects of the file have changed and report the results of that check. While not a robust solution, it can assist a system administrator in a pinch. To check the integrity of all files, run the following command:

```
rpm -Va
```

If you get no output, then all the files checked by **rpm** are unchanged. You will likely see some output as files change with new software additions and routine change to the system. An example of some changes taken from a live system are

```
linux1:/tmp# rpm -Va
.M...... c /media/cdrom
SM5....T c /etc/crontab
.......T   /lib/modules/2.4.19-4GB/modules.dep
```

A period (.) means the test passed and no changes were found for a certain test. The other possible characters and their meaning are listed in Table 14-1.

Using Table 14-1, we can now figure out what changes occurred on the system for the sample file list. The c in between the tests and the file change indicates the file is a

| Character | Meaning |
|---|---|
| . (period) | Test passed, no changes |
| 5 (five) | MD5 sum mismatch. |
| S | File size mismatch |
| L | Symbolic link change |
| T | Mtime (modification time) error |
| D | Device file mismatch |
| U | User ownership mismatch |
| G | Group ownership mismatch |
| M | Mode (file type or permission mismatch) |
| Missing | File is missing |
| ? | Couldn't read file (problem with permission probably) |

**Table 14-1.**    **rpm -Va** Output Meaning

configuration file. For /etc/crontab, we know that the file size has changed and there is a mode modification, a MD5 mismatch, and a modification time mismatch. For this particular file, these changes are out of the ordinary and having some files changed is normal for a system that is in a production environment. There is a certain group of files that should not change and this is where the value of this tool comes in. Files such as /bin/ ps shouldn't change (unless patched, and then the database should be updated), and if these types of files are discovered, more investigation would be prudent. If you are concerned with only one file, such as /bin/ps, you can run a verify command on a single file using the **rpm -Vf** command and specifying the filename. One note on using **rpm** as a security mechanism is that you may want to make a backup to tape or other nonsystem attached media of your RPM library (for SUSE and Red Hat the library is located in /var/lib/rpm). This allows you to verify your packages against a known good source in case a malicious attacker modifies your RPM database.

For a more hands-off approach to monitoring with RPM, you could utilize a cronjob to script the use of RPM checking with the command **awk** to extract a list of files that have changed and put a file on the system for later viewing. Here's a sample line in a crontab (**crontab -e**) that would extract only the files changed and put the output to /var/log/rpm_output:

```
* * * * 1 /bin/rpm -Va > /var/log/rpm_output
```

## Other Tools

Some other tools that can assist with host-based intrusion detection are

- **Advanced Intrusion Detection Environment (AIDE)**    An open source alternative to Tripwire with similar functionality. Available at http:// sourceforge.net/projects/aide/.

- **Another File Integrity Checker (AFICK)**    Another open source alternative to Tripwire. Available at http://sourceforge.net/projects/afick/.

- **Radmind**    Another file integrity checker, available at http://rsug.itd.umich.edu /software/radmind/

# Install and Run a Password Checker

Passwords are often called the weakest link in a security program, because it is human nature to seek out the easiest solution to a problem. If a user must create a password, they will not create a password that long and complex and therefore difficult to remember. Instead they will often create a password with something in their environment as a password hint. Unfortunately, it's also easy for an intruder to deduce the password, or easy for a password cracker to determine these easy-to-remember passwords. It is therefore the responsibility of the security staff to ensure that passwords meet a minimum requirement of security.

Since most organizations still rely on passwords as a single factor, or one form of authentication mechanism to access system resources, passwords are one of the most significant weaknesses facing an organization. Using free password checkers or auditing tools to enforce password policies will help you reduce the risk that poor passwords pose.

Both SUSE and Red Hat server products have sanity checking for user inputted passwords, but users are crafty and will find ways around these preventative measures. In any case, you should set up your system to check password length and complexity via the pluggable authentication modules (PAM) administration tools that come with the distribution as discussed in Chapter 8.

## Use John the Ripper to Audit Passwords

John the Ripper is an alternative to the venerable Crack program and is seen as far more sophisticated and faster than Crack. Since most systems use the MD5 version of crypt() instead of the original DES version, John the Ripper is the preferred method of password auditing due to its increased speed and functionality. It allows you to restore previous cracking sessions, can be configured to use idle processor time for cracking sessions, and has a multitude of configurable rule sets. One special note on this program as well as any other type of security vulnerability software is that you should only install it on nonproduction, nonessential machines, as this software gives you (and any users who may access it) the ability to break system passwords. There is also the possibility that the output files you create could fall into the wrong hands, giving an attacker a major head start for breaking into your system. Don't give the attacker an upper hand in compromising your system by providing all the answers to them. If you absolutely must run it on a production machine, at least make the output files and the file you use to audit with have very strict permissions (owned by root with 700 permissions, for example).

To use John the Ripper, download it from http://www.openwall.com/john/. First download the source package for compiling. You will need to ensure that you have make and gcc packages installed (included on most distribution CDs or available at http://www.rpmfind.net/) if you are compiling from the source files.

## HEADS UP!

Make sure to remove gcc if it is no longer required after compilation as these types of tools can be used by attackers to compile malicious programs. A better option is to compile any programs on another nonproduction or test system and transfer the program to the production server without installing the extra program (such as gcc). This is discussed more in depth in Chapter 4.

To compile John the Ripper, use the following commands on the file you downloaded from Openwall.com:

```
tar -xzf john-1.6.tar
cd john-1.6/src
make generic
```

After a large group of compile feedback scrolls by your screen, you will be put back at the command line. In an ideal situation, you would not try to crack the shadow file (file containing the password in an encrypted form) of a machine on the same machine where the shadow file exists. If you have to run John the Ripper on the same machine, ensure that you pay special attention to the john.pot file in the *install directory*/john-1.6/run/ directory, as that is where all the cracked passwords are stored. It is set with restrictive permissions, so do not change them or you have made an attacker's job a little easier by cracking the passwords for them!

John the Ripper includes a dictionary in *install directory*/john-1.6/run/password.lst. This is a list of 2,290 words that are typically used as passwords. You will probably find a great number of your users use even this rudimentary list of words as passwords. For ease of use and in the interest of time, you will want to acquire a larger dictionary list to allow John the Ripper to use a greater set of words for cracking passwords. A simple search of any online search engine will produce many types of dictionaries in many languages. Download a dictionary that fits your needs, concatenate the default.lst to your downloaded file, and use that dictionary as your default. You will also want to add words that are meaningful to your company, such as your company name, what street you are on, the default passwords for new accounts, and so on. If you want to use a different word list than the default one, you can tell John the Ripper to use an alternate one, like this:

```
john -wordfile:/tmp/dictionary_file.txt /etc/shadow
```

If you want to just use the small dictionary included with John the Ripper against your shadow file, type the following (assuming you are just running it against /etc/shadow):

```
john /etc/shadow
```

John will immediately begin working on your passwords to see if they are crackable. When John is running, you will notice that it takes up a very large amount of CPU time (as indicated by the command **top**). This is normal behavior as John only utilizes unused CPU time for processing. If you want to see the status of John at any time, you can press any key and you will get output similar to Figure 14-3.

There are times when you will need to interrupt John in order to complete another processor intensive process. To interrupt John's processing of your password file, press CTRL-C. To resume your previous John the Ripper session, you only need to type

```
john -restore
```

This resumes your previous John session (you can also specify the file to restore by putting the filename after the **-restore** switch. You will also want to review which

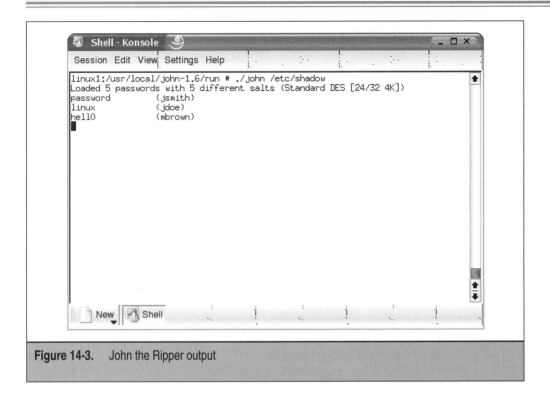

```
linux1:/usr/local/john-1.6/run # ./john /etc/shadow
Loaded 5 passwords with 5 different salts (Standard DES [24/32 4K])
password        (jsmith)
linux           (jdoe)
hell0           (mbrown)
```

**Figure 14-3.**   John the Ripper output

passwords were cracked so you can notify the user to choose an appropriate password and educate them on proper password selection. Use the **-show** *filename* option to show all cracked passwords and users associated with the password, as shown in Figure 14-4.

Besides using standard dictionary cracking mechanisms, John uses a rule set to check passwords in a focused manner. By configuring the john.ini file located in the same directory as the John binary (*install directory*/run), you can set up unique rule sets depending on your needs. Extensive documentation on creating rules is part of the John the Ripper package and is located in *install directory*/docs/RULES. You can also configure John the Ripper to run in idle mode, where John utilizes idle CPU cycles for password cracking. This is a good feature if you are running John on a machine that runs other important processes, although you should reserve this program for nonproduction, nonessential machines.

You need to notify your users that their passwords have been compromised. You can set John the Ripper to e-mail automatically, although this is not always the best route to take because of e-mail issues that can occur. Try monitoring your files and when you see a user's password has been cracked, send them an e-mail letting them know what happened (in a nonconfrontational manner) and tell them what constitutes a good password. Don't send the user the password you cracked in plaintext, as the e-mail could be intercepted, leading to an account break-in. You must also have management support for this whole process, and you absolutely must have management and or data owner approval before running any type of password-auditing programs. This is your chance

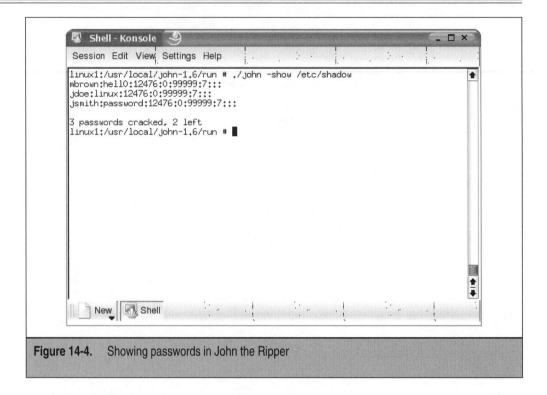

**Figure 14-4.** Showing passwords in John the Ripper

to get a user on your side and show them the value of security, so treat it as an educational experience and take the time to help the user. Word gets around when things like this happen, so keeping it friendly the first time it occurs helps the security program.

# Set Up Network Monitoring

Proactive testing of the network allows the security administrator to determine if there are weaknesses in their security architecture. Using freely available tools that are sometimes used by attackers will identify your weaknesses and allow you to correct the vulnerabilities.

## Configure and Run Nmap

Nmap (Network Mapper) is an open source tool geared for security auditing of systems. It can also be used to discover network nodes on a given network as well. Nmap can identify hosts and, based on the TCP/IP stack, give a reasonably accurate guess on what operating system a target computer is running. In addition, Nmap will note what services are available on a system, with a good guess on the service and the version. There are other types of information you can get as well with this full-featured tool, but we will focus on operating system detection and services functions.

To get the latest version of Nmap (currently 3.50), go to http://download.insecure.org/nmap/dist/?M-D. Download the latest version of both Nmap and Nmap-frontend (nmap-3.50-1.i386.rpm and nmap-frontend-3.50-1.i386.rpm, respectively, as of this writing). In a shell window, navigate to where you downloaded the file and run the following commands, substituting the filenames if you choose a different version than 3.50:

```
rpm -Uvh nmap-3.50-1.i386.rpm
rpm -Uvh nmap-frontend-3.50-1.i386.rpm
```

There are two ways to run Nmap at this point. You can utilize the command line version of Nmap or you can use the graphical front end to run your scans. We will focus on the graphical version as it is the easiest for new people to learn, but we will note the command line alternative command to each type of scan.

## HEADS UP!

Now that you have installed Nmap, you should not run Nmap or any other security auditing tools against networks or machines that you do not have explicit written permission to run these vulnerability checks on. It is considered bad form, and in some cases can be illegal, to run these programs against other people's machines and networks without specific permission to do so. Please be careful when using these tools.

## Scan Your Network

To start the graphical component of Nmap, decide if you need all the functionality of Nmap or if you can run with some of the options disabled. Not running as root limits your scanning options as described in the man page, but not so much so that you can't run an informative scan. One example of the types of scans you won't be able to run as a non-root user is the TCP SYN scan because of the requirements for building custom SYN packets. Non-root users also don't get one of the more interesting bits of functionality of OS fingerprinting, where Nmap tries to determine the operating system of the scanned system. Most of the options will still be available, but be aware that some functionality will not be available if you are not running Nmap as root.

The following starts Nmap Front End:

```
nmapfe &
```

You will see a screen similar to Figure 14-5. In the bottom of the window you see a Command text box. Nmap is one of the better designed programs in that it shows you the command that is being run, so if you find a particular scan setup that you prefer, you can see the command line alternative for the scan. This allows you to run the command line equivalent of your favorite scans if you should find yourself without a graphical user interface.

If you click the Scan button without making any modifications to switches, you will get a generic scan that will also fingerprint the OS via TCP/IP fingerprinting. The default NmapFE scan will run SYN Stealth Scan (half-open TCP connection), with an operating system scan, ICMP echo, and a default port list to scan. The output of the default NmapFE scan on a SLES8 with default install is shown in Figure 14-6.

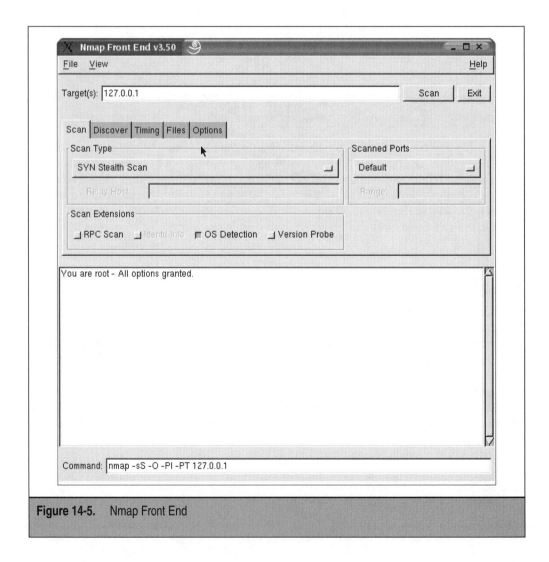

**Figure 14-5.** Nmap Front End

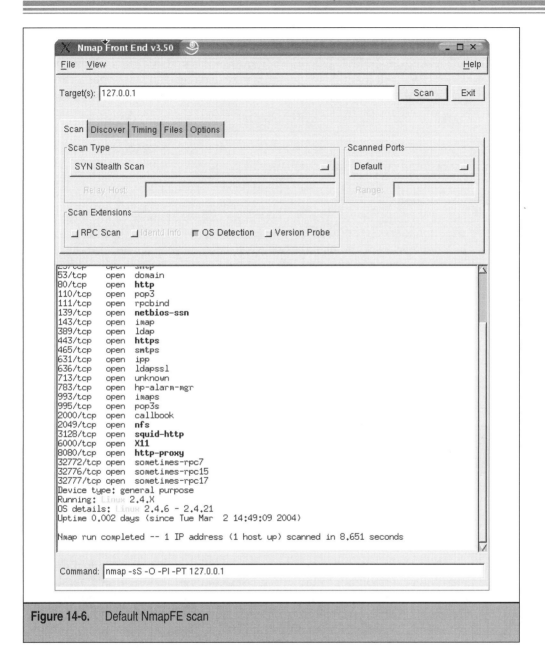

**Figure 14-6.** Default NmapFE scan

You will notice that a lot of ports are open, which are potential vulnerabilities as discussed in earlier chapters. Also notice that Nmap properly guessed our operating system as this was run against the localhost (which was a SLES8 machine). Nmap also properly guessed the uptime of the machine, which just went through a reboot.

### Identify Necessary Services Upgrades

One other interesting option for the security administrator is to check the versions of your services, which helps you identify services that may need upgrading. To get a version type scan, click on Version Probe, which will add the **-sV** option to your command line. To run the command line equivalent, type

```
nmap -sS -sV -O -PI -PT 127.0.0.1
```

This will result in output similar to Figure 14-7.

### Use Optional Scans

NMAP has many different types of scans, including some that allow you to scan more stealthily to avoid detection via network intrusion detection systems (as discussed in Chapter 11). There are many different options to use when running Nmap, including UDP scans and full TCP connect. As a valid security auditor on a network you are responsible for (with approval), some of the options to hide your activities should not be required but are useful if you want to test your intrusion detection system. To gain a further understanding of all of Nmap's functionality and capabilities, you should view the online documentation at http://www.insecure.org/nmap/nmap_documentation.html or from the man page. A thorough understanding of Nmap's capabilities will allow you to audit your network and security mechanisms in many ways, so testing and review of the documentation is highly encouraged.

The Nmap scans will help you identify what systems under your responsibility are susceptible to intrusion based on open services and can give you a view of how an attacker would see your network. Based on the results of the scans you can also identify configuration creep, which is when a system's security posture slowly degrades because of user interaction, system administration mistakes, and modifications to available services.

Nmap is a fully functional scanner, but for a true understanding of your vulnerabilities, the next scanner discussed provides a better reporting mechanism and will help you have a better understanding of your systems.

## Configure and Run Nessus

Nessus is a full-featured, open source security scanner that will identify vulnerabilities and try to test the vulnerabilities found. It is a fast and easy-to-configure vulnerability scanner that is constantly being updated by community volunteers. Another great feature of Nessus is that it can create very detailed reports with graphs and all sorts of bells and whistles that can be understood and appreciated by users who are not security professionals.

To install Nessus, download the Nessus install file, nessus-installer.sh, from http://nessus.org/download.html. You will need to have gtk-devel installed, which can be checked by typing the following command:

```
# rpm -q gtk-devel
```

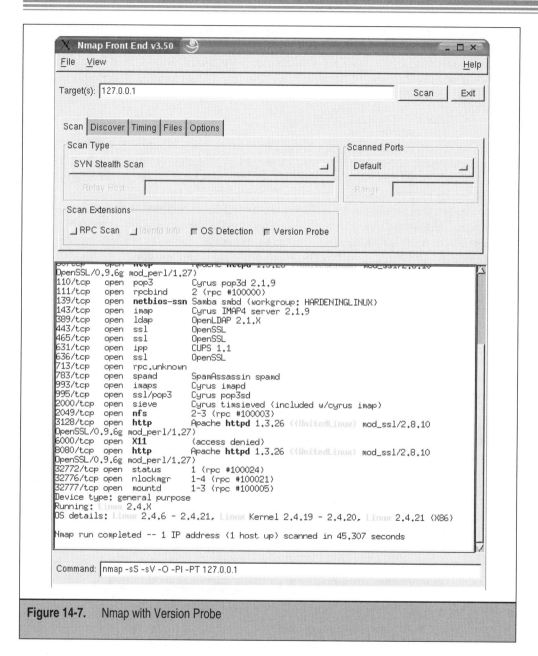

**Figure 14-7.** Nmap with Version Probe

This should result in something similar to the following:

```
gtk-devel-1.2.10-463
```

If you don't have gtk-devel installed, you should install it off your distribution CD-ROM (if you want a graphical user interface, which is the focus of this chapter). You may also need bison and flex, which are available on your distribution CD-ROM or via the Internet. If you are running SUSE, you can install the RPM from the distribution CD. If you don't have the RPM on CD, run the program you downloaded like this:

```
sh nessus-installer.sh
```

This will begin the installation process. You will be asked where you want the Nessus packages installed. The default of /usr/local/ is fine unless you have specific reasons to put it elsewhere. At this point you will be asked to press ENTER to begin the installation process, which takes a bit of time to depending on your system.

The next step is to add a user with the nessus-adduser account. You will be asked for the login, authentication (choose pass in most instances), and then a password. The next portion for rules is crucial to set Nessus up properly. The section allows you to limit the access users have to scan networks. Here is the standard syntax:

```
accept | deny ip/mask
default accept | deny
```

The format is similar to the following:

```
accept 192.168.1.0/16
default deny
```

This would allow the user who had this rule set to scan the 192.168.*x.x* network only. The IP address includes the standard CIDR notation, but you can also specify by IP address only. Press CTRL-D to finish up and accept the rule sets. The next step is to configure the Nessus daemon, but if you are happy with the default settings, Nessus will create it for you. For the first-time user, it is recommended that you leave the defaults until you are comfortable with the software. After the daemon is configured, you will need to run **nessus-mkcert** to create your SSL certificate. Now you can start **nessusd** by running the **nessusd -D** command, and then start the actual Nessus program with the command **nessus**. You will see the warning shown in Figure 14-8. After clicking OK, you will see the screen shown in Figure 14-9.

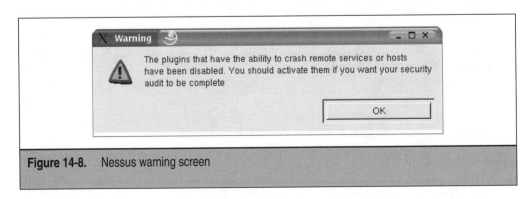

**Figure 14-8.**  Nessus warning screen

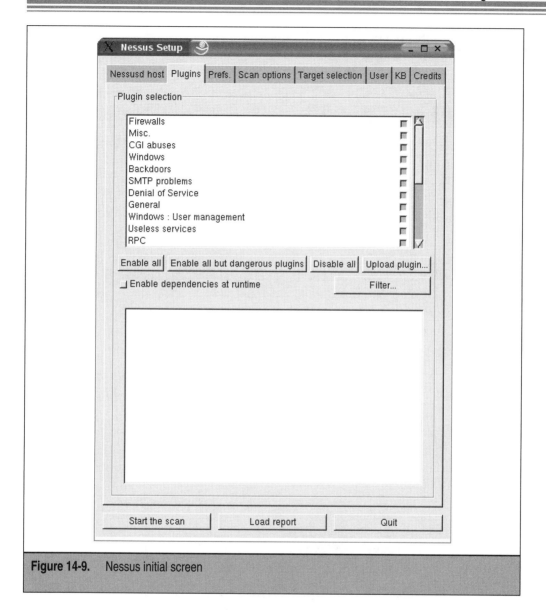

**Figure 14-9.** Nessus initial screen

It is highly recommended that you select "Enable all but dangerous plugins" (which is the default) or you may create a denial of service for machines you are trying to protect. The option tabs are fairly straightforward and are dependent upon your organization's situation, so choose options accordingly. After reviewing the options selected, click on the Target Selection tab. You will see the screen shown in Figure 14-10.

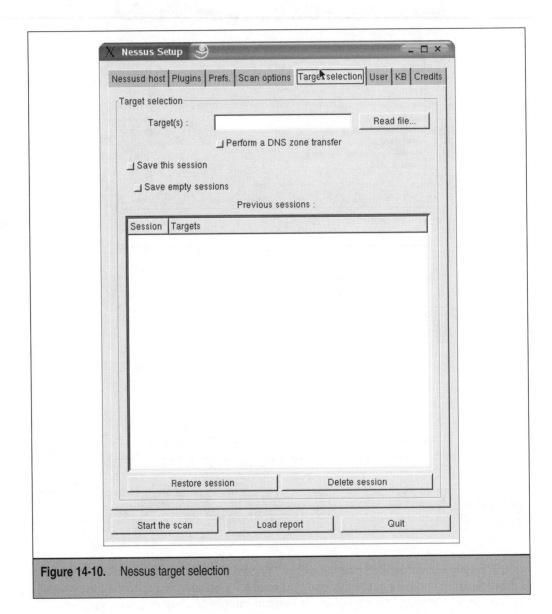

**Figure 14-10.**   Nessus target selection

The screen in Figure 14-10 is where you put in your machine or IP range to be scanned. Be very careful how you enter the information or you could inadvertently scan machines you didn't mean to. You can have your target machine listed by IP address (192.168.1.1), a hostname (linux1), or by a range of addresses (192.168.1.1-254 or 192.168.1.0/24 or 192.168.1.1-192.168.1.255). Enter in your selected machines to be audited and then click Start The Scan to begin scanning. When the scanning starts you will see a screen similar to Figure 14-11.

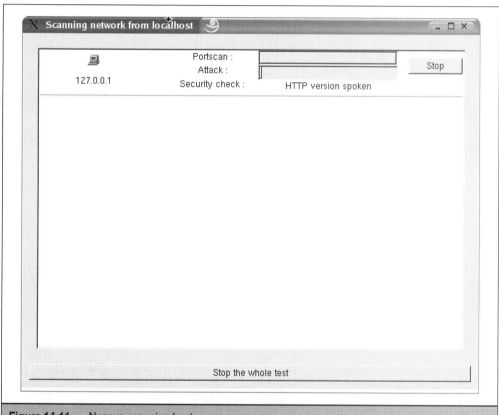

**Figure 14-11.**   Nessus scanning host

After the scan of the hosts you selected has completed, a report will pop open showing you the results of the scan. Here you can select to see results based on subnet, host, port, and severity, allowing you to drill down to specific vulnerabilities with an explanation of the vulnerability as shown in Figure 14-12.

One of the strengths of Nessus is that you can generate very easy-to-read reports that are suited for management. The reports will summarize problem areas of concern

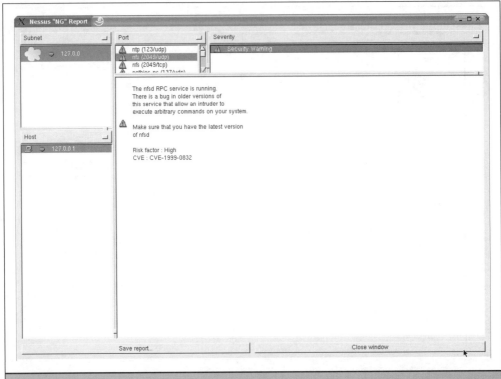

**Figure 14-12.**   Nessus report

and allow you to drill down in a convenient HTML format. Figure 14-13 shows a sample report using the HTML with Graphs option.

Monitoring your systems is an important phase in the security program, and by using GNU Public License (GPL) or commercial software, your job as the security administrator is made easier. Ensure that you continuously and vigilantly monitor your systems because they will evolve and the initial hardening you completed will slowly degrade. By using the tools listed in this chapter, you will be able to identify those problem areas and resolve them in a timely fashion, before an attacker can take advantage of the vulnerability.

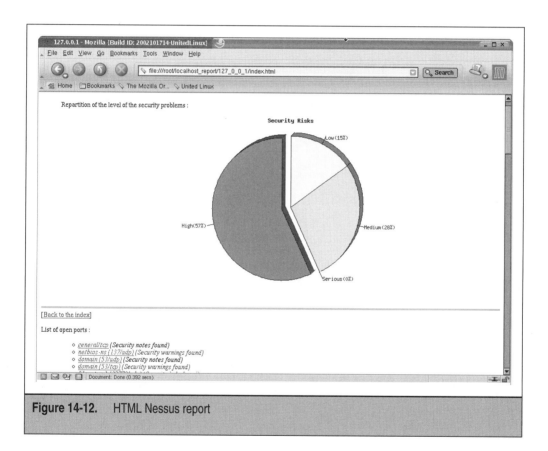

**Figure 14-12.**   HTML Nessus report

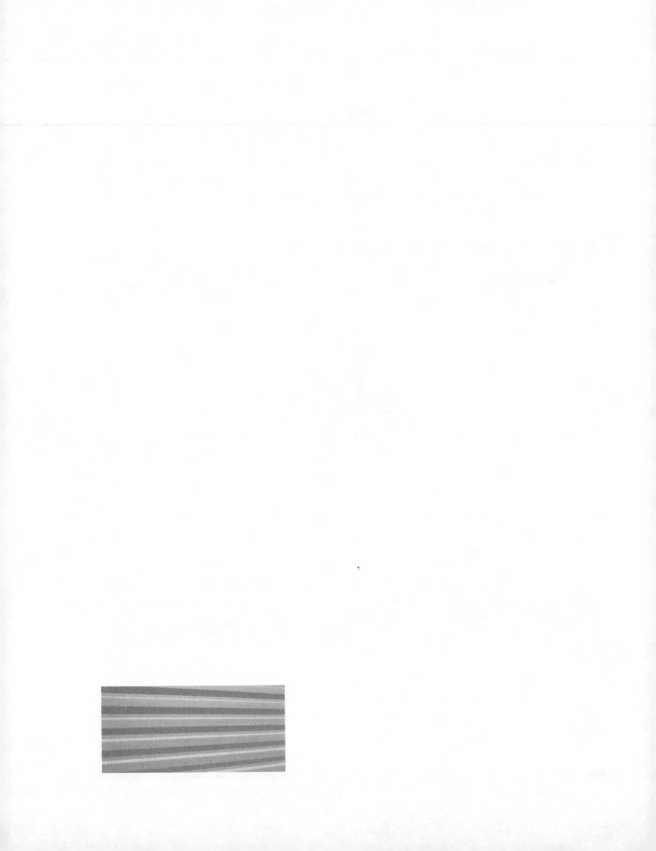

# Part IV

# How to Succeed at Hardening Linux

**353**

# Chapter 15

## Budget Acquisition and Corporate Commitment to Security

- Obtain Management Support
- Perform a Risk Assessment
- Determine Return on Investment (ROI)

The two things that are most often overlooked by security professionals are gaining management support and the acquisition of budget resources. In most environments, money is in scarce supply, while the demands on that money are not. As a security professional, you have to demonstrate the value of good security practices and resources in order to acquire more money. To do this, you must communicate the need for your security programs and projects to management by showing returns on investment, and you must involve management in a successful security program. You need to do the following immediately to ensure a successful security program:

- Obtain management support
- Perform a risk assessment
- Determine return on investment

# Obtain Management Support

In this era of ever-tightening budgets, security can be seen by the non-indoctrinated as a target for budget reduction or elimination. Most upper management does not see security as a business-critical expense that will return dividends; rather, it is seen as an expense with little direct return on investment. In order to gain more funding for security initiatives you have to show management that there is a return on their investment. Typically, security is not a profit-generating expenditure for companies not in the information security realm; it is considered more as a cost of doing business. How much is spent is determined by how well the need for an aggressive security program is articulated. The first step in involving management and gaining their support—and budget resources—is to show the business need for security.

## Show the Need for the Security Program

Showing the need for a security program seems to be an easy endeavor at first, but when approaching management with security requirements, you will need some facts to back up your claims. You will also want to gear your arguments to your audience, because speaking in techno-jargon to those not in the IT field will be meaningless and dilute the point of your requests.

Using comparable companies and their recent exploits or security posture is a good place to start. Most managers understand that there is an expected level of risk they can safely assume and still fall under duly diligent industry best standards. If your business competitors understand security and have vigorous security programs, this can be the catalyst for other management to meet or beat their security posture. Granted, this is not the most impressive way to gain acceptance from management for a security program, but it can be a quick way to get your program started until a more formal plan can be put in place. This takes from the low-hanging fruit theory of attacking a problem from the easiest point, such as a person would do when trying to garner a piece of fruit from a tree. The person wouldn't necessarily go to the most difficult or highest point of the tree; rather, they would get it from the lowest accessible point. Management support can also be gained by focusing on legal requirements, prestige, industry benchmarks, or risk assessments.

The first step in determining what security policies and programs need to be put in place is through a risk assessment.

# Perform a Risk Assessment

Risk assessments are a long-standing tool used by risk professionals to identify what a company's risks are in a quantifiable manner. There are two types of risk assessments in popular use: qualitative and quantitative. A *quantitative risk assessment* uses or attempts to assign real costs to the implementation of risk aversion methods and the costs of the incident and then assigns a quantitative figure for the likelihood of an incident. This type of risk assessment is usually in-depth and takes a great deal of time to formulate and create. It's generally not for those without prior experience in the risk assessment field, as incorrect data or assumptions can skew the results in an unexpected way, reducing the effectiveness of the security program. The benefit of this type of risk assessment is that there are hard numbers associated with risks and countermeasures. It can provide a solid ground for justifying expenditures in a way that management will understand immediately.

A *qualitative risk assessment*, on the other hand, involves subject matter experts to a greater degree, is more intuitive for the beginner, and is the predominant form of risk analysis in use today. A qualitative risk assessment involves first gathering subject matter experts in the processes within scope and then walking through possible risk scenarios. The team would then determine the degree of impact of the scenario and the possible outcome based on the degree of sensitivity of the assets used in the scenario. For the purposes of this book, we will focus on the qualitative risk assessment, due to its ease of use and quick results. If you have a disaster recovery, business continuity, or risk aversion report already completed for your business unit, you can draw heavily from the facts and figures they would have already calculated. Most disaster recovery teams will research some of the issues you will need to cover such as business downtime costs, remediation expenses, and so on.

In this chapter, we will be going over a very condensed version of what a true risk assessment is. Full-scale risk assessments often take a great deal of time and paperwork and have been the subject of entire books. You should reference some of the many risk assessment books available for further information on risk assessments.

## Determine Scope

The first step is to determine the scope of your risk assessment. Scope refers to what your risk assessment will cover—in other words, what it encompasses. It is not feasible in most corporate situations to make the scope of a risk assessment encompass the entire organization and all processes. This approach would require the cooperation of people and groups that you may not have authority over. For your first risk assessment, you should cover the most critical aspects of the business for which you have authority. As an example, Robert works for a large telecommunications company as a system administrator for the support center's Linux servers and desktops. He is trying to gain management support and money to implement a firewall solution between the support computers and the Internet. In this case, Robert might have a scope statement of

> The scope of this risk assessment is the support group's Linux server and all network connections for the server.

This simplistic scope statement explains the scope of what Robert wants to cover, allowing him to expand his scope as he progresses in his security upgrades. A scope statement of

> The scope of this risk assessment is all of the support group's information processing systems.

has significantly broadened his scope, as these systems include desktops, servers, personal digital assistants (PDAs), and such.

Make your scope realistic and flexible to allow for increase if needed. Many first-time risk assessment teams try to be overly aggressive in terms of how big of a scope they should cover, only to realize halfway through the process that there is a need to scale it down.

## Select the Team

The next step is to organize a team to determine the asset/information values (costs of equipment information to be protected) and the possible scenarios that may affect the in-scope processes, computers, and so on. If possible, try to convince management that you should select the team or at a minimum have some say in who is allowed on the team. The team should consist of subject matter experts or process owners for the in-scope processes or areas, as these people will be able to offer the most likely scenarios. The subject matter experts or process owners will also be able to provide the best resolutions to the vulnerabilities and risks covered in your risk assessment. In our previous example of Robert, the system administrator for the support desk, we would probably want to form a team consisting of the support manager, Robert (representing the system administrator), a networking staff member, a corporate security staff member, and possibly a member of the support staff. This team needs to brainstorm on the possible scenarios that could affect business processes from an information security standpoint.

# Gather Issues and Determine Impact and Probability

This team should gather the possible issues and determine the following:

- The impact of the threat (on a scale of 1–5, with 5 being highest impact)
- The probability of the threat (on a scale of 1–5, with 5 being the most likely)
- Existing safeguards
- Countermeasures

The impact of the threat means what would happen if the threat occurred. This could be cost, loss of prestige, civil and criminal penalties, and so on. The probability of the threat is what the chances are that this would happen (use prior year information if available). The numbers for the impact and vulnerability should come from a group consensus, based on the best-guess perception of the group using the severity scale. The last step is to determine what countermeasures could effectively mitigate the risk and costs of those countermeasures. A sample page of our condensed risk assessment, using Robert's situation as an example, would be as follows:

---

## Threat
An attack from the Internet through unblocked/unpatched service.

**Description**   The support Linux server is directly connected to the Internet to allow customers to view open support tickets. This computer also allows SFTP from the support desk for customer patches. The only protection from outside FTP attempts is the username/password authentication provided in Linux.

**Impact**   An attacker could attempt a brute force attack or other attack on the system directly from the Internet. An attacker could then deface the web server application, remove customer files or tickets, or use the machine to attack other computers in the network. This could cost the company up to $15,000 per day in lost revenue, and $2,200 in lost staff hours in repairs for each day the machine is not functioning.

**Existing Safeguards**   The machine requires username and password for access.

**Probability**   Known attacks have occurred in the past year from a disgruntled former employee. On February 15, 2004, the web server was attacked and all customer files removed, costing one day of downtime.

**Countermeasure**   A firewall allowing only web traffic (port 80) at a cost of $3,000 between the support server and the Internet connection.

---

Use the blank template in Figure 15-1 to create your cursory risk assessment threats.

Let's take the following scenario and fill out a sample worksheet. Tracy is leading a risk assessment team, which includes Karen from the systems administration team and Sally from the network operations group. The team has created the following scope statement for their risk assessment: "This risk assessment will cover the asset tracking web server (linux1) and network connections for the web server." The linux1 server is the only asset-tracking repository for the business unit and is used by offsite technicians to determine the location and configuration of equipment that is the core of the business. Due to frequent field hardware configuration changes, the documents are updated often and contain crucial information for the business to run normally. The team makes a list of threats and determines the top three are unpatched software, power outages, and weak passwords. They determine they will document unpatched software as the first risk worksheet because an incident based on unpatched software occurred in the last month and indirectly cost them many hours of downtime. Using this scenario, we will fill out the sample basic risk assessment worksheet shown in Figure 15-2.

After filling out a few of the risk assessment worksheets, go through them one more time with your risk assessment workgroup. This allows your group to ensure they didn't forget anything and to get a total view of the threats identified when compared to other ones noted in the risk assessments. One common result of this exercise is that the perceived highest threats may not be the ones requiring instant resolution because you may discover that other threats are far more important to mitigate.

| Date: _____ | |
|---|---|
| **Preparer:** _____ | |
| Threat | |
| Description | |
| Existing Safeguards | |
| Impact (1–5) | |
| Probability (1–5) | |
| Countermeasure | |
| Rating | Probability + Impact = Risk Rating (___ + ___ = ___) |

**Figure 15-1.**    Basic risk assessment worksheet

| Date: February 17, 2004 | |
|---|---|
| Preparer: Tracy J | |
| Threat | Unpatched software |
| Description | The linux1 server is the primary asset-tracking repository for all field equipment. Due to the need for this machine to be running at all times, patches are scheduled to be implemented once a year. |
| Existing Safeguards | Patching occurs once a year on the server. |
| Impact (1–5) | 4 (The system can be successfully attacked based on a known vulnerability.) |
| Probability (1–5) | 3 (The lack of up-to-date patches has allowed an attacker to gain access to the system, based on a problem known for six months. The patch for the problem was available six months prior.) |
| Countermeasure | Scheduled downtime every quarter for routine issues, and a policy in place that will address high or medium patch alerts within two days of patch release. |
| Rating | Probability + Impact = Risk Rating (3 + 4 = 7) |

**Figure 15-2.**    Sample completed basic risk assessment worksheet

# Prioritize Risks

As you populate your risk assessment with more threats, you should begin to prioritize the risks by adding the probability rating and the impact rating to get a total risk rating. This will allow you to focus on the most significant risks for presentation to management first. This has the side effect of enabling you to determine where your weaknesses are. The previous example listed the top three threats in the minds of the focus group as unpatched software, power outages, and weak passwords. The group created a sample risk assessment worksheet for each item and determined the rating for unpatched software as 7, power outages as 8, and weak passwords as 9. All the other threats except for denial of service fell below a rating of 5. With these ratings you can create a worksheet to show management what the experts think are the most significant risks to the organization. An example of this type of risk chart is shown in Table 15-1.

These worksheets will help you determine what the real threats are and which should be resolved first. The group had initially thought that resolving unpatched software would be the first priority, but as they progressed, they determined that weak passwords should be addressed based on the risk rating. As you work with your group to determine the threats to your organization, you might see that some of the threats can be addressed by a single countermeasure. This helps put more credence behind your findings for some

| Threat | Probability | Impact | Overall Risk Rating |
|--------|-------------|--------|---------------------|
| Weak passwords | 5 | 4 | 9 |
| Power outages | 4 | 4 | 8 |
| Unpatched software | 3 | 4 | 7 |
| Denial of service | 3 | 3 | 6 |

**Table 15-1.**   Sample Prioritization Chart

countermeasures and allows you to get management support for the issues that are most important. By prioritizing your risks based on the cumulative input from the risk assessment group, you can get surprising results. As noted previously, the risks you may have considered the most significant may have a lower risk rating than risks that were considered routine. The risk rating allows you to determine which are the most important and work on resolution of those risks first.

## Quantitative Risk Assessment Overview

Throughout the majority of the chapter, the qualitative risk assessment has been the primary focus. To show real costs and return on investment using specific numbers (as opposed to educated estimates), we'll discuss a quantitative risk assessment example. As its name implies, the quantitative risk assessment is based on hard numbers, but it still relies on some qualitative methods. Like the qualitative assessment, you need to assign a value (Asset Value or AV) to the asset or information (or impact to the organization). You must consider for example the costs to recover from the incident or loss, maintenance costs, developmental costs, and revenue loss.

The factor to consider is the Single Loss Expectancy (SLE), which is the impact of a single incident. Before determining the SLE, you need to determine the Exposure Factor (EF) of the incident. The EF is what expected percentage of the asset would be lost in a given incident. For instance, if a fire were to occur in the primary server room, only 25 percent of the in scope system would be destroyed (as it is unlikely the entire system would be destroyed because of fire suppression systems). This would give you an exposure factor of .25. The asset value multiplied by the exposure factor results in the SLE:

$$AV \times EF = SLE$$

If we had a network operations center that had an asset value of $960,000 (considering loss of revenue, replacement costs, personnel costs, etc.) with an exposure factor of .25 to a fire incident, we can now derive the SLE:

$$\$960,000 \times .25 = \$240,000$$

The next step is to consider the Annualized Rate of Occurrence (ARO) or, more simply put, the expected regularity of incident occurrence. This can be represented by 0.0 for something that will never occur to 365.0 for something that will occur every day. So, if we expected a fire every 25 years, we would have an ARO of 0.04. We can now determine our Annualized Loss Expectancy (ALE) using the following formula:

$$SLE \times ARO = ALE$$

Continuing with our previous example, we have an SLE of $240,000 and an ARO of 0.04, so our ALE would be

$$\$240{,}000 \times 0.04 = \$9{,}600$$

You could now put that information in a chart for management showing them the costs of security programs and procedures. In order to show a positive Return on Investment (ROI), we would put this information in a chart comparing the costs of mitigation programs and compare that cost to the costs we calculated in our quantitative risk assessment. We wouldn't spend $1,000,000 a year in fire suppression mechanisms when the ALE was $9,600 a year. When considering these types of risks, you must also consider non-monetary issues such as personnel safety and regulatory requirements, so even though the ROI wouldn't necessarily directly compare with the mitigation mechanism costs, the other factors come into consideration as well.

# Report to Management and Obtain Guidance

The sample risk assessment provides management with a clear-cut view of what risk they are facing in monetary terms, and how much it would cost to remove that risk. For the final report, create a short one-page summary of your findings in what is typically called an executive overview. This allows management to get a quick overview of your findings, without having to dredge through the entire report. Make sure to emphasize your most important points and the most critical security issues, as this is your attention-getting page. The rest of the report is available for management review, but most managers will review the executive summary and trust the judgment of their staff on the needs, especially if you based your recommendations on hard facts. When management sees that the countermeasure costs less than the actual risk mitigated, the business need becomes evident. This allows you to request budget and management support in your effort to mitigate your shown risks to business goals. Executive summaries are by definition a very condensed version of the original report. You should remember to keep an executive summary to one page, or in extreme cases, it should not exceed ten percent of the overall page count of the report being summarized. In your executive summary, you need to first identify the scope, what threats were identified, and the countermeasures that are recommended. You should not try to include every threat your team discovered. Limit yourself to the top five or the most urgent issues noted and how they can be mitigated. Using the previous example with Tracy's group, here is a representative executive summary with all the elements listed above.

# Executive Summary

The asset-tracking web server, also known as linux1, is the only asset-tracking repository for the business unit and is used by the offsite technicians to determine the location and configuration of equipment. Due to frequent field hardware configuration changes, the documents are updated often and contain crucial information for the business to run normally.

The subject matter experts involved in the operation of the web server formed a risk assessment group and determined the top three threats to the normal operation of this machine:

- **Weak passwords** User passwords have been found to be deficient based on previous experience and the amount of compromised accounts based on poor password selection by users.

- **Power outages** Power outages occur frequently at the data center, causing the system to shut down forcefully, sometimes causing data corruption.

- **Unpatched software** Software is currently patched once per year, leaving the systems vulnerable to known software weaknesses for up to one year after release of a patch.

To mitigate the possibility of these threats affecting the normal business operations of the organization, the following countermeasures were determined to be the most cost effective while adequately reducing the exposure to the threat:

- **User education** Security newsletters should be sent every month and immediately after significant events. If possible, users should also attend security awareness training quarterly at which time password selection and strength will be emphasized.

- **Installation of uninterruptible power supplies (UPS)** The installation of a UPS for the linux1 server will allow the system to shut down in a graceful manner, preventing data corruption.

- **Scheduled maintenance periods every quarter** Scheduled downtime should be made available every quarter at a minimum to allow the system staff to patch vulnerable software. If business requirements allow, critical patches should be allowed more frequently.

The implementation of these countermeasures will alleviate the majority of problems currently encountered by the linux1 server, providing better availability to the end user.

# Determine Return on Investment (ROI)

Return on investment is simply showing management, in terms they understand, what the results of their security investments will be. This doesn't necessarily have to be profits from the investment; it can be the culmination of savings and risk aversion from the investment. You will need to conduct a risk assessment to realize the full value of your security efforts, as they show the threats and countermeasure in a formalized, rated way. Part of the risk assessment should include costs for each type of incident. The previous one-page risk assessment showed in precise terms that the cost of mitigating the risk was far less than the impact of doing nothing. Sometimes showing the return on investment is not quite so straightforward. In those instances where you can't determine the costs of an issue and the return on investment, use the best figures you can gather (realistic and within reason). You can use the estimated costs of a previous incident that was similar in scope and convert the numbers to cover the issue you are working on. You must also keep in mind any regulatory considerations as well as insurance adjustments related to your security program.

## Perform Fact Finding

To effectively convey the importance of the security program, you will need to do some fact finding and coordinate with other groups. This step can be time intensive, but the results of your effort can be tremendous. A methodical fact-finding effort will allow you to present management with factual evidence for the need for a good security program, without opinions based on preconceived notions or guesses that can degrade your overall security message.

Determining what information you need is often the most difficult aspect of the information gathering phase. Some sample facts to gather are

- What is the average income per day of your business unit?
- What is the cost of hardware in your business unit?
- What is the average salary of the staff?
- What laws or regulations apply to your business unit?
- What penalties are associated with process failure of your business unit?

There are other facts to gather, but these are largely determined by what problem you are addressing. It is good to take some time to figure out what you are trying to accomplish and how you are going to go about meeting that goal.

After determining the facts you need to gather, you then need to get the information from those who can provide the best answers. This may include financial, legal, and human resource staff, as well as subject matter experts. Your management should have an understanding of the business relationships and who would be the most helpful in your fact-finding phase. Another good resource to consider is the office manager, who usually knows the major players in the organization and can help lead you in the right direction for information.

## Determine Revenue and Revenue Loss

The first step is to determine the typical revenue produced in one normal business day. This allows you to show what a worst case scenario of complete loss of business functions would be, upon which you can begin determining more long-term effects of business failure. Another important area to consider is if there are fines associated with failure of business activities. If your company has a contract to provide services to another company or individual, do you have an associated fine or deduction when your service doesn't meet predetermined metrics? Are there governmental fines associated with failure to deliver goods or services that could be levied for failure of business delivery? Has a similar company in your industry faced an information security incident? If so, what were the costs of the incident? The costs associated with business interruption or failure could be of tremendous impact, even causing severe degradation of business revenue. If you are a business in the government sector, you must consider the ramifications of potential fines or investigations by government oversight committees and the costs associated with those activities. Government and business entities must consider the impact of incidents on operating budgets and future budgets/revenues.

A good way to determine return on investment (or return on security investment) is to use some previous examples of security issues that caused downtime or business disruption and compare the cost of the downtime to that of the mitigation solution. For example, the fictional company ACME Sprockets has an application called Sprocket Tracker. If the Sprocket Tracker application went offline for 30 minutes, it could directly cost the company $10,000. Using that figure, you can reasonably estimate that in an average business day, you could lose $160,000. This was determined by figuring out the average work hours in a business day, dividing by 2 and then multiplying by $10,000 (average loss per 30 minutes). These are the types of calculations you will need so that you can provide management with reasonable information on potential losses associated with a security event. Figure 15-3 shows an example of determining an incident's cost for a very small company suffering a minor virus outbreak.

Using the report shown in Figure 15-2, you can propose a possible resolution or ways to mitigate the risk and directly compare the two to show the business case for the resolution. For instance, in this case, you show how a patch management system for your Windows machines, which might cost $1,000, could reduce the damage, potentially saving the organization $5,600 per incident.

## Determine Government and Industry Requirements

Other areas that can assist in the determination of return on investment and can greatly impact budget resources are governmental and industry requirements. There are many different legal requirements for security practices throughout the world, which if not

| Incident Cost Report | | |
|---|---|---|
| Incident description | Virus outbreak on Windows user's laptop, due to opening an attachment. | |
| Remediation staff hours used | Two support staff spent 15 hours over two days to remove the virus from end users. | 2 staff members at $30 hour for 15 hours = $900 |
| End user hours used | End users had to wait for staff. A total of 15 users had an average of three hours non-productive time each. | 15 users at average $60 hour for 3 hours each = $2,700 |
| Business hours down | Network problems caused three hours of downtime due to network resources being over-utilized. Typically $8,000 a day is generated in revenue. | 3 hours at $3,000 |
| Total Cost | | $6,600 |

**Figure 15-3.**   Sample incident cost report

properly followed can result in severe monetary penalties, censure, or even criminal penalties. Most security legislation is still in its beginning stages and many businesses have not seen penalties yet, but the provisions are available for regulatory or investigative agencies. Examples of current legislation (pending and enacted) include

- The Health Insurance Portability and Accountability Act (HIPAA), which sets provisions for how personal health information is handled, disclosed, and used. This is applicable in the United States.
  More information is available at http://www.hhs.gov/ocr/hipaa/.

- California SB 1386, relating to reporting of security incidents to California residents and applicable to all businesses that hold personal information on California residents. This particular legislation is seen as far reaching due to the global nature of business, and the fact that a lot of private businesses will hold information on a California citizen due to the nature of interstate and global commerce.
  More information is available at the California State Senate home page: http:// info.sen.ca.gov/pub/01-02/bill/sen/sb_1351-1400/sb_1386_bill_20020926_chaptered.html.

- The Gramm-Leach-Bliley Act (GLBA) or the Financial Services Modernization Act defines some guidance on information security obligations for companies in the United States and sets out requirements for the protection of consumers' personal financial information.
  More information can be found at http://www.ftc.gov/privacy/glbact/.

- The Sarbanes-Oxley (SOX) Act of 2002 deals with accountability for public companies. Of special interest to information security professionals is section 404. Violation of the requirements set forth in this act can lead to civil and criminal penalties for executives and directly impact a security program. The basics of this legislation are that it requires certification of a company's internal controls on a yearly basis, requiring a need for the protection of your company's data. Go to http://www.sec.gov/spotlight/sarbanes-oxley.htm.

- European Union Directive 95/46 EC on the Protection of Individuals with Regards to the Processing of Personal Data, and on the free movement of such data within the European Union. This legislation concerns the protection of personal information and how that information is stored, used, and processed. Go to http://europa.eu.int/comm/internal_market/privacy/law_en.htm.

- The Personal Information Protection and Electronic Documents Act (PIPEDA) covers the collection, use, and disclosure of personal information on Canadian citizens.
  Further details on this legislation are available at http://www.privcom.gc.ca/.

Information security has become a major concern of governments and citizens, and legislation is being enacted throughout the world. The six pieces of legislation listed previously only cover a small portion of the wide-ranging information security laws and regulations that apply to business today. Contact your legal department for further clarification on what legislation applies to your company and industry based on your operating regions, what type of information and services you provide, and other factors. The legal department should also be able to define the potential penalties accrued when a company is not in compliance with these regulations. The security controls required by governmental and industrial regulations should be brought to management's attention immediately and enacted as soon as possible as these represent the most immediate security fulfillment requirements.

## Determine Impact of Loss of Trust

Another area to consider when determining the return on security investment is the estimated losses from prestige or trust in the industry. If your company is a high profile or especially sensitive industry (financial, utility, and so on), the losses incurred by a publicized security incident could be far greater than the more obvious short-term losses on operations, recovery, and maintenance. You must also consider how it would affect future customers. This is particularly hard to determine because there are usually no definite future sales or revenue figures, so you must take average sales and consider what could potentially be lost due to lack of confidence in security. For instance, imagine if your company provides information systems services to a credit card processing facility and the company suffered a malicious event. How would future customers view your service offering and how much more difficult would it be for sales staff to close future deals? This is the most obscure portion to determine, but your best guess based on previous sales will have to suffice to give management a realistic expectation of the cost of loss of prestige and trust.

# Show Return on Investment

Now that you have gathered the appropriate information as outlined in the preceding sections, you need to show the return on investment. Most security practitioners consider information security in terms relative to insurance. Having a vigorous information security program affords an organization insurance against the outcome of poor security. Using all the information gathered, you can now determine the costs of an incident or potential incident and weigh that against the outcome of the possible scenarios.

One suggestion is to write a paper correlating all the information you gathered in conjunction with the risk assessment and provide management with an overview of the benefits of the security program. This should include the worst case scenarios along with the costs of those scenarios. Then provide a direct link to the planned and implemented security mechanisms and procedures to show how these things mitigate, reduce the likelihood, or reduce the impact of that threat. Note that the cost of the countermeasures should not exceed your costs of the risk, as this is not in the best interests of the company. For instance, the countermeasure for an intruder coming on the premises might be to hire roving security guards and erect a fence around the premises. This might be reasonable in some situations, but if the cost of the assets and information protected do not warrant this level of protection, the business requirements for this solution are diminished. Gather your information and show how the costs of implementing countermeasures will provide real benefit to the company. This will show management how important security is to the overall business objectives.

# Seek Outside Help and References

In some instances, management may want the input or guidance of an outside, independent source to provide validation for your recommendations. This is a prudent step and having the information available to management allows them to make a more informed choice and provides legitimacy to your recommendations.

## Gather Industry Statistics

Statistics are a great way to enhance your security expenditure and policy requests. There are many security statistics available online, as well as sites that provide industry research at a reasonable cost. Providing a hard-hitting statistic that shows management what others in the industry are saying or experiencing can sometimes be the determining factor between project approval and rejection. Use the experiences of others and the statistics they provide as an attention grabbing point in your research to prevent your company from becoming one of those statistics.

Statistics on security that will assist you in your security goals can be found in several places. You can also use statistics based on your own experiences, such as firewall logs, security incidents per quarter, or other pertinent facts as these statistics can have more impact than general reference ones. A few of the more popular sites for security statistics are

- CERT/CC (http://www.cert.org/stats/cert_stats.html)
- CSO Magazine (http://www.csoonline.com/)
- ISSA Journal (http://www.issa.org/)
- SANS (http://www.sans.org/)
- SecurityFocus (http://www.securityfocus.com/)
- ZDNet (http://itpapers.zdnet.com/)
- LinuxSecurity (http://www.linuxsecurity.com/)
- InfoSecurityMag (http://infosecuritymag.techtarget.com/)
- Linux Weekly News (http://lwn.net/security)
- Linux Today (http://linuxtoday.com/security/)
- Vendor web sites
- General use search engines such as http://www.google.com/ can provide the most up-to-date or relevant statistics.

## Contract a Consultant

An uninvolved third party can provide insight from a viewpoint that you may not have previously had. They can also back up your recommendations if they are based on sound research and foresight. If you are not a security professional or if you don't have a security background, this is the favored course of action. A consultant is usually versed in management and business practices, and can articulate your recommendations in a way that conveys the urgency and need for a vigorous security program. This is not to say that a consultant is going to come to your business and rubber-stamp your proposal without providing feedback or new recommendations if yours need enhancing. A good consultant will take your research and recommendations and weigh them against industry best practices or prevalent levels of security. Most consultants will also conduct some form of audit to determine the current security posture and what level of security management desires. Having the research discussed earlier in this chapter available to the consultant will allow them to create recommendations in a timely manner, with the least disruption to staff.

Locating a good consultant can be difficult. A good place to start is by contacting your local Information Systems Security Association (http://www.issa.org/) or Information Systems Audit and Control Association (http://www.isaca.org/) and talking to chapter representatives. They will usually be able to provide some references and contact information for local security consultants. When interviewing security consultants, ask what types of certifications they hold, level of education, how long they have been doing security consulting, references from the last few customers they had, as well as if they have experience in your organization's field of business. A good consultant will be happy to provide this information, and by doing your homework on your prospective consultant, you will ensure that your company gets sound, unbiased advice.

After contracting a consultant, you should start by telling them what your objectives are and provide them with access to the information required to effectively do their job. A consultant who doesn't have enough access to resources and information will prove to be useless to your company and can actually lead to results that are detrimental. Consultants are sometimes seen as the untrustworthy outsider or competitor to many in the information technology field, so you may need to assist the consultant in their fact-finding duties.

A consultant who understands your business and needs can prove invaluable to your company's security goals and often provides the final catalyst needed to implement security mechanisms and policies.

## Reference Current Industry Standards

A great place to reference your current security posture against a worldwide reference is ISO 17799 (BS 7799-2), Code of Practice for Information Security Management. This standard provides a framework that is beginning to be accepted worldwide as an information security standard. There are other industry standards available online, but ISO 17799 is rapidly becoming the de facto guideline for creating a security program that will meet the needs of most organizations. Referencing the ISO standard and using it as a guideline for your program will show management that you are utilizing tools that are in use worldwide and widely accepted as best practice in the information security industry. The ISO standards do cost money to obtain (around $250) and can be ordered at BSI Americas (http://www.bsiamericas.com/InformationSecurity/). There are other guidelines in use worldwide, even industry-specific guidelines, so you must do your research to determine what the best documentation for you will be. Some of the other guidelines for a security program or audit of a security program are

- Generally Accepted System Security Principles (GASSP), available at (http://web.mit.edu/security/www/gassp1.html).

- Generally Accepted Information Security Principles (GAISP). This is a project to rework the GASSP and move it forward. It is still a work in progress, but information about it can be found at http://www.issa.org/gaisp/.

- Commonly Accepted Security Practices and Recommendations (CASPR), available at http://www.caspr.org/ (currently inactive).

- Control Objectives for Information and Technology (COBIT), available at http://www.caspr.org/www.isaca.org/cobit.htm.

- Common Criteria, available at http://csrc.nist.gov/cc/.

# Involve Management in Creation of Security Policies and Spending

This is possibly the most crucial step to gaining management support for your security program. Management must perceive some ownership in the overall security plan. This sense of ownership will ensure that they fully support your process and influence their management and staff to support your security initiatives. The first step was to show the need for the security program through the use of costs versus return on investment. The next step is to involve management in the creation and formulation of the security plan through education. The more informed your management is, the better equipped they are to support your programs to their management. Provide timely, management audience targeted newsletters and news segments to management to show how important security is to the overall security architecture. There are many magazines (online and hard copy) and newsletters in print today, targeted at the management audience. Some of these magazines are

- Corporate Security (http://www.straffordpub.com/products/csn/)
- CSO Magazine (http://www.csoonline.com/)
- ISSA Journal (http://www.issa.org/)
- Network World Fusion (http://www.nwfusion.com/)
- InfoSecurityMag (http://www.infosecuritymag.com/)
- SC Magazine (http://www.scmagazine.com/)

When determining what your security program should entail, seek management's guidance on what solutions will be the least disruptive to the organization as a whole. Management can provide invaluable insight on the interdependencies and social relationships between business segments that you may not have been aware of. These relationships can prove beneficial when seeking to influence change across business units.

With the introduction of information security legislation on the rise worldwide, management in most companies is beginning to understand that security is not just a cost of doing business, but a requirement of doing business. Your job is to show that your security solutions can provide maximum benefit at a reasonable cost. By involving management in all aspects of your security program and showing why security is crucial to business operations, you will obtain the budget resources and management support you need to be successful.

# Chapter 16

## Establishing a Security Campaign

■ Establish the Security Campaign

■ Example Company Encrypted Protocols Policy

**W**ith all the technical and software security solutions available to security professionals today, there is a tendency to forget what is possibly the single most important factor in any security program, the user. The user's cooperation and support of a security program can mean the difference between a successful security program and one that fails miserably. If the users do not know what is expected of them, a security program will be ineffective and can lead to misinterpreted security intent. In this chapter, we will discuss what steps you should take to gain user support and establish a security campaign.

# Establish the Security Campaign

Before you can get user acceptance, you have to know what your security efforts will be. This rather obvious sounding statement seems intuitive, but one issue new security campaigns face is the fact that they are often unfocused and lack the documentation necessary to effectively convey the security strategy. A security campaign is the coordinated, focused effort of the security practitioner to communicate the security requirements to the users. This includes educating users on social engineering, proper password creation, laptop security, and so on. The security campaign can use many methods to accomplish the goals of communicating the security objectives. This can range from the traditional policy-only program to one that uses multiple forms of educational materials such as posters, e-mails, internal websites with whitepapers and tutorials, screensavers, and security events.

## Determine Goals

Regardless of the delivery method of the security program, you must determine what the goals of the security program will be. If no security program was previously in place, your job will require more investigation on the needs of the company, otherwise you will need to build upon the previous program. The first step is to determine the needs of the company and how to align the security program to those needs. There will be major differences in the scope of the security program for those working in regulated industries from those in retail sales for instance. Your risk assessment conducted in Chapter 15 will assist you in determining what you are required to do by regulation or law (federal, local, or company). The risk assessment can show you your weak areas and allow you to focus on creating policies for the deficient areas first. By viewing policy creation as a step-by-step process, you can tackle the most urgent issues in a piecemeal fashion first, rather than try to create an all-encompassing security policy that covers all aspects of information security in your company.

If your company is looking to be in compliance with an information security standard, such as ISO 17799 (BS 7799-2) standards, there is a standard set of clauses that you will use as a guideline for your policies. For instance, there are specific subsections on most major aspects of information security within companies outlined. These clauses do not

| Standard | More Information | Overview |
|----------|-----------------|----------|
| ISO 17799/BS 7799-2 | http://www.bsi-global.com/Corporate/17799.xalter | Code of Practice for Information Security Management (costs around $250) |
| GASSP | http://web.mit.edu/security/www/gassp1.html | Generally Accepted System Security Principles (not actively updated) |
| GAISSP | http://www.issa.org/gaisp/ | Still in development |
| CASPR | http://www.caspr.org/ | In very early stages of development |
| RFC 2196 | http://www.ietf.org/rfc/rfc2196.txt | The Internet Engineering Task Force's (IETF) guide for security policies |
| COBIT | http://www.isaca.org/cobit.htm | IT control standard that can be beneficial to security professionals (costs between $150 and $300) |

**Table 16-1.**   Information Security Standards

necessarily have policies accompanying them; rather, they set out a basic, high-level statement of need, giving you the framework to build your policies on. Using a well-established set of internationally recognized guidelines will make the creation of your security program more methodical and focused, as well as lend more credibility to your policy efforts. Some of the guidelines that are widely known, which you can use as a basis for your security program, are shown in Table 16-1.

Using these standards as the foundation of your security program, you can begin the next stage, the creation of policies and standards for your organization.

## Identify What Is Needed to Accomplish Goals

Now that you have determined your goals, you need to decide what steps you will take to distribute the message to the users, management, and others affected by your policy. Most security programs consist of a security policy and occasional security awareness presentations. You should create your policies before creating your security awareness program, as your awareness program should be based on your policies and industry best standards. This is great if your users remember your program throughout the year or if they read your policy often. In the real world, users must be reminded of what is expected of them in both traditional and nontraditional ways. Most innovative security programs consist of alternative ways of delivering your security message, including but not limited to:

- **Internal websites**   Create an internal website with current security information and trends.
- **Security posters**   Provide visual reminders of the security policy.
  - http://www.securityawareness.com/

- http://nativeintelligence.com/posters/security-posters.asp
- **Security screensavers** Use your choice of screensaver creation programs and come up with interesting slogans.
- **Computer-based training** Use multimedia to provide consistent, perpetual training.
  - http://www.sans.org/awareness/
- **Security trinkets (such as keychains or cubicle toys)** There are a multitude of branding companies with trinkets for sale.
- **Lunch presentations** Have the company purchase lunch as an enticement to attend frequent security awareness presentations.
- **Security contests** Give away prizes for remembering some part of a newsletter, for example.
- **Newsletters** Create a paper or e-mail newsletter with the latest security information.

Anything you can do that will keep your users' attention and get them to think about security is a great part of the security program, and offers more than plain security policies. Determining what alternative materials to use in your security program is largely dependent on your company's culture and your budget for security. The solutions above allow you to create an interesting program whether or not you have a security budget. After determining the components for delivering your security program's message, you must begin creating the actual guidelines for users to follow in the form of security policies.

## Create Policies

Before embarking on policy creation, we should make note of some oddities in the information security field. A policy is a document that specifies actions to be taken or rules to be followed to be in compliance with the directive. Note that some in the information security industry will call a policy as defined above a standard, guideline, or directive. For the purposes of this book, we will refer to the policy as the document that outlines rules or actions to be followed, while a standard will be referred to as a document that offers step-by-step instructions for complying with a policy.

Concise, easy-to-understand policies are very important in communicating your security requirements and objects to management and users. Policies are the framework for the users and management to follow allowing for the systematic and uniform application of security principles throughout the organization. Well-written policies can make the security administrator's job easier as well as getting user and management support by informing them of the requirements and meanings behind the security program.

Before embarking on your policy creation, you should determine what resources you will need to create the policy. This will primarily be staff that can assist in the creation of your security policy. The policy development team is a different group than the user forum discussed in Chapter 15. The user forum is primarily consultative in nature, while the policy development team will actually formulate the policy that is followed. You should choose a team based on the expertise of the individual and how well they can write concise, instructional policies for the staff. You will want to have an expert on each of the major policy areas you will be outlining, as the experts will usually know their areas best and what the security requirements should be.

There are different ways to approach the creation of security policies. You can create a comprehensive single document security policy that covers all aspects of security in your organization, or you can choose to write a policy for the major sections that need to be covered. The type of policy you choose is completely dependent on your organization's situation and culture. If a large corporation or government entity employs you, an all-encompassing policy might be well within normal expectations. If you are in a smaller company, there may be an expectation that you keep all documents very concise and create separate documents for every situation (or the reverse may be true). For most security professionals, an all-inclusive document that references other policies and standards is the easiest route to take. This is because you can create your policy in a way that you can cover the major aspects of information security needs in your organization quickly and then link to more specific and time-consuming policies for specialized areas. An added benefit of this technique is that all the users can view the main document for security guidance, and those who need specifics can refer to the more comprehensive policies as needed. Most comprehensive security documents have the following security elements at a minimum:

- **Acceptable use provisions**   Outline what is allowed and disallowed on organizational resources

- **E-mail provision**   Outlines all aspects of e-mail, including retention periods, proper use, and other factors

- **Information classification**   Specifies the protection levels afforded different sensitivity levels of corporate assets

- **Password and antivirus provision**   Provide guidance on proper password selection and use of anti-virus tools

- **Remote access**   How access to the organization's resources will be handled when originating from outside the organization's infrastructure

The items listed here are only the core set of provisions outlined in security policies and aren't necessarily required, but in general are included in most policies. You should also outline other specific provisions in your policy, such as third-party access guidelines and physical access guidelines.

As you begin to work on defining policies, the first step you should take is to try to refer to policies created by others in your industry. If this is not possible, you will need to rely on your own knowledge of business needs and management expectations. Talk to management and human resources to see what is expected of a security policy. You can also research online as a starting point to get a general idea of how other companies use security policies in their organization.

You are now ready to write your security policy. The basic requirements of a security policy are that it includes the following information:

- **Scope**  This identifies what the policy covers in terms of physical location, staff, procedures, or process. This sometimes identifies what the penalties are for noncompliance with the policy.

- **Overview**  This describes why the policy is being put in place, what is being protected, or any other amplifying information.

- **Policy**  This is actually where policy is being defined.

Most policies usually include the following highly recommended sections as well:

- **Revision history**  This shows the revision history of the document (when it was last updated).

- **Definitions**  Any words or acronyms that may not be readily known to readers are defined here.

- **Effective dates**  This is for special-purpose policies that are only in effect for a certain time frame, such as during a transition to a new technology.

- **Management signature**  This shows that management is behind the policy and lends credibility to the policy.

## Determine Scope

The first step in the creation of your security policy is to determine the scope of your policy. The scope or coverage of your security policy should be within your area of responsibility. Basically, you should not create a scope for your policy that is inappropriate or too broad. For example, if you are a subordinate organization or business group to a larger group, you usually must defer to the higher organization's authority and rules. This is not always the case, and most companies won't restrict you from being more aggressive in your implementation of security policies, but this is something that needs to be determined by contacting your higher-level security staff. Regardless of whether you have autonomy or not, the scope should be realistic and within your realm of influence.

We use a fictitious company named Example Company and create a sample scope statement (we will continue to use this example throughout the policy creation). The company has no dedicated security staff and after a recent risk assessment conducted by the system administration group, it is discovered that the use of unencrypted telnet was their biggest risk. Karen, who is in charge of the system administration group, decided to implement a policy of requiring SSH throughout the company. Karen determines that she is responsible for all system administration functions and that she has the sphere of influence for the entire enterprise, which is confirmed by management. Karen creates the following scope statement for her SSH policy: "This policy applies to all users and computers using Example Company corporate resources." This simple scope statement conveys in a clear and concise manner who and what the policy applies to.

## Create the Overview

The overview should include a brief statement of what the policy is about. You should also explain why the policy is being put in place and what is being protected in the overview in order to gain users' acceptance and support of the policy. An overview should be concise and provide a quick glance of the more in-depth policy that follows. For example, if you need to create a policy on the requirement for encrypted protocols on the network, a simple overview statement for this could be

> This policy defines the requirement for the use of Secure Shell (SSH), Secure File Transfer Protocol (SFTP), and Secure Copy (SCP) on the corporate network. These protocols use encryption during the transfer of the information, including usernames and passwords, and prevent interception of sensitive company information.

The basic overview above meets the requirements of identifying what the policy will be about, and then provides the user with some background information on why the policy is needed. Your overview shouldn't be too long or it distracts the user away from the actual policy and will tend to discourage the reader from reading the actual content of your policy.

## Write the Policy

The policy section is where actual rules or guidance is provided to the reader. This is the hardest part to write as it is the most in-depth and requires specific instructions. Before trying to create a policy from scratch, try to determine if there is a template for a policy similar in nature to the one you are trying to create. Depending on your organization's specific industry, you may want to try to locate policies from the same industry. For example, if you are in the utility industry, you would want to see if there are other utility companies with publicly available policies for use as a base for your policy. This is because some industries have special requirements not met by completely generic template policies. If you can't find policies specific to your industry or they are not required, here are some resources for good baseline policies:

- The SANS Security Policy Project:
  http://www.sans.org/resources/policies/

- SecurityFocus.com's Introduction to Security Policies:
  http://www.securityfocus.com/infocus/1193/

When creating a security policy, keep it as concise and brief as possible. This doesn't mean you should keep it so brief that you don't offer precise information on what is expected of the user. There shouldn't be any gray area or any segment of your policy that is left to too much interpretation. If you have to be vague on any points, make sure to note who the reader can contact for further clarification.

Now that you have the basics of what a policy consists of, let's create a sample policy using the SSH example used previously. Here is a basic policy statement:

All users of network resources are required to use encrypted protocols when accessing network resources. For users requiring shell access, SSH must be used and specifically OpenSSH, which is included on all system administration managed servers. SFTP or SCP must be used for file transfers or remote copies, respectively, using the toolset included with OpenSSH. Telnet, FTP, RCP, TFTP, Rlogin, or any other non-secure protocols are not authorized. Exceptions to this policy must be requested in writing with business case documentation and approved by the vice president of network operations.

The preceding policy statement is concise and provides a way for users to request exceptions to the policy based on business need. This particular policy could have been included in a larger, unified policy document for easier reading. For our purposes we will keep it as a single document that outlines a single security requirement.

## Finalize the Policy

Now that you have the basic policy statement, it is time to pull it all together. Figure 16-1 shows a completed sample policy with extra items added.

This sample policy is not the most aesthetically pleasing, but it conveys the point. You will want to use your company's document templates to make it more visually appealing and easier to read.

## Review Policies

Review your policies with those who will be impacted and those who understand company policies on legal and human resource issues as well as management and users. If a policy is released before the input of the staff who have a vested interest in the security policies, you may end up having to do many public revisions before a finalized policy is released. This can create confusion on what the most up-to-date policy is and generally creates confusion among all involved.

**Query Interested Parties**   To ensure that your policy meets the needs of the company and follows already established guidelines, you will need to contact different groups to determine the policy's overall viability in the organization.

Some questions you will need to ask are shown in Table 16-2.

Table 16-2 shows only a sampling of the questions you should ask. You should take notes when asking the different groups questions about your policy and modify your policy as needed. If legal, human resources, or management disagrees with or questions your policy, you should seriously reconsider the policy as it may be ineffective from the start or, even worse, violate some legal regulations. There will always be some users who don't agree with a policy, and you should note their concerns before implementing the policy. Remember that you can't please everyone, so be prepared for some disagreement and interesting discussion.

# Example Company Encrypted Protocols Policy

## Revision History

1. Added rlogin to list of protocols not allowed—February 3, 2004

2. Initial policy created—February 1, 2004

## Management Approval

*Vice President's Signature*                                    *Date*

_____                    _____

## Effective Dates

This policy is in effect from February 1, 2004 until superseded.

## Scope

This policy applies to all users and computers using Example Company's corporate resources. Failure to comply with this policy can lead to disciplinary action up to and including termination.

## Overview

This policy defines the requirement for the use of Secure Shell (SSH), Secure File Transfer Protocol (SFTP), and Secure Copy (SCP) on the corporate network. These protocols use encryption during the transfer of the information, including usernames and passwords, and prevent interception of sensitive company information.

## Policy

All users of network resources are required to use encrypted protocols when accessing network resources. For users requiring shell access, SSH must be used and specifically OpenSSH, which is included on all system administration–managed servers. SFTP or SCP must be used for file transfers or remote copies, respectively, using the toolset included with OpenSSH. Telnet, FTP, RCP, TFTP, rlogin or any other insecure protocols are not authorized. Exceptions to this policy must be requested in writing with a business case documentation and approved by the Vice President of Network Operations.

**Figure 16-1.**   Sample security policy

| Question | Whom to Ask |
|---|---|
| Does the policy make sense? | Users and management |
| Is the policy within organizational and legal requirements? | Legal and human resources |
| Is the policy enforceable? | Legal and human resources |
| Is management behind the policy? | Management |
| Are the users behind the policy? | Users |

**Table 16-2.** Policy Review Table

**Create a Security Forum**   Another way to involve your users and management is to create a user security forum. In this forum, you can gather a select group of representative users. You can present your policies and other aspects of your security program to determine what impact, if any, the program will have. This is a step that many security professionals skip, because there is a perception that user input is not needed and an unnecessary burden. One of the major problems with not consulting the users is that they are a crucial part of the security program, and if they don't agree with the policy or at least understand the reason for the program, they might rebel against it. For example, a security officer at a company proposed installing a retina scanner on the computer room doors to control access. The users found out about the proposal and began to complain to their direct management and upper management. These complaints weren't based on any facts; the users were just uncomfortable with having a device read their eyes. There was the perception that a laser would be reading their eye, and if they moved there was potential for blindness or other unfortunate results. There were other issues, but the crux of the problem was that the users hadn't been given the proper information prior to the proposal, and they were uncomfortable with the technology. The proposal was denied and an alternative technology had to be implemented because management hesitated to implement a device that so many users disagreed with. This problem could have been prevented if there had been a user forum, where the security officer could have given the facts to the users, who could then dispel the rumors before they got out of hand. This example applies to policies as well. If you wanted to implement a policy requiring users to have their bags inspected before leaving the building, there might be serious user backlash, but if the program is explained beforehand and users are consulted, the policy will have less of a shock impact on the users.

# Gain User Acceptance and Support

As stated throughout this chapter, users are a very important part of the security program. If the users do not support or are openly hostile to the policy, it will have a diminished impact and eventually fail. You want to give the users a sense of ownership of the program, allowing them to feel like they are part of the security process.

## Ask Users to Develop Security Policy

Most people do not like to have rules dictated to them, and prefer to have some say about things that affect their day. Some things must be dictated, such as policies on prohibiting illegal downloads of copyrighted material on organization assets or requiring people to wear a badge when on company premises. Other times there is leeway to allow the users to effect some type of change in order to gain broad acceptance of the program and minimize the impact. If at all possible, ask the users to assist in developing the security policy because it will make it easier for them to accept.

## Make Policy Psychologically Acceptable

If your security program is being put in place where there were no security policies or very lax ones, your users' sensitivity to the policy is amplified. Change is difficult for users, and the changes that are put into place as part of a security program are sometimes stressful. Frequently your security program will be seen as an impediment to normal working processes. For instance, if you implement a requirement for the use of sudo (which limits the commands that users can run based on preconfigured permissions) in an environment where everyone previously had access to the root account, you will be seen as someone who is preventing work from being done. The users may resist your changes and complain to management or they may become hostile toward you. This is not because you personally are trying to create an obstacle to their work, but because the status quo has been disrupted and there is a feeling of losing control. As the security professional you become the target because you are "the face" of security. You must learn to not take the user's frustrations personally. Instead, you should use the opportunity to explain the reasons behind your security policy and try to enlist the user as an ally.

## Hold a User Security Forum

Gaining user support at the beginning of the security program is important, as they can offer advice on implementation of the program in a way that will be accepted by their peers. A user security forum is an excellent way to give users ownership of the security program. Even if the user does not like the policy, having their input and listening to it can be the catalyst needed to gain support. For example, let's imagine that you are working on a password policy for your organization. Nobody likes hard passwords; in fact, most users would prefer to use much easier passwords and be done with it. Most people understand the need for strong passwords because it has been explained many times, from many different sources. Having a user security forum would allow you to explain the reason for the policy, and to put into context the overall security architecture and how the different pieces of the security puzzle create the security program. The users involved in the security forum will often take the information you have passed to the other users, creating an understanding of the policy's intent. This allows your security program to start off on the right foot.

## Provide Computer Security Advice for Home Use

Another way to gain user acceptance of the security program is to show how security applies to them. A good way to do this is to show them through newsletters, e-mails, or security awareness training how to secure their home computers or other things that affect them outside of work. Also explain how attacks occur and why attackers target home computers, and then show the parallel to the organization. For instance, most users wonder why they should bother securing their home computer. Most think that if there is no personal information on their computer, an attacker wouldn't try to target them. When users hear that attackers don't necessarily want to read their e-mail or steal the information on their drive, but would rather use their computer as a launching pad to attack other higher profile targets, they take notice. They begin to understand the risks to the organization as they draw parallels to their own systems. There are many ways to explain the parallels from their home computer to the organization's computers, as shown in Table 16-3.

## Demonstrate User Support

Getting management to openly support your security program is another way to gain user acceptance. If you have to implement an unpopular policy, having management support your initiative openly can provide the needed prop to encourage users to follow the program, even begrudgingly. Open support by line management and upper management is critical for the program to be supported by the end user, as they often take their lead on the myriad of corporate programs from their management's willingness to enforce the provisions.

Not all portions of your security program will be popular with users, but allowing users to voice their complaints and provide input into the program will lessen the resistance to the program and make the program much more effective than it would be without user support.

| Home User Risk | Corporate User Risk |
|---|---|
| Insecure computer could be used to attack other computer or host programs that open up mail relays for spam. | Insecure computers could be used to attack other networks, host mail relays, or steal corporate information. |
| Social engineers could attempt to gain access to personal information such as credit card information for later use. | Social engineers could attempt to gain access to corporate information such as usernames and passwords for later use. |
| Poor passwords could allow access to private information such as banking records. | Poor passwords could allow access to corporate financial data. |

**Table 16-3.** Parallels for Home and Corporate Security

# Evaluate Program

You have created the security program, explained the program, and gained user support. Now what? You have to evaluate the program to ensure it is working as expected.

## Evaluate Users' Understanding of Security Through Feedback

Evaluating your security program through tools described in Chapter 14 is a good start for evaluating your program from a technical point of view. To evaluate your users, there are other ways to determine the impact of your security program. The most obvious way is to ask them. Do they understand the security strategy? If so, do they support the goals of the security program? Ask these types of questions in an informal forum to avoid canned, meaningless responses. Getting raw feedback from users will serve two purposes, the first being that you can really gauge if you got your message across. The second purpose is that it can allow you to further explain the reasons behind the program and possibly convert the user to an ally. Either way, you are showing the user that you care about their input and are genuinely concerned about the impact security has on their job.

## Test Program Effectiveness

Other ways to determine the effectiveness of your security program are to conduct penetration testing or live evaluation testing. This involves hiring a consultant or disguising yourself to determine if your users comply with policies, such as methods of authenticating users who call the help desk for a password change or checking identification of users before entering the building. These types of programs are complicated to run because they require multiple layers of management approval and often do not test the true readiness of your users. If done incorrectly, penetration testing can cause more problems than it is worth, as it can open the initiator to punitive action. If you decide to take this route, ensure that all levels of management are aware of your plans and consult with a company who is knowledgeable on penetration testing.

# Maintain the Program

Do not rest on your laurels after implementing your security program, even if it is initially successful. Many highly regarded organizational security programs that started strongly failed in the long run because of apathy. You must continue to engage your users to think about security and maintain their security vigilance. Periodic security awareness training, at a minimum yearly, is important but not always possible because of monetary limitations. Having security awareness training, even in web-based or printed form, allows you to refresh the security program with the users and gets them thinking about how security impacts them. Do not depend on one method of delivery for your program, either. Security posters throughout your organization are useless if they are not rotated, as users begin to disregard them. The same applies to other facets of your security program, as you should provide variety in delivery methods to keep the users' interest in security piqued. You must also keep your policies up to date to make the information relevant to the current business climate. Review your policy every quarter at a minimum to ensure that the policy makes sense.

By including your users in all phases of your security program, you are providing them with a sense of ownership of the process. This sense of ownership translates to user acceptance of the program and ensures that your security program starts off in a successful environment.

# Appendix

## Additional Linux Security Resources

- General Linux
- General Security
- General Linux Security
- Linux Security Programs

**387**

There are many security-related web sites and sources of information on the Internet. Use these links at your own risk, as there is some conflicting information on methodologies and implementation.

# General Linux

http://www.li.org/
http://www.linux.com/
http://www.linux.org/
http://www.linux.org.uk/
http://www.linuxgazette.com/
http://www.linuxjournal.com/
http://www.linux-mag.com/
http://www.linuxplanet.com/
http://www.linuxtoday.com/
http://www.linuxworld.com/
http://www.redhat.com/
http://www.suse.com/
http://www.tldp.org/

# General Security

http://www.antionline.com/
http://www.cerias.purdue.edu/
http://www.cert.org/
http://www.ciac.org/ciac/
http://www.csrc.nist.gov/
http://www.sans.org/
http://www.securityfocus.com/
http://www.vmyths.com/

# General Linux Security

http://www.linux.com/security/
http://www.linuxsecurity.com/
http://www.linuxtoday.com/security/
http://lwn.net/security/

http://www.redhat.com/security/
http://www.sans.org/rr/catindex.php?cat_id=32
http://www.securityfocus.com/unix/
http://www.suse.com/de/security/

# Linux Security Programs

http://www.ethereal.com/
http://www.freshmeat.net/
http://www.insecure.org/nmap/index.html
http://www.nessus.org/
http://www.openssh.com/
http://www.openwall.com/john/ (John the Ripper)
http://www.rpmfind.net/
http://www.snort.org/
http://www.sourceforge.net/
http://www.tcpdump.org/
http://www.tripwire.com/

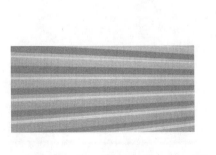

# Index

*References to figures are in italics.*

## A

## B

## C

## D

## E

# ■ F

# ■ G

# ■ H

## ■ S

## ■ U

## ■ V

## INTERNATIONAL CONTACT INFORMATION

**AUSTRALIA**
McGraw-Hill Book Company
Australia Pty. Ltd.
TEL +61-2-9900-1800
FAX +61-2-9878-8881
http://www.mcgraw-hill.com.au
books-it_sydney@mcgraw-hill.com

**CANADA**
McGraw-Hill Ryerson Ltd.
TEL +905-430-5000
FAX +905-430-5020
http://www.mcgraw-hill.ca

**GREECE, MIDDLE EAST, & AFRICA
(Excluding South Africa)**
McGraw-Hill Hellas
TEL +30-210-6560-990
TEL +30-210-6560-993
TEL +30-210-6560-994
FAX +30-210-6545-525

**MEXICO (Also serving Latin America)**
McGraw-Hill Interamericana Editores
S.A. de C.V.
TEL +525-1500-5108
FAX +525-117-1589
http://www.mcgraw-hill.com.mx
carlos_ruiz@mcgraw-hill.com

**SINGAPORE (Serving Asia)**
McGraw-Hill Book Company
TEL +65-6863-1580
FAX +65-6862-3354
http://www.mcgraw-hill.com.sg
mghasia@mcgraw-hill.com

**SOUTH AFRICA**
McGraw-Hill South Africa
TEL +27-11-622-7512
FAX +27-11-622-9045
robyn_swanepoel@mcgraw-hill.com

**SPAIN**
McGraw-Hill/
Interamericana de España, S.A.U.
TEL +34-91-180-3000
FAX +34-91-372-8513
http://www.mcgraw-hill.es
professional@mcgraw-hill.es

**UNITED KINGDOM, NORTHERN,
EASTERN, & CENTRAL EUROPE**
McGraw-Hill Education Europe
TEL +44-1-628-502500
FAX +44-1-628-770224
http://www.mcgraw-hill.co.uk
emea_queries@mcgraw-hill.com

**ALL OTHER INQUIRIES Contact:**
McGraw-Hill/Osborne
TEL +1-510-420-7700
FAX +1-510-420-7703
http://www.osborne.com
omg_international@mcgraw-hill.com

# Sound Off!

Visit us at **www.osborne.com/bookregistration** and let us know what you thought of this book. While you're online you'll have the opportunity to register for newsletters and special offers from McGraw-Hill/Osborne.

## *We want to hear from you!*

# Sneak Peek

Visit us today at **www.betabooks.com** and see what's coming from McGraw-Hill/Osborne tomorrow!

Based on the successful software paradigm, Bet@Books™ allows computing professionals to view partial and sometimes complete text versions of selected titles online. Bet@Books™ viewing is free, invites comments and feedback, and allows you to "test drive" books in progress on the subjects that interest you the most.

# Check Out All of Osborne's Hacking Books

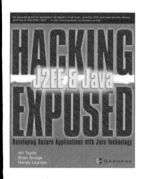

**Hacking Exposed J2EE & Java**

A. TAYLOR, B. BUEGE, R. LAYMAN

0-07-222565-3

USD $49.99

• Explains how to apply effective security countermeasures to applications which use: Servlets and Java Server Pages (JSPs)
• Enterprise Java Beans (EJBs) Web Services • Applets • Java Web Start • Remote Method Invocation (RMI) • Java Message Service (JMS)

**Hacking Exposed Web Applications**

J. SCAMBRAY, M. SHEMA

0-07-222438-X

USD $49.99

• Shows how attackers identify potential weaknesses in Web application components

• Learn about the devastating vulnerabilities that exist within Web server platforms such as Apache, IIS, Netscape Enterprise Server, J2EE, ASP.NET, and more

**Hacking Linux Exposed, Second Edition**

B. HATCH, J. LEE

0-07-222564-5

USD $49.99

• Get detailed information on Linux-specific hacks, both internal and external, and how to stop them

**Hacking Exposed Windows® 2000**

S. MCCLURE, J. SCAMBRAY

0-07-219262-3

USD $49.99

• Shows how to hack while also providing concrete solutions on how to plug the security holes in a Windows 2000 network

**Hacking Exposed Windows® Server 2003**

S. MCCLURE, J. SCAMBRAY

0-07-223061-4

USD $49.99

• Explains how to defend against the latest Windows Server 2003 attacks

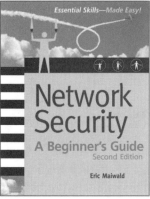